D1237632

NO LONGER PROPERTY
SCIA COLLEGE LIBRARY

Accounting for Slower
Economic Growth

EDWARD F. DENISON

Accounting for Slower Economic Growth

The United States in the 1970s

THE BROOKINGS INSTITUTION
Washington, D.C.

BRESCIA COLLEGE LIBRARY
OWENSBORO, KENTUCKY

Copyright © 1979 by

THE BROOKINGS INSTITUTION

1775 Massachusetts Avenue, N.W., Washington, D.C. 20036

Library of Congress Cataloging in Publication Data:

Denison, Edward Fulton, 1915–
   Accounting for slower economic growth.

   Includes bibliographical references and index.
   1. Labor productivity—United States.   2. Pro-
ductivity accounting.   3. National income—United
States—Accounting.   I. Title.
HC110.L3D46   330.9′73′092   79-20341
ISBN 0-8157-1802-0
ISBN 0-8157-1801-2 pbk.

330.973
D396a

1 2 3 4 5 6 7 8 9

Board of Trustees

ROBERT V. ROOSA
Chairman

LOUIS W. CABOT
Vice Chairman; Chairman, Executive Committee

VINCENT M. BARNETT, JR.
BARTON M. BIGGS
EDWARD W. CARTER
FRANK T. CARY
WILLIAM T. COLEMAN, JR.
BRUCE B. DAYTON
JOHN D. DEBUTTS
GEORGE M. ELSEY
HUNTINGTON HARRIS
ROGER W. HEYNS
CARLA A. HILLS
LANE KIRKLAND
BRUCE K. MACLAURY
ROBERT S. MCNAMARA
ARJAY MILLER
HERBERT P. PATTERSON
DONALD S. PERKINS
J. WOODWARD REDMOND
CHARLES W. ROBINSON
JAMES D. ROBINSON III
WARREN M. SHAPLEIGH
PHYLLIS A. WALLACE

Honorary Trustees

ARTHUR STANTON ADAMS
EUGENE R. BLACK
ROBERT D. CALKINS
COLGATE W. DARDEN, JR.
DOUGLAS DILLON
JOHN E. LOCKWOOD
WILLIAM MCC. MARTIN, JR.
H. CHAPMAN ROSE
ROBERT BROOKINGS SMITH
SYDNEY STEIN, JR.
J. HARVIE WILKINSON, JR.

THE BROOKINGS INSTITUTION is an independent organization devoted to nonpartisan research, education, and publication in economics, government, foreign policy, and the social sciences generally. Its principal purposes are to aid in the development of sound public policies and to promote public understanding of issues of national importance.

The Institution was founded on December 8, 1927, to merge the activities of the Institute for Government Research, founded in 1916, the Institute of Economics, founded in 1922, and the Robert Brookings Graduate School of Economics and Government, founded in 1924.

The Board of Trustees is responsible for the general administration of the Institution, while the immediate direction of the policies, program, and staff is vested in the President, assisted by an advisory committee of the officers and staff. The by-laws of the Institution state: "It is the function of the Trustees to make possible the conduct of scientific research, and publication, under the most favorable conditions, and to safeguard the independence of the research staff in the pursuit of their studies and in the publication of the results of such studies. It is not a part of their function to determine, control, or influence the conduct of particular investigations or the conclusions reached."

The President bears final responsibility for the decision to publish a manuscript as a Brookings book. In reaching his judgment on the competence, accuracy, and objectivity of each study, the President is advised by the director of the appropriate research program and weighs the views of a panel of expert outside readers who report to him in confidence on the quality of the work. Publication of a work signifies that it is deemed a competent treatment worthy of public consideration but does not imply endorsement of conclusions or recommendations.

The Institution maintains its position of neutrality on issues of public policy in order to safeguard the intellectual freedom of the staff. Hence interpretations or conclusions in Brookings publications should be understood to be solely those of the authors and should not be attributed to the Institution, to its trustees, officers, or other staff members, or to the organizations that support its research.

68756

Foreword

This is the fifth of Edward F. Denison's landmark studies of the sources of economic growth—or growth accounting, as it has come to be known. In 1962 in *The Sources of Economic Growth in the United States and the Alternatives before Us*, he first employed the quantitative techniques that distinguish his work, obtaining results that challenged conventional approaches to his subject. Five years later, assisted by Jean-Pierre Poullier, he completed a comparative analysis of the sources and rates of growth of the United States and eight European nations that was published as *Why Growth Rates Differ: Postwar Experience in Nine Western Countries*. Japan was added to his comparative analyses with the publication in 1976 of *How Japan's Economy Grew So Fast: The Sources of Postwar Expansion*, written with William K. Chung. In *Accounting for United States Economic Growth, 1929–1969*, published in 1974, Denison identified the determinants of the growth of the U.S. economy during most of the postwar period.

In recent years economic growth rates have taken a downward turn. Denison pursues the causes of the decline in the United States in this volume, providing historical perspective by examining recent changes against the backdrop of developments during the past half-century. His data show that retarded growth has been characterized by the virtual cessation of any increase in net output per person employed since 1973; employment, in contrast, has continued to expand strongly despite higher unemployment. Until 1974, Denison notes, the decline in the rate of productivity increase that began in the last half of the 1960s was not particularly disquieting, because it stemmed from factors that were transient, inevitable, or even welcome. But "beginning in 1974 the situation became more disturbing and also more puzzling"—for reasons Denison explores in detail. Most of his study is organized by reference to growth sources whose contributions are separately measured on a continuing basis, and he provides the first estimates of such sources for years after 1969.

The author, now associate director of the Bureau of Economic Analysis of the U.S. Department of Commerce and senior fellow emeritus of the Brookings Institution, carried out this project while a staff member of the Brookings Economic Studies program. His work was financed largely by a National Science Foundation grant. The Bureau of Economic Analysis supported the preparation of two articles for separate publication. The unfailing cooperation and assistance of its staff and that of the Bureau of Labor Statistics of the U.S. Department of Labor are gratefully acknowledged.

Moses Abramovitz, Jack Alterman, and Peter K. Clark provided very useful comments on a draft of the entire manuscript. Suggestions by Carol S. Carson, George Jaszi, and Jerome W. Mark helped to improve major sections, and many of the writers whose views are quoted in chapter 9 were kind enough to review the summaries of their positions.

The author also expresses his appreciation for the important contributions made to the study by Genevieve B. Wimsatt, Mark Kosmo, and Nancy Kay, who successively served as research assistants, and by Margaret H. Su, senior secretary. Penelope Harpold checked the text for accuracy. The index was prepared by Florence Robinson.

The views expressed in this book are those of the author and should not be ascribed to the officers, trustees, or other staff members of the Brookings Institution, to agencies providing financial support for the project, or to the persons whose assistance is acknowledged.

BRUCE K. MACLAURY
President

July 1979
Washington, D.C.

vii

Contents

Appendixes

Text Tables

Appendix Tables

Figure

Accounting for Slower Economic Growth

CHAPTER ONE

Introduction

The growth of American productivity was rapid by historical standards during most of the postwar period. But a decade or more ago the rate began to slacken. Until 1974 this slackening was not particularly disturbing from the standpoint of long-term growth. Estimates developed in this study show that it was in part the consequence of short-term fluctuations, notably the drop in the intensity of the use of employed labor and capital from a peak reached in 1965–66. The remainder of the slowdown resulted from developments that were inevitable or even welcome. The transfer of surplus workers from farming to nonfarm jobs in which they produce output of greater value diminished as the pool of such labor approached exhaustion. Great increases in the working-age population under 25 years of age, reinforced by increases in the ratios of employment to population in the young age groups and by the entry of many adult women into the labor force, boosted the proportion of inexperienced workers among the employed. The costs of regulations that Congress presumably felt had benefits in excess of their costs began to impinge on productivity.

National Income per Person Employed since 1973

This comfortable characterization of the productivity slowdown is not applicable to more recent years. Beginning in 1974 the situation became more disturbing and also more puzzling. The years 1974 and 1975 witnessed a sharp and rare decline in constant-dollar national income per person employed—a term to which I shall attach the somewhat wintry acronym, NIPPE—and in productivity

measures generally. Although part of the decline is attributable to the recession with which it coincided, most is not. Since 1975 NIPPE has increased, but even in 1978 it was less than 1 percent higher than five years earlier. It was much lower than would have been the case if the previous trend had continued after 1973. If in 1975 or 1976 there was still hope that the losses during the cyclical downswing might yet be made good during the recovery, this hope has had to be abandoned. NIPPE remained far below its old growth path during the remainder of the cyclical expansion then under way, and in the first half of 1979 it actually fell again.

In this introductory chapter, attention is directed to the decline in the growth rate of NIPPE in non-residential business. This sector makes up over three-fourths of the whole economy. The poor performance of NIPPE in nonresidential business was mainly responsible for the retarded growth of all the output series analyzed in subsequent chapters.

In nonresidential business, NIPPE had increased by an average of 2.4 percent a year during the quarter-century from 1948 to 1973. It then dropped by a total of 5.6 percent in 1974 and 1975. Even after a 1976 increase of 4.2 percent, NIPPE was still 1.6 percent lower in 1976 than it had been three years before. Its 1973–76 growth rate was minus 0.5 percent. More recent data indicate that NIPPE increased by a total of perhaps only 1.4 percent in 1977 and 1978. Over the whole five-year period from 1973 to 1978 the growth rate of NIPPE in nonresidential business was zero.

It is evident that the fundamental change in the pattern of growth that set in after 1973 has continued through 1978. I shall focus on the 1973–76 period, however, because my detailed analysis of growth has been carried only to 1976.

Past experience can be better interpreted by isolating the effects on output per unit of input of three factors that affect it erratically, so as to obtain an "adjusted" NIPPE. Although the effects of two of these factors—weather and work stoppages—are rather minor, the third is often important. This is the effect of changes in the intensity with which employed labor and capital are utilized that result from fluctuations in the pressure of demand. These changes are related to the business cycle, but the cycle in productivity usually is substantially ahead of that in unemployment. The cyclical position was less favorable for productivity in 1976 than in 1948 or in an average postwar year, but slightly more favorable than in 1973.

With the effects of the three irregular factors

eliminated, NIPPE grew 2.6 percent a year from 1948 to 1973 and increased appreciably every single year of that period. Drops in 1974 and 1975 in NIPPE so adjusted, which totaled 3.8 percent, thus were without postwar precedent. The adjusted 1973–76 growth rate was −0.6 percent. Not all effects of the business cycle are removed from this measure, but it will suffice for a preliminary and summary description of developments.[1]

In 1976 NIPPE in nonresidential business equaled $15,120. It would have been 2.5 percent higher if the three irregular factors (chiefly the state of demand) had been as favorable as in the average year from 1948 through 1973. Though substantial, this amount is swamped by the 10.1 percent by which NIPPE in 1976 would have been higher if its *adjusted* growth rate from 1973 to 1976 had been the same as from 1948 to 1973. (NIPPE would

---

1. Subsequent chapters also present data for potential NIPPE in nonresidential business. The decline from 1948–73 to 1973–76 in the growth rate of this series (3.9 percentage points) was even larger than that in actual NIPPE (3.0 percentage points) or "adjusted" NIPPE (3.2 percentage points). Chapter 7 explains the reasons that changes in the actual and potential rates differ as they do.

This study is organized around the concepts of total output, output per person employed, and output per unit of input. Some readers will be more familiar with output per hour. Drops in growth rates per hour in nonresidential business from 1948–73 to 1973–76 are smaller than those in NIPPE, but the difference is only 0.2 or 0.3 percentage points whether calculated on an actual, adjusted, or potential basis.

The growth rates of actual national income per hour at work in nonresidential business, 2.9 percent in 1948–73 and 0.2 percent in 1973–76, compared with rates of 3.0 percent in 1948–73 and 1.0 percent in 1973–76 (a drop of 2.0 percentage points) in the well-known Bureau of Labor Statistics (BLS) series measuring gross national product per hour paid for in the "private business economy." The difference between the 1973–76 growth rates arises chiefly from a larger increase in GNP than in national income. (From 1973 to 1978 there is much less difference.) Capital consumption continued to increase rapidly in 1973–76 so that net output series—whether national income or net national product at market prices—increased less than GNP; this is half the difference. Also, in this particular period constant-price national income (net national product valued at 1972 factor cost) grew less than net national product valued at 1972 market prices, and this is another 0.15 percentage points of the difference. Another contributor was the output of tenant-occupied dwellings, which was rising; it is included in the BLS series for "private business" and excluded from my series for nonresidential business. The series for total hours also differ—conceptually because mine includes an adjustment to exclude hours for which an individual is paid but not at work, and statistically because of the use of slightly different employment estimates.

The BLS series is available through 1978 on a preliminary basis. It shows a 1973–78 growth rate of 0.9 percent, compared with 0.8 in 1973–76 and 2.9 in 1948–73. The important thing to note is that all measures for output per person or per hour agree that there was a big drop in growth rates from 1948–73 to 1973–76 and 1973–78.

Table 1-1. Sources of Growth of National Income per Person Employed, Nonresidential Business Sector, 1948–73 and 1973–76

Percentage points

Item	1948–73	1973–76
Growth rate	2.4	−0.5
Irregular factors	−0.2	0.1
Adjusted growth rate	2.6	−0.6
Changes in labor characteristics		
Hours at work	−0.2	−0.5
Age-sex composition	−0.2	−0.3
Education	0.5	0.9
Changes in capital and land per person employed		
Nonresidential structures and equipment	0.3	0.2
Inventories	0.1	0.0
Land	0.0	0.0
Improved allocation of resources	0.4	0.0
Legal and human environment	0.0	−0.4
Economies of scale from larger markets	0.4	0.2
Advances in knowledge and n.e.c.	1.4	−0.7

Source: Table 7–3. Figures are rounded.
n.e.c. Not elsewhere classified.

---

have been $17,055, or 12.8 percent higher than the actual 1976 figure if both conditions had been met.)[2]

Sources of Retardation Summarized

To discuss the recent change in the situation it is necessary to know what was producing the previous, much higher, growth rate. The estimates of the sources of growth of NIPPE during the quarter-century from 1948 to 1973 that are developed in this study are capsulized in the first column of table 1-1. Estimating methods are described in subsequent chapters and appendixes. Here, I can only suggest the meaning of each entry and caution that the numbers, like those already cited, are estimates. I also caution that space limitations force me to write as if the economy were more mechanistic and growth sources less interrelated than may be the case.

The first three sources of growth are changes in hours of work and in characteristics of the people working. *Hours* changes subtracted 0.2 percent from NIPPE growth in 1948–73, mainly because of rising part-time employment and minor reductions

---

2. Figures for 1976 cited in these paragraphs refer to persons who were employed in 1976. They would be somewhat different if one included persons who were not employed but who would have been if the 1976 unemployment rate had been lower.

in the average hours of full-time, nonfarm wage and salary workers.

The effect on the 1948–73 growth rate of changes in the distribution of total hours worked among demographic groups, that is, in the *age-sex composition* of labor, was negative, by 0.2 percentage points. The proportion of total hours worked by highly weighted groups, particularly males 35 to 64 years of age, declined.

A person's *education* decisively conditions both the types of work he is able to perform and his proficiency in any particular occupation. The educational distribution of employed persons moved steadily and strongly upward and added an estimated 0.5 percent a year to NIPPE in 1948–73.

The contribution of capital is divided between *structures* and *equipment,* which together amounted to a positive 0.3 percentage points, and *inventories,* 0.1 points. The estimates represent the contribution of increases in the capital stock of each type *per person employed.* Capital contributed more to the growth of total national income, but much of the increase in the capital stock was matched by increased employment.

The *land* available per worker declined as employment increased, so its contribution was negative, but the figure rounds to 0.0.

The estimate that 0.4 percentage points were contributed by *improved resource allocation* covers gains from reducing the percentage of the labor in the business sector that was overallocated to farming or misallocated to self-employment and unpaid family labor in nonfarm enterprises too small for efficiency.

Selected changes in the legal and human environment, whose explanation will be deferred, subtracted from the growth rate, but the amount rounds to 0.0 points.

The gain from *economies of scale,* put at 0.4 percentage points, refers to the rise in output per unit of input that is made possible by changes in the size of markets that business serves. It covers the beneficial effects of increased specialization of all sorts.

Five of the growth sources enumerated so far contributed a positive 1.7 percentage points, while four made negative contributions totaling −0.5 points (based on unrounded data).

Since the adjusted growth rate was 2.6 percent, other output determinants must have made a net positive contribution of 1.4 points. This residual is labeled *advances in knowledge and n.e.c. (not elsewhere classified).* The contribution of advances in knowledge includes gains in measured output that result from the incorporation of new knowledge of any type into production, regardless of the source of that knowledge; the way knowledge is transmitted to those who can use it; or the way it is incorporated into production. "Not elsewhere classified" refers to the effects of a large number of determinants that are thought to have been individually small and on the average as likely to have been favorable as unfavorable in the 1948–73 period.

I believe that the residual estimate provides a reasonable approximation to the contribution made by the incorporation of advances in knowledge from 1948 to 1973. In that period my annual index for this series rose without interruption, and at a rather steady rate.

The adjusted growth rate of NIPPE fell from 2.6 percent a year in 1948–73 to −0.6 percent in 1973–76, a drop of 3.2 percentage points. Why did the growth rate of NIPPE drop so sharply, even turning negative? The new estimates make it possible to examine the sources of this change. A drop of 1.5 percentage points can be specifically allocated.

Governmental controls have required the diversion of a growing share of the labor and capital employed by business to pollution abatement and to the protection of employee safety and health. Also, rising crime has forced business to divert resources to crime prevention, and thefts of merchandise have directly reduced measured output. These particular changes in the legal and human environment in which business operates are estimated to have retarded the 1973–76 growth rate of NIPPE by 0.4 percentage points.

Another 1.1 percentage points of the drop in the growth rate of NIPPE is attributable to six determinants discussed earlier: 0.3 points to a steeper drop in working hours, 0.1 to an accelerated shift in the age-sex composition of employed labor, less than 0.1 to slower growth of fixed capital per worker, 0.1 to slower growth of inventories per worker, 0.4 to resource reallocation as the gain from this source completely disappeared, and 0.2 points to economies of scale as market growth slackened.

In contrast, the contribution of education increased by nearly 0.4 percentage points as the educational distribution of persons employed by business moved upward at an accelerated rate. Among the reasons were the facts that government stopped absorbing a disproportionately large part of the increase in the highly educated, and that the average age of adult workers declined. (Young adults have more education than older workers.) Land deducted slightly less than in 1948–73, but the difference rounds to 0.0 percentage points.

The figures just cited would have been different if unemployment had been the same in 1976 as in 1973. Some determinants would have contributed more, others less, and the total decline of NIPPE would have been even larger.[3]

Nearly 2.2 percentage points of the drop in the growth rate of NIPPE remain in the residual series for advances in knowledge and n.e.c. Its contribution fell from a positive 1.4 points to a negative 0.8 points. (After rising steadily until 1973 the series dropped sharply in 1974 and 1975, then in 1976 rose by only a normal amount from the low 1975 level.)

Why the sudden change in the contribution? As already stated, I judge that my residual series for the contribution of advances in knowledge and n.e.c. determinants provides a reasonable approximation to the contribution of advances in knowledge alone until 1973. It is implausible that this is the case in 1973–76, when the residual series suddenly turns negative. A slowdown in the introduction of new knowledge into the productive process may have contributed to the change, but most of the sudden sharp drop in the course of the residual is probably due to one or more of the miscellaneous determinants.

What happened is, to be blunt, a mystery. I investigate it in chapter 9 by examining seventeen suggested causes of worsened productivity performance in the recent past. They are confined to suggestions that, if correct, would affect the residual series rather than output determinants whose contributions were separately estimated. Some—for example, a lowered proportion of the national product devoted to research and development and an increased lag in the application of new knowledge because the average age of capital is increasing—pertain to gains from advances in knowledge. Most refer to miscellaneous determinants of output. Many of these have to do with the effects of government regulation (other than those I have specifically estimated) and taxation. Others range from the allegation that "people don't want to work anymore" to the sharp increase in fuel prices at the end of 1973. After examination, I rejected a few suggestions, expressed skepticism about some and the absence of any opinion about others, and characterized the rest as probably correct but, individually,

able to explain only a small part of the slowdown. Of course, as I point out, many different changes may have contributed to the portion of the productivity lag that appears in the contribution of advances in knowledge and n.e.c.

The retarded growth of NIPPE in nonresidential business was responsible for a sharp decline in NIPPE in the economy as a whole. This in turn has been accompanied by very slow growth of total real national income. This is the case even though employment increased at a good rate from 1973 to 1976 and would have risen at a near-record rate (as it actually did from 1973 to 1978) if a rise in unemployment could have been avoided. My estimate of the growth rate of the economy's capacity to produce at a constant unemployment rate fell from 3.9 percent in 1948–73 to 1.6 percent in 1973–76.[4] Detailed estimates after 1976 have not been made, but it seems likely that the rate over the whole 1973–78 period, though well above 1973–76, was under 2.5 percent.

Content of the Book

This book explores the changes that were responsible for retardation, as well as the few that were favorable to growth. The technique is called sources-of-growth analysis, or growth accounting. Changes in the determinants of output are measured, and the growth rate of output is divided among the determinants of output that changed and produced growth.

The methodology is essentially that used in my *Accounting for United States Economic Growth*.[5] Some minor adaptations were made to conform to new conditions or to improve the estimates. Also, separate series have been introduced for the effects on output per unit of input of new government programs for pollution abatement and for worker safety and health, and of an increase in dishonesty and crime.

Although the book focuses on developments in the 1970s, data are presented for the whole period back to 1929. The significance of recent experience emerges only when it is viewed against a historical background. Data for 1929–69, which were presented in *Accounting for Growth*, have been reestimated to incorporate revisions in the national income and product accounts (NIPA) prepared by the Bureau of Economic Analysis and in other gov-

---

3. See the section on the 1973–76 period in chapter 7 for an explanation.

4. Tables 2-3 and 2-9 provide growth rates for a variety of series and periods.
5. Edward F. Denison. *Accounting for United States Economic Growth, 1929–1969* (Brookings Institution, 1974). Hereinafter referred to as *Accounting for Growth*.

ernment statistics, and to conform to the bureau's shift from 1958 prices to 1972 prices in the construction of constant-price series.

The recent retardation of growth, the major theme of the book, is disturbing, and I do not wish to diminish the impact of the numbers already cited and those I shall present. Yet the situation is not quite so bleak as some writers suggest by their use of erroneous or misleading international comparisons. NIPPE continues higher in the United States than in any other country outside the Arabian peninsula. This is shown by all estimates that are based on quantities of output in different countries, or on conversion of values in national currencies by the use of purchasing power parities.[6] The Bureau of Labor Statistics calculated real gross domestic product per employed civilian in 1977 for seven major countries. It was 92 percent of the U.S. figure in Canada, 78 to 84 percent in France and West Germany, and 57 to 62 percent in Japan, Italy, and the United Kingdom.[7] Smaller advanced nations, including Switzerland, the Scandinavian countries, and members of Benelux, also remain below the United States.[8]

Almost all advanced countries, to be sure, have enjoyed larger percentage increases in output during the postwar period than the United States has. But as I concluded a decade ago in a comparative study of nine countries, an appropriate evaluation of the performance of the American economy "would have to be based on a comparison of United States achievements with United States possibilities. It cannot be based on casual comparisons of the United States growth rate with the rates of countries having quite different opportunities for growth."[9] Most other advanced countries, like the United States, experienced retardation in the growth of NIPPE after 1973.[10]

Because *Accounting for Growth* describes my methods in great detail and explains their rationale, it has been possible to cover those topics more briefly here. The practice of providing a complete description of all series is nevertheless retained, in part by reference to earlier publications.

The course of the nation's output is governed by changes both in its capacity to produce and in the ratio of its actual to its potential production. To distinguish the two types of changes an appropriately defined series for potential output is required. Such a series, derived by growth accounting techniques, was introduced in *Accounting for Growth*. It is also a central part of the present study. Throughout this book just as much attention is devoted to potential national income, its determinants, and its growth sources as to actual national income.[11]

Current Status of Data Utilized

The output series I use, and many details entering into the analysis, are obtained from the NIPA. In 1976 the NIPA were revised all the way back to 1929.[12] These data were fully incorporated into the present study. Additional changes in 1929–46 estimates were published in August 1978; these were

6. Most such comparisons are benchmarked to data reported by the United Nations International Comparison Project. See Irving B. Kravis and others, *A System of International Comparisons of Gross Product and Purchasing Power* (Johns Hopkins University Press for the World Bank, 1975); and Irving B. Kravis, Alan Heston, and Robert Summers, *International Comparisons of Real Product and Purchasing Power* (Johns Hopkins University Press for the World Bank, 1978).

7. U.S. Bureau of Labor Statistics, Office of Productivity and Technology, "Comparative Real Gross Domestic Product, Real GDP per Capita, and Real GDP per Employed Civilian, Seven Countries, 1950–77" (BLS, June 1978). Data cited are based on the use of output comparisons that are based on the geometric mean of U.S. and other-country price weights. The U.S. advantage in each comparison appears smaller if only U.S. price weights are used and larger if only the other country's price weights are used.

8. Angus Maddison shows the United States first among sixteen industrial countries in gross domestic product per man-hour in 1977. Belgium, Canada, and Norway are in the second to fourth positions. Maddison's data for annual hours per person permit gross domestic product per person also to be calculated. The United States again leads, followed by the Netherlands, Belgium, and Canada. (Angus Maddison, "Long Run Dynamics of Productivity Growth," *Banca Nazionale del Lavoro Quarterly Review* [Rome], no. 128 [March 1979], pp. 42–43.) International comparisons that are based on conversion of values in national currencies by exchange rates, which erratically and irregularly have placed Canada, Sweden, Switzerland, and perhaps other countries above the United States in some years, never yield satisfactory comparisons of output and productivity. In recent years wide fluctuations in exchange rates have made them especially misleading. See Jai-Hoon Yang, "Comparing Per Capita Output Internationally: Has the United States Been Overtaken?" *Review*, Federal Reserve Bank of St. Louis, vol. 60 (May 1978), pp. 8–15.

9. Edward F. Denison, assisted by Jean-Pierre Poullier, *Why Growth Rates Differ: Postwar Experience in Nine Western Countries* (Brookings Institution, 1967), p. 345. Hereinafter referred to as *Why Growth Rates Differ.*

10. See table 9-2.

11. The concept of potential output has recently come to have a variety of meanings. My definition is provided in the "potential national income" section of chapter 2. The gap between actual and potential output and the effect of changing the definition is considered in the final sections of chapter 8.

12. U.S. Department of Commerce, Bureau of Economic Analysis, *The National Income and Product Accounts of the United States, 1929–74 Statistical Tables,* A Supplement to the *Survey of Current Business* (GPO, 1977). This and subsequent reports cited below are hereinafter referred to collectively as NIPA.

anticipated and were also incorporated.[13] Also incorporated were new and revised data published in the July 1976 and July 1977 issues of the *Survey of Current Business*. Further changes in 1975 and 1976 estimates that were published in the July 1978 issue could not, in general, be incorporated.[14] Preliminary estimates shown, mainly in chapter 2, for

1977 and 1978 are based on data from the July 1978 and February 1979 issues of the *Survey of Current Business*.

13. "Revised National Income and Product Estimates, 1929–46," *Survey of Current Business,* vol. 58 (August 1978), pp. 67–70. The 1941 estimate for national income in 1972 prices differs trivially ($0.2 billion, or 0.06 percent) from that which I used.

14. The incorporation of revisions in 1976 data published in the July 1978 *Survey of Current Business* for real national income, employment, and the labor share of national income originating in nonfinancial corporations would change the 1976 estimates as follows: total national income, −0.3 percent; total employment, −0.1 percent, NIPPE, −0.2 percent; nonresidential business national income, 0.5 percent; nonresidential business employment, −0.1 percent; NIPPE in nonresidential business, −0.4 percent; the index of intensity of utilization in nonresidential business, −0.2 percent; the residual in nonresidential business, −0.2 percent. Effects on 1973–76 growth rates are only one-third this large and those on 1929–76 growth rates are imperceptible. The July 1979 *Survey of Current Business* will again change the 1976 estimates—too late for consideration in this book.

CHAPTER TWO

⇥⇥≫≪⇤

Output and Income

⇥⇥≫≪⇤

After a quarter-century in which output had expanded rapidly by standards of the past, real growth slackened abruptly after 1973. The slackening occurred in both actual and potential output. As the result of a sharp increase in the price of imported oil, growth in the nation's command over goods and services deteriorated even more than the nation's production.[1] The retardation was in output per worker, not in employment. Employment grew faster from 1973 to 1978 than it had during the preceding 25 years and it would have grown much faster still if unemployment had not risen.

The Economy as a Whole

This section introduces measures of the nation's output and related series.[2] It also describes the abrupt changes in the path of economic development that took place after 1973.

Actual National Income

National income, which is also known as net national product valued at factor cost, is used to measure the value of the nation's output in this study. It is shown in current and constant prices in table 2-1, columns 1 and 2. Both series are obtained from the national income and product accounts (NIPA) published by the U.S. Bureau of Economic Analysis (BEA).

Table 2-1 excludes Alaska and Hawaii up to

1960 and includes them thereafter. Data for 1960 are shown both ways. In the construction of indexes, such as those in table 2-2, the series are linked at 1960 so that the additional coverage does not raise the index. The same practice is followed in computing growth rates.

The nation's net output of goods and services consists of personal consumption expenditures, net private domestic investment, and government purchases of goods and services (which together account for domestic use of product) plus net exports of goods and services. National income is the value of the nation's net output when each product is valued by the factor cost of producing it. The factor cost of a product is the earnings of labor and property that are derived from its production. It differs from its market price in two main ways: indirect business taxes incorporated in market price are excluded and subsidies (which are not part of market price) are included. Total national income in current prices is thus equal to the aggregate earnings of labor and property accruing from current production of goods and services.

I measure changes in real output by national income in constant prices: the value obtained for net national product when each product is valued at its factor cost in 1972, the base year selected by the BEA.[3]

From 1948 to 1973 national income in current prices increased at an average annual rate of 6.5 percent, made up of a 3.7 percent a year increase in real (constant price) national income and a 2.8 percent a year increase in the average price of output (at factor cost).[4] By 1973 to 1978 the increase in nominal national income had risen to 9.9 percent a year. But the increase in real output had slumped to 2.1 percent a year, while the annual increase in price had jumped to 7.6 percent a year. Table 2-3

---

1. The distinction between "production" and "command over goods and services" is discussed later in this chapter.

2. For additional information concerning these series, see appendix A for national income and command over goods and services, appendix B for employment, appendix C for hours at work, and appendix L for potential national income and employment.

3. National income at factor cost and net national product at market prices, it should be understood, measure production of exactly the same bundle of goods and services. Also, an index of the quantity of any individual product is the same whether one is measuring national income or net national product. Indexes of national income and net national product differ only because they weight products differently as a result of the fact that prices of most goods and services are different at factor cost and at market price.

Factor cost valuation is a little more convenient for analysis of productivity changes. This is because a mere shift in the allocation of resources from a lightly taxed to a heavily taxed commodity (or from a subsidized to an unsubsidized one) raises the real product at market prices but leaves product at factor cost unchanged if the earnings of resources are the same in all activities.

4. As always in such cases, the true relationship between the whole and the parts is multiplicative. With less rounding, the rates were 6.51 percent, 3.65 percent, and 2.76 percent, respectively. $(1.0365 \times 1.0276 = 1.0651;$ $3.65 + 2.76 = 6.41$, less than 6.51.)

Table 2-1. Actual and Potential Total National Income in Current and Constant Prices, Unemployment, Population, Employment, and Hours Worked, 1929, 1940–41, and 1947–78

Year	National income in current prices (billions of dollars) (1)	Output in constant (1972) prices (billions of dollars) Actual national income (2)	Output in constant (1972) prices Command over goods and services (3)	Output in constant (1972) prices Potential national income (4)	Percent of civilian labor force 16 and over unemployed (5)	Population, July 1 (thousands) (6)	Employment, annual average (thousands) Actual (7)	Employment, annual average (thousands) Potential (8)	Total hours at work, weekly (millions) Actual (9)	Total hours at work, weekly (millions) Potential (10)
				Excluding Alaska and Hawaii						
1929	84.8	254.7	255.1	249.9	3.0	121,875	47,729	46,990	2,313	2,272
1940a	79.7	277.6	279.8	301.8	9.3b	132,122	51,275	55,927	2,173	2,417
1940c	78.1	270.6	272.8	301.8	14.4d	...	48,445	55,927	2,103	2,417
1941a	102.6	331.1	333.9	329.8	5.7b	133,402	55,794	57,306	2,385	2,465
1941c	101.4	325.7	328.5	329.8	9.6d	...	53,585	57,306	2,331	2,465
1947	194.6	390.8	393.1	395.3	3.7	144,126	59,601	59,351	2,482	2,476
1948	219.0	406.3	407.5	401.3	3.6	146,631	60,578	60,211	2,507	2,486
1949	212.7	402.4	403.4	411.8	5.9	149,188	59,258	61,099	2,422	2,499
1950	236.2	437.7	436.6	434.1	5.2	151,684	60,945	62,143	2,491	2,531
1951	272.3	474.8	472.4	461.7	3.1	154,287	64,769	63,872	2,642	2,595
1952	285.8	492.7	489.8	487.4	2.8	156,954	66,000	64,766	2,682	2,630
1953	299.7	509.7	508.6	505.9	2.7	159,565	66,830	65,430	2,702	2,646
1954	299.1	499.6	497.9	515.5	5.4	162,391	65,075	66,433	2,604	2,668
1955	328.0	536.7	535.1	532.8	4.2	165,275	66,534	66,749	2,663	2,667
1956	346.9	552.2	550.6	559.5	4.0	168,221	67,986	67,953	2,701	2,712
1957	362.3	560.2	559.1	574.1	4.1	171,274	68,126	68,243	2,671	2,694
1958	364.0	551.2	551.0	593.9	6.7	174,141	66,381	69,240	2,576	2,723
1959	397.1	589.1	589.0	609.2	5.4	177,073	67,868	69,322	2,645	2,717
1960e	410.5	600.2	600.4	628.3	5.4	179,893	68,469	70,019	2,654	2,738
				Including Alaska and Hawaii						
1960e	412.0	602.5	602.7	630.7	5.4	180,671	68,756	70,312	2,665	2,749
1961	424.2	614.3	615.3	651.5	6.6	183,691	68,792	71,673	2,646	2,780
1962	457.4	652.7	654.0	670.9	5.5	186,538	70,243	71,853	2,701	2,773
1963	482.8	680.1	681.0	692.4	5.6	189,242	70,853	72,632	2,721	2,791
1964	519.2	717.1	717.3	719.1	5.1	191,889	72,270	73,530	2,767	2,810
1965	566.0	765.5	766.9	755.1	4.4	194,303	74,519	75,009	2,855	2,862
1966	622.2	808.7	810.5	791.6	3.6	196,560	77,941	77,493	2,950	2,919
1967	655.8	828.8	831.2	824.0	3.8	198,712	79,596	79,365	2,979	2,968
1968	714.4	868.5	871.4	858.4	3.5	200,706	81,513	80,938	3,033	3,004
1969	767.9	891.6	894.7	897.3	3.5	202,677	83,615	82,931	3,097	3,076
1970	798.4	879.5	882.2	922.5	4.9	204,878	83,244	84,526	3,039	3,104
1971	858.1	899.9	901.9	951.8	5.9	207,053	83,144	85,856	3,020	3,133
1972	951.9	951.9	951.9	996.6	5.6	208,846	85,077	87,395	3,089	3,185
1973	1,064.6	999.8	997.5	1,041.1	4.8	210,410	88,335	89,575	3,198	3,259
1974	1,136.0	977.9	966.9	1,063.4	5.6	211,945	89,651	92,011	3,206	3,331
1975	1,217.0	955.3	945.0	1,055.9	8.5	213,566	88,077	94,858	3,118	3,385
1976	1,364.1	1,017.4	1,006.8	1,091.8	7.7	215,191	90,484	96,228	3,203	3,420
1977f	1,515.3	1,065.1	1,052.0	n.a.	7.0	216,856	93,709	98,518	3,310	n.a.
1978f	1,704.1	1,110.8	1,098.5	n.a.	6.0	218,554	97,420	100,719	3,431	n.a.

Sources: Column 1, NIPA, table 1.11; column 2, NIPA, table 1.12; column 3, see appendix A; column 4, table 2-4; column 5, Department of Labor, Bureau of Labor Statistics, with small adjustments for comparability by George L. Perry and Edward F. Denison; column 6, U.S. Department of Commerce, Bureau of the Census, reported in *Economic Report of the President, January 1979*, p. 209, except 1960 excluding Alaska and Hawaii, which is from *Current Population Reports*, series P-25, no. 481, "Estimates of the Population of the United States and Components of Change: 1940 to 1972" (GPO, 1972), table 2, p. 11; column 7, table B-1; column 8, column 7 plus table L-4, column 10; column 9, see appendix C; column 10, column 9 plus table L-3, column 12.

n.a. Not available.

a. Including work relief.

b. Persons on work relief are counted as employed.

c. Excluding work relief. Work relief data are from NIPA or were provided directly by the Bureau of Economic Analysis.

d. Persons on work relief are counted as unemployed.

e. The difference between the two 1960 rows understates true values for Alaska and Hawaii because the armed forces stationed in Alaska and Hawaii were included in the series throughout, as were some other components. Data for 1960 excluding Alaska and Hawaii were computed from data provided by the Bureau of Economic Analysis. See *Accounting for Growth* for details.

f. Preliminary.

Table 2-2. Indexes of Actual and Potential National Income in Constant Prices, Population, Employment, and Hours at Work, 1929, 1940–41, and 1947–78

Actual, 1972 = 100

Year	Actual national income				Potential national income				Popula-tion (9)	Employment		Hours at work	
	Total (1)	Per capita (2)	Per person employed (3)	Per hour worked (4)	Total (5)	Per capita (6)	Per person potentially employed (7)	Per potential hour at work (8)		Actual (10)	Potential (11)	Actual (12)	Potential (13)
1929	26.86	45.83	47.68	35.72	26.35	44.96	47.51	35.69	58.61	56.34	55.46	75.19	73.85
1940ᵃ	29.27	46.08	48.37	41.44	31.83	50.09	48.21	40.51	63.54	60.52	66.01	70.64	78.56
1940ᵇ	28.54	44.91	49.91	41.74	31.83	50.09	48.21	40.51	63.54	57.18	66.01	68.36	78.56
1941ᵃ	34.92	54.43	53.02	45.04	34.78	54.21	51.42	43.41	64.15	65.86	67.64	77.53	80.12
1941ᵇ	34.35	53.54	54.31	45.33	34.78	54.21	51.42	43.41	64.15	63.25	67.64	75.77	80.12
1947	41.21	59.46	58.58	51.08	41.69	60.15	59.51	51.80	69.31	70.35	70.05	80.68	80.48
1948	42.85	60.76	59.92	52.58	42.32	60.01	59.55	52.37	70.51	71.50	71.07	81.50	80.80
1949	42.44	59.15	60.67	53.90	43.43	60.53	60.22	53.46	71.74	69.94	72.12	78.73	81.22
1950	46.16	63.28	64.17	57.00	45.78	62.76	62.41	55.65	72.94	71.94	73.35	80.98	82.27
1951	50.07	67.48	65.50	58.30	48.69	65.62	64.58	57.72	74.20	76.45	75.39	85.88	84.35
1952	51.96	68.84	66.70	59.60	51.40	68.10	67.24	60.13	75.48	77.90	76.44	87.18	85.48
1953	53.75	70.05	68.14	61.20	53.35	69.53	69.08	62.03	76.73	78.88	77.23	87.83	86.00
1954	52.69	67.47	68.59	62.24	54.36	69.61	69.33	62.69	78.09	78.81	78.41	84.65	86.72
1955	56.60	71.21	72.07	65.38	56.19	70.69	71.31	64.82	79.48	78.53	78.79	86.57	86.69
1956	58.23	71.98	72.57	66.32	59.00	72.94	73.56	66.93	80.90	80.25	80.21	87.80	88.15
1957	59.08	71.73	73.47	68.04	60.54	73.50	75.16	69.14	82.36	80.41	80.55	86.83	87.56
1958	58.13	69.41	74.19	69.42	62.63	74.79	76.63	70.76	83.74	78.35	81.73	83.74	88.51
1959	62.12	72.96	77.55	72.25	64.24	75.44	78.51	72.75	85.15	80.11	81.82	85.98	88.31
1960	63.29	73.17	78.32	73.36	66.26	76.59	80.17	74.45	86.51	80.82	82.65	86.27	88.99
1961	64.53	73.37	79.81	75.34	68.44	77.81	81.24	76.05	87.96	80.86	84.24	85.66	90.00
1962	68.57	76.77	83.05	78.42	70.48	78.91	83.45	78.51	89.32	82.56	84.46	87.44	89.77
1963	71.45	78.85	85.79	81.11	72.74	80.27	85.20	80.51	90.61	83.28	85.31	88.09	90.35
1964	75.33	81.99	88.68	84.10	75.54	82.22	87.41	83.04	91.88	84.95	86.43	89.58	90.97
1965	80.42	86.44	91.81	87.01	79.33	85.26	89.97	85.62	93.04	87.59	88.17	92.42	92.65
1966	84.96	90.27	92.73	88.96	83.16	88.36	91.30	88.00	94.12	91.61	91.09	95.50	94.50
1967	87.07	91.51	93.06	90.28	86.56	90.98	92.79	90.09	95.15	93.56	93.29	96.44	96.08
1968	91.24	94.94	95.23	92.92	90.18	93.83	94.79	92.73	96.10	95.81	95.14	98.19	97.25
1969	93.67	96.52	95.30	93.42	94.26	97.13	96.70	94.66	97.05	98.28	97.48	100.26	99.58
1970	92.39	94.18	94.43	93.91	96.91	98.79	97.54	96.44	98.10	97.85	99.35	98.38	100.49
1971	94.54	95.36	96.74	96.70	99.99	100.86	99.08	98.59	99.14	97.73	100.92	97.77	101.42
1972	100.00	100.00	100.00	100.00	104.70	104.70	101.92	101.54	100.00	100.00	102.72	100.00	103.11
1973	105.03	104.25	101.16	101.45	109.37	108.56	103.88	103.67	100.75	103.83	105.29	103.53	105.50
1974	102.73	101.23	97.49	98.98	111.71	110.08	103.29	103.60	101.48	105.38	108.15	103.79	107.83
1975	100.36	98.14	96.94	99.42	110.93	108.47	99.49	101.23	102.26	103.53	111.50	100.94	109.58
1976	106.88	103.73	100.49	103.08	114.70	111.32	101.41	103.60	103.04	106.36	113.11	103.69	110.72
1977ᶜ	111.89	107.75	101.58	104.42	n.a.	n.a.	n.a.	n.a.	103.84	110.15	115.80	107.15	n.a.
1978ᶜ	116.69	111.51	101.90	105.05	n.a.	n.a.	n.a.	n.a.	104.65	114.51	118.39	111.08	n.a.

Source: Calculated from table 2-1.
n.a. Not available.
a. Including work relief.
b. Excluding work relief.
c. Preliminary.

shows these rates. Also shown are 1973–76 rates because some of the series with which comparisons are made are not available after 1976, and because subsequent chapters analyze that period in detail.

It will be observed that I generally show growth rates and indexes to two decimal points in order to minimize rounding errors when series are combined or time periods compared. The practice does not at all imply a high degree of accuracy; though carefully compiled, the series are only approximations even when final data are available.

Two Characteristics of Output Measures

Procedures used to analyze changes in output must conform to the way that output is actually measured. Two characteristics, both of which real national income shares with real gross and net national product, are particularly important in this context.

The first has to do with production outside the business sector—that is, the output ascribed to persons employed by general government, non-profit organizations serving individuals, and private

Table 2-3. Growth Rates of Selected Series, 1948–73, 1973–76, and 1973–78

Percent per annum

Series	1948–73	1973–76	1973–78[a]
National income			
Current prices	6.51	8.61	9.87
Implicit price deflator	2.76	7.99	7.58
Constant prices	3.65	0.58	2.13
Command over goods and services			
Current prices	6.51	8.61	9.87
Implicit price deflator	2.78	8.28	7.77
Constant prices	3.63	0.31	1.95
Potential national income			
Constant prices	3.87	1.60	n.a.
Potential command over goods and services			
Constant prices	3.85	1.32	n.a.
Population	1.44	0.75	0.76
Employment			
Actual	1.50	0.80	1.98
Potential	1.58	2.42	2.37
Total hours at work			
Actual	0.96	0.05	1.42
Potential	1.07	1.62	n.a.
Per capita data in constant prices			
National income	2.18	−0.17	1.36
Command over goods and services	2.16	−0.44	1.18
Potential national income	2.40	0.84	n.a.
Potential command over goods and services	2.38	0.57	n.a.
Per-person-employed data in constant prices			
National income	2.11	−0.22	0.15
Command over goods and services	2.10	−0.49	−0.03
Potential national income[b]	2.25	−0.80	n.a.
Potential command over goods and services[b]	2.23	−1.07	n.a.
Per-hour-at-work data in constant prices			
National income	2.66	0.53	0.70
Command over goods and services	2.64	0.26	0.75
Potential national income[c]	2.77	−0.02	n.a.
Potential command over goods and services[c]	2.75	−0.29	n.a.

Sources: Tables 2-1 and 2-2.
n.a. Not available.
a. Preliminary.
b. Per person potentially employed.
c. Per potential hour at work.

households. The total output of workers in these categories is assumed to move like total labor input. Chapter 6 provides a detailed description of the procedure.

The second characteristic refers to the treatment of new or improved products—that is, to what is called noneconomic, or unmeasured, quality change.

Milton Gilbert and Irving B. Kravis distinguished economic from noneconomic quality differences in the following way:

As between two periods of time or between two countries, a product may be of a higher quality in the sense of being more attractive to the purchaser for one of two reasons. The one is that there is a more advanced state of the arts or state of technical knowledge which enables a better product to be made without requiring the use of more resources. [That is, more resources if both were produced at the same time in the same country.] The other is . . . that the purchasers in one of the markets are either willing, because of their taste preferences, or able, because of their level of income, to pay for a product that requires more resources to produce it. The first type of higher quality is cost free, and hence is noneconomic. The second type requires higher cost, and hence is economic. The first cannot be reflected in an economic measure of relative production; the second must be. It does not matter that the ultimate benefits to the consumer from the non-economic differences in quality may be greater in some sense than those from the economic differences. . . . a quantitative measure of relative production cannot be constructed in terms of ultimate satisfactions of the users of the goods, but must be limited to the relative quantities of the goods and services they command. The economic differences are quantitative in this sense. The non-economic quality differences are not, because there is no economic unit of quantity by which to measure them.[5]

The distinction is the same as I drew in an earlier study between "measured" quality changes that are reflected in changes in the measured national product and unmeasured quality changes. Where two products existing simultaneously, such as an expensive car and an inexpensive one, sell at different prices, they are counted as different quantities of product, the quantities differing in the ratio of their selling prices. Where different commodities do not in fact exist simultaneously, they are counted as different products in the ratio of what their cost (used as a substitute for price) would be if both were known and produced at the same time.[6] The quality differences measured by this procedure are "measured" or "economic" quality differences. No account is or can be taken of the fact that some or even all consumers may have a subjective evaluation of the relative merits of products that differ from the ratio of their prices or costs.

The following statement explains the implication of quality change and new products for interpretation of intertemporal comparisons:

When we say on the basis of the official estimates that total real personal consumption expenditures per capita increased by 52 percent from 1960 to 1976, we are comparing actual consumer purchases in 1960 with the sum of (1) products purchased in 1976 that were identical with those bought in 1960 and (2) products purchased in 1976 that were *not* available in 1960 valued in terms of the products that the resources used in their production *could* have provided in 1976 if used to produce products that did exist in 1960. This is only a crude description of the estimates (which rest on a variety of sources that do not follow wholly consistent procedures) but it is approximately correct. Clearly, the estimates do not take into account either the improvements made in a great range of products without a corresponding change in their production costs or the greater range of choice open to today's consumer.[7]

There is no method of measuring output that would satisfactorily take account of unmeasured quality improvements and expanded range of choice.

It is particularly important to recall this measurement characteristic when one examines the role of advances in knowledge in growth, because advances that permit new and better final products to be provided do not contribute to growth as it is actually measured. That is to say, measured output is the same as if the resources devoted to production of new products were still used to produce products that had already been familiar in earlier periods.

Command over Goods and Services

The sudden rise in the price of oil imports since 1973 has made the method by which changes in the prices of imports and exports are handled a matter of some importance.

National income and product, as already stated, are equal to domestic use of product (whether produced in the United States or abroad) plus net exports of goods and services (the amount by which the value of exports exceeds the value of imports). This statement is unambiguous in current prices. But in constant prices alternative methods that may be used to deflate net exports yield different results.

In the NIPA (and therefore in the derivation of column 2 of table 2-1) the gross value of imports is deflated by import prices and the gross value of exports by export prices. Net exports in constant prices are then calculated by subtracting deflated imports from deflated exports. When this method is used, the movements of real national income and product are not directly affected by changes in prices of imports or exports because the effect of price changes is eliminated. Such price changes are not viewed as altering U.S. production. Productivity changes, computed with such an output measure as the numerator, consequently reflect only changes in the productivity of domestically owned resources. They are not directly affected by the terms of trade.

A rise in the relative price of imports does reduce the quantity of foreign goods the country can purchase with the proceeds of any given quantity of exports, and requires that either domestic use of product or net foreign investment (or gifts abroad) be curtailed in real terms.[8] This effect is taken into account in the series I call "command over goods and services" resulting from current production, shown in table 2-1, column 3. In its derivation, net exports in constant prices are calculated by deflating *net* exports in current prices by import

5. Milton Gilbert and Irving B. Kravis, *An International Comparison of National Products and the Purchasing Power of Currencies: A Study of the United States, the United Kingdom, France, Germany, and Italy* (Paris: Organization for European Economic Co-Operation and Development, 1954), p. 80.

6. This is a general and somewhat idealized statement of the results produced by use in deflation of the available price indexes. These indexes, in practice, have many defects and inconsistencies.

7. Adapted from Edward F. Denison, *The Sources of Economic Growth in the United States and the Alternatives before Us* (Committee for Economic Development, 1962), pp. 156–57. Hereinafter referred to as *Sources of Growth*.

8. Net exports are equal to net foreign investment plus transfer payments abroad.

prices.[9] When the values of imports and exports are equal in current prices, net exports in constant prices are always zero by this alternative procedure, whereas they may take a large positive or negative value by the regular procedure. The alternative procedure provides a measure of the quantity of goods and services over which a nation has command as a result of its production. The deflated series rises or falls if the terms of trade improve or worsen. A series so constructed, valued at 1972 factor cost, is shown in table 2-1, column 3.

In current prices command over goods and services and national income are the same, as stated earlier. It happens that from 1948 to 1973 the two concepts also yield nearly the same changes in prices and real product. But from 1973 to 1976 the measure of command over goods and services yields a larger price increase and smaller quantity increase than does the measure of production. Although production from American resources (national income) increased 0.6 percent a year, the goods that could be bought with this output increased by only 0.3 percent a year. Most of the divergence developed from 1973 to 1974, when national income in constant prices fell 2.2 percent, while command over goods and services fell 3.1 percent. Although import and export prices both rose far more than the prices of products used domestically, the increase in import prices was much the larger of the two. Over the whole 1973–78 period the growth rates of the series differed by 0.2 percentage points. In 1979 renewed increases in oil prices again widened the gap between real national income and command over goods and services.

Potential National Income

The course of national income in constant prices is greatly affected by changes in the extent to which the resources available to the nation are actually utilized. To interpret developments accurately one needs a measure of "potential" output that is un-affected by such changes, in addition to the series for actual national income. Fluctuations in the ratio of actual to potential output are dominated by changes that occur during the course of each business cycle, but utilization also varies between the peaks or troughs of different cycles.

I define potential national income in 1972 prices in any year as the value that national income in 1972 prices would have taken if (1) unemployment had been at 4 percent; (2) the intensity of utilization of resources that are in use had been at the same rate in all years, namely that which on the average would be associated with a 4 percent unemployment rate; and (3) other conditions had been those that actually prevailed in that year. To conform with current labor force definitions, "4 percent" unemployment is defined as the percentage of the civilian labor force 16 years of age and over that is unemployed. The term "on the average" refers to the average of a hypothetical random sample of years in which unemployment is 4 percent but output is changing by amounts larger than, the same as, or smaller than the trend rate of change at the time.

I stress that specification of an unemployment rate, as in the first part of the definition, is insufficient to define potential national income. The second part, which has reference to the relationship between demand intensity and intensity of utilization, is essential because, given an unemployment rate of 4 percent, the output that is obtained per unit of labor, capital, and land in use is influenced by the rate of change in output. Productivity usually is much higher (relative to its trend) when output is rising rapidly than when it is stable or falling. The third part of the definition means that the weather, labor disputes, the size of the armed forces, and all other conditions except demand are taken to be the same under potential conditions as under actual conditions. Many output determinants change erratically, and their erratic movements affect output, but they are not the consequences of changes in the state of demand or controllable by macroeconomic policy. They affect both actual and potential output, not the difference between them. This is so even though many determinants of output might have been different if the past history of business cycles and wars had been different. The capital stock, an important output determinant, requires special mention in this context. Investment and, consequently, changes in the capital stock move with the business cycle. The estimates of potential output that I present for each year are based on the capital stock that actually existed that year, not the stock that might have existed if investment had been different in previous periods (either unusual periods such as the 1930s, when net investment disappeared, or preceding years of the same business cycle).

The series for potential national income shown

---

9. The excess of exports in current prices over imports in current prices is visualized as adding to (if positive) or subtracting from (if negative) the nation's ability to pay for imports in the future; hence import prices are used to deflate this balance. A variant of the method would use export prices; the resulting series for "command over goods and services" is not much different.

Table 2-4. Derivation of Potential National Income at 4 Percent Unemployment, 1929, 1940–41, and 1947–76

Billions of 1972 dollars

Year	Actual national income (1)	Plus: Adjustment for intensity of utilization of employed inputs (2)	Plus: Adjustment for labor input[a] (3)	Equals: Potential national income (4)	Excess of actual over potential	
					Amount (5)	Percent (6)
Excluding Alaska and Hawaii						
1929	254.7	−1.6	−3.2	249.9	4.8	1.9
1940	270.6[b]	0.6	30.6[c]	301.8	−24.2[c]	−8.0[d]
1941	325.7[b]	−9.3	13.4[c]	329.8	1.3[c]	0.4[d]
1947	390.8	5.3	−0.8	395.3	−4.5	−1.1
1948	406.3	−2.9	−2.1	401.3	5.0	1.2
1949	402.4	0.8	8.6	411.8	−9.4	−2.3
1950	437.7	−8.5	4.9	434.1	3.6	0.8
1951	474.8	−7.6	−5.5	461.7	13.1	2.8
1952	492.7	1.4	−6.7	487.4	5.3	1.1
1953	509.7	3.7	−7.5	505.9	3.8	0.8
1954	499.6	7.2	8.7	515.5	−15.9	−3.1
1955	536.7	−4.8	0.9	532.8	3.9	0.7
1956	552.2	5.7	1.6	559.5	−7.3	−1.3
1957	560.2	10.3	3.6	574.1	−13.9	−2.4
1958	551.2	19.6	23.1	593.9	−42.7	−7.2
1959	589.1	8.6	11.5	609.2	−20.1	−3.3
1960	600.2	14.4	13.7	628.3	−28.1	−4.5
Including Alaska and Hawaii						
1960	602.5	14.4	13.8	630.7	−28.2	−4.5
1961	614.3	14.8	22.4	651.5	−37.2	−5.7
1962	652.7	5.9	12.3	670.9	−18.2	−2.7
1963	680.1	0.2	12.1	692.4	−12.3	−1.8
1964	717.1	−5.6	7.6	719.1	−2.0	−0.3
1965	765.5	−11.6	1.2	755.1	10.4	1.4
1966	808.7	−11.8	−5.3	791.6	17.1	2.2
1967	828.8	−2.8	−2.0	824.0	4.8	0.6
1968	868.5	−4.5	−5.6	858.4	10.1	1.2
1969	891.6	10.0	−4.3	897.3	−5.7	−0.6
1970	879.5	29.8	13.2	922.5	−43.0	−4.7
1971	899.9	27.9	24.0	951.8	−51.9	−5.5
1972	951.9	24.0	20.7	996.6	−44.7	−4.5
1973	999.8	28.3	13.0	1,041.1	−41.3	−4.0
1974	977.9	58.4	27.1	1,063.4	−85.5	−8.0
1975	955.3	41.7	58.9	1,055.9	−100.6	−9.5
1976	1,017.4	25.6	48.8	1,091.8	−74.4	−6.8

Sources: Column 1, table 2-1, column 2; columns 2 and 3, based on data in appendix L; column 4, sum of columns 1, 2, and 3; column 5, column 1 minus column 4; column 6, column 5 divided by column 4.

a. Includes the effects on resource allocation of differences between actual and potential labor input.

b. Excluding work relief.

c. The actual output of employees on work relief ($6.0 billion in 1940 and $5.4 billion in 1941) is not offset here against their potential output because it is omitted from column 1.

d. Comparison is with actual national income including work relief; see table 2-1 for data.

in table 2-1 was developed in the present study and is one of its important products. Table 2-4 shows in very summary form the adjustments made to actual national income to obtain potential national income. These series are described in appendix L, but it may be noted here that potential national income differs from actual national income for two reasons, corresponding to columns 2 and 3 of the table. First, output per unit of input differs under potential and actual conditions because the intensity with

which inputs—labor, capital, and land—that are in use are utilized varies with the strength of demand pressures. Second, the quantity, composition, and distribution of labor used in production differ under potential and actual conditions. The second adjustment is positive when unemployment exceeds 4 percent and negative when it is below 4 percent. This need not be true of the first adjustment, which is only weakly correlated with the unemployment rate because utilization is greatly affected by the direction and rate of change in total output. Consequently the two adjustments are sometimes in opposite directions.

Potential output was once defined as the level of output under conditions in which unemployment was low and prices stable. But it has become clear that construction of a time series for potential output in accord with a definition that encompasses *both* low unemployment and price stability is not feasible. Of the two, only unemployment enters my definition.[10] Knowledge of the relationship between actual and potential national income is necessary for the analysis of price pressures as well as of output changes, but I do not at all imply that prices would have been stable—or would even have risen at a rate moderate enough to be acceptable—if actual national income had been the same as potential national income. Therefore potential national income, as I define it, should not be construed as necessarily a desirable output to be used as a target. In 1978 Congress passed the Full Employment and Balanced Growth Act of 1978 (known as the Humphrey-Hawkins Act), specifying an unemployment rate of 4 percent (subject to change at a later date) as a target to be reached by 1983. But most economists regard a substantially higher unemployment rate as appropriate, at least for now, because they believe so low a rate would mean unacceptably large price increases. The act, it may be noted, also specifies an inflation rate target of 3 percent for 1983 and other desirable objectives.

In table 2-2, column 5, an index of potential national income in constant prices is shown. This index was computed by dividing potential national income each year by *actual* national income in 1972. I shall follow the practice of dividing by actual rather than potential 1972 values whenever I provide indexes on either an actual or a potential basis. The advantage is that the ratio of the "actual" index to the corresponding "potential" index in any year yields the percentage by which the actual value exceeds or falls short of the potential value. For example, division of column 1 by column 5 in table

2-2 shows that actual national income exceeded potential national income by 1.2 percent in 1948 and fell below it by 7.2 percent in 1958. In the present instance this result could also be obtained from tables 2-1 and 2-4, which give dollar amounts, but most potential series are presented only in index form.

Actual national income was below potential national income continuously from 1969 through 1978. Even in 1973, a business cycle peak, the percentage gap was larger than it had been in all but a few postwar years before 1970. Because 1948–73 growth rates will shortly be used in a number of comparisons, it is pertinent to note that the ratio of actual national income to potential national income was much lower in 1973 than in 1948, a year in which actual exceeded potential. From its low 1973 level the ratio plunged downward in 1974 and 1975 as the country experienced its deepest recession since 1938, then rose as recovery got under way in 1976 and continued in 1977 and 1978. The ratio of actual to potential national income is estimated at 96.0 percent in 1973, 92.0 percent in 1974, a postwar low of 90.5 percent in 1975, and 93.2 percent in 1976. An explicit estimate of potential national income has not yet been made for later years, but it is clear that the ratio rose from 1976 to 1978. The recession and recovery responsible for the swings in the ratio contributed to the 1973–75 drop and 1975–78 rise in actual national income.

Especially unusual and disturbing was retardation of the growth of potential output itself. From 1948 to 1973 potential national income grew 3.9 percent a year (table 2-3). From 1973 to 1975 it grew only 0.7 percent a year. Potential national income increased 3.4 percent in 1976 but its 1976–78 rate of growth was much less; even actual national income grew only 3.7 percent annually in those years. The advance in potential national income from 1975 to 1978 almost surely was insufficient even to match the 1948–73 growth rate; clearly none of the ground lost in the two preceding years was recovered. Potential national income grew at a rate of 3.9 percent in 1948–73 but at only 1.6 percent in 1973–76 and probably less than 2.5 percent over the whole period from 1973 to 1978. Such low rates have not been observed since the period of demobilization after World War II.

The situation with respect to command over goods and services was even bleaker. On a potential basis the growth rate of the nation's command over goods and services fell from 3.9 percent in 1948–73 to 1.3 percent in 1973–76.

10. The need to change the original concept of potential output has resulted in the term being used for a variety of concepts, including some that refer only to prices. For greater clarity I considered substituting "high employment" for "potential" in labeling the series, but this would not help because the government uses the terms as synonyms, even though it now bases its potential output on a 5.1 percent unemployment ratio. (See references to the "high-employment budget" in *The Budget of the United States Government, Fiscal Year 1980*, p. 46: and *Economic Report of the President, January 1979*, p. 46.) My definition of potential is unchanged from that in *Accounting for Growth*.

Population and Per Capita Output

Population has risen all through the period covered by this study. The series shown in table 2-1, column 6, is prepared by the Bureau of the Census. It includes the armed forces overseas, as do the various output and employment series. Population increase has slackened considerably since the early postwar period. It averaged over 1.4 percent a year during the 1948–73 period as a whole and less than 0.8 percent thereafter.

In consequence the declines after 1973 in all growth rates reviewed so far are reduced by about 0.7 percentage points when they are computed on a per capita basis, but they still are large. From 1948–73 to 1973–78 the declines in per capita growth rates were about 0.8 percentage points for national income and about 1.0 percentage point for command over goods and services (table 2-3).

Since changes in total population are not related to changes in the population at work, except over very long periods, they are not pertinent to an investigation of the causes of changes in output growth rates. Instead, per capita series based on the whole population are useful in the appraisal of living standards. For such an appraisal, per capita command over goods and services is more appropriate than per capita national income. The fall in this growth rate was from 2.2 percent in 1948–73 to 1.2 percent in 1973–78, a drop of nearly one-half.

Employment, Hours at Work, and Output per Person Employed

The employment series shown in table 2-1, column 7, was specially developed for this study; it is described in appendix B. Employment is defined as the number of persons employed, full-time or part-time, during an average week. For maximum statistical consistency between the national income and employment series, the *movement* of the employment series is based mainly on estimates compiled by the BEA as part of its national income and product accounts. The BEA series I use for movement of employment measure the "average number of full-time and part-time employees" (covering wage and salary workers) and the number of active proprietors of unincorporated business; estimates of unpaid family workers are then added.[11] A series so constructed would, for the most part, measure jobs rather than people, but its average level has been

adjusted to correspond to the average level of a count of employed persons rather than a count of jobs, based on the Census Bureau's Current Population Survey. This procedure yields a time series for the number of employed persons that is more consistent with the output data, and probably more accurate, than the annual CPS estimates.

Potential employment, shown in table 2-1, column 8, measures the number of persons who would have been employed if the civilian unemployment rate had been 4 percent. In 1978, when the civilian unemployment rate was 6.0 percent, potential employment reached 100.7 million, consisting of 97.4 million persons who were actually employed, 2.1 million unemployed persons who would have been employed if the unemployment rate had been 4 percent, and 1.2 million persons (net) who were not actually in the labor force but would have been employed if the unemployment rate had been 4 percent.[12]

Whereas population growth dropped by nearly one-half from 1948–73 to 1973–78, the growth rate of potential employment increased by one-half, from 1.6 percent to 2.4 percent. Changes in the age distribution and acceleration of the long rise in female labor force participation rates were main factors in the differential movement. So fast was the growth of potential employment after 1973 that despite the rise in unemployment, actual employment, too, grew much faster in 1973–78 than it had from 1948 to 1973.

The estimates for total hours at work, shown in table 2-1, column 9, were also specifically developed for this study (see appendix C). They are based on the employment series in column 6 and estimates of average hours at work that are almost entirely derived from Bureau of Labor Statistics data. The term "total hours at work, weekly" has been substituted for the term formerly used, "total hours worked weekly," because it seems slightly more accurate, but the meaning is unchanged. Hours for which persons are paid when they are not at work are excluded, but time they spend at the workplace without actually working is not eliminated.

Potential hours are shown in table 2-1, column 10. The difference between potential and actual hours consists of (1) the hours that would have been worked under potential conditions by the people corresponding to the difference between actual and potential employment and (2) the difference

---

11. Although the BEA now includes military reserves not on active duty in "full-time and part-time employees," I continue to exclude them.

12. See pp. 28–29 and 196–99 for further discussion.

between the hours that employed persons worked under actual conditions and the hours they would have worked under potential conditions. The former is much the larger component except, occasionally, when the total difference between actual and potential hours is trivial.

The series for national income and command over goods and services per person employed and per hour at work provide a gloomy picture indeed. To see what was happening, it is necessary to look at the annual series since 1973. They are shown in the informal tabulation below as indexes with 1973 equal to 100; some estimates for 1977–78 are rough.

In 1976 actual national income per person employed (NIPPE) remained below potential national income per person potentially employed for the eighth straight year (table 2-2, columns 3 and 7), but the difference was smaller than in 1973. Since the unemployment rate averaged 7.7 percent in 1976, compared with 4.8 percent in 1973, this may surprise readers accustomed to associating high actual productivity with low unemployment. The explanation has two parts. First, the large 1973–76 increase in the gap between actual and potential employment was concentrated in categories of workers (classified by demographic characteristics and education) who normally work short hours and have

	1973	1974	1975	1976	1977	1978
Actual Data						
National income						
Per person employed	100.0	96.4	95.8	99.3	100.4	100.7
Per hour at work	100.0	97.6	98.0	101.6	102.9	103.5
Command over goods and services						
Per person employed	100.0	95.5	95.0	98.5	99.4	99.9
Per hour at work	100.0	96.7	97.2	100.8	101.9	102.6
Potential Data						
National income						
Per person potentially employed	100.0	99.4	95.8	97.6	n.a.	n.a.
Per potential hour at work	100.0	99.9	97.6	99.9	n.a.	n.a.
Command over goods and services						
Per person potentially employed	100.0	98.5	95.0	96.8	n.a.	n.a.
Per potential hour at work	100.0	99.0	96.8	99.1	n.a.	n.a.

As indicators of the economy's productivity performance, actual and potential national income per person employed and per hour at work should be examined. All these series actually dropped by appreciable amounts (2.0 to 4.2 percent) over the two years from 1973 to 1975. This was very unusual. In every single postwar year until 1974 increases had been registered in potential national income per person potentially employed, potential national income per potential hour at work, and actual national income per hour at work. In every year but one (1970) actual national income per worker had also risen.

By 1976 potential national income per potential hour worked was 8.0 percent smaller and potential national income per person potentially employed was 8.7 percent smaller than would have been the case if their 1948–73 growth rates had continued from 1973 to 1976. Both series had risen from 1975 to 1976 but at less than the 1948–73 rate; preliminary indications are that this pattern was repeated from 1976 to 1978 so that the shortfalls, measured against a continuation of 1948–73 growth rates, continued to increase.

low hourly earnings. Consequently labor input per person employed rose more on an actual than on a potential basis. Second, although low unemployment is associated with high productivity on the average, the last years of cyclical expansions (such as 1973) characteristically show low productivity as output expansion slackens and stops. Such years are typically less favorable to high productivity than years, such as 1976, during which unemployment is higher but output is expanding vigorously.[13] There may also have been a special factor at work in 1973. While subnormal intensity of utilization was due in some sectors to inadequate demand, in others it seems to have been due to a shortage of materials. My techniques of measurement do not distinguish between the two.

Relationship of Productivity to Price Changes

The impact on prices of the poor productivity performance in 1974 and 1975, reinforced by deterioration in the terms of trade, was devastating. On a potential basis, command over goods and

13. See appendix I.

services had increased at average annual rates of 2.2 percent per person employed and 2.8 percent per hour worked from 1948 to 1973. (These were scarcely different from corresponding rates for real national income.) Labor earnings per year and per hour could have been increased at these rates without raising the implicit deflator for command over goods and services in the economy as a whole, provided that the labor share of national income did not change. A similar relationship was popularized by the Council of Economic Advisers during the "guidepost" period of the Kennedy and Johnson administrations, and again during wage and price control periods of the Nixon administration.[14] The CEA rightly considered it proper to use changes in potential rather than actual productivity to set guideposts. Although the ratio of actual to potential labor productivity falls in recessions and rises in booms, the effect on prices is offset because the labor share of national income rises in recessions and falls in booms. (In current prices, national income is the same as command over goods and services.) Thus *actual* prices would tend to be stable over the cycle if labor earnings rose at the same rate as *potential* productivity.

Of course, wages actually increased more than productivity from 1948 to 1973, and the implicit deflator for command over goods and services rose —at an average annual rate of 2.8 percent.[15] Most of the increase occurred after 1965, when deficit financing of the costs of the Vietnamese conflict provided the initial stimulus to accelerated inflation. In the last five years of the period (1968–73) the annual increase averaged 5.4 percent. Thus inflation was already strong and persistent as the country approached 1974–75.

Labor has become accustomed to wage increases sufficient to raise expected real earnings at least as much as the rate of increase in potential productivity, and management to granting such increases with little resistance. If price changes and productivity changes are expected to be similar to those of the recent past, and if productivity changes actually conform to this expectation on a potential basis,

then the past rate of inflation will tend to perpetuate itself.[16]

But the sudden unanticipated drop in the rate of increase of command over goods and services per hour worked, computed on a potential basis, radically changed the situation in 1974 and 1975. Wage increases that in the absence of the drop would have raised unit labor costs at the previous rate now drove them upward far more sharply and caused a price explosion. The price series jumped 9.9 percent a year from 1973 to 1975 instead of the 5.4 percent experienced from 1968 to 1973. The rise in the labor share that typically occurs when there is a cyclical retardation of productivity and prevents it from raising prices occurred as usual; indeed, the drop in nonlabor earnings from 1972 to 1975 was unusually severe because the curtailment of production was exceptionally large. But it could not offset either the part of the drop in productivity that was not due to the business cycle or the change in the terms of trade.

The description I have just given can be provided only in retrospect. During 1974–75 the situation was not obvious. Although it was soon apparent that productivity performance was poor, it was not realized immediately that the retardation was as large as it turned out to be, or that oil would have as big and lasting an impact upon prices as proved to be the case. There was also an understandable tendency to consider all or almost all of the retardation in productivity as cyclical and to expect it to be made up when business recovered (which it was not).

Temporary relief was obtained in 1976 when potential command over goods and services per hour worked and prices returned to something like their 1968–73 rates of increase. The price deflator rose 5.2 percent.

Although remembrance of 1974 and 1975 did not prevent the 1968–73 relationship between price and productivity changes from being restored in 1976, there is no assurance that the aftermath of 1974–75, reinforced by the small size of productivity gains in 1977–78, will not accentuate price increases in the future. It cannot fail to do so if wage bargains are reached that seek to establish real earnings at the level of 1973 plus an allowance for subsequent productivity gains that is based on experience in an earlier period and far exceeds actual experience. The future course of potential pro-

14. However, the data I have cited refer to the whole economy, whereas the CEA used prices and productivity changes in the private economy, and this is among the reasons it obtained a guidepost for hourly earnings as high as 3.2 percent.

15. This price index is computed as the ratio of column 1 to column 3 in table 2-1. It increased 37.3 percent in the seventeen years from 1948 to 1965, a period that included the hostilities in Korea, and 44.6 percent in the seven years from 1965 to 1973. The total increase from 1948 to 1973 was 98.6 percent.

16. Unless some other major influence, such as a change in the government surplus at high employment, intervenes to change it.

68756

330.973
D396a

Brescia College Library
Owensboro, Kentucky

ductivity will also affect prices, but what that course will be is unknown.

The preceding paragraphs are not offered as a history of prices. Prices are subject to many influences and are the subject of many entire books. Nor can the basic cause and effect relationships underlying price changes be inferred from ex post data for changes in wages, productivity, income shares, and prices. But attention must be directed to the effect on prices of the sudden change in the course of productivity after 1973. The nature, timing, and magnitude of the change in productivity that occurred at that time and its effect on prices are not sufficiently appreciated.[17]

While low productivity growth stimulates inflation, it is also evident that inflation poses a multiple threat to productivity, although the effects have not been quantified. First, as explained in chapter 9, rapid price advances tend to reduce output per unit of input by interfering with efficient operation of domestic and international markets, complicating decisionmaking, and distorting taxation. Second, inflation generally results in governments adopting macroeconomic policies designed to operate the economy below its supply capabilities. The result is not only unemployed labor but also underutilization of employed labor and capital that lowers their productivity. In addition, operation of the economy below capacity reduces investment and, if the deficiency is not subsequently made good, impairs labor productivity at a later date. Third, when dissatisfied with weaker measures, governments resort to price and wage controls. Such controls interfere with efficiency, and the recurring threat of their imposition forces firms to protect themselves against that contingency in making decisions even when controls are not in effect.

National Income by Sector

In subsequent chapters I shall investigate the sources of growth of national income. To facilitate that analysis, I have divided the economy into four parts: (1) general government, households, institutions, and "rest-of-the-world" labor; (2) the services of dwellings; (3) international assets; and (4) nonresidential business. Each of the first three has the following special characteristics: that all of the national income originating in it accrues to a single

factor of production, that the value of output in current prices is simply the earnings of that factor, and that changes in real output are ascribable to that factor. The fourth sector, nonresidential business, comprises the bulk of the economy. In 1976 it accounted for 76 percent of both national income and employment.

National income in current prices is shown by sector of origin in table 2-5 and in constant prices in table 2-6. Employment and real NIPPE are shown by sector in table 2-7. National income and employment in nonresidential business are further divided between farm and nonfarm enterprises; farming is not considered a separate sector, but its declining size relative to the nonfarm economy has been a major aspect of growth. The increasing proportion of workers in nonfarm business who work for wages and salaries is another such aspect, and table 2-7 separates nonfarm wage and salary workers from self-employed and unpaid family workers.

Description of the Sectors and Their National Income

The largest of the three single-factor sectors consists of *general government, households, institutions, and labor in the rest of the world*. Its national income in current prices ($247.8 billion in 1976) consists of the compensation of labor that final purchasers of the nation's output hire directly. Four types of purchasers are included. The largest ($191.6 billion in current prices in 1976) is general government (all government except government enterprises such as the U.S. Postal Service and municipally owned utilities). Americans that government employs abroad are included. Next biggest ($49.7 billion in 1976) are nonprofit organizations providing services to individuals; included are nonprofit hospitals and educational institutions, churches, clubs, private welfare agencies, and many other types. Private households ($6.4 billion) are included because they employ domestic servants and baby-sitters. The fourth component, labor in the rest-of-the-world industry, consists in part of the compensation of U.S. citizens employed within the United States by foreign governments and international organizations. It also includes the amount by which the compensation of Americans employed abroad by U.S. business firms exceeds the compensation of foreign residents employed here by U.S. firms. Compensation of employees in the rest-of-the-world industry was plus or minus $0.1 billion or a smaller amount except in 1960–62, when it was minus $0.2 billion. For brevity, it will usually be omitted from the title of the sector.

---

17. The *Economic Report of the President, January 1979;* and *Reaching a Higher Standard of Living, 1979,* Report of the Office of Economic Research of The New York Stock Exchange (1979), also stress the inflationary effects of slow productivity growth.

Table 2-5. National Income in Current Prices, by Sector of Origin and Industrial Branch, 1929, 1940–41, and 1947–78
Billions of dollars

Year	Whole economy (1)	General government, households, and institutions[a] (2)	Services of dwellings[b] (3)	International assets (4)	Nonresidential business Total[b] (5)	Nonresidential business Farm[c] (6)	Nonresidential business Nonfarm[b] (7)
			Excluding Alaska and Hawaii				
1929	84.8	7.2	5.3	0.8	71.5	8.6	62.9
1940[d]	79.7	10.2	3.3	0.4	65.8	6.3	59.5
1940[e]	78.1	8.6	3.3	0.4	65.8	6.3	59.5
1941[d]	102.6	11.9	3.6	0.4	86.7	8.8	77.9
1941[e]	101.4	10.7	3.6	0.4	86.7	8.8	77.9
1947	194.6	21.9	4.4	0.9	167.4	19.7	147.7
1948	219.0	23.1	5.0	1.1	189.8	22.1	167.7
1949	212.7	25.4	6.0	1.1	180.2	16.8	163.4
1950	236.2	27.4	6.9	1.3	200.6	17.9	182.7
1951	272.3	34.3	7.8	1.5	228.7	20.5	208.2
1952	285.8	38.4	9.3	1.5	236.6	19.6	217.0
1953	299.7	39.7	11.0	1.5	247.5	17.3	230.2
1954	299.1	40.5	12.5	1.9	244.2	16.5	227.7
1955	328.0	43.2	13.3	2.0	269.5	15.5	254.0
1956	346.9	46.3	14.1	2.2	284.3	15.5	268.8
1957	362.3	49.6	15.5	2.4	294.8	15.4	279.4
1958	364.0	53.5	17.0	2.3	291.2	17.8	273.4
1959	397.1	56.3	18.5	2.5	319.8	15.4	304.4
1960[f]	410.5	60.5	20.0	2.6	327.4	16.4	311.0
			Including Alaska and Hawaii				
1960[f]	412.0	60.8	20.0	2.6	328.6	16.4	312.2
1961	424.2	64.8	21.6	3.2	334.6	17.3	317.3
1962	457.4	69.8	23.6	3.6	360.4	17.7	342.7
1963	482.8	74.5	25.1	3.7	379.5	17.8	361.7
1964	519.2	80.6	26.6	4.4	407.6	16.8	390.8
1965	566.0	86.8	28.6	4.7	445.9	19.7	426.2
1966	622.2	97.7	30.9	4.1	489.5	21.2	468.3
1967	655.8	109.1	33.1	4.5	509.1	19.6	489.5
1968	714.4	121.6	33.6	4.7	554.5	20.0	534.5
1969	767.9	133.0	35.0	4.4	595.5	22.5	573.0
1970	798.4	146.4	37.2	4.5	610.3	22.9	587.4
1971	858.1	160.0	40.7	6.5	650.9	23.7	627.2
1972	951.9	174.6	45.7	7.0	724.6	29.5	695.1
1973	1,064.6	189.6	48.7	9.0	817.3	47.4	769.2
1974	1,136.0	206.2	54.6	13.0	862.2	41.0	821.2
1975	1,217.0	228.7	61.3	10.5	916.5	39.5	877.0
1976	1,364.1	247.8	68.2	14.3	1,033.8	36.1	997.7
1977[g]	1,515.3	270.7	75.5	17.3	1,151.8	n.a.	n.a.
1978[g]	1,704.1	298.0	82.8	19.4	1,303.9	n.a.	n.a.

Sources: Column 1, NIPA, table 1.11; column 2, NIPA, table 1.14, sum of rows 38, 42, and 47; column 3, NIPA, table 1.20, row 13 minus row 14; column 4, NIPA, table 1.14, sum of rows 48 and 49; column 5, column 1 minus columns 2 through 4; column 6, NIPA, table 1.18, sum of rows 11 and 19, plus NIPA, table 1.11, row 20, minus NIPA, table 1.20, line 13, plus government payments to nonoperator landlords from U.S. Department of Agriculture, Economic Research Service, *Farm Income Statistics*, Statistical Bulletin 557 (July 1976), table 14H (1976 figure by phone); column 7, column 5 minus column 6. See pp. 5–6 for sources of NIPA data.
n.a. Not available.
a. Includes compensation of employees in the rest-of-the-world industry.
b. The small amount of labor income in the dwellings industry is classified in nonfarm nonresidential business.
c. Includes net rent and government payments to nonoperator landlords. Excludes farm housing.
d. Including relief work.
e. Excluding work relief. Work relief data are from NIPA, table 6.6.
f. See table 2-1, note e.
g. Preliminary.

National income originating in general government, households, and institutions valued in constant (1972) prices is simply the value assigned to the "output" of the individuals employed in the sector. To obtain this value, the BEA extrapolates, by components, the 1972 value of output in current prices by its estimates of the quantity of labor used. (A more detailed description is provided in chapter 6.) Thus it can be stated unequivocally that changes in output in this sector, as measured, are due ex-

Table 2-6. National Income in Constant Prices, by Sector of Origin and Industrial Branch, 1929, 1940–41, and 1947–78
Billions of 1972 dollars

Year	Whole economy (1)	General government, households, and institutions[a] (2)	Services of dwellings[b] (3)	Inter- national assets (4)	Nonresidential business Total[b] (5)	Nonresidential business Farm[c] (6)	Nonresidential business Nonfarm[b] (7)
			Excluding Alaska and Hawaii				
1929	254.7	41.7	7.2	1.9	203.9	19.0	184.9
1940[d]	277.6	60.0	7.1	1.3	209.2	21.2	188.0
1940[e]	270.6	53.0	7.1	1.3	209.2	21.2	188.0
1941[d]	331.1	71.0	7.7	1.2	251.2	23.2	228.0
1941[e]	325.7	65.6	7.7	1.2	251.2	23.2	228.0
1947	390.8	74.0	9.9	1.5	305.4	20.4	285.0
1948	406.3	74.8	10.7	1.7	319.1	21.3	297.8
1949	402.4	79.6	12.0	1.8	309.0	20.4	288.6
1950	437.7	83.0	12.9	1.8	340.0	21.1	318.9
1951	474.8	97.5	14.0	1.8	361.5	19.3	342.2
1952	492.7	103.9	15.4	1.8	371.6	20.0	351.6
1953	509.7	104.3	16.5	2.0	386.9	21.0	365.9
1954	499.6	103.2	17.8	2.4	376.2	21.3	354.9
1955	536.7	105.7	18.8	2.6	409.6	22.2	387.4
1956	552.2	108.9	19.8	2.8	420.7	22.1	398.6
1957	560.2	111.9	21.2	3.0	424.1	21.4	402.7
1958	551.2	114.5	22.8	3.1	410.8	22.7	388.1
1959	589.1	116.6	24.3	3.3	444.9	22.0	422.9
1960[f]	600.2	120.8	25.8	3.4	450.2	23.3	426.9
			Including Alaska and Hawaii				
1960[f]	602.5	121.5	25.8	3.4	451.8	23.4	428.4
1961	614.3	125.5	27.3	4.3	457.2	23.9	433.3
1962	652.7	130.3	29.0	4.9	488.5	24.0	464.5
1963	680.1	133.7	30.5	5.0	510.9	24.8	486.1
1964	717.1	138.2	32.1	5.8	541.0	24.2	516.8
1965	765.5	143.5	34.1	6.1	581.8	25.2	556.6
1966	808.7	153.3	35.9	5.3	614.2	23.7	590.5
1967	828.8	162.1	38.0	5.7	623.0	24.6	598.4
1968	868.5	167.7	39.3	6.0	655.5	24.6	630.9
1969	891.6	171.7	41.1	5.6	673.2	25.5	647.7
1970	879.5	171.6	42.5	5.4	660.0	26.8	633.2
1971	899.9	172.6	43.8	7.1	676.4	28.6	647.8
1972	951.9	174.6	45.7	7.0	724.6	29.5	695.1
1973	999.8	177.0	47.8	7.6	767.4	29.0	738.4
1974	977.9	179.9	49.6	6.8	741.6	27.9	713.7
1975	955.3	183.5	52.3	4.9	714.6	29.1	685.5
1976	1,017.4	186.0	55.1	6.7	769.6	28.3	741.3
1977[g]	1,065.1	189.4	58.9	7.3	809.5	n.a.	n.a.
1978[g]	1,110.8	194.1	62.1	7.8	846.8	n.a.	n.a.

Sources: Column 1, NIPA, table 1.12, row 14; column 2, sum of NIPA, table 1.12, rows 23 and 24, and output of employees in the rest of the world, computed as the quotient of NIPA, table 1.14, row 47 and the deflator used by the Bureau of Economic Analysis for a group of international service transactions in which compensation of employees in the rest of the world is included for deflation; column 3, NIPA, table 1.21, row 11 reduced by the ratio of row 14 to row 13 in NIPA, table 1.20; column 4, NIPA, table 1.12, row 25, minus the output of employees in the rest of the world included in column 2; column 5, column 1 minus columns 2 through 4; column 6, NIPA, table 1.19, sum of rows 11 and 17, minus farm housing national income, provided by the BEA (and equal to NIPA, table 1.21, row 11 minus NIPA, table 1.12, row 20, in postwar years) and plus government payments to nonoperator landlords in current prices (see sources of table 2-4, column 6) deflated by the implicit deflator for farm national income from NIPA, table 7.10, row 17; column 7, column 5 minus column 6. See pp. 5–6 for sources of NIPA data.
n.a. Not available.
a. Includes output of labor in the rest-of-the-world industry.
b. The small amount of output of labor in the dwellings industry is classified in nonfarm nonresidential business.
c. Includes output corresponding to net rent and government payments to nonfarm landlords. Excludes farm housing.
d. Includes output of persons on work relief.
e. Excludes output of persons on work relief; data from the Bureau of Economic Analysis.
f. See table 2-1, note e.
g. Preliminary.

Table 2-7. Persons Employed, by Sector, Industrial Branch, and Type of Worker, and National Income per Person Employed, by Sector[a]

	Persons employed (thousands)							National income per person employed (1972 dollars)		
			Nonresidential business							
					Nonfarm				General govern-ment, house-holds, and institu-tions[b] (9)	
Year	Whole economy (1)	General govern-ment, households, and institu-tions[b] (2)	Total (3)	Farm (4)	Total (5)	Wage and salary workers (6)	Self-employed and unpaid family workers (7)	Whole economy (8)		Non-residential business (10)
				Excluding Alaska and Hawaii						
1929	47,729	6,442	41,287	9,878	31,409	26,408	5,001	5,336	6,473	4,939
1940[c]	51,275	10,426	40,849	8,886	31,963	26,692	5,271	5,414	5,755	5,121
1940[d]	48,445	7,596	40,849	8,886	31,963	26,692	5,271	5,586	6,977	5,121
1941[c]	55,794	11,190	44,604	8,910	35,694	30,371	5,323	5,934	6,345	5,632
1941[d]	53,585	8,981	44,604	8,910	35,694	30,371	5,323	6,078	7,304	5,632
1947	59,601	9,536	50,065	7,927	42,138	36,066	6,072	6,557	7,760	6,100
1948	60,578	9,798	50,780	7,835	42,945	36,777	6,168	6,707	7,634	6,284
1949	59,258	10,194	49,064	7,659	41,405	35,281	6,124	6,791	7,809	6,298
1950	60,945	10,727	50,218	7,504	42,714	36,542	6,172	7,182	7,737	6,770
1951	64,769	12,546	52,223	7,079	45,144	38,958	6,186	7,331	7,771	6,922
1952	66,000	13,197	52,803	6,878	45,925	39,688	6,237	7,465	7,873	7,037
1953	66,830	13,260	53,570	6,637	46,933	40,731	6,202	7,627	7,866	7,222
1954	65,075	13,088	51,987	6,618	45,369	39,291	6,078	7,677	7,885	7,236
1955	66,534	13,415	53,119	6,498	46,621	40,523	6,098	8,067	7,879	7,711
1956	67,986	13,795	54,191	6,244	47,947	41,770	6,177	8,122	7,894	7,763
1957	68,126	14,054	54,072	5,928	48,144	41,869	6,275	8,223	7,962	7,843
1958	66,381	14,378	52,003	5,652	46,351	40,114	6,237	8,304	7,964	7,900
1959	67,868	14,617	53,251	5,540	47,711	41,532	6,179	8,680	7,977	8,355
1960[e]	68,469	15,030	53,439	5,262	48,177	41,964	6,213	8,766	8,037	8,425
				Including Alaska and Hawaii						
1960[e]	68,756	15,108	53,648	5,286	48,362	42,126	6,236	8,763	8,042	8,422
1961	68,792	15,599	53,193	5,139	48,054	41,801	6,253	8,930	8,045	8,595
1962	70,243	16,265	53,978	4,921	49,057	42,910	6,147	9,292	8,011	9,050
1963	70,853	16,572	54,281	4,638	49,643	43,624	6,019	9,599	8,068	9,412
1964	72,270	17,072	55,198	4,362	50,836	44,783	6,053	9,923	8,095	9,801
1965	74,519	17,670	56,849	4,151	52,698	46,669	6,029	10,273	8,121	10,234
1966	77,941	19,114	58,827	3,768	55,059	49,129	5,930	10,376	8,020	10,441
1967	79,596	19,937	59,659	3,623	56,036	50,166	5,870	10,413	8,131	10,443
1968	81,513	20,551	60,962	3,562	57,400	51,616	5,784	10,655	8,160	10,753
1969	83,615	20,816	62,799	3,422	59,377	53,392	5,985	10,663	8,248	10,720
1970	83,244	20,765	62,479	3,308	59,171	53,224	5,947	10,565	8,264	10,564
1971	83,144	20,854	62,290	3,223	59,067	53,015	6,052	10,823	8,277	10,859
1972	85,077	21,003	64,074	3,216	60,858	54,757	6,101	11,189	8,313	11,309
1973	88,335	21,241	67,094	3,180	63,914	57,701	6,213	11,318	8,333	11,438
1974	89,651	21,461	68,190	3,182	65,008	58,635	6,373	10,908	8,383	10,875
1975	88,077	21,902	66,175	3,156	63,019	56,645	6,374	10,846	8,378	10,799
1976	90,484	22,102	68,382	3,133	65,249	58,851	6,398	11,244	8,416	11,254
1977	93,709	n.a.	70,941	n.a.	n.a.	n.a.	n.a.	11,366	n.a.	11,411
1978	97,420	n.a.	74,047	n.a.	n.a.	n.a.	n.a.	11,402	n.a.	11,436

Sources: Columns 1–7, see appendix B; columns 8–10, table 2-6 and table 2-7, columns 1–5.
n.a. Not available.
a. No employment is classified in the "services of dwellings" and "international assets" sectors.
b. Includes employment in the dwellings sector.
c. Includes persons on work relief.
d. Excludes persons on work relief. Work relief data are from NIPA, table 6.7.
e. See table 2-1, note e.

clusively to changes in the quantity of labor it uses. From 1960 to 1976, for example, the change in the amount of labor employed by general government, households, and institutions contributed $64.5 billion of the total increase of $414.9 billion in the value of real national income in the whole economy (table 2-6).

The *services of dwellings* industry may be defined as the provision of housing services. The "establishments" in this industry are owner-occupied and tenant-occupied nonfarm and farm dwellings. By definition, all residential structures and residential land in the country (except nonhousekeeping units such as hotels) are used in this industry. Factor input in this industry consists only of residential structures and land.[18] This sector absorbs a very large portion of the nation's total capital. At the end of 1976, the net (depreciated) value of residential structures was 80 percent as large as the combined value of all the fixed capital and inventories in the nonresidential business sector.[19] Similarly, residential sites comprise a very large portion of the total value of land.

The earnings in current dollars of dwellings and their sites ($68.2 billion in 1976) have been isolated and are shown in table 2-5, column 3. The net value in constant prices that the BEA placed on the output of this industry can also be isolated, and it is shown in table 2-6, column 3. Because the output of residential capital and land in the whole economy is the same as the output of the dwellings industry, the contribution of residential capital and land to the increase in total national income (as modified by changes in occupancy rates) can be computed directly from this column. Of the increase of $414.9 billion in real national income from 1960 to 1976, for example, $29.3 billion was from this source.

The third sector, *international assets,* contributed $14.3 billion to current-dollar national income in 1976. This amount is the excess of property income received by U.S. residents from abroad over property income paid by U.S. residents to foreign residents.[20] It must be separately included in national income to secure the earnings of factors of production that are supplied by residents of the nation.[21] When national income is viewed as an output measure, the adjustment is required so as to include the value of foreign output attributable to U.S. capital and to exclude the value of U.S. output attributable to foreign capital. The actual statistical series for net property income from abroad does not conform to the definition very well because only earnings actually remitted between countries are

counted (except in the case of branch profits). Consequently the series is affected not only by earnings but also by decisions as to the amount of earnings that are to be remitted.

Changes in the net flow of property income from abroad in constant prices do, nevertheless, indicate the contribution of internationally owned assets to changes in national income as measured. Thus of the $414.9 billion increase in national income in constant prices from 1960 to 1976, $3.3 billion represents the increase in net property income from abroad and hence the contribution of international assets (table 2-6, column 4).

Nonresidential business covers the entire domestic business sector of the economy, as defined by the BEA, except that the services of dwellings are excluded. It includes corporations, partnerships, sole proprietorships, mutual financial institutions, government enterprises, cooperatives, and other miscellaneous forms of business, as well as organizations such as trade associations or chambers of commerce that primarily serve business. The distinguishing feature of the sector as a whole is that it sells its products for a price. Output in this sector is, with minor exceptions, measured as the sum of series for its various components, which are obtained either by dividing expenditures in current prices by a price index or, less often, by multiplying a physical quantity series by a base-year price. Output is rarely inferred from the behavior of labor, capital, or land input. Changes in the output of the nonresidential business sector result from changes in the quantities of all types of input and changes in a great variety of determinants of output per unit of input. Nonresidential business contributed $1,033.8 billion to current dollar national income in 1976. Of the $414.9 billion increase in constant price national income from 1960 to 1976, $317.8 billion stemmed from nonresidential business, including $4.9 billion from farming.

Potential National Income by Sector

Data on a potential basis are shown by sector in table 2-8. Only in nonresidential business do potential national income and employment differ from actual national income and employment. This results from the way potential national income is estimated; the explanation has two aspects.

First, in calculating the difference between actual and potential labor input, I introduced the simplifying assumption that, if the unemployment rate had been 4 percent rather than the actual rate, the entire difference from actual employment would

---

18. The small amount of labor employed in apartment houses is classified in nonresidential business.

19. This comparison is based on current prices. Time series for the values of nonresidential and residential capital in *constant* prices appear in tables 4-1 and 6-4.

20. Property income to and from abroad excludes interest paid and received by the U.S. government.

21. This is because business national income measures production occurring within the geographic boundaries of the United States. The corresponding amount of labor earnings is included in the "general government, households, institutions, and rest-of-the-world labor" sector.

Table 2-8. Potential National Income in Constant Prices, Potential Employment, and Potential National Income per Person Employed, by Sector, 1929, 1940–41, and 1947–78[a]

Year	Potential national income (billions of 1972 dollars)		Potential employment (thousands)		Potential national income per person employed (1972 dollars)	
	Whole economy (1)	Nonresidential business[b] (2)	Whole economy (3)	Nonresidential business[b] (4)	Whole economy (5)	Nonresidential business[b] (6)
Excluding Alaska and Hawaii						
1929	249.9	199.1	46,990	40,548	5,318	4,910
1940	301.8	240.4	55,927	48,331	5,396	4,974
1941	329.8	255.3	57,306	48,325	5,755	5,283
1947	395.3	309.9	59,351	49,815	6,661	6,221
1948	401.3	314.1	60,211	50,413	6,665	6,231
1949	411.8	318.4	61,099	50,905	6,740	6,255
1950	434.1	336.4	62,143	51,416	6,986	6,543
1951	461.7	348.4	63,872	51,326	7,229	6,788
1952	487.4	366.3	64,766	51,569	7,526	7,103
1953	505.9	383.1	65,430	52,170	7,732	7,343
1954	515.5	392.1	66,433	53,345	7,760	7,350
1955	532.8	405.7	66,749	53,334	7,982	7,607
1956	559.5	428.0	67,953	54,158	8,234	7,903
1957	574.1	438.0	68,243	54,189	8,413	8,083
1958	593.9	453.5	69,240	54,862	8,577	8,266
1959	609.2	465.0	69,322	54,705	8,788	8,500
1960[c]	628.3	478.3	70,019	54,989	8,973	8,698
Including Alaska and Hawaii						
1960[c]	630.7	480.0	70,312	55,204	8,970	8,695
1961	651.5	494.4	71,673	56,074	9,090	8,817
1962	670.9	506.7	71,853	55,588	9,337	9,115
1963	692.4	523.2	72,632	56,060	9,533	9,333
1964	719.1	543.0	73,530	56,458	9,780	9,618
1965	755.1	571.4	75,009	57,339	10,067	9,965
1966	791.6	597.1	77,493	58,379	10,215	10,228
1967	824.0	618.2	79,365	59,428	10,382	10,403
1968	858.4	645.4	80,938	60,387	10,606	10,688
1969	897.3	678.9	82,931	62,115	10,820	10,930
1970	922.5	703.0	84,526	63,761	10,914	11,026
1971	951.8	728.3	85,856	65,002	11,086	11,204
1972	996.6	769.3	87,395	66,392	11,403	11,587
1973	1,041.1	808.7	89,575	68,334	11,623	11,835
1974	1,063.4	827.1	92,011	70,550	11,557	11,724
1975	1,055.9	815.2	94,858	72,956	11,131	11,174
1976	1,091.8	844.0	96,228	74,126	11,346	11,386
1977[d]	n.a.	n.a.	98,518	75,750	n.a.	n.a.
1978[d]	n.a.	n.a.	100,719	77,346	n.a.	n.a.

Sources: Column 1, table 2-4, column 4; column 2, sum of table 2-6, column 5, and table 2-4, columns 2 and 3; column 3, table 2-1, column 8; column 4, sum of table 2-7, column 3, and table L-4, column 10; column 5, column 1 divided by column 3; column 6, column 2 divided by column 4.

n.a. Not available.

a. In "general government, households, and institutions," "services of dwellings," and "international assets," potential national income is the same as actual national income (excluding work relief in 1940 and 1941). See table 2-6 for data. In "general government, households, and institutions," potential employment is the same as actual employment (excluding work relief in 1940 and 1941). Farm employment and the number of self-employed and unpaid family workers are also the same as on an actual basis. See table 2-7 for data. No employment is classified in "services of dwellings" and "international assets."

b. The small amount of labor in the dwellings industry and its output are classified in nonresidential business.

c. See table 2-1, note e.

d. Preliminary.

have been among nonfarm wage and salary workers in the business sector.[22] This is a reasonable simplification even if it is not precisely correct. Farm em-

22. My procedure also implies that in government, households, and institutions hours of work are the same under actual and potential conditions.

ployment, employment of nonfarm proprietors and unpaid family workers, employment in general government, and even employment in households and institutions are not much affected by short-term changes in the strength of total demand. A moderate change in the assumption adopted would have little effect on the results for the whole economy, because of offsets. A possible alternative assumption—that employment in each category would have been changed proportionally—is far less realistic.

For the years 1940 and 1941 one modification of this assumption is made. If unemployment had been at 4 percent, there would have been no work relief program. Work relief workers are therefore eliminated from general government, and the value of their output is deducted from actual national income. It is assumed they would have been in nonresidential business under potential conditions.[23]

Second, an adjustment for the effect of changes in intensity of demand on productivity is made only in nonresidential business. There probably is no such effect in "general government, households, and institutions," but even if there were it would not affect actual output as measured and therefore would not create a difference between actual and potential output. Any reasonable adjustment of net property income from abroad to allow for the effects of fluctuations in intensity of domestic demand would be trivial relative to the size of total national income. The situation in the services-of-dwellings sector is somewhat different in that national income is affected by the proportion of dwellings that are occupied as well as by the size of the housing stock. But fluctuations in this proportion are only trivially related to changes in the intensity of aggregate demand; they stem mainly from the relationship between long swings in the residential building cycle and variations in the number of households.

Changes after 1973

The nonresidential business sector was almost entirely responsible for the setback to NIPPE and the other output measures after 1973. In fact, retardation of growth rates was more pronounced in nonresidential business than in the economy as a whole. Relative stability of the other sectors of the economy cushioned the decline.

Within nonresidential business the growth rate

23. Those persons employed by state and local governments and nonprofit organizations under the current Comprehensive Employment and Training Act who would not have been so employed in the absence of CETA funds might have been treated similarly but were not. This group became sizable only in 1976. Total potential national income is much less affected by this decision than by the corresponding decision with respect to 1940–41 work relief not only because numbers are smaller but also because the difference between the average pay of CETA workers and that of regular workers is smaller, as is the difference between the output per worker of the two groups as measured by the pay difference.

of NIPPE fell from 2.4 percent in 1948–73 to −0.5 percent in 1973–76 on an actual basis. The reduction of 2.9 percentage points compares with a reduction of 2.3 points in the whole economy. Similarly, in nonresidential business the growth rate of potential real national income per person potentially employed fell by 3.9 percentage points, compared with a drop of 3.0 points in the whole economy.

In "general government, households, and institutions" real NIPPE usually does not change very much, and this was the case in the period under consideration. Its growth rate was 0.3 percent in both 1948–73 and 1973–76.

Part of NIPPE in the whole economy consists of the services provided by dwellings and net property income from abroad. In constant prices these components rose less, per person employed, from 1973 to 1976 than from 1948 to 1973. This contributed to the reduction in the growth rate of NIPPE. But only 0.1 percentage points out of the reduction observed on an actual basis, and 0.2 points of the reduction on a potential basis, can be explained in this way.

Selection of Time Periods for Comparison

The series of detailed output determinants that support the analysis of this book are provided for 1929, 1940, 1941, and every individual year from 1947 through 1976. Annual series were not prepared for 1930 to 1946 because the information that would be needed is lacking for many output determinants. The period is also difficult to analyze because of the Great Depression and World War II. To avoid a gap of nearly two decades, estimates were made for 1940 and 1941, years for which information is relatively full and which were also among the least abnormal years. Estimates end with 1976 because of the unavoidable time lag required for preparation and publication of data.

To place the years to be analyzed in perspective, figure 2-1 shows the indexes of total actual national income in constant prices, including work relief, in all years from 1925 through 1978. Years covered in this study are indicated by large dots. The series is plotted on a logarithmic scale so that equal vertical distances on the chart represent equal percentage differences in national income rather than differences that are equal in absolute amount. Potential national income is shown too, but observations are available only for years analyzed in this study. The 1929 and 1940 estimates are joined with

Figure 2-1. Index of Total National Income, Actual, 1925–78, and Potential, 1929–76ª
Based on data in 1972 dollars

Index, actual national income in 1972 = 100 (ratio scale)

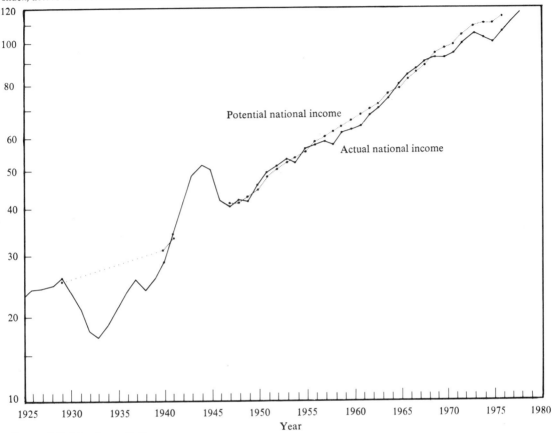

Sources: Table 2-2 and appendix B.
a. Large dots indicate years for which detailed analytical indexes are provided.

a straight line, but to do so from 1941 to 1947 would be misleading because potential as well as actual national income rose far above trend values. Note that actual national income in 1972 is equal to 100 for both series.

The year 1929, with which my analysis will begin, terminated the generally prosperous 1920s. Output was at a record high. The next year the onset of the depression began to drag production far below the economy's capacity to produce. Output did not regain its 1929 level until 1939, a whole decade later.

In 1940, the second year covered in my analysis, unemployment and emergency work relief employment remained massive but the economy was vigorously expanding. National income, including the output of emergency workers, stood 9 percent above 1929. From 1940 to 1941 national income

rose an additional 19 percent to a point 30 percent above the predepression peak.

From 1941 my indexes skip to 1947. In the interim, national income had jumped to a wartime high in 1944, then receded until 1947. At its peak in 1944 national income was 52 percent above 1941, an output level made possible by employment of an extraordinarily large percentage of the population (counting the armed forces, whose services are included in national income), by long working hours, by very intensive utilization of employed labor and capital, and doubtless by other special wartime conditions as well. The 1944 peak was not regained until 1953, nine years later. In 1947, when my analysis resumes, national income was 18.0 percent above 1941 but 21 percent below 1944.

From 1947 through 1976, the period for which

annual data are provided, national income rose by 159 percent. The increase was irregular. Percentage changes varied widely from year to year as well as over longer periods, the result both of changes in the rate at which potential output was growing and of fluctuations of actual output around the potential level. Actual declines in the calendar year series were experienced in 1949, 1954, 1958, 1970, 1974, and 1975; quarterly data show an additional decline during 1960. These interruptions to expansion were in no way comparable in size or duration to the catastrophic decline from 1929 to 1933, nor to the 1944–47 fallback from the wartime peak.

Data for thirty-three individual years are provided in this study, so it is possible to calculate the change in output or any of its determinants between any two of thirty-three years. To summarize the findings, however, it will be necessary to choose a limited number of time spans. I have selected ten.

For long-term analysis, I present data covering the entire period covered by estimates, 1929 to 1976, and for the 1929–48 and 1948–73 periods within it. The latter period is terminated when the sudden break in trend occurred. Separate data for 1973–76 are shown as a "shorter" period.

For shorter-term analysis, I have divided the forty-seven-year time span into seven periods that range from three to twelve years in length. The first, 1929–41, spans the Great Depression. The second, 1941–48, covers World War II and the immediate reconversion to peacetime production. My grouping of the postwar years is based mainly on the path of potential national income. The timing of changes in the course of major output determinants are also an important consideration, but this second criterion does not conflict with the first. A third consideration is a preference for longer periods over shorter periods because the accuracy of sources-of-growth tables must be presumed to decline as the length of the period covered diminishes. This is partly because the effects of irregular factors—some of which are difficult to measure and at least one of which (the calendar; see chapter 5) has not been measured—increase as periods are shortened. The effects of possible random errors in series for other determinants of output and the output series itself have a similar tendency. In addition some of the general procedures on which the estimates are based may be better founded for longer-term than for shorter-term analysis.

In *Accounting for Growth,* I noted (page 93) that four postwar periods of fast and slow growth could be distinguished up to 1969. The growth rates

of potential national income in these periods, based on the new data from the present study, are shown below. The last period ended in 1969 because that was when the data stopped, not because there was evidence of a slackening of growth after that date.

Period	Growth rate of potential national income
1947–49	2.07
1949–53	5.28
1953–64	3.21
1964–69	4.53

To avoid very short periods and to eliminate the use of data for 1947, a year for which the accuracy of price indexes is particularly suspect, I actually used only three postwar periods in *Accounting for Growth,* and I retain the same periods in the present study. They are shown with their growth rates, based on the new data, in the first three rows below.

Period	Growth rate of potential national income
1948–53	4.74
1953–64	3.21
1964–69	4.53
1969–73	3.79
1973–76	1.60

Estimates of potential national income are now available through 1976. Growth rates over some time spans pertinent to the selection of periods are:

1964–69	4.53	1971–73	4.59
1964–73	4.20	1973–76	1.60
1964–76	3.54	1973–75	0.71
1969–73	3.79	1975–76	3.40
1969–71	2.99		

I have decided to retain 1964–69 as one of the shorter periods for detailed analysis of the sources of growth, and to introduce 1969–73 and 1973–76 periods. Use of a single high-growth period running from 1964 to 1973 was considered since the 1969–73 growth rate of potential national income, at 3.79 percent, was still a good one. The decline from the 1964–69 rate of 4.53 percent was big enough, however, to make isolation of the sources that accounted for the drop interesting. The fact that these years had not previously been analyzed supported the decision to treat 1969–73 separately. Subdivision of 1969–73 was rejected, despite the difference between 1969–71 and 1971–73 in growth rates, because the periods would be too short and also because no lasting change in growth sources is evident. A new period clearly was required after 1973; I have continued it to 1976, when the data end. This is an incomplete period. Preliminary data indicate that growth of potential output, and especially output per worker, continued slow until at least 1978. Three years clearly is a shorter time span than is desirable from the standpoint of accuracy, and in the future this period can be lengthened. In the meantime the disadvantage of such a short period is ameliorated by the knowledge that the growth rate itself remained low for at least two more years and by the observation that the main changes in growth sources were very pronounced.

Table 2-9 shows rates of growth during each of the selected periods for total potential and actual national income both in the whole economy and in nonresidential business. Rates for both total national income and NIPPE are provided. The study will focus on these eighty growth rates. As a rule, data exclusive of work relief employment will be analyzed. This type of employment was so unusual, and the value of output per worker of work relief employees was so low, that its inclusion would complicate analysis without contributing to it.

Table 2-9. Growth Rates of Potential and Actual National Income and National Income per Person Employed in the Whole Economy and Nonresidential Business, Selected Periods, 1929–76

Percent per annum

Item	Long periods			Shorter periods						
	1929–76	*1929–48*	*1948–73*	*1929–41*	*1941–48*	*1948–53*	*1953–64*	*1964–69*	*1969–73*	*1973–76*
Whole economy										
Total potential national income	3.18	2.52	3.87	2.34	2.84	4.74	3.21	4.53	3.79	1.60
Per person potentially employed	1.63	1.20	2.25	0.66	2.12	3.01	2.16	2.04	1.81	−0.80
Total actual national income	2.98	2.49	3.65	2.07a	3.21a	4.64	3.12	4.45	2.91	0.58
Per person employed	1.60	1.21	2.12	1.09a	1.41a	2.60	2.42	1.45	1.50	−0.22
Nonresidential business										
Total potential national income	3.11	2.43	3.84	2.09	3.01	4.05	3.19	4.57	4.47	1.43
Per person potentially employed	1.81	1.26	2.60	0.61	2.38	3.34	2.49	2.59	2.01	−1.28
Total actual national income	2.86	2.39	3.56	1.75	3.48	3.93	3.06	4.47	3.33	0.10
Per person employed	1.77	1.28	2.43	1.10	1.55	2.83	2.82	1.81	1.63	−0.54

Sources: Tables 2-2, 2-6, 2-7, and 2-8.

a. Based on data excluding work relief employees. When based on data including work relief employees, growth rates of total actual national income are 2.21 in 1929–41 and 2.97 in 1941–48, and growth rates of actual national income per person employed are 0.89 in 1929–41 and 1.76 in 1941–48.

⇒⟩⟨⟨⇐

Labor Input in Nonresidential Business

⇒⟩⟨⟨⇐

The nonresidential business sector is of particular interest because it is rather homogeneous in the motivations and behavior of producing units and the way output is measured. Determinants of the sector's output will be divided between those that affect total input and those that affect output per unit of input.

The analysis of inputs rests on the general proposition that enterprises seek to minimize costs of production and hence to use the various types of labor and property in proportions that yield the lowest costs. If they succeed in doing so, or if errors by individual enterprises are offsetting, the earnings of different types of inputs will be proportional to their marginal products. The presumption of this study is that on the average, for all enterprises in the sector, the tendency toward proportionality of factor prices and marginal products under conditions of reasonably high employment is sufficiently strong for relative earnings to provide an adequate measure of the relative marginal products of different inputs, and hence of the weights appropriate for combining them.[1] Relative earnings are not only used as weights to combine labor, capital, and land to arrive at a measure of total input, but also to weight different types of input within these broad categories.

This chapter is concerned with changes in labor input. My measure of labor input does not treat

1. See *Why Growth Rates Differ,* chap. 4, for a fuller discussion of the topic of this paragraph. The presumption is stronger in the present study because government, private households, and institutions are excluded from the universe to which it pertains.

employed persons or total hours worked as an undifferentiated mass. Its construction recognizes that hours worked by different groups contribute different average amounts to the value of output; relative earnings are used as weights to combine components. Labor earns about four-fifths of national income originating in nonresidential business, so it is inferred that it represents about four-fifths of total input. Consequently if labor input or any of its components has grown at any stated rate, it will have raised total input (and hence output if economies of scale are disregarded) about four-fifths as much. Actual estimates of these contributions are provided in chapter 7.

Labor input in nonresidential business and in the whole business sector are synonymous and are thus used interchangeably in this chapter. All employed persons except those classified in general government, households, and institutions are included. The services-of-dwellings and international assets sectors, as defined, do not use labor.

This chapter presents estimates of both actual and potential labor input in nonresidential business. Its descriptions of series on an actual basis are supplemented by appendixes B through F. Series on a potential basis are further described in appendix M.

Employment

The starting point for labor input measurement is employment. Employment is defined as the number of *persons* employed. The movement of the series nevertheless is based largely on data (from the national income and product accounts of the Bureau of Economic Analysis) that measure jobs rather than persons. The Current Population Survey, the only direct source of estimates of persons employed, was used to establish the average level of employment. The series I have constructed provides estimates of the number of persons employed that are statistically more consistent with the measurement of output, and judged also to be more accurate, than the CPS estimates. Table 3-1, column 1, shows the employment series in index form.

An index of potential nonresidential business employment is shown in table 3-2, column 1. It is expressed with actual 1972 employment equal to 100 so that the actual and potential indexes can be compared directly. Division of the 1976 actual index of 106.72 by the potential index of 115.69 shows that actual employment was 92.2 percent of potential employment in the sector in 1976.

When the civilian unemployment rate is above 4 percent, potential employment exceeds actual

Table 3-1. Nonresidential Business: Indexes of Sector Labor Input, 1929, 1940–41, and 1947–76[a]
1972 = 100

Year	Employment (1)	Average weekly hours (2)	Total weekly hours (3)	Age-sex composition of total hours (4)	Intragroup changes (5)	Specified intergroup shifts (6)	Amount of education (7)	Labor input (8)	Addendum: Effect of changes in hours (9)
1929	64.69	130.52	84.43	104.30	92.38	94.53	76.64	58.94	113.98
1940	64.00	117.37	75.12	105.91	98.02	94.52	82.79	61.02	108.74
1941	69.89	118.26	82.65	105.05	97.76	95.30	83.08	67.21	110.18
1947	78.44	113.41	88.96	104.78	98.61	96.55	85.42	75.80	107.97
1948	79.56	112.81	89.76	104.55	98.41	96.61	85.94	76.67	107.26
1949	76.88	111.39	85.63	104.50	98.96	96.34	86.69	73.96	106.20
1950	78.68	111.45	87.69	104.50	98.80	96.57	87.17	76.21	106.33
1951	81.83	111.40	91.15	104.70	98.64	97.06	87.48	79.93	106.65
1952	82.73	110.90	91.75	104.90	99.22	97.22	97.98	81.68	106.98
1953	83.93	110.25	92.53	105.10	99.27	97.46	88.45	83.22	106.66
1954	81.45	109.14	88.90	105.46	99.12	97.28	89.18	80.62	105.24
1955	83.23	109.41	91.06	105.13	99.28	97.55	89.55	83.03	105.96
1956	84.91	108.72	92.31	104.64	99.11	97.80	90.01	84.28	105.38
1957	84.72	107.09	90.73	104.56	99.51	97.94	90.60	83.76	104.37
1958	81.48	106.20	86.53	104.80	99.51	97.83	91.57	80.84	103.39
1959	83.43	106.89	89.19	104.54	99.53	98.09	92.10	83.82	104.35
1960	83.72	106.23	88.95	104.19	99.42	98.20	92.74	83.90	103.71
1961	83.02	105.62	87.68	104.28	99.56	98.23	93.50	83.62	103.30
1962	84.24	105.85	89.17	104.04	99.20	98.48	93.94	85.14	103.41
1963	84.71	105.74	89.58	104.13	98.92	98.79	94.34	85.99	103.33
1964	86.15	105.57	90.94	103.67	98.99	98.94	94.78	87.53	103.40
1965	88.72	105.79	93.86	102.97	98.76	99.16	95.36	90.25	103.60
1966	91.81	104.72	96.14	102.25	99.09	99.50	95.87	92.92	103.25
1967	93.11	103.04	95.94	102.24	99.55	99.64	96.54	93.92	102.20
1968	95.13	102.55	97.57	101.98	99.58	99.76	97.17	96.03	101.87
1969	98.00	101.90	99.88	101.22	99.56	99.85	97.72	98.19	101.30
1970	97.51	100.36	97.86	101.04	99.94	99.90	98.43	97.17	100.20
1971	97.21	99.95	97.17	100.87	99.90	99.93	99.30	97.16	99.78
1972	100.00	100.00	100.00	100.00	100.00	100.00	100.00	100.00	100.00
1973	104.71	99.51	104.20	99.16	100.22	100.10	100.83	104.51	99.83
1974	106.42	98.18	104.48	98.56	100.62	100.09	101.84	105.62	98.88
1975	103.28	97.26	100.45	99.03	100.66	99.98	102.98	103.09	97.88
1976	106.72	97.20	103.73	98.26	100.62	100.09	104.09	106.85	97.89

Column headers span: Columns (5) and (6) are under "*Efficiency of an hour's work as affected by changes in hours due to:*" — (5) *Intragroup changes*, (6) *Specified intergroup shifts*.

Sources: Column 1, table 2-6, column 3; column 2, table C-1, column 3; column 3, table C-1, columns 7–9; column 4, see appendix D; columns 5 and 6, see appendix E; column 7, see appendix F; column 8, product of columns 3, 4, 5, 6, and 7; column 9, product of columns 2, 5, and 6.
a. Series excluding and including Alaska and Hawaii were linked at 1960.

employment by the sum of (1) the amount by which unemployment exceeds 4 percent of the civilian labor force; and (2) 96 percent of the amount by which the actual civilian labor force (16 years of age and over) would have been larger if the unemployment rate were 4 percent.[2] When the unemployment rate is below 4 percent, actual employment exceeds potential employment by a corresponding amount. All of the difference between actual and potential employment in the whole economy is classified in nonresidential business.

Although it is widely agreed that high unem-

2. The employment series is not confined to persons 16 years of age or more. But the amount of labor input provided by younger persons who move in and out of the labor force as the unemployment rate fluctuates is so trivial that it can be ignored.

ployment reduces the labor force, the amount by which it does so is uncertain; potential employment estimates consequently may be appreciably in error when unemployment is very high. The estimates I use are described in appendix L. They imply that each additional percentage point in the civilian unemployment rate reduces the number in the labor force in each age-sex group by the following percentage of the population in that group:

Age group	Males	Females
16–19	1.2961	0.9871
20–24	0.9373	0.4991
25–64	0.0106	0.4780
65 and over	0.4393	0.0821

Since the mid-1960s the growth of potential business employment has been both rapid and

Table 3-2. Nonresidential Business: Indexes of Potential Sector Labor Input, 1929, 1940–41, and 1947–76[a]
Actual, 1972 = 100

| Year | Employ-ment (1) | Average weekly hours (2) | Total weekly hours (3) | Age-sex composition of total hours (4) | Efficiency of an hour's work as affected by changes in hours due to: | | Amount of education (7) | Labor input (8) | Addendum: Effect of changes in hours (9) |
					Intra-group changes (5)	Specified intergroup shifts (6)			
1929	63.53	130.22	82.73	104.72	92.45	94.37	76.75	58.01	113.61
1940	75.72	116.44	88.17	103.77	98.02	95.76	82.23	70.62	109.30
1941	75.72	116.51	88.22	104.26	98.03	95.84	82.71	71.47	109.46
1947	78.05	113.68	88.73	105.01	98.51	96.51	85.42	75.67	108.08
1948	78.99	112.56	88.91	104.84	98.50	96.56	85.96	76.21	107.06
1949	79.76	111.42	88.87	104.07	99.00	96.60	86.50	76.51	106.56
1950	80.56	110.95	89.38	104.25	99.03	96.74	87.05	77.71	106.29
1951	80.42	110.93	89.21	105.17	98.77	96.96	87.52	78.64	106.23
1952	80.80	110.89	89.60	105.51	99.16	97.08	88.06	80.14	106.75
1953	81.74	110.35	90.20	105.76	99.18	97.29	88.55	81.51	106.48
1954	83.58	109.58	91.59	105.23	99.06	97.45	89.03	82.83	105.79
1955	83.56	109.21	91.26	105.22	99.42	97.61	89.51	83.41	105.99
1956	84.85	109.31	92.75	104.84	99.05	97.85	90.00	84.82	105.94
1957	84.90	108.02	91.71	104.72	99.38	98.01	90.56	84.71	105.22
1958	85.96	107.78	92.65	104.15	99.32	98.21	91.28	85.92	105.13
1959	85.71	107.56	92.19	104.27	99.47	98.27	91.95	86.40	105.14
1960	86.16	107.31	92.46	103.90	99.28	98.41	92.57	86.88	104.85
1961	87.51	106.52	93.22	103.63	99.46	98.53	93.22	88.25	104.39
1962	86.76	106.21	92.15	103.72	99.20	98.63	93.78	87.70	103.92
1963	87.49	105.69	92.47	103.73	99.03	98.93	94.17	88.49	103.55
1964	88.11	105.24	92.73	103.42	99.14	99.04	94.66	89.14	103.34
1965	89.49	105.18	94.13	102.92	98.95	99.20	95.30	90.63	103.25
1966	91.11	104.15	94.89	102.37	99.25	99.47	95.89	91.96	102.82
1967	92.75	102.92	95.46	102.29	99.59	99.64	96.56	93.56	102.13
1968	94.25	102.24	96.36	102.12	99.66	99.72	97.21	95.07	101.61
1969	96.94	102.13	99.00	101.42	99.48	99.81	97.76	97.46	101.40
1970	99.51	101.05	100.55	100.70	99.73	99.97	98.38	99.31	100.74
1971	101.45	100.39	101.85	100.12	99.74	100.07	99.21	100.97	100.20
1972	103.62	100.35	103.98	99.36	99.89	100.12	99.87	103.19	100.36
1973	106.65	100.06	106.71	98.84	100.05	100.15	100.73	106.45	100.26
1974	110.11	99.58	109.65	98.01	100.23	100.19	101.63	109.68	100.00
1975	113.86	97.93	111.50	97.46	100.51	100.30	102.46	112.24	98.72
1976	115.69	97.44	112.73	96.94	100.57	100.34	103.66	114.31	98.33

Source: See appendix M.
a. Series excluding and including Alaska and Hawaii were linked at 1960.

accelerating. Thus changes in labor supply have been highly and increasingly favorable to rapid expansion of the sector's output. To explain the acceleration in the growth rate of potential employment I turn to table 3-3, which divides the rate among components of change.

If the ratio of employment to population had been constant in each age-sex group, population changes alone would have increased employment by 1.5 percent a year in 1964–69, half again as much as in the two earlier postwar periods. This rate increased further to 1.7 percent in 1969–73 before slipping back, but only slightly, to 1.6 percent in 1973–76.

Ratios of potential employment to population have not, of course, been constant. Changes have

been dominated by rising ratios for adult women, partly offset by falling ratios for adult males and especially for older men as the average retirement age dropped.[3] Rates for young persons fell with increasing school attendance until the early 1950s, then rose again as more and more students took part-time jobs. The military draft doubtless influenced participation rates but its net effect is hard to specify. The combined effect of changes in participation rates in the various demographic groups has been erratic. After contributing nothing on balance to the growth of sector employment in 1953–64, these changes contributed a big 0.9 percent in

3. Estimates of potential employment classified by age and sex are described in appendix L.

Table 3-3. Analysis of Employment Growth, Shorter Periods, 1948–76
Growth rates in percent per annum

Item	1948–53	1953–64	1964–69	1969–73	1973–76
1. Whole economy: potential employment with constant 1970 participation rates	0.95	1.04	1.52	1.71	1.61
2. Whole economy: effect of changing participation rates[a]	0.72	−0.01	0.90	0.23	0.80
3. Whole economy: potential employment	1.68	1.03	2.43	1.95	2.42
4. Ratio of potential employment in nonresidential business to potential employment in whole economy	−0.97	−0.34	−0.49	0.46	0.32
5. Nonresidential business: potential employment	0.69	0.68	1.93	2.41	2.75
6. Nonresidential business: ratio of actual to potential employment	0.38	−0.44	0.67	−0.73	−2.06
7. Nonresidential business: actual employment	1.08	0.24	2.61	1.67	0.64

Sources: See text for explanation.
a. Effect on growth rate of potential employment in the whole economy, in percentage points.

1964–69, only 0.2 percent in 1969–73, and 0.8 percent in 1973–76.

As a result of population and participation-rate changes, growth rates of potential employment in the economy as a whole were high in all of the three most recent periods: 2.4 percent in 1964–69 and 1973–76 and 1.9 percent in the intervening 1969–73 period. Up to 1969 general government, households, and institutions employed an increasing proportion of potential employment, but during the two most recent periods their proportion fell. Mainly responsible were the armed forces, which were cut 34 percent from 1969 to 1973 and an additional 7 percent from 1973 to 1976, and public education employment, whose rapid 1953–69 rate of expansion was halved in 1969–73 and reduced to almost nothing in 1973–76. The growth rate of potential employment in business, which had been less than in the whole economy up to 1969 (0.5 percentage points less in 1964–69), consequently was greater in business in the later periods: 0.5 percent greater in 1969–73 and 0.3 percent greater in 1973–76.

The growth rate of potential employment in the business sector jumped from 0.7 percent in both 1948–53 and 1953–64 to 1.9 percent in 1964–69, 2.4 percent in 1969–73, and 2.7 percent in 1973–76. The latter rates are very high not only in comparison with earlier periods in the United States, but also with other advanced countries. Changes in the numbers available to business were favorable for high and accelerating growth of business output.

The course of actual sector employment, which depends on the percentages of available workers that are employed, was quite different. From a high of 2.6 percent in 1964–69, a period during which unemployment was reduced, the growth rate of actual employment in the sector fell to 1.7 percent

in 1969–73 and then to 0.6 percent in 1973–76. Because of the business cycle these rates are sensitive to the exact time periods compared. Extension of the last period to 1978 would greatly raise its rate, from 0.6 to 2.0 percent.

Average and Total Hours of Work

An index of average weekly hours worked by persons employed in the business sector is shown in table 3-1, column 2. Column 3 is an index of total weekly hours, equal to the product of the indexes of employment and average hours. My estimates of average hours worked in the 1947–76 period are derived from Bureau of Labor Statistics estimates. Appendix C describes them. They are estimates of hours at work, as distinguished from hours "paid for." Table 3-2, columns 2 and 3, provides indexes of average and total hours calculated on a potential basis.

Why are average actual hours different from average potential hours? First, among persons who are actually employed, actual hours differ from potential hours because intensity of demand affects both the percentage of employed persons that work only part-time and the average hours worked by full-time workers. Second, the difference between actual and potential employment is concentrated in demographic groups that work short hours, on the average, when they are employed. If unemployment is high, the first relationship tends, on balance, to drop average actual hours below average potential hours whereas the second tends to raise average actual hours above average potential hours.

Whether measured on an actual or a potential basis average hours at work have moved persistently downward. Potential hours declined in all postwar years except 1956.

Table 3-4, column 2, shows the growth rates of

Table 3-4. Growth Rates of Potential and Actual Labor Input and Components, Nonresidential Business, Selected Periods, 1929–76

Percent per annum

| Basis and period | Employment (1) | Average weekly hours (2) | Total weekly hours (3) | Age-sex composition of total hours (4) | Efficiency of an hour's work as affected by change in hours due to: | | Amount of education (7) | Labor input (8) | Addendum: Effect of changes in hours (9) |
					Intragroup changes (5)	Specified intergroup shifts (6)			
Potential labor input									
Long periods									
1929–76	1.28	−0.62	0.66	−0.16	0.18	0.13	0.64	1.45	−0.31
1929–48	1.15	−0.76	0.38	0.01	0.33	0.12	0.60	1.45	−0.31
1948–73	1.21	−0.47	0.73	−0.24	0.06	0.15	0.64	1.35	−0.26
Shorter periods									
1929–41	1.47	−0.92	0.54	−0.04	0.49	0.13	0.63	1.76	−0.31
1941–48	0.61	−0.49	0.11	0.08	0.07	0.11	0.55	0.92	−0.32
1948–53	0.69	−0.40	0.29	0.18	0.14	0.15	0.59	1.35	−0.11
1953–64	0.68	−0.43	0.25	−0.20	0.00	0.16	0.61	0.82	−0.27
1964–69	1.93	−0.60	1.32	−0.39	0.07	0.15	0.65	1.80	−0.38
1969–73	2.41	−0.51	1.89	−0.64	0.15	0.09	0.75	2.23	−0.28
1973–76	2.75	−0.88	1.85	−0.64	0.17	0.06	0.96	2.40	−0.64
Actual labor input									
Long periods									
1929–76	1.07	−0.63	0.44	−0.13	0.18	0.12	0.65	1.27	−0.32
1929–48	1.09	−0.76	0.32	0.01	0.33	0.11	0.60	1.39	−0.32
1948–73	1.10	−0.50	0.60	−0.21	0.07	0.14	0.64	1.25	−0.29
Shorter periods									
1929–41	0.65	−0.82	−0.18	0.06	0.47	0.07	0.67	1.10	−0.28
1941–48	1.87	−0.67	1.19	−0.07	0.09	0.20	0.48	1.90	−0.38
1948–53	1.08	−0.46	0.61	0.11	0.17	0.18	0.58	1.65	−0.11
1953–64	0.24	−0.39	−0.16	−0.12	−0.03	0.14	0.63	0.46	−0.28
1964–69	2.61	−0.71	1.89	−0.48	0.11	0.18	0.61	2.33	−0.41
1969–73	1.67	−0.59	1.06	−0.51	0.17	0.06	0.79	1.57	−0.36
1973–76	0.64	−0.78	−0.15	−0.30	0.13	0.00	1.07	0.74	−0.64

Source: Computed from tables 3-1 and 3-2.

both series in the selected periods. In all three shorter periods after 1964 average hours declined more rapidly than they had in the postwar period up to 1964, and in 1973–76 faster than in any period since 1929–41; this is so on both an actual and a potential basis.

As a result of the fall in average hours, total hours at work (table 3-4, column 3) have grown much less than employment (column 1). Moreover, in 1973–76 acceleration of the decline of potential average hours more than offset the acceleration of the increase in potential employment, bringing the growth rate of total potential hours in 1973–76 slightly below the 1969–73 rate. The growth rate of total potential hours in both 1969–73 and 1973–76, nearly 1.9 percent, was far above any earlier period.

The decline in actual average hours was sufficient to turn the 1973–76 growth rate of total actual hours in the sector negative. This was not unusual; the rate had previously been negative in 1929–41 and 1953–64.

The index of average hours in the business sector as a whole provides no indication of changes in the average hours worked by homogeneous groups of workers, nor does it indicate the effect of changes in average hours on labor input or output. I shall consider these subjects as soon as the distribution of hours worked among demographic groups has been examined.

The Distribution of Hours Worked, by Age and Sex

The proportions of total hours that are worked by males and females, and within each sex by individuals of different ages, change over time. An average hour worked has a different value in each demographic group. It is necessary to develop an index to allow for the effect of changes in these proportions.

Calculating such an index requires two types of information: distributions of hours worked by age and sex, and appropriate weights. Hourly earnings

Table 3-5. Nonresidential Business: Average Hourly Earnings and Percentage Distribution of Total Hours and Earnings, by Sex and Age

Sex and age group	Hourly earnings as percentage of earnings of males 35–64		Percentage of total hours worked		Percentage of total earnings	
	1929–70[a] (1)	1970–76[a] (2)	1948 (3)	1976 (4)	1948 (5)	1976 (6)
Male						
14–19	30	29	4.01	4.20	1.51	1.66
20–24	61	56	8.04	8.76	6.16	6.67
25–34	89	85	19.06	18.24	21.29	21.08
35–64	100	100	43.04	34.79	54.03	47.30
65 and over	66	66	3.59	1.68	2.97	1.51
Female						
14–19	29	26	2.01	2.75	0.73	0.97
20–24	47	44	3.71	5.68	2.19	3.40
25–34	54	54	5.25	7.79	3.56	5.72
35–64	54	54	10.73	15.42	7.27	11.32
65 and over	41	41	0.55	0.69	0.28	0.38
Total	...	...	100.00	100.00	100.00	100.00

Sources: See text and appendix D.
a. Refers to periods during which these percentages are used as weights.

are used as weights. Their use rests on the assumption that average earnings in the ten age-sex groups distinguished are proportional to the marginal products of labor, per hour worked, of these groups. If this assumption is correct, it is necessary and legitimate to consider an average hour worked by a demographic group whose average hourly earnings are twice as high as those of another group to represent twice as much labor input.

Estimated differentials in average hourly earnings in the business sector are indicated in table 3-5, columns 1 and 2. Earnings in each cell are expressed as percentages of the average earnings of males 35 to 64 years of age. Differentials in column 1 are used to compute the movement of the index from 1929 to 1970 and those in column 2 from 1970 to 1976. Weights for the earlier period actually refer to the late 1960s; if differentials were any different earlier in the period, the scattered information available gives no reliable indication of it.

Among the five groups that consist of men 35 and over and of women 25 and over, relative earnings were unchanged from the 1960s to the 1970s. Workers in these groups contributed three-fifths of all hours worked in 1976 and earned almost two-thirds of all labor earnings (table 3-5, columns 4 and 6). Relative to these groups, average hourly earnings of the remaining five groups, consisting of males under 35 and females under 25, all declined. This dip in the relative earnings of younger workers coincided with a large increase in the proportion of the labor supply that consisted of

younger workers, as well as with a sharp rise in unemployment among them.

My assumption that average earnings are proportional to marginal products of labor implies that an average hour's work by males 35 to 64 years of age, for example, was 2.3 times as valuable in the 1970s as an average hour's work by females 20 to 24 years of age ($100 \div 44$). The assumption is valid insofar as earnings differentials among age-sex groups reflect differences in the value of the work that is actually performed. It does not matter whether these differences result from differences in the value of the work the groups are able and willing to do (because of variations in skill, training, experience, and strength; in attitudes; in home, marital, and school responsibilities that inhibit the assumption of responsibility on the job or working at inconvenient hours; in continuity of labor force participation; and the like) or from failure to use abilities that are present. Such failure may occur because abilities are not recognized or because of discrimination in employment practices with respect to hiring, training, promotion, or dismissal, so that one group or another cannot reach its full work capability. Potential abilities that are unused do not affect output; a newsboy might make a competent publisher but his unused potentiality has no more effect than if it did not exist. Discrimination introduces an error into the calculation only insofar as relative earnings are affected by differences in pay for identical work. My use of earnings weights implies a judgment that this type of discrimination,

Table 3-6. Nonresidential Business: Percentage Distribution of Total Hours Worked, by Sex and Age, Selected Years, 1929–76[a]

	Males (by age group)						Females (by age group)					
Year[b]	Total	14–19	20–24	25–34	35–64	65 and over	Total	14–19	20–24	25–34	35–64	65 and over
1929	83.48	6.15	10.89	20.63	42.41	3.40	16.52	2.56	3.74	3.99	5.88	0.35
1941	80.82	4.35	10.10	20.55	42.47	3.35	19.18	1.63	4.13	5.23	7.80	0.39
1948	77.75	4.01	8.04	19.06	43.04	3.59	22.25	2.01	3.71	5.25	10.73	0.55
1953	75.71	3.61	5.34	19.22	43.92	3.62	24.29	1.86	3.25	5.45	13.04	0.70
1961	73.93	3.48	6.52	16.68	44.45	2.81	26.07	1.80	3.15	4.75	15.53	0.83
1962	73.72	3.53	6.61	16.37	44.39	2.82	26.28	1.98	3.28	4.62	15.60	0.79
1963	73.66	3.44	6.86	16.07	44.67	2.63	26.34	1.84	3.39	4.54	15.77	0.79
1964	73.33	3.57	7.18	15.92	44.11	2.56	26.67	1.84	3.64	4.48	15.89	0.82
1965	72.82	3.88	7.43	15.65	43.33	2.53	27.18	1.97	3.76	4.61	16.02	0.82
1966[c]	72.04	4.19	7.12	15.60	42.66	2.47	27.96	2.30	3.96	4.74	16.15	0.81
1966[d]	72.00	4.24	7.14	15.58	42.64	2.41	28.00	2.40	4.03	4.70	16.03	0.84
1967	71.57	3.94	7.21	15.73	42.24	2.46	28.43	2.24	4.22	4.94	16.25	0.78
1968	71.24	3.99	7.06	16.08	41.62	2.49	28.76	2.25	4.39	5.09	16.24	0.79
1969	70.28	4.05	7.17	16.16	40.46	2.43	29.72	2.37	4.80	5.27	16.44	0.83
1970	70.13	4.05	7.29	16.56	39.87	2.36	29.87	2.34	4.90	5.40	16.40	0.83
1971	70.22	4.09	7.72	16.40	39.69	2.32	29.78	2.28	5.00	5.33	16.36	0.81
1972	69.67	4.30	8.14	16.85	38.31	2.07	30.33	2.52	5.13	5.98	15.89	0.81
1973	69.27	4.63	8.51	17.16	37.12	1.84	30.73	2.77	5.25	6.43	15.48	0.79
1974	68.63	4.63	8.71	17.43	36.04	1.82	31.37	2.86	5.46	6.90	15.46	0.69
1975	68.48	4.43	8.24	17.36	36.67	1.77	31.52	2.66	5.51	7.30	15.33	0.70
1976	67.66	4.20	8.76	18.24	34.79	1.68	32.34	2.75	5.68	7.79	15.42	0.69

Source: See appendix D.

a. Distributions are based on hours worked by civilians other than wage and salary workers employed in government or private households.

b. See *Accounting for Growth*, table F-5, p. 191, for comparable estimates for 1940, 1947, 1949–52, and 1954–60.

c. Distribution comparable to earlier years.

d. Distribution comparable to later years.

failure to provide "equal pay for equal work" when all costs are taken into account, does not greatly affect differentials in earnings among age-sex groups.[4]

Columns 3 to 6 of table 3-5 indicate the importance of the various age-sex groups in total hours and in total earnings in the business sector in 1948 and 1976. It may be observed that the proportion of total hours and earnings represented by males 25 to 64 years of age is higher in the business sector than in the civilian economy as a whole. Both civilian government and private households employ much higher proportions of females than does business.

Percentage distributions of total hours worked, by sex and age, were developed for this study and are shown on an annual basis in table 3-6. (Years not shown here have been published previously.) The distributions are based on CPS data because establishment reports do not provide detail of this type on a comprehensive basis.[5]

4. See *Why Growth Rates Differ*, pp. 70–108, for additional discussion, and both that source and Edward F. Denison and William K. Chung, *How Japan's Economy Grew So Fast: The Sources of Postwar Expansion* (Brookings Institution, 1976), pp. 58–59, 188, for evidence of the similarity of differentials in various countries.

5. The distributions actually represent hours worked by

An index measuring the effect of changes in the age-sex composition of total hours worked on labor input was obtained by weighting each age-sex group's percentage of hours worked, as shown for most years in table 3-6, by its average hourly earnings weight, as shown in table 3-5. A series for 1929–70 based on the earlier weights was linked with a series for 1970–76 based on the later weights to secure a continuous index. The index is shown in table 3-1, column 4. It is equivalent to the index of average hourly earnings in the business sector that would have been observed if there had been no change in average hourly earnings within any age-sex group. The index exhibits a fairly distinct cyclical pattern: it tends to rise in recession years because recession curtails most strongly hours worked by young people.

persons other than government and private household workers, rather than hours worked in the business sector. Thus hours worked by persons employed by nonprofit institutions are inappropriately included and hours worked by persons employed in government enterprises excluded. The numbers in these groups are small proportions of the totals.

An effort was made to eliminate discontinuities that changes in procedures introduce into CPS data. (Overlapping distributions are provided for 1966, when adjustment was impossible.) The most difficult problems affect changes from 1952 to 1953, and from 1966 to 1967 (based on new CPS definitions), and these changes are subject to some uncertainty.

Table 3-2, column 4, shows an index calculated from the age-sex distribution of potential hours rather than actual hours. One reason that the actual and potential distributions differ is that fluctuations in demand affect the average hours of employed persons in different age-sex categories unevenly, but most of the difference comes from the potential hours that correspond to the gap between actual and potential employment. Males in the prime working ages are underrepresented in this gap in comparison with their share of employment. In consequence, the age-sex index is ordinarily higher on an actual than on a potential basis when unemployment exceeds 4 percent, and higher on a potential basis when unemployment is below 4 percent.

On either basis the index measuring the effect of changes in age-sex composition of hours worked on sector labor input has moved downward with only minor interruptions since 1954. The changes in the composition of hours that produced this decline were complex up to 1963, but thereafter the immediate cause was a steady reduction in the proportion of hours worked by men 35 to 64, the most heavily weighted group, rather than changes in the distribution of hours among lesser-weighted groups. The growth rate of the index computed on a potential basis fell from 0.2 percent in 1948–53 to −0.2 percent in 1953–64, −0.4 percent in 1964–69, and −0.6 percent in both 1969–73 and 1973–76 (table 3-4). The effect on potential sector output is estimated to be the same as would be that of a similar change in the growth rate of potential employment in the absence of changes in employment composition, so these are substantial amounts.

Acceleration of the decline in the age-sex composition index after 1969 had two causes: entry of the large cohorts born in the early postwar years into the working ages, and rising participation rates of both young people and women. These same developments contributed to the accelerated expansion of potential employment and the accelerated decline in average hours. The entry of so many young people and women into the labor force added to labor input and to output, but less than an employment expansion of similar size would have done if it had been distributed like existing employment.

The main changes in age-sex composition in the business sector stand out prominently if the percentage distributions are condensed into three demographic groups. Based on potential hours so as to eliminate cyclical fluctuations, such distribu-

tions were as follows in the boundary years of the postwar periods:[6]

	Both sexes, 14–24	Males, 25 and over	Females, 25 and over	Total
1948	17.9	65.8	16.3	100.0
1953	13.9	67.4	18.7	100.0
1964	16.8	61.9	21.3	100.0
1969	18.2	59.4	22.4	100.0
1973	21.5	55.7	22.8	100.0
1976	22.6	52.9	24.5	100.0

From 1948 to 1953 the share of young people fell more than the share of women 25 and over increased, resulting in an increase in the age-sex index in that period. After 1953 the percentages worked by women 25 and over and by persons under 25 both rose persistently, but it was the share of young people that rose most. From 1953 to 1973 increases were 7.6 percentage points for young people as against 4.1 points for women 25 and over. Thereafter, the situation changed. The annual increase in the share of young people dropped by more than half from the 1969–73 period to 1973–76, while the annual increase in the share of women 25 and over accelerated. The increase in total hours worked by adult women has been the main factor responsible for the secular decline in the age-sex index, whereas changes in the age distribution and the switch, occurring about 1954, from falling to rising participation rates for young workers as students increasingly took part-time jobs have been mainly responsible for shorter-term fluctuations.

Until the 1969–73 period, changes in the demographic composition of potential employment, by reducing the average value of an hour's work, worked toward a falling growth rate of potential national income per person employed. But their negative effect was the same size in 1973–76 as in 1969–73, so they did not contribute to the abrupt deterioration in that growth rate after 1973. Age distributions of the population suggest that demographic characteristics will become a factor favorable to more rapid growth in the future. They suggest that the rate of decline in the age-sex composition index computed on a potential basis probably will diminish in the latter 1970s and that by the 1980s the index may actually be rising.[7]

6. Distributions before 1966 were adjusted for comparability with later years by adding or subtracting the amount by which the 1966 percentage based on old CPS definitions differs from the 1966 percentage based on new definitions.

7. If total hours worked in business by each age-sex group moved like total population in that group, past and future growth rates of the age-sex index would be 1948–53,

The rise in unemployment from 1969 to 1973, and especially from 1973 to 1976, retarded the increases in the percentages of actual hours that were worked by young workers and women and prevented the age-sex composition index for actual hours from falling as much as the index for potential hours in these periods. This index declined less in 1973–76 than in 1969–73, so it helped to mitigate the impact on actual national income per person employed of deterioration in other output determinants. With unemployment falling as business recovered in 1977 and 1978, the actual index was moving down toward the potential index, so changes in demographic composition were less favorable on an actual than on a potential basis in those years.

The Effect of Changes in Average Hours of Work

Labor input is sometimes measured by total hours worked, with or without weighting of age-sex groups. The use of such a measure would imply that the amount of work done changes proportionally if the average hours worked by persons employed in business change for any reason. I do not regard this as plausible. To measure labor input I therefore substitute for the index of average hours (table 3-1, column 2) an index (shown in column 9) that does reflect my judgment as to the effect of changes that have occurred in average hours.

To derive this index it was first necessary to divide persons employed in the business sector into twelve categories. Wage and salary workers in nonfarm business, nonfarm self-employed and unpaid family workers, and farm workers were each divided by sex, and each of the resulting six categories were divided between full-time workers and part-time workers.[8] The number of employed persons in each of these twelve categories and their total and average weekly hours at work are shown in tables 3-7, 3-8, and 3-9. The estimates result from the adjustment of CPS data to remove inconsistencies and then to conform to my establishment-based control totals for employment and hours in the three main groups.

Full-time workers in any week are persons who worked thirty-five hours or more that week and persons who usually work thirty-five hours or more but for noneconomic reasons worked fewer hours, or none at all, that week. Thus average full-time hours, as shown in the tables, are after reduction to allow for vacations, holidays, sickness, and absences for all other noneconomic reasons. Part-time workers include all other employed persons. Most members of this heterogenous group wished to work only part-time. Some could find only part-time jobs. Some held what were usually full-time jobs but worked less than thirty-five hours in a particular week for economic reasons: lack of demand, materials shortages, or breakdowns of equipment. Some worked only part of a week because they were starting or ending a job.

In the framework of the twelve-way classification of workers just set out, average hours in business may change from any of five main causes. I shall now set out my assumptions about the effects of changes from each cause.

Intragroup Changes in Hours of Full-Time Workers

Average hours in business may change, first, because the length of the average workweek of one or more of the six groups of full-time workers that I have distinguished changes. If this happens, what are the effects?

The general shape of a curve relating hours to output for any given category of workers can be described with some assurance. If working hours are very long, the adverse effects of fatigue on productivity are so great that output per worker increases if hours are shortened (and output per hour increases much more). The effects of fatigue are reinforced by a tendency for absenteeism (which is costly) to be excessive when hours are long, and by important institutional factors. If hours are shortened further, a point is reached below which output per worker declines, while output per hour continues to increase. At this stage increases in output per hour only partially offset the reduction in hours worked. Finally, if hours become very short, the proportion of time spent in starting and stopping work may become so great that even output per hour declines as hours are shortened.

The difficulty in deriving such curves empirically is that the evidence as to the location of the critical points is inadequate. Nevertheless, it is impossible to measure labor input at all or to analyze sources

---

0.16; 1953–64, −0.13; 1964–69, −0.28; 1969–73, −0.21; 1973–76, −0.05; 1976–80, 0.08; 1980–85, 0.28; and 1985–90, 0.30.

8. Part-time work should not be confused with intermittent or temporary work. A person who works forty hours a week for half of the year counts as one-half of a full-time worker, not as a part-time worker.

Table 3-7. Wage and Salary Workers in Nonfarm Business: Employment and Hours by Sex and Full-Time or Part-Time Status, 1929, 1940–41, and 1947–76[a]

	Employment (thousands)				Total weekly hours (millions)				Average weekly hours			
	Males		Females		Males		Females		Males		Females	
Year	Full-time (1)	Part-time (2)	Full-time (3)	Part-time (4)	Full-time (5)	Part-time (6)	Full-time (7)	Part-time (8)	Full-time (9)	Part-time (10)	Full-time (11)	Part-time (12)
					Excluding Alaska and Hawaii							
1929	19,967	1,081	4,822	538	973.97	17.70	217.55	11.54	48.8	16.4	45.1	21.4
1940	18,686	1,476	5,401	1,129	815.60	24.17	218.05	24.21	43.6	16.4	40.4	21.4
1941	21,772	1,176	6,282	1,138	959.08	19.31	255.94	24.40	44.1	16.4	40.7	21.4
1947	24,638	1,333	8,547	1,548	1,057.13	21.83	339.19	33.19	42.9	16.4	39.7	21.4
1948	24,660	1,734	8,586	1,797	1,058.91	31.25	341.17	38.92	42.9	18.0	39.7	21.7
1949	22,687	2,422	8,324	1,848	970.18	48.53	329.96	40.84	42.8	20.0	39.6	22.1
1950	23,490	2,432	8,661	1,959	1,012.63	48.01	345.97	43.13	43.1	19.7	39.9	22.0
1951	25,211	2,184	9,427	2,136	1,086.49	40.92	374.70	46.53	43.1	18.7	39.7	21.8
1952	25,860	1,668	10,114	2,046	1,101.14	28.75	399.51	44.17	42.6	17.2	39.5	21.6
1953	26,652	1,685	10,444	1,950	1,122.62	28.36	409.03	42.40	42.1	16.8	39.2	21.7
1954	24,942	2,341	9,676	2,332	1,056.60	38.37	382.00	50.04	42.4	16.4	39.5	21.5
1955	26,086	2,078	10,246	2,113	1,107.04	35.69	405.51	39.37	42.4	17.2	39.6	18.6
1956	26,580	2,264	10,554	2,372	1,125.46	42.98	416.43	43.24	42.3	19.0	39.4	18.2
1957	26,439	2,247	10,637	2,546	1,108.79	41.41	414.34	48.27	41.9	18.4	39.0	19.0
1958	24,710	2,660	10,075	2,669	1,034.22	53.00	395.09	50.10	41.8	20.0	39.2	18.8
1959	26,036	2,379	10,507	2,610	1,102.63	39.58	412.55	50.01	42.4	16.6	39.3	19.2
1960	26,008	2,531	10,733	2,692	1,099.27	45.74	415.22	49.36	42.3	18.1	38.7	18.3
					Including Alaska and Hawaii							
1960	26,108	2,540	10,775	2,703	1,103.51	45.91	416.82	49.55	42.3	18.1	38.7	18.3
1961	25,624	2,668	10,624	2,885	1,085.33	47.57	411.16	53.43	42.4	17.8	38.7	18.5
1962	26,428	2,569	10,957	2,956	1,124.78	42.17	423.10	54.05	42.6	16.4	38.6	18.3
1963	26,911	2,506	11,108	3,099	1,149.24	41.42	428.31	55.23	42.7	16.5	38.6	17.8
1964	27,442	2,619	11,608	3,114	1,180.31	39.31	442.96	58.91	43.0	15.0	38.2	18.9
1965	28,481	2,650	12,134	3,404	1,225.04	43.22	467.80	63.06	43.0	16.3	38.6	18.5
1966[b]	29,688	2,751	13,103	3,587	1,263.90	45.41	500.03	67.29	42.6	16.5	38.2	18.8
1966[c]	29,629	2,882	13,040	3,578	1,263.30	48.18	498.68	66.47	42.6	16.7	38.2	18.6
1967	29,948	2,947	13,365	3,906	1,261.08	48.98	503.72	72.14	42.1	16.6	37.7	18.5
1968	30,573	2,984	13,823	4,236	1,282.97	49.59	518.91	77.32	42.0	16.6	37.5	18.2
1969	30,971	3,235	14,578	4,608	1,299.08	54.95	547.67	84.07	41.9	17.0	37.6	18.2
1970	30,450	3,416	14,369	4,989	1,263.78	61.69	536.08	89.44	41.5	18.0	37.3	17.9
1971	30,267	3,487	14,149	5,112	1,252.68	62.31	525.64	93.29	41.4	17.9	37.1	18.2
1972	31,127	3,562	14,749	5,319	1,296.91	60.79	551.20	96.18	41.7	17.1	37.4	18.1
1973	32,606	3,674	15,681	5,740	1,354.92	63.25	583.63	102.81	41.6	17.2	37.2	17.9
1974	32,582	3,811	16,138	6,104	1,335.47	67.78	596.54	111.35	41.0	17.8	37.0	18.2
1975	30,745	4,017	15,580	6,303	1,253.11	74.73	574.62	115.02	40.8	18.6	36.9	18.2
1976	31,889	3,961	16,479	6,522	1,301.49	69.90	608.82	118.53	40.8	17.6	36.9	18.2

Source: See appendix E.
a. Tables 2-6 and C-1 provide combined data for the four groups of workers.
b. Comparable to earlier years.
c. Comparable to later years.

of growth without introducing assumptions about such curves. I have discussed available evidence and expert opinion elsewhere.[9] Here, I shall merely describe the assumptions and procedures I follow to estimate the effect of changes in working hours on the work done in an hour.

Full-time wage and salary workers employed in nonfarm business are much the largest of the groups distinguished. I judge that throughout the period covered in this study the hours of this group

9. *Why Growth Rates Differ*, pp. 59–64.

have been within the range in which the effect of changes in hours on the work done in a year is partially offset by a change in output per hour resulting from the change in hours. I also judge that the size of the offset declines as hours are shortened. In the absence of solid comprehensive data, one can only guess at the size of the offsets corresponding to different hours levels. I shall assume, for males and females separately, that at the levels of average weekly hours (including vacations and holiday weeks) worked in 1960, a small change in average hours worked per week by a representa-

Table 3-8. Nonfarm Self-Employed and Unpaid Family Workers: Employment and Hours by Sex and Full-Time or Part-Time Status, 1929, 1940–41, and 1947–76[a]

	Employment (thousands)				Total weekly hours (millions)				Average weekly hours			
	Males		Females		Males		Females		Males		Females	
	Full-time	Part-time	Full-time	Part-time	Full-time	Part-time	Full-time	Part-time	Full-time	Part-time	Full-time	Part-time
Year	(1)	(2)	(3)	(4)	(5)	(6)	(7)	(8)	(9)	(10)	(11)	(12)
	Excluding Alaska and Hawaii											
1929	3,517	280	820	384	208.87	4.83	48.70	7.38	59.4	17.3	59.4	19.2
1940	3,621	381	843	426	192.43	6.58	44.80	8.18	53.1	17.3	53.1	19.2
1941	3,724	296	887	416	199.73	5.11	47.58	7.99	53.5	17.3	53.6	19.2
1947	4,341	345	943	443	226.77	5.96	49.27	8.51	52.2	17.3	52.2	19.2
1948	4,395	345	973	455	229.99	5.91	50.87	8.68	52.3	17.1	52.3	19.1
1949	4,316	341	1,002	465	226.22	5.88	52.52	8.79	52.4	17.2	52.4	18.9
1950	4,387	350	978	457	229.62	6.06	51.18	8.69	52.3	17.3	52.3	19.0
1951	4,353	341	1,016	476	227.96	5.86	53.19	9.09	52.4	17.2	52.4	19.1
1952	4,399	350	1,009	479	229.96	6.06	52.78	9.24	52.3	17.3	52.3	19.3
1953	4,397	343	991	471	229.80	5.87	51.77	9.10	52.3	17.1	52.2	19.3
1954	4,299	415	905	459	227.07	7.02	48.45	8.23	52.8	16.9	53.5	17.9
1955	4,294	338	987	479	225.45	5.83	51.86	9.58	52.5	17.2	52.5	20.0
1956	4,344	335	1,027	471	231.08	5.93	55.11	9.14	53.2	17.7	53.7	19.4
1957	4,226	491	1,067	491	226.03	8.24	55.54	9.72	53.5	16.8	52.0	18.0
1958	4,140	522	1,069	506	220.84	8.66	54.93	9.02	53.3	16.9	51.4	17.8
1959	4,098	478	1,043	560	217.19	7.79	53.04	10.92	53.0	16.3	50.8	19.5
1960	4,077	477	1,042	617	217.48	8.26	54.38	10.85	53.3	17.3	52.2	17.6
	Including Alaska and Hawaii											
1960	4,092	479	1,046	619	218.29	8.29	54.58	10.89	53.3	17.3	52.2	17.6
1961	4,028	484	1,061	680	213.80	8.67	54.63	11.85	53.1	17.9	51.5	17.4
1962	3,960	477	1,088	622	210.71	8.14	55.12	11.04	53.2	17.1	50.7	17.7
1963	3,816	529	1,041	633	204.24	9.34	50.80	11.87	53.5	17.6	48.8	18.8
1964	3,881	480	1,029	663	206.04	8.14	51.18	12.82	53.1	17.0	49.7	19.3
1965	3,821	479	1,059	670	204.97	7.54	53.79	11.21	53.6	15.7	50.8	16.7
1966[b]	3,684	488	1,140	618	197.92	7.64	57.11	10.42	53.7	15.7	50.1	16.9
1966[c]	3,603	526	1,087	714	196.30	8.47	55.47	12.85	54.5	16.1	51.0	18.0
1967	3,567	526	1,061	716	191.06	8.42	54.80	12.72	53.6	16.0	51.6	17.7
1968	3,546	522	1,038	678	190.26	8.61	54.43	11.75	53.6	16.5	52.4	17.3
1969	3,618	5'0	1,077	720	193.31	9.56	55.21	12.39	53.4	16.8	51.3	17.2
1970	3,529	628	1,052	738	186.84	10.53	53.62	12.89	52.9	16.8	51.0	17.5
1971	3,544	665	1,067	776	187.98	10.93	55.08	13.41	53.0	16.4	51.6	17.3
1972	3,546	673	1,069	813	186.17	11.44	54.62	14.12	52.5	17.0	51.1	17.3
1973	3,621	646	1,113	833	188.85	11.21	56.29	14.09	52.2	17.4	50.6	16.9
1974	3,679	738	1,107	849	189.16	12.52	55.66	14.55	51.4	17.0	50.3	17.1
1975	3,593	831	1,083	867	183.96	14.72	54.03	14.85	51.2	17.7	49.9	17.1
1976	3,635	771	1,103	889	195.85	13.16	53.46	15.31	51.1	17.1	48.5	17.2

Source: See appendix E.
a. Tables 2-6 and C-1 provide combined data for the four groups of workers.
b. Comparable to earlier years.
c. Comparable to later years.

tive group of workers has a 30 percent offset in output per man-hour. These levels, according to my estimates, were 42.3 for males and 38.7 for females.[10] I further assume that if weekly hours were ten hours longer (52.3 for males and 48.7 for females) a small change in average hours worked would be fully offset in output per man-hour. Intermediate points are set by proportional interpolation, and this same relationship is extrapolated to shorter hours. The introduction of these assump-

tions permits curves for males and females to be constructed that relate hours to the work done in an hour.[11] (See table E-1.) The curves for males imply that output per hour is a maximum at 38.0 hours a week and output per worker is a maximum at 52.3 hours. The corresponding points for females are 34.4 and 48.7, respectively. However, I needed

10. These levels correspond to about 45.6 and 41.9 hours, respectively, for full workweeks.

11. In some cases a change in hours of full-time workers is accompanied by a change in the hours that capital goods are used. The assumption here, and also for other groups, is intended to allow for the effect of any such related changes in capital hours on output so that no adjustment to measures of capital input is introduced on this account.

Table 3-9. Farm Workers: Employment and Hours by Sex and Full-Time or Part-Time Status, 1929, 1940–41, and 1947–76[a]

| | Employment (thousands) | | | | Total weekly hours (millions) | | | | Average weekly hours | | | |
| | Males | | Females | | Males | | Females | | Males | | Females | |
Year	Full-time (1)	Part-time (2)	Full-time (3)	Part-time (4)	Full-time (5)	Part-time (6)	Full-time (7)	Part-time (8)	Full-time (9)	Part-time (10)	Full-time (11)	Part-time (12)
				Excluding Alaska and Hawaii								
1929	8,222	338	836	482	481.76	5.20	42.01	10.44	58.6	15.4	50.3	21.7
1940	7,626	247	606	407	430.56	3.66	29.35	8.49	56.5	14.8	48.4	20.9
1941	7,367	302	787	454	415.93	4.48	38.11	9.48	56.5	14.8	48.4	20.9
1947	6,070	605	600	652	345.14	9.04	29.26	13.70	56.9	14.9	48.8	21.0
1948	5,915	609	603	708	338.59	9.19	29.61	14.98	57.2	15.1	49.1	21.1
1949	5,757	584	621	697	322.86	8.28	30.21	14.66	56.1	14.2	48.6	21.0
1950	5,614	670	514	706	313.56	10.05	24.74	14.77	55.8	15.0	48.1	20.9
1951	5,256	568	554	701	297.07	8.20	26.92	14.77	56.5	14.4	48.6	21.1
1952	5,186	515	533	644	287.61	7.57	25.35	13.84	55.4	14.7	47.6	21.5
1953	5,028	535	521	553	281.14	7.89	25.04	11.82	55.9	14.7	48.0	21.4
1954	4,896	634	546	542	272.82	9.05	26.30	11.54	55.7	14.3	48.2	21.3
1955	4,653	646	705	494	257.53	10.46	31.05	10.05	55.3	16.2	44.0	20.3
1956	4,295	708	605	636	237.35	11.48	28.78	12.53	55.3	16.2	47.6	19.7
1957	4,048	752	549	579	220.34	12.67	24.15	11.90	54.4	16.8	44.0	20.5
1958	3,814	831	460	547	209.21	13.08	21.29	11.01	54.8	15.7	46.3	20.1
1959	3,747	760	454	579	204.73	12.56	21.50	11.86	54.6	16.5	47.4	20.5
1960	3,570	731	437	524	195.13	11.67	20.99	10.30	54.6	16.0	48.0	19.6
				Including Alaska and Hawaii								
1960	3,587	734	439	526	196.02	11.73	21.09	10.34	54.6	16.0	48.0	19.7
1961	3,449	792	428	470	186.68	13.67	20.38	8.97	54.1	17.3	47.6	19.1
1962	3,262	783	438	438	182.02	12.38	20.24	8.68	55.8	15.8	46.2	19.8
1963	3,001	769	409	459	170.11	12.68	20.06	8.88	56.7	16.5	49.0	19.3
1964	2,826	732	388	416	157.82	11.14	18.54	8.03	55.8	15.2	47.8	19.3
1965	2,687	688	406	370	151.54	11.26	18.98	7.08	56.4	16.4	46.7	19.1
1966[b]	2,447	628	360	333	137.15	10.18	17.14	6.50	56.0	16.2	47.6	19.5
1966[c]	2,448	626	351	343	136.28	11.06	16.80	6.83	55.7	17.7	46.7	19.9
1967	2,333	651	312	327	130.09	11.45	14.87	6.55	55.8	17.6	47.6	20.0
1968	2,302	644	316	300	129.05	10.81	15.21	6.20	56.1	16.8	48.1	20.6
1969	2,178	629	307	308	122.44	10.65	15.17	6.31	56.2	16.9	49.4	20.5
1970	2,091	641	296	280	116.38	10.60	14.55	5.76	55.6	16.5	49.1	20.6
1971	2,002	650	287	284	113.50	11.00	13.83	5.81	56.7	16.9	48.2	20.5
1972	2,029	600	287	300	112.79	10.09	13.44	6.06	55.6	16.8	46.8	20.2
1973	2,030	576	298	276	110.82	9.49	14.18	5.56	54.6	16.5	47.6	20.1
1974	2,044	594	285	259	110.12	10.16	13.55	5.17	53.9	17.1	47.5	20.0
1975	2,010	604	292	250	110.10	10.20	14.21	5.06	54.8	16.9	48.7	20.2
1976	1,977	607	291	258	108.45	10.30	13.48	5.18	54.9	17.0	46.3	20.1

Source: See appendix E.
a. Tables 2-6 and C-1 provide combined data for the four groups of workers.
b. Comparable to earlier years.
c. Comparable to later years.

to use only a small part of these ranges during the postwar period: from 40.8 to 43.1 for males, and from 36.9 to 39.9 for females.

When most people consider changes in average hours, they have full-time nonfarm wage and salary workers in mind, and it is by far the biggest group. The hours of its members had dropped sharply from 1929 to 1940 in the business sector and somewhat more by 1948. After 1948, however, reductions in the hours of males were moderate. On a potential basis they were confined to two short periods if small and erratic year-to-year fluctuations are disregarded. The first decline was from

1965 to 1967.[12] Potential male hours, which had averaged 42.6 in both the 1948–65 and 1959–65 periods, slipped to an average of 42.0 in 1967–74. The second decline was from 1974, when average potential hours were still 42.0, to 1976, when they were 41.0. The second drop occurs a little earlier if actual hours are considered; it is from an average of 41.8 in 1967–72 and 41.6 in 1973 to 40.8 in 1975 and 1976. On either basis the average annual

12. Potential hours cited in this paragraph refer to the average potential hours of employed persons, shown in table L-2, column 2, but in this case there is no reason to expect data based on potential employment to be different.

decline was unusually large from 1973 to 1976. The average hours of females declined more smoothly than those of males and fell less after 1973, but their 1973–76 decline was nevertheless larger than the postwar average on either an actual or potential basis. Thus changes in the average hours of full-time nonfarm wage and salary workers contributed to the deterioration in the growth rates of both actual and potential national income per person employed. Moreover, the favorable effect of shorter hours on output per hour offset a smaller proportion of the decline in 1973–76 than in previous periods of hours reduction, according to my appraisal, and much less than in the big 1929–40 decline, which had started from the long 1929 workweek.

Full-time farm workers put in very long hours (table 3-9). Ranging from fifty-four hours to fifty-seven in postwar years, average weekly hours of full-time males have continuously exceeded the point at which the productivity offset is assumed to be complete for nonfarm wage and salary workers, while average hours of the small group of female full-time farm workers have fluctuated around that point.

The series for average full-time hours in farming are dominated by small erratic fluctuations. Over the whole postwar period the average level for each sex declined, but by less than two hours a week.[13]

I assume, separately for each sex, that on farms changes in average full-time weekly hours have not affected the amount of work done in a week; the productivity offset is presumed to be complete. Consequently changes in average hours of male or female full-time farm workers do not affect my measure of labor input. This is fortunate because hours of farm workers are difficult to define and to measure. Indeed, this limitation on the data is a supplementary reason for making the assumption stated.

The reasons to ignore changes in hours of full-time farm workers in measuring labor input also apply to full-time nonfarm proprietors and unpaid family workers. The hours of both males and females in this category (shown in table 3-8) have consistently been near or above the point at which the productivity offset is judged complete for nonfarm wage and salary workers. In addition the hours

of this group reflect to a large degree local custom with respect to the time establishments are open, and for this reason alone changes have a large efficiency offset. As in farming, the series for hours are dominated in the postwar period by irregular fluctuations but also show some decline. This decline was small and perhaps confined to females until after 1971, when it seems to have become rather larger, especially for females. I adopt the same assumption and procedures for full-time nonfarm proprietors and unpaid family workers as for full-time farm workers: changes in hours do not affect output or labor input.

Changes in the average hours of the six categories of full-time workers (I count males and females separately) account for only 38 percent of the postwar decline in average hours in nonresidential business. Average full-time hours fell 0.20 percent a year from 1948 to 1976 when the weights of the six categories are held constant.[14] This compares with a 0.53 percent decline from all causes in the average hours of all workers combined. The remaining 0.33 percentage points result from changes in the composition of employment and, to a very small extent, a faster drop in average part-time hours.

Changes in Average Hours Resulting from Shifts in the Distribution of Full-Time Workers

The proportion of full-time workers who are nonfarm wage and salary workers has increased at the expense of farm workers and nonfarm self-employed and unpaid family workers. Among males, the latter two groups fell from 29.3 percent of full-time business employment in 1948 to 15.0 percent in 1976. The corresponding percentage of females fell from 15.1 to 7.8. Farm employment fell most. Because the nonfarm wage and salary group works shorter hours than other full-time workers, these shifts reduced the average hours worked by all full-time workers of each sex. If this were permitted to reduce the index of labor input, it would mean that a typical farm worker or nonfarm self-employed or unpaid family worker is counted as far more labor input than a typical nonfarm wage and salary worker. It would also mean that a decline in labor input could be avoided when a shift occurs only if workers shifting worked as long in

---

13. This statement allows for the difference in 1966 between the estimates with old and new definitions, as shown in table 3-9.

14. An average of 1948 and 1976 employment weights were used in this calculation.

their new jobs as they had in their old jobs. I believe this result is unrealistic and undesirable.

I therefore adopt the convention that a year of full-time employment (when performed by the same individual or by individuals with similar characteristics) represents the same amount of labor input in any of these three groups rather than the alternative convention that an hour of work in each type of employment is equivalent.[15] For example, if full-time workers shift from one group to another, and if they work the average hours of their old group before moving and of their new group after moving, average hours fall, but my index of labor input is unchanged.

Shifts in the distribution of full-time employment of each sex among the three categories was responsible for 0.13 percentage points of the 0.53 percent average annual decline in average hours from 1948 to 1976. This part of the decline in average hours had no effect on my measure of labor input.

Other Causes of Changes in Average Hours

When average hours of workers in nonresidential business change for the remaining reasons, I estimate that the amount of work done changes proportionally.

The third reason is that the average hours of part-time workers declined by a larger percentage than those of full-time workers. It accounts for only 0.02 percentage points of the average annual decline from 1948 to 1976.

The fourth reason was the big increase in part-time employment. The part-time percentage for both sexes combined rose from 11.1 in 1948 to 19.0 in 1976 in the business sector. For women and girls the increase was from 22.6 percent to 30.0 percent, for men and boys from 7.1 percent to 12.5 percent. About 0.14 percentage points out of the 1948–76 average annual decline of 0.53 percent in average hours resulted from the increased proportion of part-time workers.

The fifth reason was the increase in the percentage of full-time workers who are females, from 22.5 percent in 1948 to 32.3 percent in 1976. Since the average hours of full-time male workers exceeded those of full-time females by more than 12 percent in both years, this change in composition reduced average hours. It was responsible for 0.04 percentage points of the average annual decline of

0.53 percent in the average hours of all workers in the sector from 1948 to 1973.[16]

Indexes for Effects of Changes in Hours

The indexes shown in column 9 of tables 3-1 and 3-2 measure the effect of changes in hours on actual and potential labor input, respectively, when the assumptions just set out are introduced. A 1 percent change in this index changes labor input by 1 percent. Column 9 is the product of three indexes, which themselves provide additional information. Column 2, average weekly hours, shows what the effect of changes in average hours would have been if, regardless of their origin, they had affected labor input proportionally. Column 5 measures the amount of the change in column 2 that is offset by my assumptions that changes in average hours of full-time workers within a category affect the amount of work done less than proportionally (for farm and self-employed workers, not at all). Column 6 measures the amount of the change in column 1 that is offset by my assumption that full-time workers who are similar except for their working hours represent the same labor input whether they are nonfarm wage and salary workers, farm workers, or nonfarm self-employed workers.[17]

Effect of Changes in Average Hours during Recent Periods

Table 3-4, column 9, shows that in 1969–73 the adverse effect of changes in weekly hours on both actual and potential labor input was much the same as in the 1948–73 period as a whole and a little less than in 1964–69.

---

15. I explain my preference for this convention in *Accounting for Growth,* pp. 42–43.

16. As stated, this reduced the growth rate of labor input by 0.04 percentage points. This reduction is in addition to the effect of the change on the demographic composition of total hours, which is captured in the index for the effects of changes in age-sex composition.

17. There is one complication. Weighting by sex was introduced in column 4. Hence the influence of a change in the average hours of one sex on labor input is proportional to that sex's share of total labor earnings, not of total hours worked. To secure annual changes in the indexes for "intragroup changes" and "intergroup shifts" (columns 5 and 6), it was therefore necessary to calculate changes for males and females separately and weight them by total labor earnings. This procedure results in a consistent measure of labor input when the indexes for hours and age-sex composition are multiplied, but there is a minor inconsistency in the index measuring the effect of hours changes alone (column 9) in the sense that this series is the product of column 2, which is not weighted by sex, and columns 5 and 6, which are so weighted. The inconsistency could be eliminated only by applying age-sex weighting separately to changes in employment and average hours instead of to total hours.

But from 1973 to 1976 changes in average hours cut more than 0.6 percent a year from the growth rates of both potential and actual labor input. This was much more than in any of my previous periods and more than twice as much as the average curtailment from 1948 to 1973. The 1973–76 drag exceeded that in the immediately preceding 1969–73 period by 0.36 percentage points on a potential basis and by 0.28 points on an actual basis. Thus changes in working hours contributed importantly to the decline in output per person employed in 1973–76. The main factor was the sharp and unusual decline in the average hours of full-time nonfarm wage and salary workers. Also contributing was an accelerated increase in the proportion of persons working part-time.

Education of Workers

Educational background decisively conditions both the types of work a person is able to perform and his proficiency in any particular occupation. A continuous upward shift in the educational background of the American labor force has upgraded the skills and versatility of labor and contributed to the rise in national income. It has enhanced the skills of individuals within what is conventionally termed an occupation, often with considerable changes in the work actually performed; it has also permitted a shift in occupational composition from occupations in which workers typically have little education and low earnings toward those in which education and earnings are higher. Education also heightens a person's awareness of job opportunities and thereby the chances that he is employed where his marginal product is greatest. A more educated work force—from top management down—also is better able to learn about and use the most efficient production practices.

Past studies have identified increasing education as a major source of growth in the United States since at least 1910, and especially since about 1930. During the 1970s the amount of education held by persons employed in business has risen faster than ever before.

Table 3-10 shows percentage distributions among nine education levels of persons employed in the business sector.[18] The wide dispersion of the

population and labor force among levels of education in the United States is unusual. Other advanced countries have had smaller percentages at both the bottom and the upper ranges of the distribution, with a heavy concentration at the level corresponding to the completion of compulsory education. Most countries, however, have been moving toward the American mold. Within the United States the distribution of females employed in business is less dispersed than that of males. More females have had four years of high school, and percentages at both the bottom and top of the distribution are smaller.

The major characteristic of table 3-10 is the pervasive and massive upgrading of the educational background of workers that it reveals. I wish to stress first the pervasiveness of the increase.

Attention to the relationship between education and growth sometimes focuses on college graduates, and indeed there has been a notable increase in their number. From 6 percent in 1948, the percentage of males who had completed four or more years of college increased to 12 percent in 1969 and 17 percent in 1976.[19] However, the change at the bottom of the distribution was larger. Those with zero to seven years of school completed dropped from 24 percent in 1948 to 11 percent in 1969 and 7 percent in 1976. The percentage with a completed high school education but not a completed college education changed even more, rising from 29 in 1948 to 48 in 1969 and 54 in 1976. The female distribution also displays a pervasive upswing.

For many years the percentages in the one-to-three-years-of-high-school group (which includes but is not dominated by junior high school graduates) were rather stable, while the percentages in all groups with less education persistently fell by substantial amounts and those with more education rose. In the 1970s, however, the dividing point has risen to the high-school-graduate level; the percentages at that level have now become rather stable, while the percentages with one to three years of high school are dropping sharply.

The size of the increase in average education is also impressive. One measure is time spent in school. The average number of years of education completed by persons employed in the business

---

18. These distributions have smaller percentages with advanced education than distributions for the whole economy because they omit professors, teachers, and clergymen. They also omit domestic servants, who are among the least educated workers.

19. Table 3-10 refers to persons 18 and over at earlier dates and 16 and over at later dates, with an overlap at March 1972. For text comparisons, data for the earlier years have been adjusted by the differences between the distributions at the overlap date.

Table 3-10. Percentage Distribution of Persons Employed in the Business Sector, by Sex and Years of School Completed, Full-Time Equivalent Basis, Survey Dates, 1948–76[a]

Years of school completed	October 1948[b] (1)	March 1959[b] (2)	March 1964[b] (3)	March 1969[b] (4)	March 1970[b] (5)	March 1971[b] (6)	March 1972[b] (7)	March 1972[c] (8)	March 1973[c] (9)	March 1974[c] (10)	March 1975[c] (11)	March 1976[c] (12)
Males												
Total	100.00	100.00	100.00	100.00	100.00	100.00	100.00	100.00	100.00	100.00	100.00	100.00
No school years completed	8.76	0.98	0.67	0.46	0.42	0.46	0.43	0.43	0.44	0.39	0.34	0.32
Elementary, 1–4		4.78	3.56	2.74	2.46	2.33	2.17	2.17	2.07	1.92	1.75	1.65
Elementary, 5–7	14.64	10.77	8.90	7.27	7.07	6.49	6.15	6.21	5.73	5.33	4.84	4.65
Elementary, 8	21.04	16.45	14.13	11.21	10.82	10.03	9.32	9.25	8.17	7.77	6.90	6.36
High school, 1–3	20.17	20.35	19.78	18.48	17.91	17.16	17.22	18.19	17.54	16.84	16.00	15.68
High school, 4	23.10	28.34	32.50	36.17	36.77	37.44	37.87	37.10	38.15	38.28	38.50	38.80
College, 1–3	6.58	8.99	10.23	11.94	12.67	13.26	13.63	13.31	14.03	14.61	15.45	15.69
College, 4	5.71	5.74	6.25	7.06	7.27	7.71	7.86	7.81	8.22	8.61	9.51	10.00
College, 5 or more		3.58	3.97	4.66	4.62	5.12	5.35	5.53	5.65	6.25	6.71	6.85
Females												
Total	100.00	100.00	100.00	100.00	100.00	100.00	100.00	100.00	100.00	100.00	100.00	100.00
No school years completed	4.37	0.50	0.34	0.23	0.21	0.21	0.19	0.19	0.14	0.26	0.25	0.26
Elementary, 1–4		1.92	1.67	1.25	1.00	0.99	1.09	1.06	1.03	0.84	0.65	0.72
Elementary, 5–7	9.88	7.17	5.93	4.89	4.19	4.12	3.78	3.75	3.56	3.44	3.02	2.75
Elementary, 8	18.15	13.37	11.72	8.33	8.14	7.65	6.97	6.90	6.19	5.57	5.38	4.92
High school, 1–3	18.77	19.92	19.58	18.41	18.16	17.09	16.96	18.07	17.45	17.15	15.87	15.97
High school, 4	37.33	43.85	46.02	50.23	50.60	50.61	51.44	50.50	51.04	49.59	50.25	49.88
College, 1–3	7.51	9.20	10.14	11.80	12.70	13.66	13.51	13.29	13.99	15.56	16.15	16.28
College, 4	3.98	3.07	3.42	3.35	3.49	3.85	4.16	4.22	4.53	5.25	5.85	6.42
College, 5 or more		1.01	1.20	1.49	1.52	1.82	1.90	2.02	2.07	2.34	2.58	2.80

Source: See appendix F.

a. See *Accounting for Growth*, table I-15, p. 244, for distributions at seven additional dates.

b. Distributions are for persons 18 years of age and over.

c. Distributions are for persons 16 years of age and over. Columns 7 and 8 differ for reasons besides the change in the lower age limit. See pp. 166–67.

sector is shown in table 3-11. For males it rose 27.4 percent (2.6 years) from 1948 to 1976, and 7.3 percent just from 1969. Increases for female workers were smaller but still big: 16.8 percent from 1948 and 5.6 percent from 1969.

Table 3-11. Full-Time Equivalent Employment in Nonresidential Business: Average Years of Education, and Average Days of Education per Year for Persons with No College Training, 1948, 1969, and 1976[a]

Date	Males		Females	
	Average years of education[b] (1)	Average days per year[c] (2)	Average years of education[b] (3)	Average days per year[c] (4)
October 1948	9.46	124.3	10.22	128.0
March 1969	11.23	144.6	11.31	145.5
March 1976	12.05	152.0	11.94	152.6

Sources: Columns 1 and 3, calculated from table 3-10; columns 2 and 4, see appendix F.

a. Data refer to persons 18 years of age and over.

b. Calculated from table 3-10 but with 1976 data adjusted to eliminate 16–17-year-olds. Data cover all education categories. Averages used for grouped data are given in *Accounting for Growth*, p. 240, note 50.

c. Midyear estimates for persons with four years of high school education or less.

The number of days in school that a year of education represents also increased as the length of the school year for students in rural and town schools was raised toward that in big city school systems (which did not itself increase) and as absenteeism declined in all types of schools. These changes were reflected, with a long time lag, in the number of days that employed persons had spent in school for each year of school they had completed. Although persons who entered college—even in the nineteenth century—can be assumed to have made up any deficiencies in preparation that resulted from abbreviated attendance in lower schools, in the rest of the distribution increased attendance must be taken into account. Among employed male workers who had not attended college the average number of days of education per year of school completed rose 22.3 percent from 1948 to 1976 and 5.1 percent just from 1969 (table 3-11). Changes were again somewhat less for females.

Years or days spent in school, however, are not the appropriate weights to combine education groups, and hence a series measuring average time cannot measure changes in the education component of labor input. The appropriate series is one in which education groups are weighted, not by the time their members spent in school, but by the relative values, or marginal products, of the work their members perform. Such information can be inferred from data on earnings.

Because differences in amounts of education are associated with differences in other individual characteristics that affect earnings, care must be taken to base the weights on earnings differentials between earners who differ only in amount of education and corresponding experience. (Long education usually means less experience at any given age.)

Earnings differentials were computed for 1959 and 1969, based on data from the decennial census of population, and are shown in table 3-12. Average full-time equivalent earnings of men at each education level are expressed as a percentage of the earnings of men with eight years of elementary education in columns 1 and 2. In the derivation of these percentages only earnings of males 25 to 64 years of age were used. Men in any occupation were excluded if most of its members were employed in general government, households, and institutions. Earnings were computed on a full-year, full-time equivalent basis, because men with relatively little education work irregularly or part-time more often than those with more education. Males 25 and over were classified into thirty-two groups based on age, region, color, and attachment to farm or nonfarm occupations. Earnings differentials between education levels were computed for each of the thirty-two groups, and the percentages in table 3-12, columns 1 and 2, are a weighted average of them. This procedure eliminated from earnings differentials the effects of correlation among education, the four characteristics just listed, and (because only data for males were used) sex.

Finally, as explained in appendix F and more fully in *Accounting for Growth,* the standardized differentials so obtained were squeezed to eliminate the effect of correlation among education, earnings, and academic aptitude and socioeconomic status of parents. The adjusted differentials that resulted, shown in table 3-12, columns 3 and 4, are used as the proper weights to construct an index that measures the effect of changes in amount of education on labor input.

Earnings data are less satisfactory before 1959 but support the view that at least from 1939 to 1959 differentials were rather stable, except for

Table 3-12. Nonresidential Business: Standardized Earnings and Weights, 1959 and 1969

Percentage of earnings or weight of persons with 8 years of elementary education

Years of school completed	Standardized earnings[a]		Weight	
	1959 (1)	1969 (2)	1959 (3)	1969 (4)
None	71.6	82.1	75	87
Elementary, 1–4	86.5	89.7	89	93
Elementary, 5–7	95.5	95.6	97	97
Elementary, 8	100.0	100.0	100	100
High school, 1–3	112.6	112.6	111	111
High school, 4	127.3	125.6	124	122
College, 1–3	153.9	148.5	147	142
College, 4	201.3	195.6	189	184
College, 5 or more	264.2	243.2	219	207

Sources: Data for 1959, *Accounting for Growth*, table I-13, p. 240; for 1969, see appendix F.

a. Full-year earnings of males 25 years of age and over. Percentages are weighted averages of similar percentages for thirty-two separate categories of men.

some erratic fluctuations of moderate size.[20] From 1959 to 1969 percentage differentials narrowed. The narrowing was minor, however, except for men with zero or one to four years of education whose relative earnings rose, and those with five or more years of college whose relative earnings declined. Standardized earnings of men with four years of college exceeded those of men with four years of high school by 58 percent in 1959 (before adjustment for academic aptitude and socioeconomic status) and this had slipped only to 56 percent in 1969.

CPS data for mean income, which are much less satisfactory than those from the decennial census but which are available annually from 1967 to 1975, were also analyzed. They did not suggest any different or later change in differentials by amount of education.[21]

The distributions by level of education at dates shown in table 3-10 and other dates for which distributions were available were multiplied by the education weights shown in table 3-12, to obtain indexes for the effect of education on labor input, expressed with the weight of persons with eight years of education equal to 100. Actually, three overlapping indexes were computed for each sex and linked. The first, ending with March 1969, was

20. See *Why Growth Rates Differ*, pp. 373–74; and Edward F. Denison, "Measuring the Contribution of Education to Economic Growth," in E. A. G. Robinson and J. E. Vaizey, eds., *The Economics of Education* (St. Martin's, 1966), p. 226.

21. Appendix F describes the analysis of both the decennial census data and the CPS data.

based on persons 18 and over and 1959 education weights. The second, running from March 1969 to March 1972, was based on persons 18 and over and 1969 education weights. The third, starting with March 1972, was based on persons 16 and over and 1969 education weights.

To obtain annual estimates from the data for survey dates, an interpolation procedure was introduced that takes account of the positive relationship between the education index and the level of unemployment. Because unemployment is concentrated among the less educated, the distribution of employed persons by level of education shifts upward when unemployment rises.

An adjustment to these indexes was introduced to take account of the increase, for persons leaving school at the elementary and secondary levels, in the number of days of attendance per school year. The adjustment is based on the propositions that (1) only for persons who *regularly* attended *big-city* schools does the highest school grade completed provide a constant measure of the amount of education obtained; and (2) at any given date the number of days of school attended provides an appropriate ratio to convert the education received by other students to equivalence with that received by students who regularly attend big-city schools at the same grade level or who are of the same age. (Grade level and age are roughly interchangeable.) The statistical implementation of this proposition is an approximation.

The adjusted indexes for each sex were converted to time series indexes (shown in table F-5). They were weighted by total earnings to obtain the final index for both sexes combined.

The education index takes account only of the quantitative aspects of formal education. It is assumed that persons who reached any given educational level had studied a curriculum equally appropriate for their subsequent participation in economic life regardless of the date at which they were educated. If changes occurred in the "quality" of education, other than by extension of the school year and improved attendance, this is not reflected. Above all, it should be noted that the index is intended only as a component of labor input, not as an indication of all the economic effects of education. In particular, any effect of an increase in the level of education on the rate at which knowledge of how to produce at low cost advances is not captured by the index. Nor should it be.

The index just described is on an actual basis and is shown in table 3-1, column 7. A similar index on a potential basis appears in table 3-2. Growth rates of both are shown for the standard periods in table 3-4.

The rise of both indexes, already fast, accelerated after 1969. The growth rate on a potential basis had been 0.61 percent over the 1948–69 period as a whole and 0.65 percent in 1964–69. It mounted to 0.75 percent in 1969–73 and 0.96 percent in 1973–76. On an actual basis the acceleration was even greater, with the rate reaching 1.07 percent in 1973–76.

This acceleration was not anticipated, and it is interesting to inquire whether special factors were at work. Table 3-13, which compares 1969–75 with 1948–69, will be used to assist this inquiry.[22] It turns out that the biggest reason that the index for business employment accelerated is that the average age of employed adults declined.

Rows 1 to 7 of table 3-13 take account only of changes in the distributions by years of school completed; they do not allow for changes in days of school attendance per year. Row 3 shows growth rates of indexes based on distributions of the whole civilian labor force rather than full-time equivalent business employment, but calculated with the same weights. The rise in the growth rate from 1948–69 to 1969–75 was 0.17 points for males and 0.23 points for females. Line 2 shows that this increase was largely due to changes in average age. These affect the average education of the labor force because younger persons have more education than older persons, on the average. The average age of both male and female members of the civilian labor force dropped by nearly two years from 1969 to 1975, whereas that of males had declined only trivially from 1948 to 1969 and that of females had increased by more than two years. These changes in age distribution were not, it should be emphasized, the result of a changing proportion of teenagers. Differences between the periods with respect to changes in average age are about the same for each sex if the calculation is confined to persons 20 and over. When the effects of changes in average age are eliminated, row 1 shows, acceleration in the growth rates of education indexes for the civilian labor force, based on years of education, was only 0.03 percentage points for males and 0.05 for females.

Higher unemployment in 1975 than in 1969 contributed to acceleration of the growth rate of

22. The later period is terminated at 1975 because changes in the education distributions after March 1976 are preliminary.

Table 3-13. Analysis of the Acceleration in the Growth Rate of the Education Index for Labor Input from 1948–69 to 1969–75, by Sex

Growth rates in percent per annum

Item	Males			Females		
	1948–69	*1969–75*	*Change*	*1948–69*	*1969–75*	*Change*
1. Index for civilian labor force, age standardized[a]	0.55	0.58	0.03	0.43	0.48	0.05
2. Effect of change in average age[a,b]	0.01	0.15	0.14	−0.05	0.13	0.18
3. Index for civilian labor force (1+2)[a]	0.56	0.73	0.17	0.38	0.61	0.23
4. Effect of changes in unemployment[a,b]	−0.01	0.08	0.09	0.00	0.04	0.04
5. Index for civilian employment (3+4)[a]	0.55	0.81	0.26	0.38	0.65	0.27
6. Effect of changes in business share of employment[a,b]	−0.05	0.00	0.05	−0.11	0.00	0.11
7. Index for full-time equivalent business employment (5+6)[a]	0.50	0.81	0.31	0.27	0.65	0.38
8. Effect of changes in days per year[b]	0.15	0.10	−0.05	0.14	0.12	−0.02
9. Final education indexes (7+8)	**0.65**	**0.91**	**0.26**	**0.41**	**0.77**	**0.36**
10. Reduction due to changing from 1959 to 1969 weights[b]	0.00	0.07	0.07	0.00	0.06	0.06
11. Indexes if 1959 weights had been retained	0.65	0.98	0.33	0.41	0.83	0.42

Sources: Rows 3, 5, 6, table F-4 and *Accounting for Growth*, table I-18, p. 252; rows 7 and 9, table F-5; other rows, see text.
a. Indexes computed without allowance for changes in days per year of education.
b. Effect on growth rate, in percentage points.

the education index on an actual basis. This is indicated by the fact that similarly computed indexes for total civilian employment (row 5) increased more than those for the civilian labor force (row 3) in 1969–75 but by the same or a slightly smaller amount in 1948–69. The difference between periods was 0.09 percentage points for males and 0.04 points for females (row 4).

Changes in the division of employment between business and other activities were also of some importance. In 1969–75, growth rates for both males and females of education indexes for full-time equivalent business employment (row 7) were the same as those for total civilian employment (row 5), whereas in the earlier period they had been lower. Differences in the earlier period had reflected the absorption by government and nonprofit organizations of a disproportionate share of the increase in college graduates; expansion of employment in teaching was especially notable. The elimination of the adverse effect of changes in the distribution of civilian employment contributed 0.05 percentage points to acceleration in the growth rate of the education index for males and 0.11 points for females (row 6).[23]

The increase in the number of days of school attendance per year of education contributed less in 1969–75 than in 1948–69 (row 8), so it held down the rise in the growth rates of the indexes.

The adverse change was 0.05 percentage points for males and 0.02 points for females.

Rows 10 and 11 of table 3-13 show that in 1969–75 growth of the indexes would have been even faster were it not for the narrowing of earnings differentials between education groups, which was interpreted as indicating that the return to additional education had diminished. The change in weights held down the increases in growth rates by 0.06 or 0.07 points for each sex.

This review makes it clear that changes in the age distribution and shifts in the division of employment between business and other parts of the economy were responsible for the accelerated rise in the education index computed on a potential basis.[24] The rise in unemployment among the less educated added a further stimulus when the index for employed persons was computed on an actual basis. If one eliminates the effect of a changing age distribution and slightly narrowed earnings differentials, the education of the whole civilian labor force was rising only slightly faster in 1969–75 than in 1948–69.[25]

Average test scores for new high school graduates as well as for pupils in lower grades have declined during the past decade. This is widely regarded as resulting at least partially from the falling quality of education. This is probably correct, even though it is true that achievement may

23. These differences reflect not only the distribution of employment between business and other activities but also the divisions of employment at different educational levels between full-time and part-time workers.

24. Appendix M describes the derivation of this index.
25. This is deduced from table 3-13 by adding rows 1, 8, and 10. The acceleration is 0.05 percentage points for males and 0.09 points for females.

be hard to distinguish from IQ, and that no tests measure the contribution of schools alone. If the average quality of education *held by employed persons* had also declined, the acceleration in the increase in education that my index measures might have been offset by a qualitative decline. But a decline for workers cannot be inferred from a decline for students, as I shall now explain.

Members of the 1948 work force who were 65 years old started school about 1888, while the youngest members had just completed or were still attending school in 1948. Hence the quality of education of persons employed in 1948 depended on the average quality of schools during the sixty years from 1888 to 1948. The similar range for those employed in 1969 was 1909 to 1969, and for those employed in 1976, 1916 to 1976. For a change in educational quality to have offset the quantitative acceleration from the 1948–69 period to the 1969–76 period would have required the average quality of education of students to have increased less (or decreased more) from its 1909–69 average to its 1916–76 average than it had from its 1888–1948 average to its 1909–69 average.[26]

The reason this is unlikely, even if educational quality is inferred from test scores, is that test scores have moved in cycles. They declined from 1916 to 1925, increased substantially from the middle and late 1920s through the depression and into the early 1940s, declined during the 1940s and until the early 1950s, increased strongly during the 1950s and early 1960s, and declined strongly from 1965, and especially 1971, until the middle 1970s.[27]

The fact that recurrent cycles, rather than a steady trend, characterize student scores assures that changes in a series for the average test scores received by employed persons when they were students would be small and gradual—very muted

in comparison with movements in student scores. To determine the direction of change between any two dates would require complicated calculations.[28]

Total Labor Input

A comprehensive index of labor input in nonresidential business is obtained by multiplying the separate indexes already described. It is shown on an actual basis in table 3-1, column 8, and on a potential basis in table 3-2, column 8. Growth rates of both series in the selected periods appear in table 3-4, column 8.

The growth rate of potential labor input in the sector climbed from 0.8 percent a year in 1953–64 to 1.8 percent in 1964–69, 2.2 percent in 1969–73, and 2.4 percent in 1973–76. The 2.4 percent rate in the last period compares with about 1.4 percent in all the "long periods" for which rates were calculated and was a strong force toward rapid growth in this period, even though it was overridden by unfavorable developments.

Actual labor input was following quite a different course. After jumping from 0.5 percent in 1953–64 to 2.3 percent in 1964–69, it slipped to 1.6 percent in 1969–73 and 0.7 percent in 1973–76, a rate that would be much higher if the period were extended to 1978 when unemployment had been reduced.

The determinants of these rates have been dis-

---

26. This is an oversimplification since the averages should weight different years in accordance with their importance to the educational stocks of employed persons in 1948, 1969, or 1976, as the case may be, and some weight should be attached even to years before these ranges since many people work beyond 65.

27. Based on Paul Taubman and Terence Wales, *Mental Ability and Higher Educational Attainment in the 20th Century*, National Bureau of Economic Research Occasional Paper 118 (Berkeley: Carnegie Commission on Higher Education, 1972); Frank Armbruster, "The U.S. Primary and Secondary Educational Process" (Hudson Institute, 1975); Christopher Jencks, "The Wrong Answer for Schools Is: (b) Back to Basics," *Washington Post*, February 19, 1978; Marshall Smith, "The Test Score Collapse," Brookings Institution Seminar, September 1976; and Willard Wirtz and others, *On Further Examination: Report of the Advisory Panel on the Scholastic Aptitude Test Score Decline* (New York: College Entrance Examination Board, 1977).

28. Something should also be said about the relationship of possible long-term trends in IQ scores at different grade levels to my estimates. Since I assume that in the long run the distribution of the population by natural aptitude has not changed, the upswing in its distribution by highest grade completed, when combined with the observation that at any point in time average aptitude is highest at higher grade levels, implies that aptitude at some or all education levels must have dropped. (My adjustment of earnings differentials for differences in academic aptitude prevents this from biasing my education index upward.) The drop in IQ at a given grade would lead to a drop in achievement scores unless it were offset by some other change, such as improvement in educational quality.

Taubman and Wales in *Mental Ability and Higher Educational Attainment*, chap. 4, show that in actuality the average quality (as measured by IQ's or the like) of entering college students increased until about 1946 and then held steady until the 1960s. Avoidance of a decline until the mid-1960s was possible because 60 percent of the most able high school graduates entered college in the 1920s and 90 percent by the 1960s. Meanwhile, the average IQ of high school graduates who did not enter college was declining, not only because this group was losing its better academic talent to the education groups above it, but also because the proportion of each age group that completed high school was rising. Selectively draining the better talent from lower education groups provided an offset but it was only partial. A similar pattern probably prevailed in the education categories below four years of high school.

cussed individually, and repetition is unnecessary. The dominant effect of employment on changes in the growth rate of labor input is evident from table 3-4.

The measure of labor input is as comprehensive as I can make it, but it does not cover all of the characteristics of workers that are related to output, that may change over time, and hence that may contribute to increases or decreases in production.

Changes in the work effort per hour worked that is exerted by workers of a given age, sex, and level of education, are not captured by the index unless they result from changes in the length of working hours. It is conceivable that the omission is important; I shall return to this subject in chapter 9.

Time lost because of sickness is appropriately omitted from labor input, but the health of workers while they are at work, which may affect their output, is also omitted. I do not believe that changes during the period covered by this study have been sufficient to affect total labor input perceptibly. (I exclude here possible effects of alcohol and drugs; alcohol is discussed in chapter 5.)

Changes in experience are measured by the technique of weighting by age. The experience of women of a given age may have changed because of a change in the work habits of married women, particularly those with children, but the direction of any change is unclear.[29] A perceptible error in the labor input index from this source is scarcely conceivable in view of the small size of any change and the small weight of female workers in the total index. I know no other reasons to suspect a significant change during the postwar period in the relationship between age and experience for workers of a given sex.

The education index measures only the effects of changes in formal education, beginning with the first grade, that is received in regular schools or institutions of higher education, and equivalent programs. The effects of changes in the average amount of other types of education or training (which must be distinguished from "experience") received by persons of the same age and sex, and with the same amount of formal education, are omitted. These include kindergarten and nursery schools, courses taken from commercial and trade schools, adult self-education programs (including correspondence school courses), the new manpower training programs, apprenticeship programs, and short-term courses and seminars provided by employers that are not a normal accompaniment of a worker's job. Total resources going into all these programs are small in comparison with those used in regular formal education.

Color is not among the characteristics of workers that were considered in the construction of the labor input index and it is not clear that it should be, but in any case it appears that the effect of including color would be negligible because the composition of employment has not changed much.

All these characteristics of workers, and some others, have been considered in my previous studies.[30]

---

29. Single women typically have more experience than married women of the same age, and their proportion of all women workers has been declining rapidly. On the other hand, the experience of older married women presumably has risen because of earlier entry or reentry into the labor force after children are born. The rise in part-time work further clouds the picture.

30. *Sources of Economic Growth,* pp. 84, 166–69; *Why Growth Rates Differ,* especially chaps. 8 and 9 and apps. F and G; and *Accounting for Growth* (from which the preceding discussion is drawn), pp. 48–50.

➤➤➤◀◀◀

Capital, Land, and Total Input in Nonresidential Business

➤➤➤◀◀◀

An index of the total quantity of labor, land, and capital used to produce goods and services in the nonresidential business sector is constructed in this chapter. Capital is divided between two types: (1) inventories and (2) nonresidential structures and equipment. The index of total factor input is a weighted average of the indexes of labor, land, and the two types of capital. I shall first describe the weights and procedures used to combine the four indexes, and then the series that are used to measure capital and land inputs. Labor input was measured in chapter 3.

The Weighting Structure

To combine the four inputs, the weight used for each input is its estimated share of their combined earnings. The reason that earnings are used as weights can be stated briefly. At current prices, national income originating in the sector consists of the earnings of the labor, land, inventories, and nonresidential structures and equipment used in the sector, together with some amount of "pure" profit. The total earnings of each factor can be viewed as equal to the number of units of the factor and its price, or earnings, per unit. The marginal product of each factor is the extra output that would be added by one additional unit of that factor when the quantities of the other factors are held

constant. If enterprises combine the four factors in such a way as to minimize costs, they will use them in such proportions that the marginal products per unit of the several factors are proportional to their prices, or earnings, per unit. Unless this condition is satisfied, enterprises could reduce costs by substituting one factor for another. Departures from this situation are assumed to be small or offsetting so that total earnings of the four inputs are proportional to the number of units of each times its marginal product.[1]

It follows that if a small percentage increase in the number of units of all the factors would increase output of the sector by x percent, then a percentage increase of the same amount in the number of units of only one factor would increase output by x times the share of that factor in total earnings in the sector.

I shall measure total input as if a given percentage increase in all inputs would increase output by that same percentage, even though I do not believe this to be the case. The business sector actually operates under increasing returns to scale so that an increase of, say, 1 percent in every input would raise output by more than 1 percent, but this extra gain is classified as a change in output per unit of input rather than as an increase in total input (see chapter 5). Weights summing to 100 percent are therefore used so that if every input were to increase by 1 percent, total input would also increase by 1 percent.

The average values of the weights in the postwar years were as follows:

	Percent
Labor	81.0
Nonresidential structures and equipment	10.9
Inventories	4.2
Land	3.9

Appendix table G-2 shows the weights for all periods (which in the postwar years are pairs of adjacent years) and appendix G describes the procedures followed to secure them.[2]

National income includes an ingredient of "pure" profit (presumably positive in most postwar years) which could not be eliminated from the earnings of capital and land. If there are no offsetting biases (some possibilities were noted in *Accounting for Growth*), shares of capital and land are overstated relative to the share of labor in an

---

1. There is no need to specify the scale of a unit.

2. I discussed the statistical problems encountered in deriving the earnings weights and the extent to which they are sensitive to choices among alternative estimating procedures in *Accounting for Growth*, app. J.

average year, but no correction for this was attempted. The annual series were smoothed, however, in order to eliminate the effects of pronounced fluctuations in profits that occurred in the course of postwar business cycles—fluctuations that do not reflect changes in the relative marginal products of labor, capital, and land at standardized utilization rates.[3] These adjustments permit use of the same weights in the construction of input indexes on actual and potential bases.

Until 1969 there was little trend in the weights and fluctuations were moderate. The labor weight then rose to an average of 83 percent in 1969–76, compared with 80 percent in 1947–69, while the other three shares all declined. The long-range significance of these changes is yet to be determined. The labor share has averaged much the same as in other industrial countries; the percentage in the United States lies near the top of a fairly narrow range.[4]

Capital Input

To measure the two types of capital input in the nonresidential business sector (inventories, and nonresidential structures and equipment), I make use of the values in constant 1972 prices of the stock of privately owned capital of each type that is used in the sector.[5] The average of the stock at the beginning and end of the year was used.

Measurement of Inventory Input

The values of inventories in 1972 prices and an index of these values, which is used to measure the inventory component of total input, are shown in table 4-1, columns 1 and 2. The series is the one from which the Bureau of Economic Analysis

(BEA) measures the change in business inventories in 1972 prices, a component of its constant-dollar GNP series. Raw materials, work in process, finished goods, supplies, spare parts, crops (but not growing crops), and livestock are all included.

Derivation of Stock of Structures and Equipment

Two series are shown in table 4-1 for the value of the stock of nonresidential structures and equipment in 1972 prices: gross stock and net stock (gross stock minus accumulated depreciation). Both are from the BEA capital stock study, and are estimated by the perpetual inventory method. Capital stock series cannot be constructed without adopting certain conventions. For each type of capital good these series are based on useful service lives 85 percent as long as those estimated in the Bureau of Internal Revenue's Bulletin F (revised January 1942). These are averages; discards of goods installed in any year are distributed over a period ranging from 45 percent to 155 percent of the average service life by use of a modified Winfrey S-3 curve. To compute net stock, depreciation is calculated in accordance with the straight-line formula. These are the same conventions that are used to compute "capital consumption allowances with capital consumption adjustment" in the NIPA, and the data are drawn from the same tabulations.[6]

Measurement of Input of Structures and Equipment

Given the capital stock data, how should input of nonresidential structures and equipment be measured? If all capital goods were like the "wonderful

---

3. Data for the depressed 1930s, World War II, and the immediate postwar conversion years were replaced by shares interpolated between 1929 and 1948. These adjustments prevent changes in the movement of the total input index over a period of years from being sensitive to the particular date at which the various inputs (especially capital inputs) were added.

4. Edward F. Denison and William K. Chung, *How Japan's Economy Grew So Fast: The Sources of Postwar Expansion* (Brookings Institution, 1976), pp. 29–30; and *Why Growth Rates Differ*, pp. 33–44. Comparisons with most countries have been based on the labor share in the whole economy or with only the "dwellings" and "international assets" sectors excluded. Such percentages can be readily calculated for the United States based on data from the present study by combining tables 2-5 and G-1.

5. Some minor difficulties in delineating the appropriate borderline between nonresidential business capital and government capital were discussed in *Accounting for Growth*, app. K.

6. For a fuller description see Bureau of Economic Analysis, *Fixed Nonresidential Business and Residential Capital in the United States, 1929–75*, PB-253725 (National Technical Information Service, June 1976). In presenting data in that volume BEA groups components somewhat differently than I do. In the series it labels "fixed nonresidential business capital" it includes nonresidential capital owned by nonprofit organizations (which is excluded from table 4-1) and excludes private hotels, motels, and other "nonhousekeeping" residential structures (which are included in table 4-1).

The series in table 4-1 differ from the corresponding series in table 5-2 of *Accounting for Growth* in the following respects: (1) the base year for capital valuation is changed from 1958 to 1972; (2) service lives are reduced from 100 percent of Bulletin F to 85 percent; (3) BEA revised the investment and price data used in the calculations (formerly, BEA offered alternative constant-price series for structures, and in *Accounting for Growth*, data based on "price series 2" were used); (4) the method BEA uses to value capital goods transferred between sectors (chiefly, sales of government surplus in 1945–48) is changed, as explained in BEA, *Fixed Nonresidential Business and Residential Capital*, pp. T-19 to T-22.

Table 4-1. Nonresidential Business: Capital Stock Values in Constant Prices and Indexes, 1929, 1940–41, 1947–78[a]

Values in billions of 1972 dollars; indexes, 1972 = 100

	Inventories		Nonresidential structures and equipment					
			Values		Ratio of net stock to gross stock	Indexes		
Year	Value (1)	Index (2)	Gross stock (3)	Net stock (4)	(5)	Gross stock (6)	Net stock (7)	Weighted average (8)
1929	93.6	34.33	605.3	323.0	0.534	42.66	39.41	41.79
1940	92.2	33.82	561.8	262.3	0.467	39.60	32.00	37.52
1941	101.4	37.17	563.1	265.1	0.471	39.69	32.35	37.69
1947	118.8	43.55	585.0	284.6	0.486	41.23	34.72	39.48
1948	121.4	44.51	615.9	311.1	0.505	43.40	37.96	41.97
1949	121.9	44.71	639.8	330.6	0.517	45.09	40.34	43.85
1950	125.0	45.83	661.0	345.7	0.523	46.59	42.18	45.44
1951	137.0	50.27	685.4	361.9	0.528	48.31	44.16	47.23
1952	146.0	53.57	710.2	377.2	0.531	50.05	46.02	49.01
1953	149.0	54.63	735.2	392.0	0.533	51.82	47.82	50.79
1954	148.6	54.50	759.9	406.1	0.534	53.56	49.55	52.52
1955	151.4	55.53	785.0	420.8	0.536	55.33	51.34	54.30
1956	158.2	58.02	812.9	438.8	0.540	57.29	53.54	56.33
1957	161.8	59.36	841.1	457.5	0.544	59.28	55.82	58.39
1958	161.7	59.31	864.4	471.1	0.545	60.92	57.48	60.04
1959	164.0	60.15	884.5	481.6	0.544	62.34	58.75	61.42
1960	169.4	62.13	907.4	494.5	0.545	63.95	60.34	63.02
1961	173.0	63.47	930.7	507.7	0.546	65.59	61.94	64.66
1962	178.6	65.49	954.9	521.8	0.546	67.30	63.67	66.37
1963	186.5	68.40	982.5	538.5	0.548	69.25	65.71	68.34
1964	194.0	71.17	1,013.3	558.8	0.551	71.42	68.18	70.59
1965	203.4	74.58	1,052.9	587.4	0.558	74.21	71.67	73.56
1966	217.4	79.72	1,103.2	624.8	0.566	77.75	76.23	77.06
1967	231.7	84.98	1,155.5	662.3	0.573	81.44	80.81	81.28
1968	242.0	88.78	1,207.5	697.0	0.577	85.10	85.05	85.09
1969	251.7	92.32	1,263.6	733.2	0.580	89.06	89.46	89.16
1970	259.2	95.05	1,319.1	766.5	0.581	92.97	93.52	93.11
1971	264.6	97.05	1,368.8	793.1	0.580	96.47	96.77	96.55
1972	272.6	100.00	1,418.9	819.6	0.578	100.00	100.00	100.00
1973	285.6	104.77	1,477.3	853.2	0.578	104.12	104.10	104.12
1974	297.8	109.24	1,539.8	889.5	0.578	108.52	108.53	108.52
1975[b]	296.9	108.95	1,591.8	915.1	0.575	112.19	111.65	112.05
1976[b]	295.4	108.36	1,635.3	932.7	0.570	115.25	113.79	114.89
1977[b]	303.2	111.23	1,684.7	955.5	0.567	118.73	116.58	118.19
1978[b]	312.8	114.75	1,741.8	984.4	0.565	122.76	120.10	122.10

Sources: Column 1, NIPA, table 5.10. Column 2 was computed from column 1. Columns 3 and 4 are the sums of (1) corporate fixed nonresidential business capital from Bureau of Economic Analysis, *Fixed Nonresidential Business and Residential Capital in the United States, 1929–75*, PB-25735 (National Technical Information Service, June 1976), pp. 46, 79, 85, 303, and recent data from relevant BEA worksheets; (2) fixed nonresidential business capital of sole proprietorships and partnerships, from ibid., p. 79, and BEA worksheets; (3) private nonhousekeeping residential capital, from ibid., p. 303, and BEA worksheets; and (4) personal fixed nonresidential business capital (a component of "other private business" in ibid., p. 85) from BEA worksheets. Column 5 is the ratio of column 4 to column 3. Columns 6 and 7 were computed from columns 3 and 4. Column 8 is derived from annual percentage changes in column 3 (weighted 3) and column 4 (weighted 1).

a. Indexes are computed from capital stock data in millions of dollars. The values have been rounded to a tenth of a billion. All data are averages of values at the start and end of the year.

b. Data for capital stock in all years incorporate revisions in NIPA data provided in the July 1978 *Survey of Current Business*. Estimates for 1978 are consistent with NIPA data in the February 1979 *Survey*.

one hoss shay," their ability to perform services would not change during their service lives. In that case the gross stock, which places an unchanging value on each capital good throughout its useful service life, would provide the correct capital stock series for capital input measurement. Use of this assumption probably would lead to no great error, but it is extreme. The performance of at least some types of capital goods deteriorates unless mainte-

nance and repair costs (which are deducted to obtain net output) are increased as a good ages; it may deteriorate in any case. Also, newer capital goods are more likely to be in the place and use in which they are most advantageous to production.

To introduce an allowance for rising maintenance expense and deterioration of capital services with the passage of time, I have adopted the following expedient. To measure input of structures

Table 4-2. Growth Rates of Capital Input in the Nonresidential Business Sector
Percent

Period	Total capital input		Capital input per person employed		Capital input per person potentially employed	
	Inventories (1)	Nonresidential structures and equipment (2)	Inventories (3)	Nonresidential structures and equipment (4)	Inventories (5)	Nonresidential structures and equipment (6)
Long						
1929–76	2.48	2.17	1.40	1.09	1.18	0.88
1929–48	1.38	0.02	0.28	−1.06	0.22	−1.12
1948–73	3.48	3.70	2.35	2.56	2.25	2.46
Short						
1929–41	0.66	−0.86	0.02	−1.49	−0.80	−2.30
1941–48	2.61	1.55	0.73	−0.31	1.99	0.94
1948–53	4.18	3.89	3.07	2.78	3.47	3.18
1953–64	2.43	3.04	2.19	2.79	1.74	2.34
1964–69	5.34	4.78	2.66	2.12	3.35	2.80
1969–73	3.21	3.95	1.52	2.25	0.78	1.50
1973–76	1.21	3.31	0.57	2.66	−1.50	0.55
Addenda:						
1973–78	1.84	3.24	−0.15	1.22	−0.66	0.71
1973–75	1.98	3.74	2.68	4.45	−1.31	0.40
1975–78	1.74	2.90	−2.00	−0.88	−0.22	0.92

Source: Computed from tables 2-6, 2-7, and 4-1.

and equipment I have used a weighted average of indexes of the gross stock and net stock, with the gross stock weighted three and the net stock one.[7] This series is shown in table 4-1, column 8. The procedure implies that on the average a capital good with one-half of its useful service life exhausted contributes seven-eighths as much to net output (when net output itself is measured by the use of straight-line depreciation and after deduction of maintenance costs) as a good that is unused but otherwise identical, and three-fourths as much shortly before its retirement.

Growth of Capital Input

Capital has increased at an irregular pace in the past, as is evident from the growth rates shown in the first two columns of table 4-2. The period from 1929 to 1948, which spans the Great Depression and World War II, had on the whole been one of slow growth of capital. The postwar years to 1969 divide into three parts. The short 1948–53 and 1964–69 periods experienced very rapid growth of both inventories and fixed capital while in the longer intervening period, 1953–64, capital in-

creased much more slowly. This is the same pattern that was observed in sector employment and output.

The rate of increase in the stock of nonresidential structures and equipment in the latest of these periods, 1964–69, was far above earlier rates, and at the time, investment in such assets was generally acknowledged to be unsustainably high. The 4.8 percent growth rate of nonresidential structures and equipment input in 1964–69 compares with about 3.7 percent over the whole 1948–69 or 1948–73 periods, and only 2.2 percent over the entire 1929–76 period.

Growth of fixed capital input slackened in 1969–73, as expected, but only to the still-high rate of almost 4.0 percent. Even in 1973–75, the time when productivity sagged so badly, the rate eased back only to 3.7 percent, and it thus averaged 3.9 percent over the whole eight-year span from 1969 to 1975. At 3.9 percent the growth rate from 1969 to 1975 was the same as the rate during 1948–53, which had been the highest in any short period since 1929 except for 1964–69. It was nearly double the 2.2 percent rate in the prosperous period from 1926 to 1929.

The whole eleven-year span from 1964 to 1975 was thus one of rapid growth of fixed capital. Not until 1976, by which time the deepest postwar recession had cut sharply into fixed investment, did the rate of increase in capital input drop much. The

---

7. More exactly, annual percentage changes in gross stock and net stock were computed and averaged by these weights, and the weighted annual percentage changes were linked to obtain the input index.

reduction in that year was enough to cut the 1973–76 growth rate to 3.3 percent.[8]

The growth rate of capital in the form of inventories, at 5.3 percent, was even higher than that of fixed capital in 1964–69—both absolutely and in comparison with previous periods. It subsequently dropped more, to 3.2 percent in 1969–73 and 3.4 percent in 1969–74. Though slightly below the postwar average, these rates were above any previous period since 1929 except 1948–53 and 1964–69. The recession affected inventories more quickly than fixed capital, and the stock actually declined slightly in 1975 and 1976, cutting the 1973–76 growth rate to 1.1 percent.

By any reasonable past standard, the increase in fixed capital after 1969 was favorable to rapid growth of sector output through 1975, and the increase in inventories was favorable through 1974, even though the increases were less than in the extraordinary 1964–69 period. Weak growth of capital started only with 1976 in the case of fixed capital and 1975 in the case of inventories.

Changes in growth rates of capital, especially fixed capital, coincided with those in sector employment during the 1948–76 period. Consequently, growth of capital per worker was more stable than that of total capital (table 4-2, columns 3 and 4). Indeed, based on my standard short periods, the growth rate of fixed capital input per person employed was rather stable: 2.8 percent in 1948–53, 2.8 percent again in 1953–64, 2.1 percent in 1964–69, 2.2 percent in 1969–73, and 2.7 percent in 1973–76. The rates were moderately lower after 1964 than before and this contributed to diminished growth of national income per person employed (NIPPE). But there was no adverse change after 1973 that could account for the sudden drop in NIPPE; indeed, the 1973–76 rate almost matched the rates in the early postwar periods.

It is true, as column 6 of table 4-2 makes clear, that growth of fixed capital input per person *potentially* employed in the sector dipped sharply in 1969–73 and again in 1973–76. This was substantially adverse to the growth of potential national income per person potentially employed. If employment had suddenly returned to its potential level, the increase in fixed capital per worker since the last time that state was reached (1969) would have been found to be unusually small. This is an important fact, but it is not pertinent to an explanation of the retardation of growth observed in actual NIPPE.

8. The capital data are on an annual-average basis. Investment was already down within 1975.

The growth of inventories per person employed slipped further below its postwar average than growth of fixed capital in 1969–73 and especially in 1973–76. On a potential basis it was actually negative in the latter period. Thus inventories contributed to the decline in NIPPE on both an actual and potential basis, but they were not a dominant factor.

Tables 4-1 and 4-2 carry the capital stock series up to 1978. In the case of fixed capital, 1973–78 growth rates are close to 1973–76 rates both for total capital input and capital input per person potentially employed, but much lower for capital input per person actually employed. It may be inferred that fixed capital was a more important factor in the retardation of the growth of actual output per worker over the whole 1973–78 period than in 1973–76 alone. In the case of inventories, 1973–78 growth rates are higher than 1973–76 rates both for total capital input and for capital input per person employed, but as with fixed capital, lower for capital input per person actually employed.

Contributions of fixed capital and inventories to the growth of net output in nonresidential business are the products of the growth rates of their input indexes and the percentages that their earnings represent of the total factor costs that are incurred by nonresidential business (after adjustment for the business cycle). The shares of the two capital inputs diminished somewhat in the 1970s, implying that each 1 percent increase in capital input would raise sector output by a smaller percentage than in earlier years. This accentuated the decline from 1964–69 in the size of the capital contributions that the decline in growth of capital inputs alone would have produced. Shown in detail in chapter 7, the contribution of capital (fixed capital and inventories together) to the growth rates of the major series for sector national income is summarized below in percentage points:

	Sector national income		Potential sector national income	
	Total	Per person employed	Total	Per person employed
1948–73	0.56	0.39	0.56	0.38
1964–69	0.79	0.35	0.80	0.48
1969–73	0.52	0.28	0.52	0.18
1973–76	0.35	0.27	0.34	0.00

In 1973–76 capital contributed 0.2 percentage points less to the growth rates of total actual and potential sector national income than it had in the 1948–73 period as a whole or the preceding 1969–73 period, and about 0.45 points less than in

1964–69 when its contribution was biggest.[9] The contribution to NIPPE slipped less, by only 0.1 percentage points from either 1948–73 or 1964–69 and scarcely at all from 1969–73. The contribution to potential national income per person potentially employed, on the other hand, fell to nothing from a substantial 0.4 percentage points in 1948–73, 0.5 points in 1964–69, and 0.2 points even in 1969–73. This pattern foreshadowed a substantial drag from capital on actual output per worker as actual employment moved toward potential after 1976.

Saving and Investment Ratios

Growth of capital stock results from saving and investment. As an aid to understanding the behavior of the capital stock better it is instructive to examine these flows, particularly ratios of saving and investment to national product. The behavior of these ratios also has implications for attempts to alter future growth of investment and output.

In the framework of the national income and product accounts, gross private investment is equal to gross private saving plus government saving (defined as the government surplus on income and product account). Similarly, net private investment is equal to net private saving plus government saving. These equalities are a matter of definition.[10] In actual statistics they may not hold exactly because estimates are statistically inconsistent. In the construction of table 4-3, which shows aggregate saving and investment ratios, statistical equality was obtained by subtracting one-half of the statistical discrepancy in the national accounts from private investment and adding the other half to private saving.

In the preceding paragraph, and in table 4-3, investment is defined to include private investment in dwellings and (except in columns 7 and 8 of the table) net foreign investment, in addition to investment in structures, equipment, and inventories in the nonresidential business sector. Outlays made by government units (including government enterprises) for durable assets and inventories are omitted.

The most stable ratio is that of gross private saving to gross national product (table 4-3, column 1).

In the twenty-nine years from 1948 through 1976 gross private saving averaged 15.84 percent of GNP. The mean deviation of the annual percentages from this average was only 0.54 percent of GNP and in only three years (1967, 1969, and 1975) was the deviation as much as one percentage point.[11]

There is no indication of a rising or falling trend in the gross private saving rate. It averaged 15.7 percent in 1948–62 and 16.0 percent in 1963–76. It averaged about the same, 15.9 percent, during 1973–78, which includes the recent period of slow growth.

The net private saving rate—the ratio of net private saving to net national product—was of course much lower. It averaged 7.50 percent in 1948–76. It was also less stable than the gross saving rate, though not notably so. The mean deviation of the annual percentages from their mean was 0.66 percent of net national product. Fluctuations, like those in the gross ratio, seem largely random. Again, there is no appreciable trend; the net private saving ratio averaged 7.4 percent in 1948–62 and 7.6 percent in 1963–76. In 1973–78, however, the ratio averaged 6.5 percent, nearly a point below the postwar mean.

Saving available for private investment is augmented by a government surplus, while a government deficit absorbs part of private saving and thus reduces the amount available for investment. From 1948 to 1974 governments absorbed private saving, but not to a major extent. The surplus or deficit averaged −0.16 percent of gross national product and −0.18 percent of net national product. The 1975–76 deficits were so big that extending the period to 1948–76 more than doubles these percentages, to −0.37 and −0.41, respectively. From 1975 to 1977 the deficit averaged −2.39 percent of GNP and −2.67 percent of net national product before returning to near balance in 1978. In these years

---

9. The capital contributions to actual and potential sector national income differ only because of rounding and a minor interaction term.

10. What the BEA terms "capital grants received by the United States (net)" appear in the accounts in four years (NIPA, table 5.1). When they do, they must be added to saving or subtracted from investment to secure equality.

11. The national accounts permit two estimates of gross private saving, which differ by the statistical discrepancy. The average size of the statistical discrepancy was almost as big as the average deviation of the saving rate from its average. In only about half the years do both saving estimates indicate the saving rate was above or below its 1948–76 average.

I called attention to the stability of the gross private saving rate from 1929 to 1957 and explored some of the implications in "A Note on Private Saving," *Review of Economics and Statistics,* vol. 40 (August 1958), pp. 261–67. Paul A. David and John L. Scadding showed the stability to have extended much further back in time in "Private Savings: Ultrarationality, Aggregation, and 'Denison's Law,'" *Journal of Political Economy,* vol. 82, no. 2, pt. 1 (March-April 1974), pp. 225–49.

Table 4-3. U.S. Aggregate Saving and Investment Ratios, 1948–78[a]

	Percent of gross national product			Percent of net national product			Net private domestic investment as percent of net national product	
Year	Gross private saving (1)	Government surplus (2)	Gross national saving and gross private investment[b] (3)	Net private saving (4)	Government surplus (5)	Net national saving and net private investment[b] (6)	Current prices (7)	Constant (1972) prices (8)
1948	15.4	3.3	18.7	8.2	3.5	11.8	10.7	9.7
1949	15.0	−1.3	13.6	7.1	−1.4	5.7	5.6	5.4
1950	14.9	2.8	17.8	7.2	3.1	10.3	11.4	10.2
1951	15.7	1.8	17.5	7.9	2.0	9.9	10.4	9.1
1952	15.7	−1.1	14.6	7.9	−1.2	6.6	7.1	6.4
1953	15.5	−1.9	13.7	7.5	−2.1	5.4	6.5	6.1
1954	15.9	−2.0	14.0	7.5	−2.2	5.4	5.9	5.5
1955	16.0	0.8	16.8	7.8	0.9	8.7	9.1	8.2
1956	16.1	1.2	17.4	7.6	1.6	10.3	8.4	7.5
1957	16.2	0.2	16.4	7.4	0.2	7.7	6.8	6.1
1958	16.5	−2.8	13.6	7.4	−3.1	4.1	4.4	4.3
1959	15.9	−0.3	15.5	7.1	−0.4	6.7	7.1	6.8
1960	14.9	0.6	15.5	6.0	0.7	6.7	6.3	6.1
1961	15.5	−0.8	14.7	6.7	−0.9	5.8	5.3	5.4
1962	15.9	−0.7	15.2	7.6	−0.7	6.9	6.8	6.8
1963	15.3	0.1	15.4	7.1	0.1	7.3	7.0	7.1
1964	16.3	−0.4	16.0	8.4	−0.4	8.0	7.2	7.4
1965	16.8	0.1	16.8	9.2	0.1	9.3	8.6	8.7
1966	16.7	−0.2	16.6	9.3	−0.2	9.1	9.1	9.0
1967	17.1	−1.8	15.2	9.4	−2.0	7.4	7.4	7.4
1968	15.7	−0.6	15.0	7.8	−0.7	7.1	7.2	7.4
1969	14.4	1.1	15.6	6.2	1.2	7.4	7.5	7.6
1970	15.3	−1.0	15.4	6.7	−1.0	5.8	5.6	5.8
1971	16.3	−1.7	14.7	7.8	−1.9	5.9	6.3	6.5
1972	15.5	−0.3	15.2	7.1	−0.3	6.9	7.8	7.8
1973	16.2	0.5	16.7	7.9	0.5	8.5	8.6	8.5
1974	15.1	−0.2	14.7	5.9	−0.2	5.5	6.0	6.1
1975	17.3	−4.2	13.1	7.4	−4.7	2.7	2.1	1.9
1976	16.1	−2.0	14.1	6.2	−2.2	4.1	4.3	4.1
1977	15.6	−1.0	14.6	5.8	−1.1	4.7	6.1	5.6
1978	15.2	−0.1	15.1	5.5	−0.1	5.4	6.8	6.2

Source: Computed from NIPA and incorporates data from July 1978 and February 1979 issues of *Survey of Current Business*.

a. Ratios computed from data in which gross and net national product and gross and net investment have been reduced, and gross and net private saving raised, by half the value of the statistical discrepancy in the NIPA.

b. Percentages shown are for gross and net investment. Percentages for gross and net saving are the same except in 1970, 1971, 1972, and 1974. In these years there is a difference, not exceeding 0.1 percentage points, because of capital grants paid or received by the United States.

large surpluses at the state and local level offset part of the large federal deficits. The government surplus or deficit has fluctuated widely, mainly because of the effect of the business cycle on tax liabilities and government expenditures. The full-employment surplus or deficit has also varied, of course.

Because of the pattern of government saving, private investment ratios have averaged a little lower and fluctuated more than twice as much as private saving ratios. From 1948 through 1974 gross private investment averaged 15.60 percent of GNP, and net private investment averaged 7.41 percent of net national product. Corresponding percentages in 1948–76 were 15.46 and 7.12. Neither percentage displayed any weakness until 1974, when inventory investment fell off as noted in the discussion of capital stock. Both percentages fell to

postwar lows in 1975 and were still low, though rising, from 1976 to 1978. In 1974–78 the gross investment ratio averaged only 14.1 percent and the net ratio 4.5 percent. In 1978 the gross investment ratio, at 15.1 percent of GNP, was still below the postwar average, but that for investment in nonresidential structures and equipment alone was up to its level even in prosperous past periods. The years 1977 and 1978 saw the emergence of balance of payments deficits that made net foreign investment negative by huge amounts, aiding the financing of domestic investment.

Columns 1 through 6 of table 4-3 are based on output, saving, and investment data expressed in current rather than constant prices. This is appropriate for consideration of saving and investment decisions because in any year such decisions are necessarily based on price and income relationships prevailing in that year, not those prevailing in some future or past "base" year. It is investment in constant, not current, prices, however, that is related to the growth of the capital stock, and hence of capital input and output measured in constant prices.

Columns 7 and 8 of table 4-3 compare current and constant price data for net private domestic investment as a percentage of net national product.[12] The comparison shows that the constant-price net investment ratio rose 12 percent relative to the current-price ratio from the average of 1948–52 to the average of 1970–74. This reflects the circumstance that the implicit deflator for net private domestic investment rose less than that for net national product. The smaller price rise for investment was helpful to growth in the sense that an investment ratio that was stable in money terms would have risen in real terms. The relative decline in investment prices was confined to the years before 1961. After 1970, and especially after 1974, the situation reversed. From the 1970–74 average to the 1975–78 average the constant price net investment ratio fell 7.9 percent relative to the current price ratio. Sharply higher relative prices for construction, both residential and nonresidential, were responsible. The rise during this period in the relative price of investment accentuated the effect of a lower current-dollar investment rate on capital stock growth.

Even on a constant-price basis, the relationship between investment ratios and growth of capital input is not a simple one. Net investment, to be sure, does measure the dollar change in the net capital stock, but it is the ratio of investment to capital stock, not to output, that determines the growth rate of the capital stock and is pertinent to the growth of output. Moreover, if my judgments are correct, in the case of fixed capital the change in the gross stock, which is equal to gross investment minus retirements, is more closely related to growth of services of fixed capital than is the change in the net stock, which is equal to gross investment minus capital consumption. Growth rates of gross and net stock tend to converge in the long run, and rates tend to be high or low for both in any particular place and period, but they sometimes diverge considerably. Also to be remembered is that investment in the nonresidential business sector is only part of total private investment and its share is not constant.[13]

Although the preceding section showed that capital contributed only moderately to the recent retardation of growth rates (except for potential output per person potentially employed), it does not follow that a program to restore growth should ignore capital as an important ingredient. Any effort to raise the growth rate by increasing investment would require a judgment as to whether the problem would be to stimulate incentives for investment, incentives for saving, or both.

In this century at least, the impetus to past major changes in the growth of capital have come from the investment side. The general stability of private saving ratios throughout the postwar period—and indeed for a much longer time span if the periods of major wars and major depressions are discarded—suggests that significant changes in the U.S. growth rate in this century cannot be ascribed to changes in the private propensity to save. This continued to be the case in the period of recent slow growth of output and capital stock. The stability, it is to be noted, prevailed despite major changes in rates of inflation, interest rates, the level and structure of taxes, real per capita income, government and private retirement programs, other forms of public and private insurance against contingencies, and many other aspects of the economic environment. It suggests that policymakers should be cautious in appraising their ability to influence private saving behavior.

There is no similar difficulty in financing more investment by raising government saving—by raising tax rates of reducing expenditures—if investment demand is known to be sufficiently strong to assure that a more stringent fiscal policy will not instead simply reduce demand, production, and investment—and tax revenues as well. But much of the time this condition is not met.

It seems clear to me that in the period after 1974 the problem was weak investment demand. Investment was not small because saving was inadequate to support a larger investment volume, as one might suppose if he thinks of private saving being absorbed by government deficits. Rather, with the gross private saving rate stable, it was weak investment demand that created the large government deficits by dropping the economy's production and real income far below capacity and thus curtailing government revenues and inducing additional gov-

---

12. Net private domestic investment differs conceptually from net private investment only in that net foreign investment (often negative) is omitted. Column 7 differs from column 6, however, for the additional reason that for comparability with column 8, the statistical discrepancy was omitted from both numerator and denominator in computing column 7.

13. Residential construction usually makes up almost all of the rest, but in 1975 net foreign investment reached 0.8 percent of GNP and in 1978 it fell to −1.2 percent.

ernment expenditures. Underutilization, of course, further weakened investment demand. Under these conditions any attempt to raise government saving by raising taxes or reducing government expenditures would have further lowered output and in all probability reduced investment even more. It is impossible to say just how much of the drop in the investment rate was the secondary effect of the drop in utilization, but it is likely that the drop in investment would not have been large if the rate of utilization could have been maintained.

Any program to stimulate capital stock growth over an extended period—or for that matter even in the short run as of the time of writing—probably would have to rely on strengthening incentives to invest rather than to save. In making this statement, however, I do not want to suggest that I or anyone else knows of acceptable measures that can be counted on with confidence to stimulate investment enough to raise the growth rate by any considerable amount.

If one wished to embark on such a program, a sensible place to start under present conditions would be with reductions in taxes on profits, either by lowering rates or, if measurement and administrative problems can be overcome, by some form of inflation adjustment. The purpose would be to raise rates of return on capital. Even before-tax rates of return on corporate capital have been decidedly low by historical standards in the last half of the 1970s. (Whether they would have been low if utilization had been at the postwar average is uncertain.) The extraordinarily high effective tax rates resulting from the effect of inflation on "book" profits brought the after-tax rate of return much below the rate in earlier postwar years. The prospect that future inflation will cause this situation to continue, and even to worsen if inflation should accelerate, cannot but discourage investment, and especially investment in long-lived assets because the difference between original cost depreciation and replacement cost depreciation is directly related to service lives. Uncertainty and costs arising from government regulation and possible future changes in regulation, including the possibility of reimposition of price controls, also discourage investment but it is not easy to see how such uncertainty could be removed.

Conditions Related to Capital That Affect Output per Unit of Input

Changes in the age, allocation, and intensity of use of the capital stock affect output per unit of input rather than the contribution of capital, according to my classification. It is convenient, however, to refer to these topics here.

Age of Fixed Capital

After declining until 1970 the average age of fixed capital began to increase and has continued to do so. I do not believe this has been a significant factor in the retardation of growth, but many observers do, so it is necessary to examine the facts and explain my view.

The average useful service lives used in the capital stock study range from eight years for tractors and for office, computing, and accounting machinery to fifty-one years for railroad structures. For all structures and equipment in the stock the average service life was about twenty-four years in the mid-1970s (if components with different service lives are weighted by depreciation).[14]

The percentage of the original service life of durable capital goods that still remains is equal to the ratio of net stock (based on straight-line depreciation) to gross stock. This is the best available measure of the "newness" of capital goods because it is not affected by changes in the distribution of capital among types of goods with different service lives.[15] The higher the net-gross ratio, the newer is the capital stock. The series is shown in table 4-1, column 5.

The net-gross ratio rose steadily from 0.486 in 1947 to 0.581 in 1970, meaning that fixed capital was becoming newer (even with the effect of changes in mix eliminated). From 1970 to 1978 the net-gross ratio fell steadily from 0.581 to 0.565, meaning the capital stock was growing older (with the effect of changes in mix eliminated). Even in 1978, however, the stock was not "old"; it was newer than it had been in any year from 1925, when the series starts, through 1965.

What are the effects of changes in average age? I shall first calculate them using the assumption of an extreme "vintage" model of "embodied" technical progress, and then explain (as I have been doing for many years) why the effects are hugely overestimated if not wholly a mirage.

Table 4-4 shows the calculations; I shall describe

14. See *Why Growth Rates Differ*, pp. 146–48, for a discussion of alternative weights. Depreciation weights are used here because this is the only basis on which the average service life is readily calculated from aggregate figures. It is equal to average age of the gross stock divided by (one minus the net-gross ratio).

15. In contrast, series for average age rise if the composition of the stock moves toward longer-lived assets and decline if it shifts toward shorter-lived assets—as actually happened over the postwar period.

Table 4-4. Derivation of the Effect of Changes in Average Age on the Growth Rate of National Income in Nonresidential Business According to an Extreme Vintage Model, Selected Periods, 1948–76

Item	1948–73	1948–53	1953–64	1964–69	1969–73	1973–76
1. Change in ratio of net stock to gross stock	0.072	0.028	0.018	0.029	−0.003	−0.007
2. Decline in average age of capital, in years (with composition held constant)	1.74	0.67	0.44	0.69	−0.06	−0.18
3. Annual decline in average age of capital, in years	0.07	0.14	0.04	0.14	−0.02	−0.06
4. Effect on growth rate of output, in percentage points	0.10	0.19	0.06	0.19	−0.02	−0.08

Sources: Row 1, calculated from table 4-1, column 5 (based on unrounded ratios); row 2, row 1 times twenty-four-year service life; row 3, row 2 divided by length of period; row 4 equals product of row 3 and contribution of advances in knowledge to growth rate in 1948–73, estimated at 1.40 percent per annum.

the arithmetic for the 1948–73 period. The net-gross ratio fell by 0.072 points (or by 7.2 percent of the average service life) from 1948 to 1973. If the average service life was twenty-four years, this implies a reduction of 1.74 years (7.2 percent of 24) in the average age of capital (with the effect of mix changes eliminated). A reduction of 1.74 years over a twenty-four-year period is an average annual reduction of 0.07 years (or 26 days). Estimates presented in the following chapter suggest that from 1948 to 1973 output rose 1.40 percent a year as a result of advances in knowledge. (I use this same figure for all periods.) The extreme vintage model supposes that all "technological progress," which I identify for the moment with advances in knowledge, is carried by structures and equipment. If so, each year's vintage of fixed capital goods will produce 1.40 percent more output than an equal amount of capital from the previous year's vintage with no change in labor, inventories, or any other output determinant. If this is so, a reduction of one year in the average age of capital will raise output 1.40 percent above what it would have been with no change in average age. Hence the annual decline of 0.07 years in average age raised the growth rate of national income by 0.10 percentage points (0.07 times 1.40) in the 1948–73 period, according to this model. As shown in table 4-4, similar calculations indicate the change in average age subtracted nearly 0.1 percentage points from the national income growth rate in 1973–76 and accounts for a decline of 0.2 points from the 1948–73 period, 0.3 points from 1964–69, and 0.1 points from 1969–73. I have presented these results to show that allowance for the age of capital could explain only a little of recent output behavior even under extreme assumptions. But I want to stress that I believe these results to be wrong, and the actual effect to have been unimportant.

In *Why Growth Rates Differ* I outlined as follows the reason that a change in age distribution could not under normal circumstances have the effect that vintage models suppose even on the unreasonable supposition that all advances in knowledge are embodied in structures and equipment:

During any span of time, different types of capital goods undergo very different amounts of quality improvement. The greater the quality improvement in new goods of any type, the greater the obsolescence of existing capital for which the new goods are a substitute. Other things being equal, the rate of return on replacement investment, and hence the incentive to invest, is highest for types of capital goods that have experienced the most obsolescence. Any substantial amount of gross investment permits investment opportunities created by sizable quality improvements in new capital goods to be grasped. It is only the less profitable investments, involving replacement of capital goods for which quality change has been small, that are sensitive to variations in the amount of gross investment (on which changes in average age depend). Similarly, the advantage of improvements will be greater in some uses than others even for the same type of good, and new acquisitions will be used first where the gains are greatest. The gain in the average quality of the capital stock that vintage models imagine to be derived from additional new investment is not realized because the change in average age automatically is largely offset by a reduction in the average amount of quality improvement incorporated in new capital.[16]

Investment Required to Meet Government Regulations

Much recent business investment was required by new governmental regulations and therefore not available to increase the measured output or to reduce costs. It is sometimes suggested that such capi-

16. *Why Growth Rates Differ*, pp. 145–46. See that source for earlier citations.

tal should be deleted from capital input. I find it more informative to consider that diversion of capital (and labor) to meet government requirements reduces output per unit of input, and I consider the topic in chapters 6 and 9. The magnitude of the capital diversion, however, will be indicated here.

The net stock of nonresidential business capital that had been installed to conform with new regulations related to pollution abatement, over and above the amount that would have been required if 1967 practices had continued, was valued annually through 1975. This incremental value was put at $27.6 billion in current prices in 1975.[17] The corresponding incremental value of net capital stock required to meet new regulations for employee safety and health was estimated at $5.9 billion, bringing the total incremental value for the two types of program to $33.5 billion. This was almost 2.6 percent of the total net stock of nonresidential structures and equipment in nonresidential business. The growth of this percentage from 1967, when it was zero by definition, is shown below. The percentage has continued to grow rapidly since 1975, but explicit estimates are not available.[18]

Year	Percent of net stock	Year	Percent of net stock
1967	0.00	1972	1.18
1968	0.10	1973	1.53
1969	0.25	1974	2.02
1970	0.52	1975	2.58
1971	0.83		

Thus it is true that the net stock available for production of measured output grew appreciably less than the total net stock—over 0.5 percent a year less from 1973 to 1975. This compares with 0.3 percent from 1969 to 1973, 0.05 percent in 1964–69, and nothing in earlier periods. The percent of

17. The total value of the net stock of pollution abatement capital was $9.0 billion larger. Data are averages for the year.

18. The incremental stock of pollution abatement capital is from Edward F. Denison, "Effects of Selected Changes in the Institutional and Human Environment upon Output per Unit of Input," *Survey of Current Business,* vol. 58 (January 1978), table 2, p. 26 (Brookings General Series Reprint 335); the incremental stock of safety equipment on business-owned autos and trucks from ibid., table 5, p. 33; the incremental stock of other safety and health capital (except in mining) from my estimates described in ibid., p. 37; and the incremental stock of safety and health capital in mining from estimates obtained by multiplying the stock in nonmining industries by the ratio of gross investment in safety and health capital in mining from 1972 to 1975 to similar investment in nonmining industries. The total stock of nonresidential structures and equipment in the nonresidential business sector in current prices is from the same source as the constant-price series shown in table 4-1, column 4.

gross stock so diverted was smaller. These two types of regulation were not the only types requiring business investment, but they are believed to be the most important.

Allocation of Capital

If the allocation of capital (like that of any other input) approaches closer to the allocation that would maximize output per unit of input, or departs further from it, the shift will affect the growth rate. Except for the expansion of government regulations, the introduction of the investment tax credit may have had the most pervasive effects on the efficiency of investment allocation.

The investment tax credit (ITC) badly distorts relative incentives to invest in different types of assets and must be presumed to have increasingly distorted the distribution of capital as the proportion of the stock installed while ITC was in effect increased. First enacted as part of the Revenue Act of 1962, the ITC has been successively suspended, repealed, and reenacted. It was "permanently" reinstated by the Revenue Act of 1971 at a maximum 7 percent rate (4 percent for utilities), later raised to 10 percent (including utilities) under the Tax Reduction Act of 1975 for the years 1975 to 1980.

If the tax credit were equal to the same percentage of gross investment in durable assets for assets of all service lives, it would discriminate in favor of shorter-lived durable assets. Consider, for example, a country with a stationary capital stock (so that net stock, based on straight-line depreciation, is always half the gross stock) that consists of assets with service lives of four years and of forty years. Annual gross investment is equal to 50 percent of the average value of the net stock for the four-year asset but to only 5 percent for the forty-year asset. Since the ITC is a percentage of the amount of gross investment rather than of the size of the stock, the four-year assets receive ten times as much subsidy as the forty-year assets.

The actual tax law is much more complicated. The Council of Economic Advisers discussed the distorting effects of the credit in its January 1977 report and summarized the provisions at that time as follows:

At present the law provides for a credit against current tax liabilities of corporate and noncorporate businesses, equal to 10 percent of the value of qualified investments. Qualified investments are generally new depreciable assets used in production, excluding structures, with service lives of 3 years or more. The credit is applied on a sliding scale in such a way that one-third of the full credit is allowed for assets with service lives of

3 or 4 years, two-thirds for assets with service lives of 5 or 6 years, and the full credit for those assets with service lives of 7 years or more. The ITC rates thus range from 3⅓ to 10 percent, depending on the life of the asset. The credit claimed in any year cannot exceed a company's total tax liability for the year, and the maximum credit that generally may be taken is $25,000, plus 50 percent of the tax liability in excess of $25,000. Credits not usable in the current year because of this limitation may be deducted against tax liabilities 3 years back and 7 years forward on a first-in, first-out basis, that is, the oldest credits are used first. Under current law the basis for calculating depreciation allowances on new equipment is not reduced by the amount of the credit.[19]

The Council of Economic Advisers estimated the change in the after-tax internal rate of return on various types of assets when that rate is 10 percent before account is taken of ITC. Table 4-5 shows these estimates. Short-lived assets—inventories and equipment with less than a three-year service life— got no subsidy. Neither did structures, the assets with the longest service lives (mostly in the range of twenty-six to forty years, according to BEA data). In the intermediate range the ITC raises the rate of return by amounts fluctuating up from 19 percent on equipment with a three-year service life to a maximum of 33 percent on equipment with a seven-year service life, then down to 13 percent on equipment with a thirty-year life.

Altering the rate of return by amounts ranging from nothing to one-third can hardly fail to distort the distribution of the capital stock and reduce its average efficiency. Failure to assist inventory investment biases business decisions against stockpiling of raw materials, finished goods, and spare parts to provide for periods of peak demand or equipment breakdown and in favor of maintenance of excess capacity or simply sustaining the loss of shortages. Failure to assist investment in long-lived assets discriminates against replacement of entire factories or other production complexes—which some keen observers hold essential to secure maximum productivity gains—and instead encourages piecemeal replacement of equipment. As the Council of Economic Advisers points out, discrimination by type of asset inevitably also favors some industries over others, and has been especially adverse to industries most in need of long-term investment.

The ITC was amended in 1978 to cover structures, but this does not affect the period under review. Even though they are now eligible, structures,

19. *Economic Report of the President, January 1977,* p. 163.

Table 4-5. Change in After-Tax Internal Rate of Return under Present 10 Percent Investment Tax Credit, All Businesses, as of 1977

Type and service life of asset	Investment tax credit (percent)	Change in after-tax internal rate of return (percentage points)[a]
Inventories	0.0	0.00
Equipment (years of service)		
1	0.0	0.00
2	0.0	0.00
3	3.3	1.92
4	3.3	1.57
5	6.7	2.77
6	6.7	2.42
7	10.0	3.30
8	10.0	2.99
9	10.0	2.73
10	10.0	2.52
15	10.0	1.91
20	10.0	1.60
25	10.0	1.42
30	10.0	1.31
Structures	0.0	0.00

Source: *Economic Report of the President, January 1977,* pp. 163–65.
a. Assumes that the net income stream from the investment is constant, that the after-tax internal rate of return before the investment tax credit equals 10 percent, and that the credit does not affect future costs or revenues.

like long-lived equipment, receive only a minimal subsidy from the ITC.

Heightened inflation, experienced in the 1970s, also tends to worsen the allocation of capital. It adds to uncertainty about the future. Moreover, with the present tax system inflation penalizes investment in long-lived depreciable assets more than investment in short-lived depreciable assets because the difference between original cost and replacement cost is greater the less frequently the stock turns over. Thus inflation reinforces the similar bias that ITC introduces. The tax system also penalizes ownership of inventories heavily in the presence of inflation, again reinforcing a bias introduced by ITC. Business could usually avoid this penalty by using last-in-first-out (LIFO) accounting, but many firms do not do so to avoid reporting lower profits.

An increase in misallocation as the proportion of capital put in place while the investment tax credit was operative and the inflation rate high may be assumed. The quantitative effect on the growth rate of output per unit of input, however, may not have been large if one can judge from similar cases.[20]

20. Arnold C. Harberger has developed methods for estimating such costs. See his *Taxation and Welfare* (Little, Brown, 1974). See also *Sources of Growth,* chap. 17, especially pp. 184–91.

Capital Utilization Not Measured Separately

My index of the input of structures and equipment refers to the fixed capital stock standing ready for use by business. It does not measure variations in the average hours that capital is actually used or other aspects of intensity of use, such as the speed with which machines are operated.

In the short run, capital utilization fluctuates with variations in the pressure of demand, but in this respect capital input is no different from land input or labor input. My input series may be regarded as measures of the labor, capital, and land physically present in business establishments and available for use in production. Changes in the intensity of their use that result from variations in the pressure of demand on these "employed" resources therefore affect my series for output per unit of input. In chapter 5, I try to isolate this effect for all the factors combined.

The hours that capital is used may also change in the longer run, but such changes, if they occur, are merely manifestations of changes in other output determinants that are separately measured so they need not be given separate consideration. A possible exception is the prevalence of shift work when industry weights are held constant. My estimate, based on limited data, is that a series for the prevalence of shift work based on use of constant industry weights, were it available, would not change much apart from short-term fluctuations related to demand pressure.[21]

Land Input

An ideal index of land input would take each parcel of land available in the base period and use an input index for each parcel that would remain 100 unless

21. In the past information has been largely confined to manufacturing and mining. The Bureau of Labor Statistics, using the Current Population Survey, obtained data representative of all full-time nonfarm wage and salary workers for May 1977. It found that 84 percent worked at least half their hours between 8 A.M. and 4 P.M. (described as day shifts), 8 percent worked at least half their hours between 4 P.M. and midnight (evening shifts), and 3 percent worked at least half their hours between midnight and 8 A.M. (night shifts). The remaining 5 percent worked more than twelve or less than six hours a day and were classified as on "other shifts." (U.S. Department of Labor Release 78-188, March 16, 1978.)

The proportion working on other than the first shift cannot be calculated from this classification, but it could not exceed 16 percent and is more likely to have been around 11 percent. Inclusion of part-time employees probably would have raised the percentage. Since only one such survey has been made, no trend can be obtained.

there was some change in its quality. The indexes for the separate parcels would then be weighted by their base period economic rent. In the absence of a change in land area or in the quality of any parcel, the total land input index necessarily would always remain 100. This would continue to be the case if the weights for the parcels were changed frequently and short-period, fixed-weight indexes were linked to obtain a continuous series.

The total land area of the country has not, in fact, changed and the area of private nonresidential land has changed very little during the period covered. Hence the index could not change much unless net transfers between nonresidential business and other sectors were highly concentrated in land with very high economic rent when in nonresidential business use—more concentrated than seems possible. Some adjustment for changes in the quality of agricultural, mineral, and forestland would be desirable, but I have not found this feasible nor does it seem likely that such changes could affect the index appreciably, even allowing for discoveries and depletion of minerals.

I shall assume land input in the nonresidential business sector to have been constant. Consequently changes in land made no contribution to the growth of total national income, actual or potential. The quantity of land per person employed declines when employment increases, and its increasing scarcity relative to labor makes land a negative factor in the growth rate of NIPPE. Its weight is so small, however, that the adverse effect usually is not large. Because the growth of potential employment was very fast from 1973 to 1976, land does account for 0.07 percentage points of the decline from 1948–73 to 1973–76 in the growth of potential national income per person potentially employed in nonresidential business. The contribution of land to the various output series in all standard periods is shown in chapter 7.

Total Factor Input

Table 4-6 repeats the sector output indexes and the input indexes for the four major types of input. In addition, indexes of total capital input and total factor input are introduced. They were computed by weighting the annual percentage changes in the component series by the earnings weights shown in table G-2 and then linking the annual percentage changes. Series are shown on both an actual and potential basis. (For capital and land inputs, the

Table 4-6. Nonresidential Business: Indexes of Sector Inputs, and Sector National Income per Unit of Total Factor Input, 1929, 1940–41, and 1947–76, Actual and Potential Basis[a]

Actual, 1972 = 100

			Indexes of inputs										
Year	Actual sector national income in 1972 prices (1)	Potential sector national income in 1972 prices (2)	Actual labor (3)	Potential labor (4)	Inventories (5)	Nonresidential structures and equipment (6)	All reproducible capital (7)	Land (8)	Actual total factor input (9)	Potential total factor input (10)	Actual sector national income per unit of input (11)	Potential sector national income per unit of input (12)	Potential discrepancy factor (13)
1929	28.24	27.57	58.94	58.01	34.33	41.79	38.97	100.00	56.56	55.80	49.93	49.20	100.44
1940	28.97	33.29	61.02	70.62	33.82	37.52	35.99	100.00	57.40	64.41	50.48	52.66	98.16
1941	34.79	35.35	67.21	71.47	37.17	37.69	37.23	100.00	62.32	65.41	55.83	54.65	98.91
1947	42.30	42.92	75.80	75.67	43.55	39.48	40.56	100.00	69.48	69.38	60.88	61.82	100.08
1948	44.19	43.50	76.67	76.21	44.51	41.97	42.52	100.00	70.67	70.32	62.53	61.81	100.08
1949	42.80	44.10	73.96	76.51	44.71	43.85	43.86	100.00	69.09	70.92	61.95	62.50	99.49
1950	47.09	46.59	76.21	77.71	45.83	45.44	45.29	100.00	71.13	72.18	66.20	64.78	99.64
1951	50.07	48.25	79.93	78.64	50.27	47.23	47.91	100.00	74.56	73.57	67.15	65.49	100.15
1952	51.46	50.73	81.68	80.14	53.57	49.01	50.14	100.00	76.43	75.26	67.33	67.25	100.23
1953	53.59	53.06	83.22	81.51	54.63	50.79	51.70	100.00	77.92	76.65	68.78	69.07	100.22
1954	52.10	54.31	80.62	82.83	54.50	52.52	52.90	100.00	76.24	77.93	68.84	69.89	99.71
1955	56.60	56.19	83.03	83.41	55.53	54.30	54.46	100.00	78.43	78.73	72.17	71.31	100.09
1956	58.27	59.28	84.28	84.82	58.02	56.33	56.61	100.00	79.86	80.28	72.97	73.92	99.89
1957	58.74	60.66	83.76	84.71	59.36	58.39	58.47	100.00	79.86	80.60	73.55	75.36	99.88
1958	56.90	62.81	80.84	85.92	59.31	60.04	59.66	100.00	77.81	81.78	73.13	77.22	99.45
1959	61.62	64.40	83.82	86.40	60.15	61.42	60.50	100.00	80.41	82.39	76.63	78.38	99.72
1960	62.35	66.24	83.90	86.88	62.13	63.02	62.73	100.00	80.80	83.11	77.17	79.94	99.71
1961	63.10	68.23	83.62	88.25	63.47	64.66	64.29	100.00	80.87	84.49	78.03	81.10	99.58
1962	67.42	69.93	85.14	87.70	65.49	66.37	66.08	100.00	82.40	84.39	81.82	83.10	99.71
1963	70.51	72.21	85.99	88.49	68.40	68.34	68.30	100.00	83.49	85.44	84.45	84.78	99.68
1964	74.66	74.94	87.53	89.14	71.17	70.59	70.69	100.00	85.15	86.42	87.68	86.96	99.71
1965	80.29	78.86	90.25	90.63	74.58	73.56	73.77	100.00	87.86	88.19	91.38	89.60	99.80
1966	84.76	82.40	92.92	91.96	79.72	77.06	77.71	100.00	90.69	89.97	93.46	91.57	100.02
1967	85.98	85.32	93.92	93.56	84.98	81.28	82.19	100.00	92.31	92.07	93.14	92.69	99.97
1968	90.46	89.07	96.03	95.07	88.78	85.09	86.00	100.00	94.65	93.92	95.57	94.81	100.03
1969	92.91	93.69	98.19	97.46	92.32	89.16	89.94	100.00	97.02	96.48	95.76	97.06	100.05
1970	91.08	97.02	97.17	99.31	95.05	93.11	93.58	100.00	96.76	98.56	94.13	98.55	99.89
1971	93.35	100.51	97.16	100.97	97.05	96.55	96.67	100.00	97.20	100.36	96.04	100.33	99.82
1972	100.00	106.17	100.00	103.19	100.00	100.00	100.00	100.00	100.00	102.64	100.00	103.59	99.85
1973	105.91	111.61	104.51	106.45	104.77	104.12	104.28	100.00	104.30	105.93	101.54	105.43	99.94
1974	102.35	114.15	105.62	109.68	109.24	108.52	108.70	100.00	105.78	109.17	96.76	104.65	99.91
1975	98.62	112.50	103.09	112.24	108.95b	112.05b	111.25b	100.00	103.98	111.48	94.85	101.13	99.79
1976	106.21	116.48	106.85	114.31	108.36b	114.89b	113.21b	100.00	107.36	113.55	98.93	102.82	99.76

Sources: Column 1, table 2-6, column 5; column 2, table 2-8, column 2; column 3, table 3-1, column 8; column 4, table 3-2, column 8; columns 5 and 6, table 4-1, columns 2 and 8; columns 7–10, see text; column 11, quotient of columns 1 and 9; column 12, table 5-2, column 1; column 13, column 2 divided by product of columns 10 and 12.

a. Series excluding and including Alaska and Hawaii are linked at 1960.

b. Slightly different indexes, not incorporating revisions introduced in the July 1978 *Survey of Current Business*, were used to calculate columns 9 and 10 and estimates of the sources of growth shown in subsequent tables.

series are the same.) Both actual and potential series are shown with actual 1972 values equal to 100.

Table 4-6 also shows output per unit of input. On an actual basis this series (column 11) is obtained by dividing the index of output (column 1) by the index of total factor input (column 9). Output per unit of input on a potential basis is obtained by a different procedure, explained in appendix M, which introduces a small discrepancy (shown in column 13) between output and the product of in-

put and output per unit of input. Table 4-7 shows the growth rates during the standard periods of the series shown in table 4-6.

On an actual basis, total factor input was responsible for 18 percent of the drop of 3.5 percentage points in the growth rate of sector output from 1948–73 to 1973–76, and for 27 percent of the drop of 3.2 percentage points from 1969–73 to 1973–76. The decline in output per unit of input was much more important.

Output per unit of input much more than accounts for the drop of 2.4 percentage points in the growth rate of potential output from 1948–73 to 1973–76; potential input growth had actually speeded up. During the three most recent short periods the growth rate of potential input scarcely changed, so output per unit of input was entirely responsible for the decline in output growth over this time span.

Table 4-7. Nonresidential Business: Growth Rates on Actual and Potential Basis of National Income, Inputs, and National Income per Unit of Total Factor Input
Percent per annum

Period	Actual sector national income in 1972 prices (1)	Potential sector national income in 1972 prices (2)	Indexes of inputs								Actual sector national income per unit of input (11)	Potential sector national income per unit of input (12)	Potential discrepancy factor (13)
			Actual labor (3)	Potential labor (4)	Inventories (5)	Nonresidential structures and equipment (6)	All reproducible capital (7)	Land (8)	Actual total factor input (9)	Potential total factor input (10)			
Long													
1929–76	2.86	3.11	1.27	1.45	2.48	2.17	2.29	0.00	1.37	1.52	1.47	1.58	−0.01
1929–48	2.39	2.43	1.39	1.45	1.38	0.02	0.46	0.00	1.18	1.22	1.19	1.21	−0.02
1948–73	3.56	3.84	1.25	1.35	3.48	3.70	3.65	0.00	1.57	1.65	1.96	2.16	−0.01
Short													
1929–41	1.75	2.09	1.10	1.76	0.66	−0.86	−0.37	0.00	0.81	1.33	0.94	0.88	−0.13
1941–48	3.48	3.01	1.90	0.92	2.61	1.55	1.92	0.00	1.81	1.04	1.63	1.77	0.17
1948–53	3.93	4.05	1.65	1.35	4.18	3.89	3.99	0.00	1.97	1.74	1.92	2.24	0.03
1953–64	3.06	3.19	0.46	0.82	2.43	3.04	2.88	0.00	0.81	1.10	2.23	2.12	−0.05
1964–69	4.47	4.57	2.33	1.80	5.34	4.78	4.93	0.00	2.64	2.23	1.78	2.22	0.07
1969–73	3.33	4.47	1.57	2.23	3.21	3.95	3.77	0.00	1.83	2.36	1.48	2.09	−0.03
1973–76	0.10	1.43	0.74	2.40	1.12	3.31	2.74	0.00	0.97	2.34	−0.86	−0.83	−0.06

Source: Computed from table 4-6.

⇉≪⇇

CHAPTER FIVE

Output per Unit of Input in Nonresidential Business

⇉≪⇇

Determinants of output per unit of input are numerous. In the very long run, two are responsible for most of the productivity increase. One is advances in knowledge of how to produce at low cost; the other is gains from economies of scale made possible by expansion of the size of markets as the economy grows. Many other determinants describe reasons that productivity falls short of the maximum that would be possible if resources were allocated and used with perfect efficiency, given the state of knowledge and the size of markets. These affect the growth rate only during a transitional period within which the economy moves to either a more or a less efficient position. Such shifts may take place over quite long time spans, however. Burdens imposed on business by government, services provided to business by government, and other aspects of the environment within which business operates may change in ways that affect productivity. Irregular factors dominate short-term movements of output per unit of input and are sometimes important even in comparisons of years that are decades apart.

Changes in output per unit of input are divided among some of its determinants in this chapter. The division cannot be either complete or precise, but even partial and approximate estimates are useful if made with care. The order in which determinants are examined is dictated solely by convenience for the process of estimation; it has no other logic.

The first column of table 5-1 repeats the series for output per unit of input in the sector that is presented in table 4-6. Subsequent columns provide indexes of the effects of changes in individual determinants on the composite index. The indexes for total output per unit of input and its components shown in table 5-1 are all measured on a scale such that a difference of, say, 1 percent in the value of an index in any year would change total national income in nonresidential business by an estimated 1 percent.[1] Table 5-2 shows the indexes for components of output per unit of input on a potential basis. As usual, these indexes are presented with actual values in 1972 equal to 100.

Reallocation of Labor a Diminishing Growth Source

The more nearly resources are allocated to the uses in which their contributions to the value of output are greatest, the larger is output per unit of input. Mainly because shifting patterns of demand for labor have long been reducing the requirements for farm labor while the actual transfer of labor has lagged, overallocation of labor to farming has been a chronic condition. Indeed, it has been by far the biggest type of misallocation of resources among uses.

As farm employment shrank, the fraction of total business employment thus misallocated declined. Farming used about 22.4 percent of total labor input in the nonresidential business sector in 1929, 14.5 percent in 1947, and 4.2 percent in 1976. Thus the percentage of total business labor misallocated to farming would have been much reduced even if the percentage of farm labor that was excessive had not declined—which it has. The farm percentage of the sector's national income, measured in 1972 prices, is smaller than its percentage of labor input and has declined less: from 9.3 percent in 1929 to 6.7 percent in 1947 and 3.7 percent in 1976. The drop in the farm percentage of the sector's labor input from 1947 to 1976 (10.3 percentage points) was over three times as large as the drop (3.0 points) in the farm percentage of the sector's national income in constant prices. Appendix table H-1 provides similar data for other years.

The gain in output per unit of input resulting

---

1. In this respect these indexes are similar to that for total factor input in table 4-6, column 9, but not, of course, to indexes for the separate inputs as they are presented in table 4-6.

Table 5-1. Nonresidential Business: Indexes of Sector Output per Unit of Input, 1929, 1940–41, and 1947–76
1972 = 100

| | | | | | | | | Effects of irregular factors | | | | |
| | | Gains from reallocation of resources from: | | Effects of changes in legal and human environment | | | | Changes in intensity of utilization of employed resources resulting from: | | Other determinants | | |
Year	Output per unit of input (1)	Farming (2)	Nonfarm self-employment (3)	Pollution abatement (4)	Employee safety and health (5)	Dishonesty and crime (6)	Effect of weather on farm output (7)	Work stoppages (8)	Fluctuations in intensity of demand[a] (9)	Total (semi-residual) (10)	Economies of scale (11)	Advances in knowledge and miscellaneous (residual) (12)
1929	49.93	88.35	97.11	100.41	100.17	100.33	100.19	100.04	104.12	55.25	86.41	63.94
1940	50.48	89.20	96.61	100.41	100.17	100.33	99.40	100.03	103.00	56.67	87.63	64.67
1941	55.83	90.74	97.43	100.41	100.17	100.33	99.90	99.99	107.28	58.39	88.03	66.33
1947	60.88	93.68	97.47	100.41	100.17	100.33	99.58	99.96	101.56	65.35	90.61	72.12
1948	62.53	93.93	97.46	100.41	100.17	100.33	100.06	99.97	104.27	64.88	90.89	71.38
1949	61.95	93.73	97.14	100.41	100.17	100.33	99.87	99.92	103.03	65.56	91.14	71.93
1950	66.20	94.19	97.30	100.41	100.17	100.33	100.24	99.95	105.97	67.41	91.38	73.77
1951	67.15	95.10	97.75	100.41	100.17	100.33	99.83	100.00	105.52	67.94	91.86	73.96
1952	67.33	95.38	97.83	100.41	100.17	100.33	99.83	99.88	102.92	69.67	92.51	75.31
1953	68.78	95.77	98.04	100.41	100.17	100.33	100.05	99.98	102.33	70.91	93.02	76.23
1954	68.84	95.54	97.83	100.41	100.17	100.33	100.07	100.00	101.36	71.42	93.33	76.52
1955	72.17	95.96	98.07	100.41	100.17	100.33	100.19	99.98	104.53	72.56	93.49	77.61
1956	72.97	96.55	98.15	100.41	100.17	100.33	100.03	99.97	101.93	74.85	93.88	79.73
1957	73.55	96.83	98.18	100.41	100.17	100.33	99.84	100.01	100.86	76.11	94.28	80.73
1958	73.13	96.91	97.94	100.41	100.17	100.27	100.07	99.99	98.61	77.42	94.50	81.93
1959	76.63	97.16	98.27	100.41	100.17	100.28	99.84	99.84	101.36	78.75	94.74	83.12
1960	77.17	97.46	98.32	100.41	100.17	100.22	100.06	100.00	100.11	79.72	94.97	83.94
1961	78.03	97.53	98.28	100.41	100.17	100.20	100.06	100.02	100.07	80.64	95.23	84.68
1962	81.82	97.89	98.54	100.41	100.17	100.20	99.99	100.01	102.07	82.46	95.56	86.29
1963	84.45	98.25	98.81	100.41	100.17	100.17	100.10	100.01	103.26	83.52	95.90	87.09
1964	87.68	98.60	98.88	100.41	100.17	100.15	99.94	100.00	104.39	85.57	96.33	88.83
1965	91.38	98.88	99.22	100.41	100.17	100.16	100.09	100.00	105.41	87.61	96.94	90.38
1966	93.46	99.33	99.62	100.41	100.17	100.14	99.83	100.00	105.34	89.16	97.59	91.36
1967	93.14	99.51	99.75	100.41	100.17	100.09	100.00	99.97	103.78	89.84	98.07	91.61
1968	95.57	99.62	99.93	100.37	100.17	100.04	99.96	99.96	104.02	91.82	98.50	93.22
1969	95.76	99.83	99.92	100.31	100.14	99.98	99.91	99.97	101.80	94.01	99.05	94.91
1970	94.13	99.89	99.95	100.21	100.11	99.91	100.00	99.92	98.84	95.26	99.41	95.83
1971	96.04	99.96	99.87	100.10	100.05	99.89	100.18	99.96	99.22	96.80	99.56	97.23
1972	100.00	100.00	100.00	100.00	100.00	100.00	100.00	100.00	100.00	100.00	100.00	100.00
1973	101.54	100.12	100.16	99.89	99.96	99.95	99.96	100.00	99.63	101.88	100.71	101.16
1974	96.76	100.13	100.10	99.67	99.87	99.83	99.96	99.96	95.77	101.49	101.09	100.40
1975	94.85	100.07	99.91	99.44	99.75	99.67	100.09	99.99	97.61	98.22	101.27	96.99
1976	98.93	100.17	100.08	(99.20)[b]	(99.60)[b]	(99.67)[b]	99.90	99.98	99.99	100.32	101.44	98.90

Sources: Column 1, table 4-6, column 11; columns 2–3, see appendix H; columns 4–6, Edward F. Denison, "Effects of Selected Changes in the Institutional and Human Environment upon Output per Unit of Input," *Survey of Current Business*, vol. 58 (January 1978), table 15, p. 41 (Brookings Reprint 335); columns 7–9, see text; column 10, column 1 divided by the product of columns 2 through 9; column 11, see text; column 12, column 10 divided by column 11.

a. Includes changes in intensity of utilization due to materials shortages and miscellaneous causes.
b. Estimates for 1976 were not prepared for columns 4 to 6. The table assumes approximately the same change in columns 4 and 5 in 1976 as in 1975 and no change in 1976 in column 6.

from reduction in the overallocation of labor to farming is calculated from two estimates. First, it is estimated that if labor input in the nonfarm portion of nonresidential business had been larger by 1 percent in any year, nonfarm output in the sector would have been larger by 0.8 percent, approximately the labor share of national income. Second, it is estimated that if labor input in farming had been smaller by 1 percent in any year, farm output (farm national income in 1972 prices) would have

been smaller by 0.33 percent. This estimate supposes that the reduction in labor would be concentrated on small farms with little output to about the same extent as was the actual reduction of labor in farming.

These two estimates permit a calculation of the percentage by which national income in the nonresidential business sector as a whole would have been raised each year if labor input in the sector had been divided between farm and nonfarm work

Table 5-2. Nonresidential Business: Indexes of Potential Sector Output per Unit of Input, 1929, 1940–41, and 1947–76
Actual, 1972 = 100

Year	Output per unit of input (1)	Gains from reallocation of resources from: Farming (2)	Gains from reallocation of resources from: Nonfarm self-employment (3)	Effects of changes in legal and human environment: Pollution abatement (4)	Effects of changes in legal and human environment: Employee safety and health (5)	Effects of changes in legal and human environment: Dishonesty and crime (6)	Effects of irregular factors: Effect of weather on farm output (7)	Changes in intensity of utilization of employed resources resulting from: Work stoppages (8)	Changes in intensity of utilization of employed resources resulting from: Fluctuations in intensity of demand (9)	Other determinants: Total (semiresidual) (10)	Other determinants: Economies of scale (11)	Other determinants: Advances in knowledge and miscellaneous (residual) (12)
1929	49.20	87.95	96.87	100.41	100.17	100.33	100.19	100.04	103.31	55.25	86.41	63.94
1940	52.66	91.31	98.16	100.41	100.17	100.33	99.40	100.03	103.31	56.67	87.63	64.67
1941	54.65	91.62	98.08	100.41	100.17	100.33	99.90	99.99	103.31	58.39	88.03	66.33
1947	61.82	93.56	97.41	100.41	100.17	100.33	99.58	99.96	103.31	65.35	90.61	72.12
1948	61.81	93.81	97.37	100.41	100.17	100.33	100.06	99.97	103.31	64.88	90.89	71.38
1949	62.50	94.00	97.47	100.41	100.17	100.33	99.87	99.92	103.31	65.56	91.14	71.93
1950	64.78	94.34	97.50	100.41	100.17	100.33	100.24	99.95	103.31	67.41	91.38	73.77
1951	65.49	94.89	97.59	100.41	100.17	100.33	99.83	100.00	103.31	67.94	91.86	73.96
1952	67.25	95.12	97.61	100.41	100.17	100.33	99.83	99.88	103.31	69.67	92.51	75.31
1953	69.07	95.49	97.79	100.41	100.17	100.33	100.05	99.98	103.31	70.91	93.02	76.23
1954	69.89	95.65	98.05	100.41	100.17	100.33	100.07	100.00	103.31	71.42	93.33	76.52
1955	71.31	95.92	98.09	100.41	100.17	100.33	100.19	99.98	103.31	72.56	93.49	77.61
1956	73.92	96.49	98.16	100.41	100.17	100.33	100.03	99.97	103.31	74.85	93.88	79.73
1957	75.36	96.81	98.23	100.41	100.17	100.33	99.84	100.01	103.31	76.11	94.28	80.73
1958	77.22	97.19	98.42	100.41	100.17	100.27	100.07	99.99	103.31	77.42	94.50	81.93
1959	78.38	97.28	98.49	100.41	100.17	100.28	99.84	99.84	103.31	78.75	94.74	83.12
1960	79.94	97.59	98.57	100.41	100.17	100.22	100.06	100.00	103.31	79.72	94.97	83.94
1961	81.10	97.78	98.70	100.41	100.17	100.20	100.06	100.02	103.31	80.64	95.23	84.68
1962	83.10	98.00	98.76	100.41	100.17	100.20	99.99	100.01	103.31	82.46	95.56	86.29
1963	84.78	98.36	99.03	100.41	100.17	100.17	100.10	100.01	103.31	83.52	95.90	87.09
1964	86.96	98.66	99.03	100.41	100.17	100.15	99.94	100.00	103.31	85.57	96.33	88.83
1965	89.60	98.89	99.26	100.41	100.17	100.16	100.09	100.00	103.31	87.61	96.94	90.38
1966	91.57	99.30	99.56	100.41	100.17	100.14	99.83	100.00	103.31	89.16	97.59	91.36
1967	92.69	99.49	99.73	100.41	100.17	100.09	100.00	99.97	103.31	89.84	98.07	91.61
1968	94.81	99.58	99.87	100.37	100.17	100.04	99.96	99.96	103.31	91.82	98.50	93.22
1969	97.06	99.78	99.85	100.31	100.14	99.98	99.91	99.97	103.31	94.01	99.05	94.91
1970	98.55	99.93	100.06	100.21	100.11	99.91	100.00	99.92	103.31	95.26	99.41	95.83
1971	100.33	100.04	100.11	100.10	100.05	99.89	100.18	99.96	103.31	96.80	99.56	97.23
1972	103.59	100.08	100.19	100.00	100.00	100.00	100.00	100.00	103.31	100.00	100.00	100.00
1973	105.43	100.16	100.25	99.89	99.96	99.95	99.96	100.00	103.31	101.88	100.71	101.16
1974	104.65	100.20	100.29	99.67	99.87	99.83	99.96	99.96	103.31	101.49	101.09	100.40
1975	101.13	100.26	100.45	99.44	99.75	99.67	100.09	99.99	103.31	98.22	101.27	96.99
1976	102.82	100.32	100.52	(99.20)[b]	(99.60)[b]	(99.67)[b]	99.90	99.98	103.31	102.32	101.44	98.90

Sources: Column 1, product of columns 2 through 10; columns 2–3, see appendix M; columns 4–8, table 5-1; column 9, see text of appendix L; columns 10–12, table 5-1.

a. Includes changes in intensity of utilization due to materials shortages and miscellaneous causes.

b. Estimates for 1976 were not prepared for columns 4–6. The table assumes approximately the same change in columns 4 and 5 in 1976 as in 1975, and no change in 1976 in column 6.

in the following year's proportion. This percentage is my estimate of the gain from one year to the next in output per unit of input that resulted from the shift of resources from farming to nonfarm jobs. The annual percentages were linked to obtain a continuous index, shown in table 5-1, column 2.

Persons who are underemployed or whose labor is very wastefully utilized are also present among the nonfarm self-employed and unpaid members of their families. These individuals work in enterprises that are not only small but also highly inefficient.

Little or no paid labor is hired, which holds down out-of-pocket expenses and enables an enterprise to survive when it could not do so if labor had to be paid in cash. Turnover among such enterprises is high as hopeful newcomers replace their unsuccessful predecessors. But many endure as long as their owners can subsist on the small earnings obtained, and they disappear only with their owners' disability or death. Members of this "fringe" group among the self-employed contribute little to the value of production, but if hired by larger enterprises, they could contribute as much to output as other workers.

Such persons are only a fraction—today, a small fraction—of the total number of self-employed and unpaid family workers engaged in nonfarm activities. However, the reduction in the share of nonfarm business employment that is represented by self-employed and unpaid family workers appears to have occurred among this fringe group rather than among those who are independent professionals; who operate more sizable establishments; who do well as craftsmen, repairmen, and the like; or who are simply unqualified for paid jobs. The reduction in the percentage of labor input in nonfarm nonresidential business that consists of self-employed and unpaid family workers was from 15.2 percent in 1929 to 14.5 percent in 1947 and 9.8 percent in 1976 (table H-1).

The transfer of workers from the fringe group among the self-employed to paid employment contributed to the rise in productivity. The index shown in table 5-1, column 3, is my estimate of the effect on output per unit of input in the sector. It was calculated on the assumption that as the importance of self-employment diminished, an increase in wage and salary employment only one-fourth as large as the decline in self-employment was required to obtain production of equal value. This assumption, which is retained from earlier studies, takes into consideration not only that those leaving self-employment had a low value of output per person, but also that the work they formerly did could often be absorbed by those remaining in that status. No allowance is made for possible savings in capital or land.

The indexes of gains from the reallocation of labor are influenced by the business cycle because a rise in unemployment affects the distribution of labor input among farm employment, nonfarm self-employment and nonfarm wage and salary employment. As explained in chapter 2, my estimates of potential national income are calculated in accordance with the convention that actual and potential employment differ only in nonfarm wage and salary employment. The consequence is that the indexes for gains from reallocation are higher on a potential basis than on an actual basis when the unemployment rate is over 4 percent. The indexes on a potential basis are substantially free of cyclical movements.

The growth rates of the reallocation indexes measure the estimated amounts that reallocation contributed to the growth rates of sector national income and national income per person employed. They are shown in table 5-3, columns 2 and 3.

Diminution of gains from resource reallocation is a prominent cause of the decline in the rate of growth of potential national income and potential national income per person potentially employed. The gain from the shift of labor out of farming fell regularly. By 1969–73 the shift contributed only 0.1 percentage points, 0.2 percentage points less than its average contribution from 1948 to 1969. In 1973–76 the contribution fell further to only 0.05 percentage points, one-quarter of a point below 1948–69. The disappearance of the shift from farming as a big source of productivity gain was inevitable. Farms once provided a large pool of labor that could be tapped for other activities without reducing agricultural production much, but the pool is nearly dry.

Nonfarm self-employment has also diminished considerably as a percentage of total employment, but the decline has been much slower than in farming and three times as much employment remains. The shift of labor from nonfarm self-employment contributed approximately 0.1 percentage points to the growth rate of potential national income in all the postwar periods except 1964–69, when the contribution reached 0.17 percentage points.

The two sources combined were responsible for a drop of about 0.2 percentage points in the growth rate of potential output from all three of the preceding short periods to 1969–73, and about 0.3 points from all three periods to 1973–76. These are substantial amounts.

The reduction of gains from reallocation was an even more important cause of the decline in the growth rates of actual national income than of potential national income during the 1970s. Unemployment in nonfarm wage and salary jobs temporarily lifted the actual percentage of employment on farms and in nonfarm self-employment in 1976, so the shift of labor contributed less to the 1973–76 growth of actual than of potential national income. In fact, it contributed nothing at all. This compares with an average contribution of 0.4 percentage points in 1948–69.

Growth Reduced by Changes in the Institutional and Human Environment

In the last decade the institutional and human environment within which business must operate has changed in several ways that adversely affect output per unit of input. Columns 4 to 6 of table 5-1 mea-

Table 5-3. Nonresidential Business: Growth Rates of Potential and Actual Output per Unit of Input and Components, Selected Periods, 1929–76

Percent per annum

Basis and period	Output per unit of input (1)	Gains from reallocation of resources from: Farming (2)	Nonfarm self-employment (3)	Effects of changes in legal and human environment: Pollution abatement (4)	Employee safety and health (5)	Dishonesty and crime (6)	Effect of weather on farm output (7)	Changes in intensity of utilization of employed resources resulting from: Work stoppages (8)	Fluctuations in intensity of demand[a] (9)	Other determinants: Total (semi-residual) (10)	Economies of scale (11)	Advances in knowledge and miscellaneous (residual) (12)
Potential												
Long periods												
1929–76	1.58	0.28	0.08	−0.03	−0.01	−0.01	−0.01	0.00	0.00	1.28	0.34	0.93
1929–48	1.21	0.34	0.03	0.00	0.00	0.00	−0.01	0.00	0.00	0.85	0.27	0.58
1948–73	2.16	0.26	0.12	−0.02	−0.01	−0.02	0.00	0.00	0.00	1.82	0.41	1.40
Shorter periods												
1929–41	0.88	0.34	0.10	0.00	0.00	0.00	−0.02	0.00	0.00	0.46	0.16	0.31
1941–48	1.77	0.34	−0.10	0.00	0.00	0.00	0.02	0.00	0.00	1.52	0.46	1.05
1948–53	2.24	0.36	0.09	0.00	0.00	0.00	0.00	0.00	0.00	1.79	0.46	1.32
1953–64	2.12	0.30	0.11	0.00	0.00	−0.02	−0.01	0.00	0.00	1.72	0.32	1.40
1964–69	2.22	0.23	0.17	−0.02	−0.01	−0.03	−0.01	−0.01	0.00	1.90	0.56	1.33
1969–73	2.09	0.10	0.10	−0.10	−0.04	−0.01	0.01	0.01	0.00	2.03	0.42	1.61
1973–76	−0.83	0.05	0.09	−0.23	−0.12	−0.09	−0.02	−0.01	0.00	−0.51	0.24	−0.75
Actual												
Long periods												
1929–76	1.47	0.27	0.06	−0.03	−0.01	−0.01	−0.01	0.00	−0.09	1.28	0.34	0.93
1929–48	1.19	0.32	0.02	0.00	0.00	0.00	−0.01	0.00	0.01	0.85	0.27	0.58
1948–73	1.96	0.26	0.11	−0.02	−0.01	−0.02	0.00	0.00	−0.18	1.82	0.41	1.40
Shorter periods												
1929–41	0.94	0.22	0.03	0.00	0.00	0.00	−0.02	0.00	0.25	0.46	0.16	0.31
1941–48	1.63	0.49	0.00	0.00	0.00	0.00	0.02	0.00	−0.41	1.52	0.46	1.05
1948–53	1.92	0.39	0.12	0.00	0.00	0.00	0.00	0.00	−0.37	1.79	0.46	1.32
1953–64	2.23	0.27	0.08	0.00	0.00	−0.02	−0.01	0.00	0.18	1.72	0.32	1.40
1964–69	1.78	0.25	0.21	−0.02	−0.01	−0.03	−0.01	−0.01	−0.50	1.90	0.56	1.33
1969–73	1.48	0.07	0.06	−0.10	−0.04	−0.01	0.01	0.01	−0.54	2.03	0.42	1.61
1973–76	−0.86	0.02	−0.03	−0.23	−0.12	−0.09	−0.02	−0.01	0.12	−0.51	0.24	−0.75

Source: Computed from tables 5-1 and 5-2.

a. Includes changes in intensity of utilization due to materials shortages and miscellaneous causes.

sure the effects of three such changes: (1) new requirements to protect the physical environment against pollution; (2) increased requirements to protect the safety and health of employed persons; and (3) a rise in dishonesty and crime. The common characteristic of these changes is that they have reduced the measured output that is produced by any given amount of input.

By 1975, the last year for which estimates were made, output per unit of input in the nonresidential business sector of the economy was 1.8 percent smaller than it would have been if business had operated under 1967 conditions. Of this amount, 1.0 percent is ascribable to pollution abatement and 0.4 percent each to employee safety and health programs and to the increase in dishonesty and crime. The reductions had been small in 1968–70 but rose

rapidly from 1970 to 1975. The increase in their size cut the annual change in output per unit of input from 1972 to 1973 by 0.2 percentage points, the change from 1973 to 1974 by 0.4 percentage points, and the change from 1974 to 1975 by 0.5 percentage points. They contributed importantly to the decline in national income per person employed in 1973–75.

Although the three indexes were prepared for this study, they were published separately in an article that described them and their derivation in detail.[2] Only a summary is therefore required here.

The three series (like many others I use) rest on

2. Edward F. Denison, "Effects of Selected Changes in the Institutional and Human Environment upon Output per Unit of Input," *Survey of Current Business*, vol. 58 (January 1978), pp. 21–44 (Brookings Reprint 335).

less adequate information than one would like and are by no means precise. Nevertheless, they are believed sufficient to add appreciably to an understanding of recent productivity experience. They are the same on a potential output basis as on an actual basis.

Programs to abate pollution and protect the safety and health of workers have benefits as well as costs. Consequently the merits of these programs cannot be judged from their adverse effect on productivity alone.[3] This effect is sufficiently large, however, to indicate the urgency of finding the most efficient means of attaining the objectives of the programs and of realistically evaluating the gains.

Costs Incurred to Protect the Physical Environment

Legislation relating to pollution passed before the mid-1960s expressed governmental concern about pollution but did not importantly affect business costs. Subsequent legislation did. At the federal level, this legislation included the Water Quality Act of 1965 and the Water Pollution Control Act Amendments of 1972, the Motor Vehicle Air Pollution Control Act of 1965, the Air Quality Act of 1967, the Clean Air Amendments of 1970, numerous amendments to these basic air and water pollution laws, and provisions affecting other types of pollution. State and local governments also introduced new laws and regulations and more vigorous enforcement of existing provisions. The effect of the new environmental controls was not immediate and their impact on business costs and productivity can be ignored through 1967. I attempt annual estimates beginning with 1968; they are meant to cover controls imposed by all levels of government.

Some of the expenditures made to protect the environment reduce measured output per unit of input. The reason is that the labor and capital whose services they purchase provide no measured output whereas they would have done so if not diverted to environmental protection.

Expenditures for environmental protection that are made by government or by consumers are not in this category because, like all other government and consumer purchases, they are themselves counted as expenditures for final products in the national income and product accounts (NIPA). Consequently they merely replace other final products that could have been produced by the inputs absorbed by environmental protection.

In contrast, costs of environmental protection that are incurred by business on current account, whether for purchases from other enterprises or for the direct hiring of labor, are not counted as purchases of final products in the NIPA. Because they absorb inputs that would otherwise be used to produce final products, they lower output per unit of input below what it would have been in the absence of the diversion of inputs to environmental protection. The dollar cost of the environmental expenditures, when expressed as a percentage of measured output plus these expenditures themselves, measures both the percentage of input diverted to unmeasured production and the percentage reduction in measured output per unit of input that they cause.[4]

Capital goods acquired by business for pollution abatement are counted as final products when they are purchased, so their production in place of other final products does not immediately reduce measured output per unit of input. What does reduce measured output per unit of input is the use of part of the stock of capital for pollution abatement, because the proportion of the stock of capital goods present at any date that business devotes to pollution abatement is not available to produce products that are counted as final. Given the total stock of capital, measured output is reduced by the value of the services that this capital would have provided if used to produce final products.

This value is measured as the sum of depreciation on pollution abatement capital and an imputed net return on this capital. It represents the opportunity cost of using capital for pollution abatement. Depreciation is calculated from esti-

3. In the article cited in the preceding footnote I noted that my purpose in developing the series "is to aid analysis of growth and productivity; it is not to judge the wisdom of government programs, which have benefits as well as costs. It must also be stressed that . . . many of the costs occasioned by pollution abatement, employee safety and health programs, and dishonesty and crime do not reduce output per unit of input and therefore are not included in cost estimates cited. In particular, costs imposed directly upon governmental units and consumers do not have this effect. A major part of the estimating process was the division of costs between those that change output per unit of input and those that do not" (p. 22).

4. The estimates rely on the presumption, common in economic analysis, that if a commodity represents a certain percentage of the value of the nation's output, then the percentage of the nation's total factor input that is used to produce that commodity is about the same. Consequently percentage distributions of output and input are similar. The percentage distribution of total factor input corresponds to the percentage distribution of output more closely if output is valued by national income (at factor cost) than if it is valued by net national product (at market prices), which includes indirect business taxes in addition to the earnings of labor and property.

mates of the stock of pollution abatement capital, using a formula (the straight-line method), service lives, and procedures as consistent as practical with those used in the NIPA. The imputed net return, which I call the net opportunity cost of using capital for pollution abatement, is calculated as the product of the net stock of pollution abatement capital and the ratio of nonlabor earnings (net of depreciation) in nonfarm corporations to the value of the net stock of capital and land in such corporations. Rather than the actual ratio, which is described in appendix G, I use a series from which the effects of business cycle swings have been removed in order to prevent the adverse effect of pollution abatement costs on output per unit of input from diminishing in recessions because of cyclical drops in the general ratio of earnings to capital stock. To do this, I substituted trend values for the actual ratios. Two periods from which least squares trends might reasonably be computed are 1947–69 and 1947–73. Use of either period implies that the 1974–75 figures were greatly reduced by recession. For the pollution abatement calculation, I have averaged the values from these two trend lines, securing a cyclically adjusted series that drops from 0.112 in 1967 to 0.111 in 1969 and to 0.106 in 1975.

This chapter is confined to nonresidential business, and thus environmental expenditures associated with dwellings, chiefly for trash collection and sewage disposal, are omitted from all the pollution cost estimates.

The classification of costs between government and consumers, on the one hand, and business, on the other, usually depends on who makes the expenditure in the first instance. But this is not necessarily so if there is a recognizable change in a final product as the result of the initial business expenditure. Pollution abatement devices installed in motor vehicles (autos and trucks) are the outstanding example. Such devices add to the unit values of motor vehicles but do not raise motor vehicle prices as measured by the Bureau of Labor Statistics and the Bureau of Economic Analysis (BEA). This is so because these agencies consider that the difference in unit value between vehicles with and without these devices represents a difference in real product rather than in price. The outcome is the same as if purchasers bought the pollution abatement devices separately from vehicles. Consequently the devices on vehicles bought by consumers and government must be classified in the category of pollution abatement and control purchases by these groups (and omitted from expenditures that reduce output per

unit of input), while devices on vehicles bought by business must be classified as capital outlay for pollution abatement equipment by business (and included in the stock of pollution abatement capital against which depreciation and net opportunity cost are charged).

Business incurred costs for the disposal of sewage and solid wastes and to limit air, water, and other forms of pollution before 1967 and would have continued to do so in the absence of new environmental controls. Consequently the total cost of pollution abatement must be distinguished from the incremental cost.

Total cost, as I shall use the term, refers to the concept that the BEA uses when it provides estimates of national expenditures for pollution abatement and control. It is, in brief, the difference between costs with techniques actually used and costs that would be incurred with the minimum cost method that business would choose if it were indifferent to pollution.[5]

By incremental cost, I mean the excess of total cost over a baseline cost that may be defined as either (1) the cost that would have been incurred in the absence of an increase in the stringency of environmental requirements since 1967, or (2) the cost that would have been incurred if the 1967 level of abatement costs had continued unchanged after allowance for growth and price-level changes. These two alternative definitions, it may be noted, are not precisely synonymous, but data are not sufficiently refined to permit any distinction between them to be drawn in practice. To obtain the effect of increased pollution controls on an index of output per unit of input, one must know incremental costs.

My series for the incremental cost of pollution abatement to nonresidential business is the sum of 10 component series less the value of materials and fuel reclaimed as a result of the incremental outlays for pollution abatement. Table 5-4 shows these components and total incremental cost, which rose from zero in 1967 to $9,549 million in 1975. The estimates for each year are expressed in current prices of that year. The series had to be pieced together from various sources. Some guessing was also required. The most important source of information is the Abatement and Control Expenditures Branch of the BEA's Environmental and Nonmarket Economics Division.

5. John E. Cremeans and Frank W. Segel, "National Expenditures for Pollution Abatement and Control, 1972," *Survey of Current Business*, vol. 55 (February 1975), pp. 8–11.

Table 5-4. Incremental Pollution Abatement Costs That Reduce National Income per Unit of Input in Nonresidential Business

Item	1967	1968	1969	1970	1971	1972	1973	1974	1975
	Costs (millions of dollars)								
Current costs									
1. Motor vehicle emission abatement[a]	0	86	180	257	396	558	867	1,409	1,831
2. Air and water pollution abatement except motor vehicle emissions	0	71	180	431	742	1,115	1,521	2,221	3,217
(a) Direct labor cost	0	24	61	147	252	379	517	686	933
(b) Equipment leasing, materials, supplies, services, and other	0	47	119	284	490	736	1,004	1,535	2,284
3. Payments to use public sewer systems	0	20	40	60	100	139	179	218	242
4. Solid waste disposal	0	26	56	87	127	167	225	289	362
Depreciation									
5. Motor vehicle emission abatement[a]	0	3	10	19	31	48	72	111	174
6. Air and water pollution abatement except motor vehicle emissions	0	17	50	116	198	295	426	660	976
7. Solid waste disposal	0	1	2	5	9	14	24	37	53
Net opportunity cost of invested capital									
8. Motor vehicle emission abatement[a]	0	3	10	17	28	42	60	89	136
9. Air and water pollution abatement except motor vehicle emissions	0	56	144	341	589	883	1,285	1,947	2,756
10. Solid waste disposal	0	1	3	7	13	23	33	51	68
Less									
11. Value of materials and energy reclaimed	0	8	17	27	48	74	93	136	266
12. Total incremental cost	0	276	658	1,313	2,185	3,210	4,599	6,896	9,549
	Percent of input diverted to pollution abatement								
13. Total incremental cost	0.000	0.046	0.103	0.201	0.312	0.412	0.525	0.741	0.967

Source: Denison, "Effects of Selected Changes in the Institutional and Human Environment upon Output per Unit of Input," tables 1 and 4, pp. 26 and 31.
a. Business vehicles only.

The percentage that incremental costs of pollution abatement represented each year of the value of output plus these costs was next computed. To refine the calculation slightly, incremental costs were first divided into two parts. Lines 2a, 8, 9, and 10 of table 5-4 are direct factor costs. They were divided by national income to obtain the percentage of output that they represent. The other costs in table 5-4 include indirect taxes in their values and were divided by net national product. The sum of the two percentages was 0.976 percent in 1975, so if environmental protection had been as it was in 1967, the resources used in production in 1975 would have provided a measured net product 0.976 percent larger than they actually provided—or what is equivalent, the output of these resources was 0.967 percent smaller than if environmental protection had been as it was in 1967. Similar percentages for the preceding years are shown in the last line of table 5-4. The percentages of inputs *not* diverted to pollution abatement activities that have no measured product (99.588 in 1972 and 99.033 in 1975) were converted to index form with 1972 = 100. This index, shown in table 5-1, column 3, measures the course that output per unit of input would have followed if nothing had changed except pollution

abatement.[6] The 1967 index is used in all earlier years.

Changes in pollution abatement costs did not affect the growth rate until the 1964–69 period. They subtracted 0.02 percentage points in 1964–69, 0.10 points in 1969–73, and 0.23 points in 1973–75.

6. I stressed in "Effects of Selected Changes in the Institutional and Human Environment upon Output per Unit of Input" that these percentages refer to the reduction in the output of the resources that were used in 1975 and, more generally, to output per unit of input in 1975. I stated (p. 25) that they were applicable to "total output in the sector only if the change in provision for environmental protection did not change the amount of total input." And in note 8 I said that "total input might change, for example, if provision for environmental protection raised total investment, and thereby the capital stock, by raising total capital needs of business, or if it lowered total investment by lowering profits." However, "such a qualification is not needed when the percentages are used, as I do use them, to measure effects on output per unit of input, because an induced change in total input would change total output rather than output per unit of input" (p. 25).

The Council on Environmental Quality was in error when it stated that "Denison assumes that if pollution abatement took 6 percent of total plant and equipment investment in a particular year, then 'productive' plant and equipment investments were approximately 6 percent lower during that year than they would have been had there been no pollution control investment." (CEQ, *Environmental Quality: The Ninth Annual Report of the Council on Environmental Quality* [Government Printing Office, 1978], p. 434.)

Thus they contributed to the decline in productivity growth over this time span and especially to the sharp dip in 1974 and 1975.

The 1973–75 period represented a peak, at least temporarily, in the amount by which pollution abatement costs were impairing productivity growth. The deduction fell back to 0.08 points in 1975–78. During these years the ratio of input diverted to pollution abatement to total input continued to rise, but less rapidly than before.[7]

Costs Incurred to Protect the Safety and Health of Workers

Major changes in legislation, regulations, and other provisions controlling the protection of the safety and health of workers have become effective since 1967. In the measurement of national income and product, expenditures made to conform with the new requirements are treated in the same way as expenditures to conform with requirements to protect the physical environment. As in the environmental case, to obtain the effect on output per unit of input it is necessary to estimate the proportion of input in nonresidential business that has been diverted from the production of measured national income and net national product. This requires knowledge of the incremental costs that business has incurred to conform to the new provisions. The costs that must be counted are, as before, current costs (labor and purchases from other enterprises), depreciation, and the net opportunity cost of invested capital. The proportion of output diverted to

7. Estimates were not available for years after 1975 when the tables were assembled. See note, table 5-1, concerning estimates used for 1976.

protect employee safety and health is estimated as the sum of three major components.

The first component consists of new safety features on motor vehicles. Price and output measures treat these features, like antipollution devices, as additions to real product. As a result, only safety features added to vehicles that are sold to business need to be considered here. Safety features on business vehicles may, of course, protect the general public as well as employees who drive and ride in them, but the effect on output per unit of input is the same. Only capital costs—depreciation and the net opportunity cost of invested capital—were counted. From the 1968 model year on, changes in automobiles have been made every year to meet actual and anticipated federal safety standards. The biggest cost for trucks resulted from an expensive requirement for improvements to air brake systems on trucks produced after March 1, 1975. The total incremental capital cost for automobiles and trucks, shown in table 5-5, reached nearly $900 million or 0.09 percent of nonresidential business output in 1975 and it was rising rapidly.

The second component consists of the incremental costs of protecting employee safety and health in the mining of coal, metal, and nonmetallic minerals. Recent developments have involved federal and state governments and unions. The major federal laws were the Federal Metal and Nonmetallic Mine Safety Act of 1966 and the Federal Coal Mine Health and Safety Act of 1969. The tightening of state regulation often accompanied or preceded federal actions. In coal, the union itself inspects for safety, and union locals may shut down mines until violations are corrected.

Productivity in all three mining industries has

Table 5-5. Incremental Costs for Protection of Employee Safety and Health That Reduce National Income per Unit of Input in Nonresidential Business

Item	1967	1968	1969	1970	1971	1972	1973	1974	1975
	Costs (millions of dollars)								
1. Safety equipment on motor vehicles[a]	0	22	66	126	194	266	386	593	886
2. Mining (except oil and gas)[b]	0	0	95	215	522	803	975	1,468	2,224
3. Other industries[b]	0	0	0	0	54	232	419	693	972
4. Total incremental cost	0	22	161	341	770	1,301	1,780	2,754	4,082
	Percent of input diverted to protection								
5. Safety equipment on motor vehicles[a]	0.00	*	0.01	0.02	0.03	0.03	0.04	0.06	0.09
6. Mining (except oil and gas)[b]	0.00	0.00	0.02	0.04	0.08	0.11	0.12	0.17	0.24
7. Other industries[b]	0.00	0.00	0.00	0.00	0.01	0.03	0.05	0.07	0.09
8. Total incremental cost	0.00	*	0.03	0.06	0.12	0.17	0.21	0.30	0.42

Source: Denison, "Effects of Selected Changes in the Institutional and Human Environment upon Output per Unit of Input," tables 5, 7, 9, and 10, pp. 33, 35, 36, 38, except row 1, which is the product of row 5 and nonresidential business national income, and row 4, which is the sum of rows 1, 2, and 3.
* Less than 0.005 percent.
a. Depreciation and net opportunity cost of invested capital. Business vehicles only.
b. Current costs, depreciation, and net opportunity cost of invested capital. Excludes costs of safety equipment on motor vehicles.

declined in recent years after long periods of strong advance. The estimate of the incremental cost of safety and health protection is based on the amounts by which trends in output per hour worked have deteriorated and the opinion of informed persons that the change in trends resulted from stronger controls for the protection of safety and health. The percentage by which output per unit of labor input in nonresidential business was reduced by the strengthening of safety and health controls in mining was estimated. The same percentage was used for the reduction of output per unit of input, implying that the ratio of depreciation and the net opportunity cost of invested capital to labor cost in mining was not altered by the controls. The percentage for each year is shown in table 5-5, row 6. It reached 0.24 percent, equivalent to perhaps $2.2 billion, in 1975.[8]

The third component consists of the costs incurred by business in all industries except mining as a result of the Williams-Steiger Occupational Safety and Health Act of 1970, effective April 28, 1971. Through 1975, the last year estimated, only moderate costs seem to have been imposed on business by this legislation. This was partly because Occupational Safety and Health Administration regulation consisted mainly of the codification of existing standards in the field of safety, and safety (as distinguished from health) has been promoted by business for many years both on its own volition and under the prodding of state agencies and insurers. Health regulation is likely to be much more costly because it is new and will require greater changes in existing practices.

Only the capital components of incremental cost could be estimated directly for OSHA regulation. These were put at $522 million in 1975, including $285 million for depreciation and $235 million for the net opportunity cost of invested capital. To complete the estimates, current costs were assumed to bear the same ratio to annual capital costs (0.86 in 1975) as they did for air and water pollution abatement (excluding motor vehicle emission abatement). Row 7 of table 5-5 shows the ratio of the incremental cost of employee safety and health regulation in industries other than mining to the sum of nonresidential business net national product and this cost. It had reached 0.09 percent by 1975.

8. The dollar amounts, which do not affect the growth analysis, were estimated in order to complete table 5-5. The percentages were multiplied by nonresidential business national income, which was used in preference to net national product because the cost was mainly for direct labor.

Row 8 of table 5-5, which combines the three components, shows the percentage of input diverted to the protection of employee safety and health after 1967. By 1975 the percentage had reached 0.42 percent. From this series an index, shown in table 5-1, column 5, was calculated that measures the course that output per unit of input would have followed if nothing had changed except the costs of protecting the safety and health of workers. The procedure was the same as for the pollution abatement index.

The growth rates of this index in the standard periods are shown in table 5-3, column 5. The diversion of labor and capital to the protection of the safety and health of workers reduced the growth rate of measured output by about 0.1 percentage points in 1973–76 in comparison with all earlier periods.

Costs of Dishonesty and Crime

Criminal acts, including those committed against business, have increased in the United States. The increase in crime, and the apparent decline in the ability to rely on the honesty of other people, is an important change in the human environment within which business must operate.

Business is affected by an increase in dishonesty and crime among the public in general—and among customers, employees, and suppliers in particular—in two ways, both of which reduce measured output per unit of input. First, in an effort to limit its losses business may divert resources from the production of measured output to protection against criminal and dishonest acts. A highly visible example has been the appearance of guards in many drug and grocery stores. In comparison with the period before crime increased, input in these stores is raised but output is not. From the standpoint of the economy, labor that could otherwise be used to produce measured output is no longer available for that purpose. Second, business sustains increased costs as a result of criminal acts that nevertheless occur. The theft of merchandise is the main example. The production of merchandise that is stolen from inventories before it reaches a final buyer absorbs inputs that are measured, but the merchandise stolen is not counted as output. Costs resulting from various other types of crime, such as the cost of repairing property damaged by vandalism, also reduce output per unit of input.

Some costs of protection are so indirect that measurement seems nearly impossible, and it was not attempted. For example, extensive dishonesty among the public completely bars self-service at retail stores in some areas, and high crime rates may prevent placing businesses in cities or neighborhoods that would otherwise provide the most advantageous locations.

Data for crime costs are inadequate. They are increasingly so as one moves back in time. It is clear, however, that the increase in crime started much before 1967, the starting point for the estimates for pollution abatement and worker safety and health. To avoid a discontinuity, I have carried the series back to 1957.

The index measuring the effects of changes in dishonesty and crime on output per unit of input (table 5-1, column 1) is the product of separate indexes, which are shown in table 5-6, for the costs of protection and the cost of losses.

The costs of protection can be divided between the protection that firms provide for themselves, particularly the direct hiring of guards and detectives, and the purchase of protective services from firms specializing in this activity. The former costs were found not to have increased and could be disregarded. Estimates of the latter costs were based on receipts of specialized firms as reported periodically in the *Census of Business,* supplemented by

Table 5-6. Indexes of Effects of Changes in Costs of Dishonesty and Crime on Output per Unit of Input in Nonresidential Business
1972 = 100

| Year | Type of cost | | |
	Protection (1)	Losses (2)	Total (3)
1957	100.13	100.20	100.33
1958	100.11	100.16	100.27
1959	100.10	100.18	100.28
1960	100.10	100.12	100.22
1961	100.09	100.11	100.20
1962	100.09	100.11	100.20
1963	100.08	100.09	100.17
1964	100.08	100.07	100.15
1965	100.08	100.08	100.16
1966	100.07	100.07	100.14
1967	100.07	100.02	100.09
1968	100.05	99.99	100.04
1969	100.03	99.95	99.98
1970	100.01	99.90	99.91
1971	100.01	99.88	99.89
1972	100.00	100.00	100.00
1973	100.00	99.95	99.95
1974	99.95	99.88	99.83
1975	99.94	99.73	99.67

Source: Denison, "Effects of Selected Changes in the Institutional and Human Environment upon Output per Unit of Input," table 13, p. 40.

annual series for the compensation of their employees.

The main source of data on losses was the series prepared by the Bureau of Domestic Commerce (now the Industry and Trade Administration) of the Department of Commerce. This series was available for only 1971, 1973, 1974, and 1975, and recourse to an indirect method that utilized Federal Bureau of Investigation data was necessary for other years.

Although crime costs were generally rising, so that the index measuring the course that output per unit of input would have followed in their absence was falling, this pattern apparently was temporarily interrupted in 1972, and even in 1973 the index was still above 1971. The growth rate of the index in the 1973–76 period (which was negative) was almost 0.1 percentage points less than in 1948–73 or 1969–73, so costs of crime contributed to the decline in the growth of output in this period.

Combined Effects

Together, changes in the three aspects of the institutional and human environment for which measurement was attempted subtracted 0.44 percentage points from the growth rate in 1973–76. This compared with only 0.15 points in 1969–73, 0.06 points in 1964–69, and almost nothing in earlier periods. Thus they contributed importantly to the decline in output growth observed in the 1973–76 period.

To underscore a comment at the beginning of this section, the purpose of my estimates of the effect of selected changes in the institutional and human environment is to aid analysis of growth and productivity; it is not to judge the wisdom of the government programs examined, which have benefits (not included in the measure of output) as well as costs. The finding that the government regulations for which measurement was attempted contributed importantly to the decline in the growth of measured output does not provide direct evidence that these efforts are or are not worth their cost. It does, however, provide support to efforts to minimize the cost of achieving the objectives of these programs.

Weather in Farming, Labor Disputes, and the Calendar

Irregular fluctuations in output per unit of input may be due to one-time random events that defy systematic identification and measurement. But they result chiefly from recurrent and identifiable conditions. Four appear important enough to require discussion: (1) irregular fluctuations in farm output associated chiefly with the weather and other natural conditions, (2) work stoppages resulting from labor disputes, (3) variations in the number and composition of days in the year, and (4) variations in the intensity with which employed resources are used as a result of changes in the pressure of demand. The first three are discussed in this section, and the fourth, which is much the most important, in the following section.

Irregular Fluctuations in Farm Output

Variations in weather and such natural conditions as pest infestation introduce irregular fluctuations into farm output. Their effect on productivity in the nonresidential business sector as a whole was approximated by a simple device. Actual national income in the nonresidential business sector each year was compared with a hypothetical figure obtained by substituting for the actual farm output component of that total its five-year average, centered in that year.[9] The ratio of the actual to the hypothetical national income figure was then calculated each year. The index of these ratios is shown with 1972 = 100 in table 5-1, column 7. The average postwar value of the index was 99.98; thus a figure higher than this indicates better than average conditions.

Irregular fluctuations in farm output occasionally have an appreciable effect on year-to-year changes in output per unit of input. They cut its 1975–76 rise by 0.2 percent. But they were not important over longer periods. They were responsible for only 0.02 percentage points of the drop in the growth rate from 1948–73 to 1973–76.

Work Stoppages Due to Labor Disputes

Work stoppages resulting from labor disputes tend to reduce output per unit of input even though time not worked, whether in industries involved in disputes or in other industries, is excluded from labor input. Capital and land left idle are not eliminated from the input measure, and the productivity of workers remaining at work may be impaired. An index of the effect of work stoppages on output per unit of input in the sector is shown in table 5-1,

column 8. Because it is impossible to take account of the fact that every strike is different, the series is necessarily crude.[10] But it suffices to show that fluctuations in the incidence of work stoppages have not affected output per unit of input importantly.

Length and Composition of the Year

The third recurrent irregular factor concerns inconsistent data rather than real developments in the economy. The problem, in brief, is as follows:

A year may consist of fifty-two weeks and a Sunday, fifty-two weeks and two weekdays, or anything in between. Total factor input and all its components, however, are measured on a weekly average basis or the equivalent. No input series is affected by differences in the length of the year, so these can be ignored in considering changes in input series.[11] Output, in contrast, purports to measure total output during a calendar year. If it actually did so, output and therefore output per unit of input would be affected by differences in the calendar. In that case annual output could be "seasonally adjusted" for differences in the calendar if the relative importance in production of different days of the week were known, much as a "trading day" adjustment is used to seasonally adjust monthly retail sales. But in actuality the series by which output is measured does not correspond to true output; it is affected by the calendar but in a way that cannot be ascertained. The reason is that employee compensation, the largest component of national income, is not reported on an accrual basis but instead corresponds to wages paid each year. Workers are most often paid on a weekly basis. For employers paying every Friday, the most common weekly payday, employee compensation includes fifty-two payroll periods in most years but fifty-three when there is an extra Friday. The frequency with which payroll periods end on each of the days of the week is unknown, as is the fre-

9. Declines during the postwar period in the hypothetical series for normal farm output were considered unrealistic. When they occurred, the five-year average was replaced by a figure interpolated between the five-year averages for the preceding and following years. Such adjustments were few and small.

10. The estimates were made by the same method I used in *Accounting for Growth.* The Bureau of Labor Statistics slightly changed the method of publishing data on man-days idle because of labor disputes, effective in 1974, but close approximations to the old series were obtained. No adjustments (such as were introduced in 1952 and 1959) were made after 1969 for strikes having specially pronounced secondary effects. An adjustment for the 1970 General Motors strike was considered but rejected because employment data for supplying industries did not show pronounced dips.

11. The situation is quite different for holidays. The series for labor input (though not the capital and land series) take full account of changes in their frequency and the days of the week on which they fall.

quency of daily, weekly, biweekly, semimonthly, monthly, and other pay periods. Payments surely were appreciably bigger (because of the calendar) in 1948 and 1976, which had fifty-three Thursdays and Fridays, than in 1967 and 1975, which had only a fifty-third Sunday (an unlikely payday). The direction of the difference between other years can sometimes be inferred. But even a qualitative statement as to the direction of error is not always possible, and information is wholly inadequate for the construction of a continuous time series for calendar effects. None has been attempted. Inability to isolate calendar effects necessitates major qualification of comparisons of actual changes in productivity and even of changes over two- and perhaps some three-year periods.[12]

Table 5-7 lists years in this study ranked from those with only an extra Sunday, the calendar least favorable to high measured productivity, to those with both an extra Friday and other weekday, the most favorable calendar.[13] It may be noted that all terminal years of the standard periods contained at least an extra workday so that growth rates are not distorted by the most extreme calendar differences. The calendar was more favorable in 1976 than in 1973, so the low 1973–76 growth rate is artificially raised by calendar differences.

1973–76 Productivity Decline Not Caused by Fluctuations in Intensity of Demand

The business cycle strongly influences changes in productivity. As the strength of demand for business products fluctuates up or down, business responds by adjusting production. In most industries, including almost all those engaged in distribution or the provision of services, production adjusts automatically and simultaneously when sales vary; a lag may occur in industries filling orders from inventory. Although business also adjusts total input, the magnitude of the adjustment is less than for output and the timing of the adjustment is not and cannot be the same for input as for output. In consequence the intensity with which employed

Table 5-7. Composition of the Year, 1929, 1940–41, and 1947–78

Days in addition to 52 weeks[a]	Years
Sunday	1950, 1961, 1967, 1978
Saturday	1949, 1955, 1966, 1977
Saturday and Sunday	1972
Weekday	1929, 1941, 1947, 1951, 1953, 1957, 1958, 1959, 1962, 1963, 1969, 1970, 1973, 1974, 1975
Weekday and Sunday	1956
Friday	1954, 1965, 1971
Friday and Saturday	1960
Two weekdays	1940, 1952, 1964, 1968
Friday and weekday	1948, 1976

a. "Weekday" is used to denote Monday through Thursday.

resources are used not only fluctuates but does so in a complex and irregular fashion; the irregularity is greatly intensified by the phenomenon of labor hoarding—or more generally by the tendency of changes in employment to lag behind changes in output.

Such fluctuations in intensity of use greatly affect the movement of output per unit of input. In the typical business cycle output per unit of input is highest, relative to trend, during the phase of the cycle in which output is expanding rapidly—unless the level of output is still far below potential. Output per unit of input drops when expansion of total output slackens with the approach of the business cycle peak. It remains low until the trough of the next recession is passed, then turns up with total output.

Each cycle nevertheless has its own characteristics. Moreover, intensity of utilization is much higher at the peak or trough of some cycles than of others, so that merely comparing peaks (for example) of successive cycles does not satisfactorily eliminate the distortion caused by differences in intensity of utilization.

Table 5-1, column 9, provides my estimate of the effect on output per unit of input of fluctuations in the intensity of utilization of employed resources resulting from fluctuations in demand pressure. The value of the index averaged 102.33 from 1948 to 1973 and 101.86 from 1948 to 1976, so index values above these figures indicate years in which this condition was more favorable than the average in these periods and lower values indicate years in which it was less favorable. The index fluctuates within a wide range: more than 10 percent in the postwar period and 12 percent if the prewar years shown are included. The range would be even

12. In *Accounting for Growth*, pp. 311–13, I estimated that output per unit of input might be 0.7 percent higher when the calendar is most favorable than when it is least favorable if national income truly measured output in a year but that the actual difference is larger because of the pay period complication.

13. The ranking is an approximation. It is not certain, for example, that two weekdays other than Friday are more favorable than a Friday or a Friday and Saturday.

greater if extreme years such as 1933 and 1942 were counted.

Because fluctuations in demand affect productivity so much, a major effort was made to measure this effect satisfactorily when *Accounting for Growth* was written. The method is retained with some improvements in the present study. Special characteristics of the 1974–76 period introduced some new problems, however. I discuss the topic, fully describe procedures, and examine the results in appendix I. The reader is encouraged to examine that appendix.

Intensity of utilization of employed labor and capital was low throughout the 1970s. It was enough lower in 1973 than in 1948 to subtract nearly 0.2 percentage points from the 1948–73 growth rate, and it deducted nearly 0.1 points even from the 1929–76 growth rate (table 5-3). This determinant also helps to explain why output per unit of input fell so much in 1974 and 1975 and recovered in 1976. Indeed, it accounts for a large fraction of all the annual fluctuations in output per unit of input.

What fluctuation in intensity of utilization due to demand pressure does not do is account for the poor performance of productivity from 1973 to 1976. My series shows intensity of utilization actually to have been a bit higher in 1976, a year of expansion, than in 1973, a year in which business output stabilized and turned down, so it was a *positive* factor that contributed over 0.1 percentage points to the 1973–76 growth rate. This contrasted strongly with experience in the two preceding periods. Intensity of utilization was much lower in 1969 than in 1964, and much lower in 1973 than in 1969. This had *subtracted* 0.5 percentage points or more from both the 1964–69 and 1969–73 growth rates. The growth rate of output per unit of input would have been 0.6 or 0.7 percentage points higher in 1973–76 than in the 1964–69 and 1969–73 periods if changes in the intensity of utilization had been the only reason for a change in growth rates. Other determinants much more than offset this change.

I have discussed the series under consideration as if in the short run stronger demand was universally favorable to high output per unit of input. Within the range observed in this study, I believe it almost always was favorable, but "one can visualize a situation in which demand is so strong that shortages and bottlenecks develop, or workers become indifferent to performance, to such an extent that the favorable effects of fuller utilization are

overborne."[14] The possibility that shortages of materials may reduce utilization should be particularly noted because some observers believed that such shortages were limiting output in 1973. My methods do not distinguish between the effects of a shortage of materials and those of a shortage of customers.

The methodology actually is such that the series captures the effects of short-term fluctuations in intensity of utilization stemming from any cause except work stoppages. I have described it as referring to fluctuations in intensity of utilization resulting "from fluctuations in intensity of demand" because changes in demand pressure are by far the main influence.

The intensity of utilization resulting from fluctuations in the pressure of demand is constant under the conditions that define potential national income, and it is so shown in table 5-2. The index value of 103.31 means that when this determinant is at its potential value, output per unit of input is 3.31 percent higher than when it is at its level in 1972. The way by which the level of the series was established is described in appendix L.

The Semiresidual

Appendix table I-1, column 6, presents an "adjusted" productivity series from which were removed the effects on output of all determinants considered so far except fluctuations in the intensity of utilization related to the pressure of demand. That series, not surprisingly, changes much less than the original output series. Removal of the effect of fluctuations in the intensity of utilization due to the pressure of demand then yields the series, labeled the "semiresidual," that is shown in table 5-1, column 10. Most of the irregularity in year-to-year movements that was still present in the "adjusted" productivity series is eliminated by this step.[15]

The semiresidual reflects the influence on output of economies of scale, advances in knowledge, and all other determinants whose effects have not been measured. To separate the effects of economies of scale from those of advances in knowledge is extremely difficult, as is generally recognized, and the semiresidual is shown separately to permit examination of a series that is unaffected by the

14. *Why Growth Rates Differ*, p. 277.
15. See appendix I, especially p. 185. Calendar differences appear to contribute importantly to remaining irregularity.

attempt. After growing rather steadily from 1948 to 1973, at a rate averaging 1.8 percent a year, growth of the semiresidual turned negative, at −0.5 percent a year, in 1973–76.

Economies of Scale Reinforce Retardation

Growth of an economy automatically means growth in the average size of the local, regional, and national markets for end products that business serves. Growth of markets brings opportunities for greater specialization—both among and within industries, firms, and establishments—and opportunities for establishments and firms within the economy to become larger without impairing the competitive pressures on firms that stimulate efficiency. Longer production runs for individual products become possible, as do larger transactions in buying, selling, and shipping in almost all industries, including wholesale and retail trade. This is important, because the length of runs and the size of the transactions in which business deals are major determinants of unit costs. Larger regional and local markets permit greater geographic specialization and less transporting of products. The opportunities for greater specialization, bigger units, longer runs, and larger transactions provide clear reason to expect increasing returns in the production and distribution of many products, and examples of increasing returns are plentiful.

There are almost no necessary offsets from industries operating under decreasing returns to scale because increasing cost is almost never a necessary concomitant to the growth of demand for a product. Although individual establishments and firms can become too large for efficiency, their number can be multiplied without limit. There is no necessity to carry specialization beyond the point at which it is efficient.[16] When land is counted as an

input there is no reason to expect decreasing returns to scale for any product unless some very unusual situation is present.[17]

To me it seems clear from general knowledge and many studies that the business economy of the United States operates under increasing returns to scale, and that the size of the gains is large enough to contribute importantly to the growth of total output. One can go further and quantify this contribution only by arriving at some judgment as to the size of the gains from economies of scale realized as the economy grows. In previous studies I introduced such a judgment and estimated the size of the gains even though this procedure could yield only what Phyllis Deane described as "notional" estimates of the contributions of this growth source.[18] It seemed to me then, and still seems, useful to present estimates even though they are based only on one's best judgment, or guess, and the estimates are subject to a substantial margin of possible error.

I repeat that procedure here. I base the calculation on the assumption that an increase in any other determinant of output that would have sufficed to raise nonresidential business national income by 1.0 percent under conditions of constant returns to scale actually increased it by 1.125 percent: that is, that economies of scale amounted to 12.5 percent or one-eighth. This meant that cost reductions resulting from economies of scale associated with the growth of the national market were credited with being the source of one-ninth of the growth rate of sector output.[19]

---

facturing," in L. Auerbach, ed., *Appropriate Scale for Canadian Manufacturing* (Ottawa: Science Council of Canada, 1978), pp. 9–26; and D. J. Daly, *Canada's Comparative Advantage* (Ottawa: Supply and Services for Economic Council of Canada, forthcoming). A number of articles by other writers have also appeared.

17. An assumption that an economy operates under constant returns to scale when land is not counted as an input (as in some studies) implies increasing returns to scale when land is counted as an input (as in this study).

18. Phyllis Deane, book review of *Why Growth Rates Differ*, in *American Economic Review*, vol. 58 (September 1968), pp. 980–82.

19. This is approximately the same assumption I used in *Sources of Growth* and *Why Growth Rates Differ*. (See *Accounting for Growth*, p. 72.)

In *Accounting for Growth* I raised the estimate of the size of gains in the sector from 12.5 percent to 15 percent. In explaining this change I stressed that no new information warranting a change in my original judgment had been obtained. Rather, the change stemmed from a correlation analysis, based on a fit of pertinent series for the period covered that yielded a quantitative estimate of 15 percent. This was within the range that had previously seemed to me reasonable, and I made the change so as to have a systematic basis for the estimate. I commented (p. 75): "This is the

---

16. Amplification of the general statements in the paragraph above and references to some of the evidence will be found in *Why Growth Rates Differ*, chap. 17, especially pp. 226–27. Two important new studies bearing on economies of scale are Frederic M. Scherer and others, *The Economics of Multi-Plant Operation: An International Comparisons Study* (Harvard University Press, 1975); and C. F. Pratten, *Economies of Scale in Manufacturing Industry*, University of Cambridge Department of Applied Economics Occasional Paper 28 (Cambridge, England: Cambridge University Press, 1971). D. J. Daly of York University in Toronto has done a number of papers of interest. One unpublished paper, "The Empirical Applicability of the Alchian-Hirshleifer Modern Cost Theory" (York University, n.d.), emphasizes product-specific economies of scale. Reviews of the evidence and applications to Canada have been published in D. J. Daly, "Economies of Scale and Canadian Manu-

The estimates assume that the addition made to the contribution of other growth determinants by economies of scale was an unchanging 12.5 percent throughout the 1929–76 period. If technological and managerial knowledge did not change, the size of this percentage almost surely would diminish as the economy becomes bigger. But as markets and the scale of output grow, knowledge of technology and business organization develops about, and adapts to, the new situation that exists with enlarged markets, and opportunities for scale economies are constantly replenished.[20] This replenishment, to be sure, may not suffice to offset fully the tendency that would otherwise be present for gains to diminish as output rises. If such is the case, I underestimate the gains in the earlier part of the period relative to the latter part. In a previous study I made a token allowance for this possibility which is not retained in the present study. But unless the reduction is much bigger than I thought probable then, or do now, such an allowance would scarcely change the estimates.

It was necessary to develop an appropriate output series to which this fraction could be applied. Economies of scale, in the sense used here, are related to the size of markets that business is organized to serve, and ideally one would use an output series that corresponds to these markets. Clearly, one does not wish to use actual output, which fluctuates in response to the pressure of demand and for other reasons. But neither is a measure of potential output appropriate. After an extended period of underutilization, such as the 1930s, the later 1950s and early 1960s, or the mid-1970s, business does not anticipate and is not organized to serve markets as large as those that would prevail at the potential level. The series actually used, which is

best method of deriving an estimate that I can devise, and I shall use it to replace the assumption made in my previous studies. But no reader should suppose that I imagine it to be highly reliable."

As a result of revisions in the national income data, the method used in *Accounting for Growth,* when applied to the new series, yields correlation coefficients too low to warrant any reliance on the regressions. (Also, results are now so sensitive to choice of time period that the estimate of gains from economies of scale is much lower with the time period used in *Accounting for Growth* but close to the old estimate if calculations are based on 1948–76 instead.) Under these circumstances it has seemed best to revert to the original assumption that gains amount to 12.5 percent in nonresidential business. But I stress that I intend no more than to express my view of the general magnitude of such gains, and that I should find it impossible to demonstrate that 12.5 is a better or worse estimate than 15.

20. New evidence of this is provided by Pratten, *Economies of Scale in Manufacturing Industry,* pp. 303–05.

shown and described in appendix J, retains the pattern of periods of fast and slow growth in actual national income but the effect of irregular factors has been eliminated and some additional smoothing was introduced.

Gains from economies of scale associated with growth of the national market had contributed about 0.4 percentage points to the growth rate in 1948–73 (table 5-3). This was about one-ninth of the growth rate of sector national income—a result assured over long periods by the method of estimate—and about one-fifth of the growth rate of output per unit of input. The contribution was about the same in 1969–73 as in the full period, then was cut nearly in half in 1973–76. The drop resulted from, and augmented the lower contribution of, other determinants of output. Although its exact size is uncertain, the drop surely was pronounced.

Gains from economies of scale, as the term is used here, are the same on a potential basis as on an actual basis. So-called short-run economies of scale that are associated with fluctuations in output are measured in the indexes for the effects of fluctuations in intensity of utilization.

Advances in Knowledge and Miscellaneous Determinants

Series have now been provided for all output determinants that are independently measured. Column 12 of table 5-1 provides an index of the combined effects of all remaining determinants. This index moved persistently upward until 1973. The dominant force behind the upward movement was the incorporation of new knowledge into production, and I have labeled this residual series "advances in knowledge and miscellaneous" determinants (or at times, n.e.c.—not elsewhere classified).

The index turned sharply downward in 1974 and 1975. Although incorporation of new knowledge may possibly have been retarded, the main explanation for the sudden drop in this series surely must be sought elsewhere.

Advances in Knowledge

As knowledge relevant to production advances, the output that can be obtained from a given quantity of resources rises. The advance in knowledge is the biggest and most basic reason for the persistent long-term growth of output per unit of input.

The term "advances in knowledge" must be construed comprehensively. It includes what is usually defined as technological knowledge—knowledge concerning the physical properties of things and of how to make, combine, or use them in a physical sense. It also includes "managerial knowledge"—knowledge of business organization and of management techniques construed in the broadest sense. Advances in knowledge comprise knowledge originating in this country and abroad, and knowledge obtained in any way: by organized research, by individual research workers and inventors, and by simple observation and experience.

The term must, however, be limited in a study of the sources of growth of any output series to those advances in knowledge that allow the same amount of *measured* output to be obtained with less input. In the business sector, this limitation has to do mainly with "unmeasured quality change." The introduction of new and improved products for final sale from the business sector to consumers and government provides the buyer with a greater range of choice, or enables him to meet his needs better with the same use of resources, but it does not in general contribute to growth as measured; it results in "noneconomic" or "unmeasured" quality change. Hence advances in knowledge that permit business to supply final products different from those previously available are excluded.[21] One other significant exclusion is imposed by the way price indexes are compiled. The development of new forms of business organization in retail trade (self-service stores and supermarkets, for example) or in personal service establishments directly serving the public does not raise measured output or productivity in the United States. With these important exceptions, the definition is comprehensive.

I have found no way to measure changes in the state of knowledge directly. The effect of the adoption of advances in knowledge on output per unit of input in the sector can only be approximated indirectly. In *Accounting for Growth* I expressed the opinion that the net impact on the residual of miscellaneous determinants was small until 1969, particularly after 1948. With somewhat more reservation, I think the period can be extended to 1973. If this judgment is correct, then up to 1973 the residual index shown in table 5-1, column 12, approximates the effect on output per unit of input of the introduction of advances in knowledge. The word "approximates" must be stressed. The residual index picks up the effects not only of miscellaneous determinants that were not separately

estimated but also of errors in the series that enter into its calculation, insofar as these are not offsetting.

A correct series for the effects of changes in knowledge on output per unit of input has a unique characteristic. Barring calamities such as the fall of the Roman Empire, it can move in only one direction: up. Until 1973 the series actually rises between every pair of years shown except from 1947 to 1948, despite the fact that no statistical procedures introduced would assure it and despite irregular factors, such as the calendar, whose effects could not be estimated.[22]

Variations in the rate of increase in the series from year to year or between brief periods obviously cannot be taken as indications of changes in the rate at which knowledge is incorporated into production, let alone the rate at which knowledge advances. Over reasonably long time spans the index does provide an indication of the importance of advances in knowledge to growth, and I know of no method except the residual method by which any indication can be obtained.

The growth rate of the residual index, computed from 1948 to either 1969 or 1973, was 1.4 percent a year.[23] I interpret this to mean that advances in knowledge were sufficient to increase output per unit of input by 1.4 percent a year (or by a total of 42 percent over the quarter-century from 1948 to 1973). This was a high rate by historical standards. It compares with 1.1 percent a year in 1941–48 and only 0.3 percent a year over the depression period from 1929 to 1941.[24] It is not likely that it was matched in periods before 1929.

The rate of advance in the residual index was steady from 1948 to 1969. Differences among subperiods, shown in table 5-3, column 12, were trivial and certainly should not be construed as indicating changes in the advance of knowledge. From 1969

---

21. See also p. 124 and note 10 there.

22. The exception probably results from overestimation of real national income in 1947.

23. As noted in appendix I, p. 182, a plausible alternative to the series presented here would lower the growth rate of the semiresidual and hence of this index from 1948 to 1973 and in all subperiods of this time span by 0.1 percentage points and raise by the same amount the growth rate of the index for the effect of intensity of utilization due to fluctuations in intensity of demand.

24. The 1941–48 and 1948–69 rates are close to those obtained in *Accounting for Growth*, but the 1929–41 rate is reduced from 0.55 percent to 0.31 percent. The reduction stems from a lower growth rate of sector NI, and this in turn resulted chiefly from the introduction of a new method of deflating the services rendered directly to final consumers by financial institutions and by the change of the base year from 1958 to 1972.

to 1973 the growth rate of the index was higher, 1.6 percent. The apparent acceleration at about this time also appears if different years are used to divide periods. Nevertheless, it would be rash to draw any stronger conclusion than that the rate of advance probably did not decline. The period is too short, and the difficulties of estimation, particularly of the intensity of utilization, too great to warrant stressing a rise of 0.2 percentage points in the growth rate of the residual. But even a finding that up to 1973 the contribution of advances in knowledge probably did not decline is of interest in view of the much earlier inception of declines in the growth rates of both output per hour worked and total expenditures for research and development.

The growth rate of the residual index fell to −0.75 percent in 1973–76. This was the dominant development of the period. However, discussion of the residual in this period is deferred until chapter 9.

Composition of Miscellaneous Determinants

On previous occasions I have set out the composition of the miscellaneous determinants of output.[25] They may be grouped among the following six types:

1. Changes in the personal characteristics of workers that are not measured in labor input, such as effort exerted, experience on the present job, and training other than formal education.

2. Changes in the extent to which the allocation of individual workers among individual jobs departs from that which would maximize national income.[26]

3. Changes in the amount by which output obtained with the average production technique actually used falls below what it would be if the best techniques were used, because of changes in obstacles imposed (usually by government or labor union regulation) against efficient utilization of resources in the use to which they are put.

4. Changes in the cost of business services to government, such as collecting taxes or filing statistical reports, and changes in the adequacy of government services to business, such as provision of law courts or roads for business use.

5. Changes in aspects of the legal and human environment within which business must operate *other* than those whose effects I have measured (pollution abatement, worker safety and health, and dishonesty and crime).

6. Changes in productive efficiency that take place independently of changes in any of the other determinants. Economists are sometimes reluctant to admit the existence of this determinant because it is inconvenient. I am convinced that efficiency, so defined, differs among countries and surmise that it may vary over time within a country. One plausible explanation is that efficiency actually achieved is affected by the strength of competitive pressures upon firms to minimize costs.

To illustrate the ways in which miscellaneous determinants may affect growth rates, I shall discuss two that have been affected by changes in legislation. Resale price maintenance was found in *Sources of Growth* to be a particularly important example of the introduction of laws that prevented efficient allocation and use of the means of production. These laws have recently been swept away, a development that should have raised productivity. Alcoholic beverages may impair the quality of work. The repeal of prohibition (Eighteenth Amendment) in 1933 could therefore have lowered productivity.

Resale Price Maintenance

State fair trade, or resale price maintenance, laws came in two forms. Laws with a nonsigner clause permitted one retailer to contract with a manufacturer or wholesaler to sell a branded product at a certain price, which then became the legal price for all retailers, enforceable through the courts. In a much weaker form of resale price maintenance only retailers signing such a contract were bound by it.[27]

Fair trade laws did not exist in 1929. By 1937 thirteen states had laws, but they were unimportant because under the Sherman Act of 1890 the states could apply them only to intrastate commerce. The Miller-Tydings Amendment in 1937 authorized

---

25. See *Accounting for Growth*, pp. 77–79, and Edward F. Denison, "Classification of Sources of Growth," *Review of Income and Wealth*, Series 18 (March 1972), pp. 1–25.

26. Miscellaneous determinants also include changes in the extent to which the allocation of total input of each type among industries or products (or among firms categorized by size, degree of risk, or other significant characteristics) departs from that which would maximize national income except for the allocation of labor to farming and nonfarm self-employment. The effects of reallocation from farming and nonfarm self-employment were separately measured; I believe them to be much the most important cases in this category.

27. American law never allowed what Europeans call "collective" resale price maintenance, under which groups of manufacturers act jointly to establish and enforce retail prices for all their products.

states to apply resale price maintenance to inter-state commerce. Fair trade had spread to twenty-eight states one year later and to forty-five states, all with a nonsigner clause, by 1941. The situation stabilized until the later 1950s, except that a few state laws were weakened or became inoperative as a result of court decisions.[28]

In *Sources of Growth* I had assumed that 10 percent of retail sales were subject to price maintenance in 1957; that gross margins on these sales were twice what they would be in its absence; and that this doubling of margins represented overuse of resources (from retention in business of an unnecessarily large number of retailers) rather than monopoly profits. With nearly 11 percent of national income originating in retail trade, these magnitudes implied that price mantenance laws had reduced national income by 1.0 percent in 1957 and (since there were no such laws in 1929) cut the annual growth rate over the twenty-eight years from 1929 to 1957 by 0.04 percentage points.[29]

At the end of the 1950s resale price maintenance began to lose strength. The nonsigner clause was gradually eliminated on a state-by-state basis, some laws were repealed, and enforcement by the courts became less certain. By 1974 the number of states retaining a nonsigner clause had fallen from forty-five to thirteen (though these included such populous states as California, Illinois, Ohio, and New York), twenty-three states had only laws of the weak form, and fourteen (plus the District of Columbia) had no laws at all. *Consumer Reports* reported that the percent of retail sales subject to fair trade laws had fallen from 10 percent in 1959 to 4 percent or less in 1974. During 1975 some fifteen states repealed their laws. The last twenty-one state laws were invalidated as of March 1976 by repeal of the Miller-Tydings Amendment in December 1975, and thus fair trade laws ended in the United States. The Council of Economic Advisers had estimated that fair trade laws cost consumers $1.5 billion in 1969, and in signing the repealer President Ford mentioned $2 billion a year, presumably as the 1975 amount.[30]

These estimates may not be comparable to my estimate of 1 percent of national income in 1957 ($3.6 billion at a lower price level) but there clearly *had* been a sharp diminution in costs from 1957 to these dates. Based on my 1957 estimate, elimination of fair trade laws contributed 0.05 percentage points to the 1957–76 growth rate, whereas it had subtracted 0.04 points in 1929–57.[31]

Fair trade legislation is interesting for three reasons. First, it illustrates that over reasonably long time periods the effect on the growth rate of even major changes in a particularly costly program affecting the allocation and use of resources is measured in hundredths of a percentage point. Second, RPM provides a rare and heartening instance of the recent elimination of legislation strongly adverse to efficiency. Third, RPM illustrates the difficulty frequently encountered in fitting estimates of the effects of legislation into an unduplicated classification of growth sources. RPM impaired efficiency by inducing the use of unneeded resources in retail trade. Insofar as this consisted of the labor of proprietors and unpaid family workers, RPM operated by retarding the reallocation of labor out of self-employment. I estimate the gains from this reallocation separately, and the two estimates arc not additive. Only insofar as RPM increased the amounts of *paid* labor and of capital in retailing did it clearly affect the index of the residual.[32]

Consumption of Alcoholic Beverages

The Eighteenth Amendment, which prohibited the sale of alcoholic beverages, was probably the greatest and most direct attempt by the federal government to raise productivity. Its repeal in 1933 fell within the period covered by this study. It is interesting to speculate about the effect.

Ralph E. Berry, Jr., of Harvard and James P. Boland of Policy Analysis, Inc., estimate the economic cost of lost production due to alcohol abuse in the civilian economy at $11.4 billion in 1971.[33]

28. There was a hiatus in enforcement of the nonsigner clause between the first decision of the Supreme Court regarding *Schwegmann* v. *Calvert Distillers Corp.* in 1951 and the McGuire Act of 1952, which reinstated the clause.

29. *Sources of Growth*, pp. 191–93.

30. Data in this paragraph are from *Business Week*, February 17, 1975, pp. 82–84, and December 29, 1975, p. 25; *U.S. News and World Report*, October 27, 1975, p. 82; *Consumer Reports*, vol. 39 (November 1974), pp. 781–84; S. C. Hollander, "United States of America," in Basil S. Yamey, ed., *Resale Price Maintenance* (Chicago: Aldine

Publishing Co., 1966); and Lewis A. Engman, "The Case for Repealing 'Fair Trade'," *Antitrust Law and Economics Review*, vol. 7 (April 1975), pp. 79–84.

31. Based on the council's 1969 estimate, the contribution was 0.03 points from 1969 to 1976. All these amounts refer to the whole economy and would be a little larger in nonresidential business alone.

32. See *Why Growth Rates Differ*, p. 271. In *Sources of Growth* I did not estimate gains from the reallocation of labor from self-employment, and considered the effect of resale price maintenance a separate growth source.

33. *The Economic Cost of Alcohol Abuse* (Free Press, 1977), pp. 51–54.

This was 1.36 percent of civilian national income. The estimate identifies lost output as equal to the wages lost by "abusers" as a result both of working fewer hours per year than otherwise similar workers and of having lower hourly earnings while working. Only the latter portion is an indication of lower output per unit of input, so the percentage reduction in productivity was somewhere between zero and 1.36 percent, according to this estimate.[34]

Irving Fisher of Yale, one of America's leading economists, estimated in 1927 that "a 10 percent increase in productivity is a safe minimum" estimate of the gain that would result from "effective prohibition."[35] Moreover, Fisher argued strongly that prohibition *was* effective in greatly reducing drinking and that this reduction contributed strongly to productivity growth in the 1920s. Fisher's estimate included the reduced productivity of moderate drinkers, whereas the Berry and Boland estimate is confined to "abusers." Citing (among others) studies purporting to show that two to four glasses of beer a day reduce the amount of typesetting by 8 percent, increase the time required for heavy mountain marches by 22 percent, and impair the accuracy of shooting under severe army tests by 30 percent, and that the equivalent of six to eight glasses lessens capacity for mental work by 25 to 40 percent, Fisher generalized that each daily glass of beer reduces productivity by 2 to 4 percent.

Fisher drew a vitriolic response from no less a figure than Clarence Darrow. Darrow and Victor S. Yarros expressed pity for Yale students subjected to Fisher's evidence and reasoning. They asserted that *"there is no proof whatever that a glass of beer reduces productivity even ⅛ of 1 percent.* The probability is that it tends to increase productivity slightly, as any other food would if consumed at the proper time and in the right quantity."[36] They also argued that Fisher radically overestimated the effectiveness of prohibition.

Economist Clark Warburton, pursuing the subject in his doctoral dissertation, also reached a conclusion different from that of Fisher: "It may reasonably be concluded that prohibition has not been a factor of measurable significance in the increased industrial productivity of recent years [that is, during the twenties]."[37]

If the Berry-Boland estimate is about right, changes in the cost of alcohol *abuse* could hardly have affected the growth rate much in any period even if prohibition was very effective. If Fisher was right, the low 1929–41 growth rate of productivity could be attributed in substantial part to repeal, and even the 1929–76 rate was reduced. For example, if alcohol use normally cuts productivity by 10 percent but this loss was halved by prohibition in 1929, then repeal cut the 1929–41 growth rate of the residual by 0.43 percentage points and the 1929–76 rate by 0.11 points. I cannot disprove this possibility but found more persuasive Warburton's argument that prohibition did not affect productivity much. If Warburton was correct, changes in alcohol consumption are not likely to have been a major source of productivity change in any period covered by this study.

Other Miscellaneous Determinants

In the past I have examined others among the miscellaneous determinants of output without discovering any that seemed likely to have had a large effect on long-term growth. The behavior of the residual suggests that in the very recent past these determinants must have had a major effect. Developments in this period are considered in chapter 9.

---

34. The authors describe the estimate as "conservative" but also as "the best approximation available at present."
35. *Prohibition at Its Worst*, 5th ed., revised (Macmillan, 1927), p. 158. Earlier in his book Fisher asserted that "10 to 20 percent" is too low.

36. *The Prohibition Mania* (Boni and Liveright, 1927), pp. 105–106 (emphasis in the original).
37. *The Economic Results of Prohibition* (Columbia University Press, 1932), p. 261.

CHAPTER SIX

Determinants of Output in the Smaller Sectors

Measures of production and employment in the three sectors other than nonresidential business were provided in chapter 2. This chapter examines two of these sectors—(1) general government, households, and institutions, and (2) the services of dwellings—in greater detail. National income originating in the third sector consists of the net inflow of property income from abroad; I shall not analyze that inflow further. As explained in chapter 2, there is no difference between potential and actual output or employment in these parts of the economy.

General Government, Households, and Institutions

In the sector that includes general government, households, institutions, and labor in the rest-of-the-world industry, the change in national income in constant prices is measured by labor input. Therefore, only determinants of labor input need to be considered. Annual indexes are provided in table 6-1. It would be desirable to classify changes in labor input among the same determinants as in nonresidential business, but this is feasible only in part.

Employment

The first column of table 6-1 shows the index of full-time and part-time employment. The employment increase in the sector was rapid, if somewhat irregular, until about 1969. It averaged 3.6 percent a year from 1948 to 1969 and even more, 4.1 per-

cent, from 1964 to 1969. During these periods governments and nonprofit organizations increased their employment much more rapidly than did business.

In the 1970s the situation was reversed. Sector employment grew only 0.5 percent a year in 1969–73 and 1.3 percent in 1973–76. The sector's share of total employment slipped from 24.9 percent in 1969 to 24.4 percent in 1976. The decline was four times this large on a potential basis.

Table 6-2, which provides full-time equivalent employment in major components of the sector, shows that the armed forces were much the most important element in the employment slowdown during the 1970s. Their manpower shrank by almost two-fifths from 1969 to 1976 in contrast to the previous sharp expansion during the buildup for the fighting in Vietnam. Also contributing to deceleration were bigger employment drops in private households and the rest-of-the-world industry than had occurred in the earlier periods and smaller increases in employment in federal civilian government, nonprofit membership organizations, private education, and (in comparison with 1964–69 only) public education.

Effects of Changes in Hours and Employment Composition

The course of total hours worked in the sector was further retarded after 1969 by an accelerated decline in average hours per employee (table 6-1, column 3). Average hours had declined 0.4 percent a year in 1948–69 and only 0.2 percent in 1964–69. The reduction was 0.6 percent a year in 1969–73 and 0.5 percent in 1973–76.

To understand the remaining labor input series in table 6-1, the reader needs a description of the way the Bureau of Economic Analysis measures the output of workers employed in the sector. The following paragraphs refer to data beginning with 1947. The BEA used a different method of measuring labor input in earlier years.[1]

In deflating direct government purchases of labor, the BEA attempts to apply the equivalent of specification pricing, which is used to deflate other commodities and services in the national accounts.

1. The new method actually began with the 1946–47 change for some components, the 1947–48 change for others, and the 1948–49 change for still others. I treat it as if it were introduced uniformly with the 1947–48 change.

In the small rest-of-the-world component, which is omitted from the description in the text, the BEA deflates current-dollar net compensation of employees by the deflator for a group of miscellaneous services in the balance of payments. Average hours of work are assumed not to change.

Table 6-1. General Government (Excluding Work Relief), Households, and Institutions: Indexes of Sector Labor Input and Components, 1929, 1940–41, and 1947–76[a]

1972 = 100

| | | Effect of changes in hours on a year's work | | | | | |
Year	Employment (1)	Total (2)	Average hours (3)	Implied efficiency offset (4)	Inclusion of military reserves on active duty (5)	Other labor characteristics (6)	Total labor input (7)
1929	30.8	110.3	137.5	80.6	99.6	70.6	24.0
1940	36.4	111.3	122.1	91.4	99.8	75.4	30.5
1941	43.0	109.8	120.1	92.1	99.3	80.1	37.8
1947	45.6	108.6	112.5	96.9	99.6	86.0	42.6
1948	46.9	108.2	110.7	97.6	100.2	84.9	43.1
1949	48.8	108.8	110.2	98.3	100.5	86.3	45.9
1950	51.3	108.6	110.3	97.9	100.5	85.8	47.8
1951	60.0	109.7	111.8	98.2	100.0	85.3	56.2
1952	63.2	110.1	112.3	98.0	99.9	86.2	59.9
1953	63.5	109.5	112.1	97.7	100.0	86.5	60.1
1954	62.6	108.5	110.8	97.8	100.1	87.5	59.4
1955	64.2	107.1	109.5	97.6	100.3	88.5	60.9
1956	66.0	106.1	108.2	97.6	100.4	89.6	62.7
1957	67.3	106.1	107.7	97.8	100.7	90.4	64.5
1958	68.8	104.8	106.6	97.9	100.5	91.5	66.0
1959	70.0	104.2	105.9	97.9	100.5	92.1	67.2
1960	71.9	104.4	106.1	97.8	100.5	92.7	69.6
1961	74.3	103.6	105.2	98.0	100.5	93.4	71.9
1962	77.4	103.1	104.7	98.1	100.3	93.5	74.6
1963	78.9	103.0	104.6	98.1	100.3	94.3	76.6
1964	81.3	102.6	103.9	98.4	100.4	94.9	79.2
1965	84.1	102.3	103.6	98.5	100.2	95.5	82.2
1966	91.0	101.1	102.2	98.8	100.2	95.4	87.8
1967	94.9	102.7	103.3	99.1	100.3	95.3	92.8
1968	97.8	102.2	102.7	99.6	100.0	96.0	96.0
1969	99.1	102.3	102.6	99.6	100.1	97.0	98.3
1970	98.9	101.1	101.3	99.8	100.2	98.3	98.3
1971	99.3	100.6	100.5	100.0	100.1	99.0	98.9
1972	100.0	100.0	100.0	100.0	100.0	100.0	100.0
1973	101.1	100.0	100.1	100.0	100.0	100.2	101.4
1974	102.2	99.6	99.3	100.3	100.0	101.3	103.0
1975	104.3	98.9	98.6	100.4	99.9	102.0	105.1
1976	105.2	99.2	98.5	100.8	99.9	102.1	106.5

Sources: Column 1, table 2-7, column 2; column 2, product of columns 3, 4, and 5; column 3, table C-1, column 2; column 4, see appendix K; column 5, see note 4 in this chapter; column 6, column 7 divided by product of columns 1 and 2, see appendix K for explanation; column 7, table 2-6, column 2.

a. A change in the method of measuring labor input and output affects the comparability of changes in data before 1947 with those in later years; columns 2, 4, 6, and 7 are affected. Columns 1, 3, 4, and 6 exclude military reserves on inactive duty in all years.

Just as a three-ton truck is considered to represent more product than a half-ton pickup if it costs more, so the services of a physician or a general are considered to represent more product (and therefore more labor) than the services of an employee in a group that earns less.

The detail in which this principle can be applied is limited, however. Also, the characteristics of workers taken into consideration differ from those I used to measure labor input in the business sector. The BEA first divided the base-year (1972) compensation of government employees among industry or activity components. Compensation in each component was then extrapolated by a series for weighted total hours worked, with employee hours

in various civil service or pay board grades, military ranks, and similar groupings assigned weights that are proportional to 1972 hourly earnings. (Modifications were introduced to eliminate the effects of grade escalation.)

The use of total hours as an extrapolator implies that changes in average hours affect output proportionally in government, with no efficiency offset corresponding to that for which allowance was made in the business sector (in the "intragroup changes" series).[2] To measure output in constant prices in

2. The BEA makes no explicit assumption about the effect of hours changes; here and in the following paragraph I am only describing the implications of its procedures for growth analysis.

Table 6-2. Full-Time Equivalent Employment in Major Components of the Government, Households, and Institutions Sector
Thousands

Employment category	Full-time equivalent employment					Average annual increase			
	1948	1964	1969	1975	1976	1948–69	1964–69	1969–75	1969–76
Federal civilian government	1,378	1,752	1,998	1,984	1,993	30	49	−2	−1
Federal military[a]	1,478	2,720	3,463	2,154	2,123	95	149	−218	−191
Public education	1,418	3,076	4,050	4,998	5,046	125	195	158	142
State and local government, nonschool	1,723	3,034	3,634	4,575	4,621	91	120	157	141
Rest of the world	7	−56	−10	−13	−17	−1	9	−1	−1
Private households	1,574	1,513	1,467	1,037	1,074	−5	−9	−72	−56
Nonprofit membership organizations	649	1,258	1,586	1,697[c]	n.a.	45	66	18	n.a.
Private medical and health services[b]	825	1,618	2,375	3,517	n.a.	74	151	190	n.a.
Private education[b]	429	759	963	1,026	n.a.	25	41	10	n.a.
Total[b]	9,481	15,674	19,526	20,975	n.a.	479	771	240	n.a.

Source: NIPA, table 6.8.
n.a. Not available because of a change in the Standard Industrial Classification.
a. Excludes military reserves on inactive duty.
b. Wage-salary employment of business firms in private medical and health services and private education is included. Total excludes nonprofit organizations in industries not listed.
c. Correction of published NIPA data.

households and institutions, on the other hand, the BEA extrapolated base-year compensation of employees in each industry component by full-time equivalent employment. This procedure implies that changes in average hours reduce output proportionally (there is no efficiency offset) if they result from a change in the mix of full-time and part-time workers but do not change output at all (the efficiency offset is complete) if they result from changes in the average hours of full-time workers.

This last characteristic of output measurement necessitates the introduction of column 4 in table 6-1. In its absence the 1948 index value of 110.7 for average hours in column 3 would indicate erroneously that labor input and output per person employed, as measured by the BEA, were 10.7 percent bigger in 1948 than they would have been if average hours had been at their 1972 level. Column 4, the index for the implied efficiency offset, removes this error. The 1948 product of columns 3 and 4, 108.0, shows that labor input and output were only 8.0 percent bigger than if average hours had been at the 1972 level. Since the offset is confined to households and institutions, the smaller part of the sector, most of the postwar change in hours in the sector is not offset.[3]

The BEA includes the compensation of military reserves on inactive duty, who are numerous but put in only about five and one-half hours a week, in the value of government output. I have excluded them from the series described so far. Column 5 of table 6-1 measures their effect on sector national in-

come (or labor input).[4] It is classified as an effect of the change in working hours because (provided reservists hold other jobs) fluctuations in the total time worked by military reservists imply changes in average hours worked by persons employed in the economy as a whole. Though it is likely that most reserves are primarily employed in the business sector, when the sectors are combined the classification is correct.

The total effect of changes in average hours, shown in table 6-1, column 2, is the product of the series for average hours, the efficiency offset, and the effect of including military reserve hours.

The composition of employment shifted persistently toward the higher-paid industries and segments and, within government segments, the higher pay categories. This raised labor input and national income per worker. The amount, which is measured by the index in table 6-1, column 6, was considerable. The growth rate of the index had been 0.6 percent in 1948–69 (though only 0.4 percent in 1964–69). It reached 0.8 percent in 1969–73 but returned to 0.6 percent in 1973–76.

The BEA's method of measuring output from 1929 to 1947 was different in two respects from the method used for later years. First, in government as well as in households and institutions constant-price national income was extrapolated by full-time

3. Appendix K provides additional explanation of columns 4 and 6 of table 6-1.

4. Column 5 is computed by dividing the index of sector national income (column 7) by the index of "sector national income minus compensation of military reserves on inactive duty," both with 1972 equal to 100 and valued in 1972 prices. To obtain the latter series I calculated the compensation of military reserves on inactive duty in 1972 prices by extrapolating 1972 compensation in current prices by the aggregate hours worked by such reserves.

Table 6-3. National Income by Sector and Output Determinants in the Smaller Sectors: Growth Rates and Contributions to Growth Rate of Sector and Total National Income, Selected Periods, 1929–76

Growth rates and contributions in percentage points

Sector and determinant	Longer periods			Shorter periods						
	1929–76	1929–48	1948–73	1929–41	1941–48	1948–53	1953–64	1964–69	1969–73	1973–76
	Growth rate of sector national income, or contribution of determinant to it									
Whole economy	2.98	2.49	3.65	2.07	3.21	4.64	3.12	4.45	2.91	0.58
General government, households, institutions	3.22	3.12	3.48	3.85	1.89	6.88	2.54	4.44	0.76	1.67
Employment	2.66	2.24	3.13	2.83	1.25	6.28	2.28	4.06	0.50	1.34
Effect of changes in hours	−0.23	−0.10	−0.31	−0.04	−0.21	0.23	−0.59	−0.06	−0.54	−0.29
Average hours	−0.71	−0.14	−0.40	−1.13	−1.16	0.25	−0.69	−0.25	−0.61	−0.52
Implied efficiency offset	0.48	1.01	0.10	1.12	0.83	0.02	0.06	0.25	0.10	0.26
Inclusion of military reserves	0.00	0.03	−0.01	−0.03	0.12	−0.04	0.04	−0.06	−0.03	−0.03
Other labor characteristics	0.79	0.98	0.66	1.06	0.85	0.37	0.85	0.44	0.80	0.62
Services of dwellings	4.43	2.11	6.17	0.56	4.81	9.05	6.24	5.07	3.85	4.85
Quantity of housing	4.26	1.50	6.37	0.22	3.74	9.80	6.43	4.92	3.82	4.39
Occupancy ratio	0.17	0.61	−0.20	0.34	1.07	−0.75	−0.19	0.15	0.03	0.46
International assets	2.72	−0.58	6.17	−3.76	5.10	3.30	10.16	−0.70	7.93	−4.11
Nonresidential business	2.86	2.39	3.56	1.75	3.48	3.93	3.06	4.47	3.33	0.10
	Weight for calculation of contributions									
Whole economy	1.0000	1.0000	1.0000	1.0000	1.0000	1.0000	1.0000	1.0000	1.0000	1.0000
General government, households, institutions	0.1729	0.1734	0.1805	0.1810	0.1940	0.1923	0.1990	0.1926	0.1868	0.1790
Services of dwellings	0.0410	0.0273	0.0367	0.0262	0.0248	0.0287	0.0381	0.0453	0.0467	0.0499
International assets	0.0071	0.0059	0.0059	0.0057	0.0039	0.0041	0.0058	0.0074	0.0068	0.0073
Nonresidential business	0.7790	0.7934	0.7769	0.7871	0.7773	0.7749	0.7571	0.7547	0.7597	0.7638
	Contributions to growth rate of whole economy									
Whole economy	2.98	2.49	3.65	2.07	3.21	4.64	3.12	4.45	2.91	0.58
General government, households, institutions	0.56	0.54	0.63	0.70	0.37	1.32	0.51	0.86	0.14	0.30
Employment	0.46	0.39	0.57	0.52	0.24	1.21	0.46	0.79	0.09	0.24
Effect of changes in hours	−0.04	−0.02	−0.06	−0.01	−0.04	0.04	−0.12	−0.01	−0.10	−0.05
Average hours	−0.12	−0.20	−0.08	−0.20	−0.23	0.05	−0.14	−0.05	−0.11	−0.09
Implied efficiency offset	0.08	0.18	0.02	0.20	0.16	0.00	0.01	0.05	0.02	0.05
Inclusion of military reserves	0.00	0.00	0.00	−0.01	0.03	−0.01	0.01	−0.01	−0.01	−0.01
Other labor characteristics	0.14	0.17	0.12	0.19	0.17	0.07	0.17	0.08	0.15	0.11
Services of dwellings	0.18	0.06	0.23	0.01	0.12	0.26	0.24	0.23	0.18	0.24
Quantity of housing	0.17	0.04	0.24	0.00	0.09	0.28	0.25	0.22	0.18	0.22
Occupancy ratio	0.01	0.02	−0.01	0.01	0.03	−0.02	−0.01	0.01	0.00	0.02
International assets	0.02	0.00	0.04	−0.02	0.02	0.01	0.06	−0.01	0.06	−0.03
Nonresidential business	2.22	1.89	2.76	1.38	2.70	3.05	2.31	3.37	2.53	0.07

Sources: Upper panel computed from tables 2-5, 6-1, and 6-4. Middle panel computed from table 2-5; percentage distributions of national income among the sectors were calculated for the first and last years of the period, these percentages were interpolated to obtain a synthetic interpolated percentage for the next-to-last year, and the distributions for the first and next-to-last year were averaged; see *Accounting for Growth* p. 22. Lower panel is the product of corresponding series in upper panel and the sector weight from the middle panel.

equivalent employment rather than total hours, implying a complete efficiency offset to changes in average full-time hours throughout the sector. Consequently before 1948 the change in the index of average hours is largely canceled by the change in the index for the efficiency offset. Second, the weighting of hours by pay grade within government sectors was not introduced, so the index in column 6 of table 6-1 reflects changes in the distribution of employment only among industries and segments.

Contributions to Growth Rates

The second row of table 6-3 shows the growth rate of national income originating in general government, households, and institutions in each of the standard periods. The next six rows show the contributions made to that rate by changes in the determinants of labor input. Because there is only labor input in this sector, the contributions are the same as the growth rates of the corresponding indexes in table 6-1 (except for slight upward adjustments to absorb the interaction term).

Government, households, and institutions persistently represented from just over 17 to almost 20 percent of national income in 1972 prices. This is shown in the center section of table 6-3 ("weight for calculation of contributions"). This section provides the ratio that must be multiplied by the growth rate of sector labor input (which equals sector output) to obtain the contribution of changes in labor input in the sector to the growth rate of national income in the whole economy. It must also be multiplied by each determinant's contribution to the growth rate of sector national income to obtain its contribution to the growth rate of national income in the whole economy. Although the sector's share of employment increased from period to period up to 1964–69, its share of real output and therefore its weight did not, because output per worker (as measured) increased much less rapidly in this sector than in nonresidential business. (See table 2-7, columns 9 and 10.) From 1964–69 to 1973–76 the weight of the sector fell appreciably as the employment shift was reversed.

Contributions to the growth rate of national income in the whole economy are shown in the bottom panel of table 6-3. Increases in labor input in the sector contributed more than 0.6 percentage points to the 1948–73 growth rate, which was equal to 17.3 percent of the growth rate. The contribution reached 1.3 percentage points in 1948–53 and 0.9 points in 1964–69, periods that included buildups of the armed forces and of civilian employment in defense agencies as a result of the Korean and Vietnamese conflicts. The contribution was as much as 0.5 points in the intervening 1953–64 period despite a reduction in the armed forces.

From 0.9 percentage points in 1964–69 the contribution fell to only a little over 0.1 percentage points in 1969–73 and 0.3 points in 1973–76. The inclusion in 1976 employment of 306,000 workers employed by state and local governments and nonprofit organizations under the Comprehensive Employment and Training Act was a factor in the small rise that did take place in the latter period. But many CETA workers either would have been hired without the CETA program or else replaced workers who would have been hired.

Changes in employment were responsible for the bulk of the labor contribution and of changes in it from period to period, as table 6-3 makes clear. The contributions of the other determinants, which affected output and labor input per worker, were not trivial but they tended to be offsetting. Changes in average hours before 1947 were large but largely canceled by the implied efficiency offset. After 1947, when the effects of most hours changes were not canceled, the decline in average hours was smaller. Total hours worked by military reserves fluctuated widely but had only a minor impact on national income. The contribution of "other labor characteristics" is positive in all periods and fairly important in most. It reflects the shift in the composition of labor within the sector toward categories in which compensation and value of output per hour worked are higher (more precisely, were higher in 1972) than in the categories from which the shifts occurred. The estimate is similar in principle and intent to the contribution of changes in education and age-sex composition to growth in the nonresidential business sector but it cannot be divided by these categories.

The contributions of this sector and its output determinants to growth rates of economy-wide potential national income differ slightly from their contributions to growth rates of actual national income, but only because the sector weights are slightly different. The two sets of estimates are too much alike to necessitate separate presentation or discussion of series on a potential basis.

Services of Dwellings

The services of dwellings sector uses almost as much fixed capital as nonresidential business and, by value, a large fraction of all land. But it uses no inventories or (as I define the sector) labor.

Output, Utilization, and Capital Input

National income in the housing sector depends not only on the supply of dwellings and the costs associated with their maintenance and operation but also on the division of the housing stock between units that are occupied and those that are vacant.[5]

Table 6-4, column 1, shows an index of real national income originating in the sector.[6] Column 2 shows what this index would have been if the ratio of the space rent of occupied nonfarm dwellings to the space rental value of all nonfarm dwellings had been the same as in the base year 1972, and therefore measures the effect of changes in the supply of housing. The occupancy ratio, it will be noted, is based on the rental values of units, not their numbers. Column 3 shows the effect of variations in the occupancy ratio on national income originating in the sector.

The index of the occupancy ratio displays long gradual swings that have little or no relationship to the business cycle. The index (1972 = 100) rose from 93.3 in 1929 to 105.8 in 1947, slipped to a

5. Units, such as seasonal dwellings, that are reserved for the use of their owners or tenants are treated as if occupied in the national accounts, and their rental value is included in personal consumption expenditures. I define them as "occupied" in the present discussion.

6. It will be recalled from chapter 2 that labor employed in apartments is not included in this sector.

Table 6-4. Services of Dwellings: Indexes of Sector Output and Its Determinants and Estimates of Private Residential Capital Stock, 1929, 1940–41, and 1947–76

| | Output and determinants, indexes (1972 = 100) | | | Private residential capital stock | | | |
| | | | | Billions of 1972 dollars | | Indexes (1972 = 100) | |
Year	Sector national income (1)	Sector national income at constant (1972) occupancy ratio (2)	Effect of changes in occupancy ratio (3)	Gross stock (4)	Net stock (5)	Gross stock (6)	Net stock (7)
1929	15.8	16.9	93.3	530.7	343.7	41.4	41.3
1940	15.5	16.3	95.6	567.9	330.4	44.3	39.7
1941	16.8	17.3	97.2	576.5	334.7	44.9	40.2
1947	21.7	20.5	105.8	600.3	334.2	46.8	40.2
1948	23.4	22.4	104.7	619.4	349.2	48.3	42.0
1949	26.3	25.4	103.4	639.4	364.9	49.9	43.9
1950	28.2	27.2	103.8	662.6	383.4	51.7	46.1
1951	30.6	30.2	101.4	687.5	403.5	53.6	48.5
1952	33.7	33.3	101.0	709.0	419.9	55.3	50.5
1953	36.1	35.8	100.8	730.1	435.7	56.9	52.4
1954	38.9	38.7	100.8	752.7	452.8	58.7	54.4
1955	41.1	40.9	100.5	778.7	473.0	60.7	56.9
1956	43.3	43.3	100.1	805.4	493.6	62.8	59.3
1957	46.4	46.5	99.7	829.4	511.1	64.7	61.5
1958	49.9	50.2	99.5	852.6	527.7	66.5	63.5
1959	53.2	53.5	99.4	879.2	547.4	68.5	65.8
1960	56.5	56.8	99.4	907.3	568.3	70.7	68.3
1961	59.7	60.1	99.4	933.4	586.9	72.8	70.6
1962	63.5	63.9	99.3	960.5	606.3	74.9	72.9
1963	66.7	67.3	99.2	990.8	628.5	77.2	75.6
1964	70.2	71.1	98.8	1,023.1	652.4	79.8	78.5
1965	74.6	75.8	98.4	1,055.4	676.0	82.3	81.3
1966	78.6	79.7	98.6	1,085.3	696.7	84.6	83.8
1967	83.2	83.9	99.1	1,112.3	714.2	86.7	85.9
1968	86.0	86.5	99.4	1,141.4	733.6	89.0	88.2
1969	89.9	90.3	99.5	1,173.5	755.4	91.5	90.8
1970	93.0	93.1	99.8	1,204.0	775.5	93.7	93.2
1971	95.8	95.8	100.0	1,238.6	799.1	96.6	96.1
1972	100.0	100.0	100.0	1,282.7	831.6	100.0	100.0
1973	104.6	105.0	99.6	1,329.5	866.2	103.6	104.2
1974	108.5	108.2	100.3	1,367.2	891.2	106.6	107.2
1975	114.4	113.9	100.5	1,394.6	905.4	108.7	108.9
1976	120.6	119.4	101.0	1,423.3	920.7	111.0	110.7

Sources: Column 1, table 2-6, column 3; column 2, column 1 divided by column 3; column 3, see appendix K; columns 4 and 5, average of beginning and end-of-year values from Bureau of Economic Analysis, *Fixed Nonresidential Business and Residential Capital in the United States, 1925–75* (National Technical Information Service, 1976) (total privately owned from p. 22, less private nonhousekeeping from p. 303) and, for recent years, BEA worksheets; columns 6 and 7, computed from columns 4 and 5.

low of 98.4 in 1965, and crept back to 101.0 in 1976. The growth rate of the index, which had been −0.2 percent in 1948–69, moved just above 0.0 percent in 1969–73 and to 0.5 percent in 1973–76, so a rise in the use of housing was a factor, albeit a minor one, that was favorable to growth in the 1970s. The bottom panel of table 6-3 shows that its contribution to the *economy-wide* growth rate of national income had been −0.01 percentage points in the 1948–73 period as a whole. It was zero in 1969–73 and reached 0.02 percentage points in 1973–76.

Table 6-3 and the first three columns of table 6-4 make it clear that growth of the housing supply itself has been by far the more important element in

the fast growth of the housing sector. The growth rate of its net output from 1948 to 1973, with effects of occupancy changes eliminated, was 6.4 percent, far above the 3.65 percent growth rate of all output in the economy. The increase in the housing supply contributed 0.24 percentage points to the growth rate of economy-wide national income in that period.

Compared with 6.4 percent in 1948–73, the growth rate was 3.8 percent in 1969–73 and 4.4 percent in 1973–76. The importance of the housing sector had increased so much owing to previous growth, however, that the drop from the 0.24 percentage point contribution made by an expanding housing supply to economy-wide national income growth in 1948–73 was, proportionally, much smaller. The contribution was 0.18 percentage points in 1969–73 and 0.22 points in 1973–76. Hence the housing supply was responsible for only a small amount of the deceleration in the growth of total national income.

Estimates of the Stock of Residential Structures

To analyze the growth of the BEA national income series it is essential to use data from the national income and product accounts (NIPA) for the services of dwellings to measure the contribution of residential capital, as I have done. Any other procedure would merely introduce into the analysis errors arising from inconsistent estimates.

As I have pointed out before, however, the very fast growth of the services of dwellings in the NIPA is puzzling because the value of the stock of dwellings, measured in constant prices, was much slower.[7] Capital stock estimates from the BEA's capital stock study are shown in table 6-4, columns 4–7.

The fast growth of national income originating in the services-of-dwellings industry results, statistically, from the fast growth of the rent component of the NIPA series for personal consumption expenditures (measured in constant prices). It is derived from the rent series by deducting purchases from other industries and depreciation, and adjusting to a factor-cost basis. Given consistent data, the ratio of space rent to the gross stock of capital and land should be constant for an individual dwell-

ing unit. The aggregate ratio, adjusted for changes in occupancy, may rise if the ratio should happen to be higher for new units than those already present, and the ratio of national income to capital stock may also be changed by the movement of maintenance and depreciation.[8] Thus some divergence between the indexes of services provided by housing as derived from the NIPA (table 6-4, column 2) and the gross stock of housing from the BEA capital stock study (table 6-4, column 6) is justifiable. But the divergence actually observed is much too big; I believe it can result only from inconsistent data.[9] The apparent inconsistency hampers any attempt to relate changes in housing services to changes in capital stock data and hence to investment in new housing.

The growth of the gross capital stock series not only was much lower than that for sector national income at a constant occupancy ratio—in 1948–73, 3.1 percent a year compared with 6.4 percent—but also fluctuated less and in a different pattern. This rate was 3.3 percent in 1948–53, 3.1 percent in 1953–64, 2.8 percent in 1964–69, 3.2 percent in 1969–73, and 2.3 percent in 1973–76. The two series do show the 1973–76 rate to have been below the 1948–73 rate by roughly the same proportion (26 percent versus 31 percent).

---

7. For an earlier discussion, see *Accounting for Growth*, pp. 179–80.

8. Incremental housing costs resulting from legislation for pollution abatement may also affect the ratio, but they appear to have been trivial.

9. My guess is that understatement of the rise in the price series for rents is the main cause of the long-run divergence. The deflator for residential construction may also be overstated.

CHAPTER SEVEN

Sources of Growth of Nonresidential Business Output

Estimates needed to analyze the sources of growth of national income have now been completed. In this chapter and chapter 8 they are brought together in the form of tables showing the sources of growth of four output measures in ten selected time periods.

Data presented in this chapter refer to output of the nonresidential business sector. They are of particular interest because the nonresidential business sector is more homogeneous than the whole economy. Its production is sold on the market, and market transactions establish the value of this output in current prices. Value in constant prices is obtained by dividing current values by price indexes, or by an equivalent procedure. Thus output is measured in a way that is generally uniform and statistically independent of input measures. Only rarely does an assumption that output and input move alike enter the process of estimation.[1] But it is not only in statistical measurement that the sector is more homogeneous than the economy as a whole. Nearly all production is carried on by business enterprises that are organized for profit; use various types of labor, capital, and land in their operations; and must seek to combine these factors in proportions that minimize their costs if they are to achieve their goal of profit maximization.

For many purposes, however, it is essential to deal with the economy as a whole. Chapter 8 provides estimates for the whole economy that are simi-

lar to those provided in this chapter for nonresidential business alone. In considering the estimates provided in the present chapter, the reader must bear in mind that only a partial picture of the economy is presented.

Meaning and Derivation of Estimates

Output at any date depends on many determinants, and it is changes in these determinants that cause output to change—that is, economic growth. An analysis of the sources of growth over any time span identifies the determinants that have changed and the contribution that changes in each have made to the change in output. The size of the contribution of a determinant depends on its importance and the amount by which it has changed. If it has not changed at all its contribution is zero.

Forty growth rates in nonresidential business are divided among sources of growth in this chapter. They refer to growth rates of total actual national income, total potential national income, total actual national income per person employed, and total potential national income per person potentially employed, each for ten time periods.

Method of Calculation

To secure the estimates of the sources of growth of total actual national income in the nonresidential business sector shown in table 7-1, the following procedure was used in each time period. The growth rate of sector national income was allocated between total factor input and output per unit of input in proportion to the growth rates of the two series. The contribution of output per unit of input was allocated among its components in proportion to the growth rates of the individual indexes. The contribution of total input was allocated among labor, inventories, nonresidential structures and equipment, and land in proportion to the products of the growth rates of the input indexes and their average weights during the period. The contribution of labor input was allocated among its components in proportion to the growth rates of the separate labor input indexes. Finally, discrepancies between totals and the sums of more detailed components that arise because of rounding were eliminated.

The estimate for each component is only slightly different from that which would be obtained without the allocation procedure: that is, by measuring the contribution of total input, total output per unit of input, and each component of output per unit of input as the growth rate of its index, and each component of input as the product of the growth rate

---

1. Valuation of financial services provided to individuals is the only significant example.

Table 7-1. Nonresidential Business: Sources of Growth of Actual Sector National Income, Selected Periods, 1929–76
Contributions to sector growth rates in percentage points

Item	Longer periods			Shorter periods						
	1929–76	1929–48	1948–73	1929–41	1941–48	1948–53	1953–64	1964–69	1969–73	1973–76
Sector national income	**2.86**	**2.39**	**3.56**	**1.75**	**3.48**	**3.93**	**3.06**	**4.47**	**3.33**	**0.10**
Total factor input	**1.38**	**1.19**	**1.58**	**0.81**	**1.83**	**1.99**	**0.81**	**2.67**	**1.84**	**0.97**
Labor	1.03	1.12	1.02	0.87	1.51	1.32	0.38	1.88	1.32	0.62
Employment	0.86	0.88	0.90	0.51	1.48	0.86	0.20	2.10	1.40	0.53
Hours	−0.26	−0.25	−0.23	−0.22	−0.30	−0.09	−0.24	−0.33	−0.31	−0.54
Average hours	−0.51	−0.61	−0.41	−0.65	−0.53	−0.37	−0.33	−0.57	−0.50	−0.65
Efficiency offset	0.15	0.27	0.06	0.37	0.08	0.14	−0.02	0.09	0.14	0.11
Intergroup shift offset	0.10	0.09	0.12	0.06	0.15	0.14	0.11	0.15	0.05	0.00
Age-sex composition	−0.10	0.01	−0.17	0.05	−0.05	0.09	−0.10	−0.38	−0.43	−0.25
Education	0.53	0.48	0.52	0.53	0.38	0.46	0.52	0.49	0.66	0.88
Capital	0.35	0.07	0.56	−0.06	0.32	0.67	0.43	0.79	0.52	0.35
Inventories	0.11	0.07	0.15	0.03	0.15	0.22	0.10	0.23	0.11	0.04
Nonresidential structures and equipment	0.24	0.00	0.41	−0.09	0.17	0.45	0.33	0.56	0.41	0.31
Land	0.00	0.00	0.00	0.00	0.00	0.00	0.00	0.00	0.00	0.00
Output per unit of input	**1.48**	**1.20**	**1.98**	**0.94**	**1.65**	**1.94**	**2.25**	**1.80**	**1.49**	**−0.87**
Advances in knowledge and n.e.c.	0.93	0.58	1.41	0.31	1.06	1.33	1.40	1.34	1.61	−0.75
Improved resource allocation	0.33	0.35	0.37	0.25	0.50	0.51	0.35	0.46	0.14	−0.01
Farm	0.27	0.33	0.26	0.22	0.50	0.39	0.27	0.25	0.08	0.02
Nonfarm self-employment	0.06	0.02	0.11	0.03	0.00	0.12	0.08	0.21	0.06	−0.03
Legal and human environment	−0.05	0.00	−0.04	0.00	0.00	0.00	−0.01	−0.06	−0.17	−0.44
Pollution abatement	−0.03	0.00	−0.02	0.00	0.00	0.00	0.00	−0.02	−0.11	−0.23
Worker safety and health	−0.01	0.00	−0.01	0.00	0.00	0.00	0.00	−0.01	−0.05	−0.12
Dishonesty and crime	−0.01	0.00	−0.01	0.00	0.00	0.00	−0.01	−0.03	−0.01	−0.09
Economies of scale	0.35	0.27	0.42	0.15	0.46	0.47	0.32	0.56	0.42	0.24
Irregular factors	−0.08	0.00	−0.18	0.23	−0.37	−0.37	0.19	−0.50	−0.51	0.09
Weather in farming	0.00	−0.01	0.00	−0.02	0.03	0.00	−0.01	0.00	0.01	−0.02
Labor disputes	0.00	0.00	0.00	0.00	0.00	0.00	0.01	0.00	0.01	−0.01
Intensity of demand	−0.08	0.01	−0.18	0.25	−0.40	−0.37	0.19	−0.50	−0.53	0.12

Sources: Derived from tables 2-9, 3-4, 4-7, 5-3, and G-2. Procedure described in text.
n.e.c. Not elsewhere classified.

of its index and its average weight (using the labor weight for all labor input components). For example, over the 1948–73 period the growth rates of total input and total output per unit of input were 1.57 and 1.96, amounts that compare with contributions of 1.58 and 1.98 when the growth rate of output, 3.56, is allocated between them.[2]

Sources of growth of total potential national in-

2. If the allocation procedure were not used, the contribution of any determinant might be said to measure what the growth rate of output would have been if that determinant had changed as it did but there had been no change in other determinants. With its use, it is preferable to define the contribution of each determinant as the amount by which the growth rate of output would have been reduced (or increased, if the contribution is negative) if that determinant had not changed but all other determinants had changed as they actually did. This description is more accurate not only because of the treatment of the statistical interaction term but also, and more importantly, because each of the indexes and the weights were obtained by taking all of the other conditions affecting output as they actually existed throughout a period, not as they would have been had they remained unchanged for that time span.

come in the sector shown in table 7-2 were obtained by a procedure paralleling that used for total actual national income, but using indexes referring to potential conditions.[3]

Derivation of the sources of growth of actual output per person employed (table 7-3) and of potential output per person potentially employed (table 7-4) was similar to that of the corresponding estimates for total output, but employment itself disappears from the tables and the growth rates of nonlabor inputs are computed per person employed (or potentially employed).

3. Because construction of certain indexes was partially independent of the derivation of the potential national income series itself, in most periods they imply growth rates of potential national income that are a little different from those actually obtained. The differences, which are shown in index form in table 4-6, column 13, and are discussed in appendix M, were of any consequence in only two of the ten periods, 1929–41 and 1941–48. They were eliminated in the sources of growth tables by adjusting the components to remove this discrepancy along with discrepancies arising from rounding and statistical interaction.

Table 7-2. Nonresidential Business: Sources of Growth of Potential Sector National Income, Selected Periods, 1929–76
Contributions to sector growth rates in percentage points

	Longer periods			*Shorter periods*						
Item	*1929–76*	*1929–48*	*1948–73*	*1929–41*	*1941–48*	*1948–53*	*1953–64*	*1964–69*	*1969–73*	*1973–76*
Sector national income	**3.11**	**2.43**	**3.84**	**2.09**	**3.01**	**4.05**	**3.19**	**4.57**	**4.47**	**1.43**
Total factor input	**1.53**	**1.22**	**1.66**	**1.19**	**1.19**	**1.77**	**1.09**	**2.29**	**2.37**	**2.30**
Labor	1.17	1.15	1.10	1.25	0.83	1.09	0.66	1.49	1.85	1.96
Employment	1.03	0.91	0.99	1.05	0.55	0.56	0.55	1.58	1.99	2.23
Hours	−0.25	−0.24	−0.22	−0.22	−0.29	−0.09	−0.22	−0.30	−0.23	−0.52
Average hours	−0.50	−0.61	−0.39	−0.66	−0.44	−0.32	−0.35	−0.49	−0.42	−0.71
Efficiency offset	0.14	0.27	0.05	0.35	0.06	0.11	0.00	0.06	0.12	0.14
Intergroup shift offset	0.11	0.10	0.12	0.09	0.09	0.12	0.13	0.13	0.07	0.05
Age-sex composition	−0.13	0.01	−0.19	−0.02	0.07	0.14	−0.16	−0.32	−0.53	−0.52
Education	0.52	0.47	0.52	0.44	0.50	0.48	0.49	0.53	0.62	0.77
Capital	0.36	0.07	0.56	−0.06	0.36	0.68	0.43	0.80	0.52	0.34
Inventories	0.12	0.07	0.15	0.03	0.17	0.23	0.10	0.23	0.11	0.04
Nonresidential structures and equipment	0.24	0.00	0.41	−0.09	0.19	0.45	0.33	0.57	0.41	0.30
Land	0.00	0.00	0.00	0.00	0.00	0.00	0.00	0.00	0.00	0.00
Output per unit of input	**1.58**	**1.21**	**2.18**	**0.90**	**1.82**	**2.28**	**2.10**	**2.28**	**2.10**	**−0.87**
Advances in knowledge and n.e.c.	0.94	0.58	1.43	0.31	1.08	1.35	1.40	1.38	1.62	−0.78
Improved resource allocation	0.36	0.37	0.39	0.46	0.25	0.45	0.41	0.40	0.20	0.15
Farm	0.28	0.34	0.27	0.35	0.35	0.36	0.30	0.23	0.10	0.06
Nonfarm self-employment	0.08	0.03	0.12	0.11	−0.10	0.09	0.11	0.17	0.10	0.09
Legal and human environment	−0.05	0.00	−0.05	0.00	0.00	0.00	−0.02	−0.06	−0.16	−0.45
Pollution abatement	−0.03	0.00	−0.02	0.00	0.00	0.00	0.00	−0.02	−0.11	−0.24
Worker safety and health	−0.01	0.00	−0.01	0.00	0.00	0.00	0.00	−0.01	−0.04	−0.12
Dishonesty and crime	−0.01	0.00	−0.02	0.00	0.00	0.00	−0.02	−0.03	−0.01	−0.09
Economies of scale	0.34	0.27	0.42	0.16	0.47	0.48	0.32	0.58	0.42	0.24
Irregular factors	−0.01	−0.01	−0.01	−0.03	0.02	0.00	−0.01	−0.02	0.02	−0.03
Weather in farming	−0.01	−0.01	−0.01	−0.02	0.02	0.00	−0.01	−0.01	0.01	−0.02
Labor disputes	0.00	0.00	0.00	−0.01	0.00	0.00	0.00	−0.01	0.01	−0.01

Sources: Derived from tables 2-9, 3-4, 4-7, 5-3, and G-2. Procedure described in text.
n.e.c. Not elsewhere classified.

For many growth sources, contributions to the growth rates of two or more of the four output measures are the same or would be the same were it not for small differences due to rounding, statistical interaction, and the necessity, just discussed, of "forcing" the components of potential output to agree with totals.

Classification of Growth Sources

The classification of growth sources followed here is based chiefly on my judgment as to what groupings are useful, but availability of information dictated decisions in some borderline cases. Lack of information limits severely the amount of detail that can be provided for some sources. The classification has the characteristic, of course, that the sum of the contributions of the sources equals the growth rate. The same change cannot be credited to two determinants. It also has the characteristic that the contribution of each determinant is measured against a no-change situation. If a determinant does not change, its contribution to growth is zero.[4]

The value of any set of estimates of the sources of growth depends on the user's understanding of the classification adopted. Earlier chapters described the determinants. In *Accounting for Growth* and my other writings I have discussed many points of classification more fully.

The reader should note particularly the following aspects of the classification:

1. Gains from economies of scale refer to the rise in output per unit of input that is made possible by changes in the size of the markets that business is organized to serve. I classify the contribution of economies of scale as a separate growth source in order to show their contribution separately and to keep their entire contribution in output per unit of

4. See Edward F. Denison, "Classification of Sources of Growth," *Review of Income and Wealth*, Series 18 (March 1972), pp. 1–25, for a discussion of these and other characteristics of the classification of growth sources.

Table 7-3. Nonresidential Business: Sources of Growth of Actual Sector National Income per Person Employed, Selected Periods, 1929–76

Contributions to sector growth rates in percentage points

Item	Longer periods			Shorter periods						
	1929–76	*1929–48*	*1948–73*	*1929–41*	*1941–48*	*1948–53*	*1953–64*	*1964–69*	*1969–73*	*1973–76*
Sector national income	**1.77**	**1.28**	**2.43**	**1.10**	**1.58**	**2.83**	**2.82**	**1.81**	**1.63**	**−0.54**
Total factor input	**0.30**	**0.08**	**0.46**	**0.16**	**−0.05**	**0.89**	**0.57**	**0.03**	**0.15**	**0.33**
Labor	0.16	0.23	0.11	0.36	0.03	0.45	0.18	−0.22	−0.07	0.09
Hours	−0.26	−0.26	−0.24	−0.22	−0.30	−0.09	−0.24	−0.33	−0.30	−0.54
Average hours	−0.51	−0.62	−0.41	−0.65	−0.53	−0.37	−0.33	−0.57	−0.49	−0.65
Efficiency offset	0.15	0.27	0.06	0.37	0.08	0.14	−0.02	0.09	0.14	0.11
Intergroup shift offset	0.10	0.09	0.11	0.06	0.15	0.14	0.11	0.15	0.05	0.00
Age-sex composition	−0.10	0.01	−0.17	0.05	−0.05	0.08	−0.10	−0.38	−0.43	−0.25
Education	0.52	0.48	0.52	0.53	0.38	0.46	0.52	0.49	0.66	0.88
Capital	0.18	−0.10	0.39	−0.17	0.01	0.48	0.40	0.35	0.28	0.27
Inventories	0.06	0.02	0.10	0.00	0.04	0.16	0.09	0.11	0.05	0.02
Nonresidential structures and equipment	0.12	−0.12	0.29	−0.17	−0.03	0.32	0.31	0.24	0.23	0.25
Land	−0.04	−0.05	−0.04	−0.03	−0.09	−0.04	−0.01	−0.10	−0.06	−0.03
Output per unit of input	**1.47**	**1.20**	**1.97**	**0.94**	**1.63**	**1.94**	**2.25**	**1.78**	**1.48**	**−0.87**
Advances in knowledge and n.e.c.	0.93	0.58	1.41	0.31	1.05	1.33	1.40	1.34	1.61	−0.75
Improved resource allocation	0.33	0.35	0.37	0.25	0.50	0.51	0.35	0.46	0.13	−0.01
Farm	0.27	0.33	0.26	0.22	0.50	0.39	0.27	0.25	0.07	0.02
Nonfarm self-employment	0.06	0.02	0.11	0.03	0.00	0.12	0.08	0.21	0.06	−0.03
Legal and human environment	−0.05	0.00	−0.04	0.00	0.00	0.00	−0.01	−0.06	−0.17	−0.44
Pollution abatement	−0.03	0.00	−0.02	0.00	0.00	0.00	0.00	−0.02	−0.11	−0.23
Worker safety and health	−0.01	0.00	−0.01	0.00	0.00	0.00	0.00	−0.01	−0.05	−0.12
Dishonesty and crime	−0.01	0.00	−0.01	0.00	0.00	0.00	−0.01	−0.03	−0.01	−0.09
Economies of scale	0.34	0.27	0.41	0.15	0.46	0.47	0.32	0.56	0.42	0.24
Irregular factors	−0.08	0.00	−0.18	0.23	−0.38	−0.37	0.19	−0.52	−0.51	0.09
Weather in farming	0.00	−0.01	0.00	−0.02	0.02	0.00	−0.01	−0.01	0.01	−0.02
Labor disputes	0.00	0.00	0.00	0.00	0.00	0.00	0.01	−0.01	0.01	−0.01
Intensity of demand	−0.08	0.01	−0.18	0.25	−0.40	−0.37	0.19	−0.50	−0.53	0.12

Sources: Derived from tables 2-9, 3-1, 3-4, 4-6, 4-7, 5-3, and G-2. Procedures described in text.
n.e.c. Not elsewhere classified.

input (since its wording clearly implies such a classification). I have measured the contributions of all other sources as if the economy were operating under constant returns to scale. It must be understood, however, that growing markets are a reflection of a rising national income.[5] Hence their size is governed by the contributions of all other determinants except irregular factors. An alternative classification would eliminate economies of scale as a growth

5. The size of markets is, of course, also affected by barriers to international trade. Such barriers are artificially imposed by countries or their trading partners and can be changed by their actions. Like other aspects of the efficient allocation and use of resources, misallocation resulting from barriers to international trade is regarded as constituting a different, separate output determinant, and the contribution to growth made by changes in the importance of misallocation as a separate growth source. In an analysis of growth in Europe I have shown estimates of the effect of changes in international trade barriers. International trade barriers are among many miscellaneous determinants for which my best estimate of contributions to growth in the United States is approximately zero.

source and allocate their contribution among the other determinants.[6]

2. The line between the contributions of capital and of advances in knowledge is drawn in such a way that the former measures growth that results from saving and investment (in this chapter, the portion invested in nonresidential business) and the latter measures comprehensively growth that results from advances in knowledge that permit goods and services to be produced with less input. The distinction is basic because completely different causes govern the behavior of the two determinants, and the actions that would be appropriate to influence them differ fundamentally. Improvements in the de-

6. In *Accounting for Growth* I obtained estimates corresponding to this alternative classification for the longer periods by allocating the contribution of economies of scale among the other determinants in proportion to their contributions to total actual national income in the sector. (See pp. 113–16 of that book and, for the whole economy, pp. 130–33 and 135–37.)

Table 7-4. Nonresidential Business: Sources of Growth of Potential Sector National Income per Person Potentially Employed, Selected Periods, 1929–76

Contributions to sector growth rates in percentage points

Item	Longer periods			Shorter periods						
	1929–76	1929–48	1948–73	1929–41	1941–48	1948–53	1953–64	1964–69	1969–73	1973–76
Sector national income	**1.81**	**1.26**	**2.60**	**0.61**	**2.38**	**3.34**	**2.49**	**2.59**	**2.01**	**−1.28**
Total factor input	**0.24**	**0.07**	**0.44**	**−0.21**	**0.54**	**1.06**	**0.40**	**0.30**	**−0.05**	**−0.41**
Labor	0.14	0.23	0.11	0.22	0.30	0.53	0.10	−0.10	−0.14	−0.29
Hours	−0.25	−0.24	−0.22	−0.21	−0.28	−0.09	−0.22	−0.31	−0.23	−0.53
Average hours	−0.50	−0.61	−0.39	−0.65	−0.44	−0.32	−0.35	−0.49	−0.42	−0.72
Efficiency offset	0.14	0.27	0.05	0.35	0.06	0.11	0.00	0.05	0.12	0.14
Intergroup shift offset	0.11	0.10	0.12	0.09	0.10	0.12	0.13	0.13	0.07	0.05
Age-sex composition	−0.13	0.00	−0.19	−0.02	0.08	0.14	−0.17	−0.32	−0.53	−0.53
Education	0.52	0.47	0.52	0.45	0.50	0.48	0.49	0.53	0.62	0.77
Capital	0.15	−0.11	0.38	−0.34	0.27	0.56	0.32	0.48	0.18	0.00
Inventories	0.05	0.01	0.10	−0.05	0.14	0.19	0.07	0.14	0.03	−0.05
Nonresidential structures and equipment	0.10	−0.12	0.28	−0.29	0.13	0.37	0.25	0.34	0.15	0.05
Land	−0.05	−0.05	−0.05	−0.09	−0.03	−0.03	−0.02	−0.08	−0.09	−0.12
Output per unit of input	**1.57**	**1.19**	**2.16**	**0.82**	**1.84**	**2.28**	**2.09**	**2.29**	**2.06**	**−0.87**
Advances in knowledge and n.e.c.	0.93	0.57	1.41	0.29	1.10	1.35	1.39	1.38	1.59	−0.78
Improved resource allocation	0.36	0.37	0.39	0.42	0.25	0.45	0.41	0.41	0.20	0.15
Farm	0.28	0.34	0.27	0.32	0.35	0.36	0.30	0.24	0.10	0.06
Nonfarm self-employment	0.08	0.03	0.12	0.10	−0.10	0.09	0.11	0.17	0.10	0.09
Legal and human environment	−0.05	0.00	−0.05	0.00	0.00	0.00	−0.02	−0.06	−0.16	−0.45
Pollution abatement	−0.03	0.00	−0.02	0.00	0.00	0.00	0.00	−0.02	−0.11	−0.24
Worker safety and health	−0.01	0.00	−0.01	0.00	0.00	0.00	0.00	−0.01	−0.04	−0.12
Dishonesty and crime	−0.01	0.00	−0.02	0.00	0.00	0.00	−0.02	−0.03	−0.01	−0.09
Economies of scale	0.34	0.26	0.42	0.14	0.47	0.48	0.32	0.58	0.41	0.24
Irregular factors	−0.01	−0.01	−0.01	−0.03	0.02	0.00	−0.01	−0.02	0.02	−0.03
Weather in farming	−0.01	−0.01	−0.01	−0.02	0.02	0.00	−0.01	−0.01	0.01	−0.02
Labor disputes	0.00	0.00	0.00	−0.01	0.00	0.00	0.00	−0.01	0.01	−0.01

Sources: Derived from tables 2-9, 3-2, 3-4, 4-6, 4-7, 5-3, and G-2. Procedures described in text.
n.e.c. Not elsewhere classified.

sign of capital goods that raise their net contribution to output are not regarded as representing a change in capital input (except insofar as they change the cost of producing a capital good). Consequently my series for capital input is, properly, so measured that capital does not capture the contribution of inventions and other advances in knowledge that are manifested in the form of improved capital goods design, and this is the principal point to be noted.[7]

7. There is a sense, however, in which the distinction between capital and advances in knowledge is somewhat compromised by another measurement procedure. As time passes, the same capital goods can be produced with a diminishing quantity of inputs because advances in knowledge lower their production costs. Given this situation, what should be considered the same amount of saving or investment at different dates? My estimates imply that identical bundles of unused capital goods (including inventories) acquired at two dates represent the same amount of capital (in constant prices) and hence by implication the same amount of investment, and correspondingly that the amounts of saving needed to provide funds to purchase identical bundles of capital goods represent the same amount of saving. By this definition, my estimates for the

3. The contribution of education is a measure of the contribution to output made by the increased skills and versatility of workers as a result of additional formal education when the state of knowledge in the society is given. Neither the fact that advances in knowledge permit new knowledge to be transmitted in educational institutions nor the possibility that a more educated population may advance the frontiers of knowledge more rapidly is reflected

contribution of capital correspond to the effects of saving and investment, as is desired. Alternatively it may be argued that the proper way to equate saving and investment made at two dates is by the quantity of consumption goods forgone to release resources for the production of investment goods. Adoption of this definition would reduce my estimates of the contribution of capital and raise my estimates of the contribution of advances in knowledge because the same amount of saving and investment defined as consumption forgone yields increasing quantities of capital goods as time passes.

In *Accounting for Growth* (pp. 133–35) I provided rough estimates of the amounts of the contributions of various types of capital to the growth rate of total national income that would have to be transferred to advances in knowledge to conform to this definition.

in the education estimate. Both are regarded as parts of the processes by which new knowledge originates, is disseminated, and enters into the process of production.

4. My intent is to measure the contribution of each input independently of changes in the efficiency with which it is allocated among uses. Gains or losses in output that result from changes in the degree to which the allocation of each resource approaches the optimum are classified in output per unit of input (preferably in the resource allocation category; otherwise in the n.e.c. portion of "advances in knowledge and n.e.c.").

Sources of Growth over Long Periods

In this section the sources of growth in long periods are briefly reviewed. Attention is focused on 1948–73, with some note taken of 1929–48.

Total Potential and Actual Sector National Income

The sources of the long-term growth of total output in nonresidential business are portrayed best by table 7-2, which refers to the *potential* national income of the sector. The results in the 1929–48 and 1948–73 periods are summarized below in the informal tabulation that condenses growth sources into eight groups:

growth rate having been lower by almost three-eighths in 1929–48 than in 1948–73.

"More work done" covers changes in the employment, hours, and age-sex composition components of labor input. These components are interrelated. When a sixteen-year-old takes an after-school job he raises employment, but not output, as much as if he were an experienced full-time worker. The overstatement is offset by reductions in the contributions made by changes in age-sex composition and hours per worker. "More work done" was responsible for 0.58 percentage points, or 15 percent, of sector growth in 1948–73. The detailed estimates show that changes in potential employment of the size experienced would have contributed 0.99 percentage points to the growth rate if there had been no change in working hours or in employment composition. The shortening of working hours offset 0.22 percentage points of this amount, and the shift away from males in the prime working ages in the age-sex composition of hours worked, 0.19 points.[8]

Rising educational attainment contributed 0.52 percentage points to the 1948–73 growth rate, 14 percent of the total. Over this period male workers with eight years of school or less fell from 44 percent to 16 percent of the male total; females in this education range fell from 32 percent to 11 percent

	Contribution to growth rate of potential national income in sector			
	Percentage points		Percent of growth rate	
	1929–48	*1948–73*	*1929–48*	*1948–73*
All sources	2.43	3.84	100.0	100.0
More work done, with account taken of age-sex composition	0.68	0.58	28.0	15.1
Increased education per worker	0.47	0.52	19.3	13.5
More capital	0.07	0.56	2.9	14.6
Advances in knowledge and n.e.c.	0.58	1.43	23.9	37.2
Improved resource allocation	0.37	0.39	15.2	10.2
Changes in legal and human environment	0.00	−0.05	0.0	−1.3
Economies of scale	0.27	0.42	11.1	10.9
Irregular factors	−0.01	−0.01	−0.4	−0.3

Six groups were of major importance in the periods shown. They are the increase in the amount of work done, the rise in the education of employed persons, the expansion of the stock of capital, the advance in knowledge of how to produce at low cost, improvement in the allocation of resources, and—the consequence of these changes—economies of scale made possible by the expansion of markets. Two, "advances in knowledge and n.e.c." and capital, were almost entirely responsible for the

8. I estimate that the adverse effect of hours reduction was slightly less in 1929–48 than in 1948–73, even though the yearly decline in average hours was much bigger in 1929–48, because the reasons for the change in average hours were quite different. Intergroup shifts affected average potential hours similarly in the two periods, but in 1929–48 the remainder of the decline stemmed chiefly from the reduction of full-time hours from a high level which, I estimate, was offset to a considerable extent by greater efficiency per hour. After 1948 rising part-time employment, to which there is no offset in greater efficiency per hour worked, increased in relative importance and the efficiency offset to shorter full-time hours diminished as hours were shortened.

of the female total. Males with at least one year of college increased from 12 percent to 28 percent, females from 11 percent to 21 percent.

The contribution of capital was 0.56 percentage points or 15 percent of the total in 1948–73. It is likely that the capital shortage at the start of the 1948–73 period, resulting from the near absence of capital stock growth during the two preceding decades, gave a special stimulus to capital formation in the early part of the period.

The combined contribution of more work done, education and capital—that is to say, of total factor input—came to 1.66 percentage points in 1948–73. It was nearly matched by the 1.43 percentage points, or 37 percent of the growth rate, contributed by advances in knowledge. This was by far the biggest growth source—provided, of course, that my judgment is correct that up to 1973 its importance is approximated by the residual.

The reduction in the proportion of the sector's

centage points, or 1 percent. The reduction of 0.01 percentage points ascribed to irregular factors reflected better weather for farming in 1948 than in 1973.

The 1948–73 growth rate of *actual* sector national income was 3.56 percent, as against 3.84 percent for potential sector national income. Of the difference, 0.08 points is due to a smaller increase from 1948 to 1973 in "work done" when it is measured on an actual basis and 0.18 points to a decline from 1948 to 1973 in intensity of utilization.

Potential and Actual Sector National Income per Person Employed

The sources of growth of potential national income per person potentially employed are shown in table 7-4. Results in 1929–48 and 1948–73 are condensed in the informal tabulation below. This distribution differs from that of total potential sector national income in several respects.

| | Contributions to growth rate of potential national income per person potentially employed in sector | | | |
| | *Percentage points* | | *Percent of growth rate* | |
	1929–48	*1948–73*	*1929–48*	*1948–73*
All sources	1.26	2.60	100.0	100.0
More work done per worker, with account taken of age-sex composition	−0.24	−0.41	−19.0	−15.8
Increased education per worker	0.47	0.52	37.3	20.0
More capital per worker	−0.11	0.38	−8.7	14.6
More land per worker	−0.05	−0.05	−4.0	−1.9
Advances in knowledge and n.e.c.	0.57	1.41	45.2	54.2
Improved resource allocation	0.37	0.39	29.4	15.0
Changes in legal and human environment	0.00	−0.05	0.0	−1.9
Economies of scale	0.26	0.42	20.6	16.2
Irregular factors	−0.01	−0.01	−0.8	−0.4

labor that was underutilized or inefficiently utilized in farming contributed 0.27 percentage points to its 1948–73 growth rate. A similar reduction in the proportion of the sector's labor that fell within the "fringe" category of nonfarm self-employed and unpaid family workers contributed 0.12 points. Addition of the two components yields 0.39 percentage points or 10 percent of the growth rate as the contribution of improved resource allocation.

Gains from economies of scale, which are especially difficult to isolate, are estimated to have contributed 0.42 percentage points to the 1948–73 sector growth rate, 11 percent of the total.

Changes in the costs imposed by environmental and worker safety and health programs, and crime, became important only at the end of the period and reduced the 1948–73 growth rate by only 0.05 per-

First, employment disappears from the classification, so the first group of sources covers only the effects of changes in average working hours and in the age-sex composition of hours worked. These are interrelated, chiefly because changes in the composition of employment by age and sex were mainly responsible for a rising proportion of part-time workers. This reduced average working hours without any efficiency offset. The two sources together subtracted 0.41 percentage points from the 1948–73 growth rate, equal to 16 percent of the rate itself.

Second, inputs of inventories and nonresidential structures and equipment are measured per person potentially employed. With potential employment rising, the contribution of capital to growth of potential national income per person employed in 1948–73 (0.38 percentage points) was necessarily smaller than its contribution to growth of total potential national income in the sector, but happened still to be 15 percent of the growth rate. In 1929–48 capital input per person employed had dropped, so the contribution of capital was negative.

Third, the amount of land available per person employed became less plentiful as employment increased. This is estimated to have subtracted 0.05 percentage points from the growth rate of national income per person employed (NIPPE) calculated on a potential basis, equal to 2 percent of that rate.

The remaining determinants contribute the same amounts in percentage points to growth rates of potential NIPPE and national income (aside from small discrepancies due to interaction terms and rounding) but these amounts are larger percentages of the growth rate per person employed since the rate itself is lower. The contribution of "advances in knowledge and n.e.c." alone amounted to 54 percent of the 1948–73 growth rate of potential national income per person potentially employed—or, perhaps a better way to express it, 45 percent of the total contribution of determinants that contributed positively to growth.

Data for actual NIPPE in this period, shown in table 7-3, are almost identical with those on a potential basis except that the actual growth rate itself is 0.17 percentage points lower because labor, capital, and land in use were used less intensively in 1973 than in 1948.

Sources of the Decline in National Income per Person Employed

I come now to the crucial question of this chapter: what determinants were responsible for the recent decline in the growth rate of national income per person employed?

The postwar growth rates on both potential and actual bases are summarized in the following tabulation, which also shows the amount by which the rate in each of the short postwar periods exceeded or fell short of the rate in the "long period" from 1948 to 1973:

| | NIPPE growth rate | | Excess over 1948–73 | |
	Potential basis	Actual basis	Potential basis	Actual basis
1948–73	2.60	2.43	...	...
1948–53	3.34	2.83	0.74	0.40
1953–64	2.49	2.82	−0.11	0.39
1964–69	2.59	1.81	−0.01	−0.62
1969–73	2.01	1.63	−0.59	−0.80
1973–76	−1.28	−0.54	−3.88	−2.97

Growth of output per hour is usually regarded as having been receding since about 1966. The years since that date fall in my last three "shorter" periods. For potential and actual output per person employed, differences between the growth rate in each of these periods and the 1948–73 rate are shown by source in table 7-5. It will be recalled that in 1948–73, the base period for this table, all determinants except one contributed approximately the same amounts to the potential and actual growth rates. The exception was the series for intensity of utilization of employed resources associated with fluctuations in the intensity of demand. This determinant was responsible for the difference between the actual growth rate of 2.43 percent and the potential rate of 2.60 percent.

The 1964–69 Period

There was no decline in the underlying growth trend in the 1964–69 period. The growth rate of *potential* national income per person potentially employed actually was higher in 1964–69 than in any other short period except 1948–53. It was practically the same as the rate for the longer period, 1948–73. Moreover, there is an absence of major differences between the sources of growth in 1948–73 and 1964–69. The biggest difference, only 0.16 percentage points, was in the contribution of economies of scale. It was bigger in 1964–69 because this was a period of exceptional growth in total national income, due mainly to sharp employment expansion. Capital contributed 0.10 points more. The late sixties witnessed an investment boom of such proportions that capital stock growth exceeded the growth of potential employment by an above-average amount despite the fast growth of potential employment. Offsetting these favorable developments were deductions from the growth rate that were larger in 1964–69 by 0.13 percentage points in the case of age-sex composition and 0.09 points in the case of working hours.

The growth rate of *actual* NIPPE was a substantial 0.62 percentage points lower in 1964–69 than in 1948–73, but this was entirely because 1964 and 1969 were in different phases of the business cycle. The year 1964, like most other years of large output expansion, was one of high intensity of utilization and substantial unemployment. The year 1969, like most other years in which output peaks, was one of low intensity of utilization and minimal unemployment. The larger drop in intensity of utilization, per year elapsed, from 1964 to 1969 than from 1948 to 1973 accounts for more than half of the

Table 7-5. Sources of Growth of Potential and Actual National Income per Person Employed in Nonresidential Business: Differences between Contributions to Growth Rates in Recent Short Periods and in 1948–73

Excess over contribution in 1948–73 in percentage points

| Source of growth | 1964–69 | | 1969–73 | | 1973–76 | |
	Potential (1)	Actual (2)	Potential (3)	Actual (4)	Potential (5)	Actual (6)
National income per person employed	−0.01	−0.62	−0.59	−0.80	−3.88	−2.97
Labor						
Hours	−0.09	−0.09	−0.01	−0.06	−0.31	−0.30
Age-sex composition	−0.13	−0.21	−0.34	−0.26	−0.34	−0.08
Education	0.01	−0.03	0.10	0.14	0.25	0.36
Capital						
Inventories	0.04	0.01	−0.07	−0.05	−0.15	−0.08
Nonresidential structures and equipment	0.06	−0.05	−0.13	−0.06	−0.23	−0.04
Land	−0.03	−0.06	−0.04	−0.02	−0.07	0.01
Advances in knowledge and n.e.c.[a]	−0.03	−0.07	0.18	0.20	−2.19	−2.16
Improved resource allocation						
Farm	−0.03	−0.01	−0.17	−0.19	−0.21	−0.24
Nonfarm self-employment	0.05	0.10	−0.02	−0.05	−0.03	−0.14
Legal and human environment						
Pollution abatement[a]	0.00	0.00	−0.09	−0.09	−0.22	−0.21
Worker safety and health[a]	0.00	0.00	−0.03	−0.04	−0.11	−0.11
Dishonesty and crime[a]	−0.01	−0.02	0.01	0.00	−0.07	−0.08
Economies of scale[a]	0.16	0.15	−0.01	0.01	−0.18	−0.17
Irregular factors						
Weather in farming[a]	0.00	−0.01	0.02	0.01	−0.01	−0.02
Labor disputes[a]	−0.01	−0.01	0.01	0.01	−0.01	−0.01
Intensity of demand	...	−0.32	...	−0.35	...	0.30

Source: Computed from tables 7-3 and 7-4.
n.e.c. Not elsewhere classified.
a. Differences between "potential" and "actual" columns are due only to interaction terms and rounding.

difference between the growth rates of NIPPE in the two periods. Other changes were not wholly offsetting, as they were on a potential basis, because the 1964–69 rise in the ratio of actual employment to potential employment was concentrated among demographic groups with low earnings and among the less educated. The rise in the ratio also meant that changes in capital and land per worker were less favorable than if employment had grown only at the potential rate.

The 1969–73 Period

The growth rates of both actual and potential NIPPE were decidedly lower in 1969–73 than earlier in the postwar period, but this was not particularly disturbing from the standpoint of the country's long-term growth. Part of the reduction on an actual basis was associated with a further drop in the intensity of use of employed labor and capital. Other developments were inevitable and some were even welcome. As the pool of surplus labor in farming dwindled, the gain from the shift of workers to

nonfarm jobs diminished. Changes in the age distribution of the population together with increases in the ratios of employment to population among the young age groups and women boosted the proportion of inexperienced workers among the employed. Costs of regulation that Congress presumably felt had benefits in excess of their costs began to impinge upon productivity.

On a *potential* basis the growth rate was 0.59 percentage points or 23 percent lower in 1969–73 than in 1948–73. The sources of this difference are shown in table 7-5, column 3. Note first that the estimated contributions of some determinants were bigger in 1969–73 than in 1948–73—that of education by 0.10 percentage points, that of "advances in knowledge and n.e.c." by 0.18 points, and that of three other determinants by a combined 0.04 points. Other determinants together contributed 0.91 percentage points less. The biggest single factor was the age-sex composition of hours worked, responsible for 0.34 percentage points of the reduction. Capital (inventories and fixed capital together) was responsible for 0.20 percentage points.[9] Gains from reallocation of resources were responsible for 0.19 points, costs of pollution abatement and worker safety and health programs for 0.12 points, and other causes together for 0.10 points.

The growth rate on an *actual* basis was 0.80 percentage points lower in 1969–73 than in 1948–73. The sources of this difference are detailed in table 7-5, column 4. The intensity of utilization of employed resources was lower and the unemployment rate was higher in 1973 than in 1969. Both changes were greater, per year elapsed, from 1969 to 1973 than from 1948 to 1973. The sharper drop in intensity of utilization was responsible for 0.35 percentage points of the drop in the growth rate. The sharper drop in the ratio of actual to potential employment indicated by the unemployment rate also had some unfavorable effects—hours of work and resource allocation contributed more to the decline in actual than in potential growth—but on balance was favorable to the growth in NIPPE. Changes in age-sex composition of hours worked and in capital and land input per worker deducted less from the growth rate on an actual than on a potential basis and the change in education added more. The general pattern of change, however, was much the same on an actual basis as on a potential basis except for intensity of demand.

The growth sources for which direct estimates were prepared fully account for the difference between 1948–73 and 1969–73 growth rates. In fact, they slightly more than account for the drop: the contribution of the residual was about 0.2 percentage points higher in 1969–73. Until after 1973 there was no mystery about the declining growth rate of productivity.

The 1973–76 Period

NIPPE was actually lower in nonresidential business in 1976 than in 1973. The drop was even greater on a potential basis. The reasons for the sudden switch from growth to retrogression are only partially understood.

The growth rate of *potential* national income per person potentially employed was an astounding 3.88 percentage points lower in 1973–76 than in 1948–73. Table 7-5, column 5, shows that education was the only determinant that contributed

more in 1973–76. All other determinants together contributed 4.13 percentage points less in 1948–73. Of this amount nearly one-half is ascribable to determinants for which direct estimates were made. Among them no one source was dominant.

The sharper reduction of potential hours, particularly hours of full-time nonfarm business wage and salary workers, in 1973–76 was responsible for 0.31 percentage points of the deficiency from the 1948–73 growth rate. The impact of hours reduction was greater than in any other period estimated (table 7-4).

Changes in age-sex composition were responsible for 0.34 points of the growth rate difference, the same as in the previous period.

The smaller rate of increase in capital per person potentially employed in 1973–76 than in 1948–73 was responsible for 0.38 percentage points (inventories 0.15, fixed capital 0.23) and the sharper decline in land per person for 0.07 points.

Another 0.24 points of the deficiency is ascribed to resource reallocation. The amount contributed by the shift from farming had declined from 0.27 percentage points in 1948–73 to 0.06 points in 1973–76 while the contribution of the shift from nonfarm self-employment had declined only from 0.12 points to 0.09 points.

Some 0.40 percentage points of the difference between the growth rates of the two periods is ascribable to changes in three aspects of the institutional and human environment. Of this amount pollution abatement legislation was responsible for 0.22 percentage points, worker safety and health programs for 0.11 points, and the increase in dishonesty and crime for 0.07 points.

My estimates show economies of scale to be responsible for 0.18 percentage points of the difference between periods. The estimate for this period is only a guess, but I do not doubt that economies of scale were a factor of appreciable significance. Irregular factors were responsible for 0.02 points.

More than one-half of the difference between growth rates in the two periods—2.19 percentage points—results from the contribution of the residual series for advances in knowledge and miscellaneous determinants. Reasons are explored in chapter 9.

The gap between growth rates in the two periods is smaller when the comparison is based on *actual* rather than potential data. This is no cause for gratification. The drop in the growth rate of NIPPE on an "actual" basis, almost 3 percentage points, was alarming. The thrust of my analysis is that the situ-

---

9. It will be recalled that this item refers to the effect that the *actual* change in capital would have had on NIPPE if employment had been at its *potential* level in 1969 and 1973. I discuss this point in connection with the 1973–76 period.

ation is even worse when comparisons are based on potential data.

One reason that the gap between 1973–76 and 1948–73 growth rates was smaller on an actual basis than on a potential basis was that intensity of utilization associated with the pressure of demand rose from 1973 to 1976 whereas it fell from 1948 to 1973. This offset 0.30 points of the deterioration due to other determinants (table 7-5, column 6).

The other reason is that changes in the contributions of age-sex composition, education, capital, and land were all less adverse on an actual than on a potential basis. The opposite was true of hours of work and gains from resource reallocation, but the amounts involved were smaller. These differences reflect the fact that the ratio of actual to potential employment fell more per year from 1973 to 1976 than from 1948 to 1973. The effects were similar to, but larger than, those pointed out in the discussion of the preceding short period.

The decline from 1948–73 to 1973–76 in the contribution of capital, it is to be noted, is larger on a potential basis than on an actual basis, 0.38 percentage points as against 0.12 points. For nonresidential structures and equipment alone it is 0.23 percentage points on a potential basis as against only 0.04 points on an actual basis.

The difference between actual and potential figures when these or similar periods are compared has a counterpart in statements from various sources about the ratio of capital to labor that at first glance seem to be contradictory. On the one hand, it is said that this ratio has ceased to increase as it used to and that this has been an important reason for the poor performance of output per man-hour. G. William Miller, former chairman of the Board of Governors of the Federal Reserve Board and now secretary of the treasury, is among those who have expressed this view.[10] On the other hand, it is said that the increase in the ratio did not slow down much so this could not be a major cause of the slowdown. Jerome Mark, assistant commissioner of the Bureau of Labor Statistics, for example, found no deceleration until after 1974.[11] The main reason for the contradictory conclusions is that the first group divides capital by potential employment or (as in the case of Chairman Miller) by the labor force including the unemployed, while the second group divides capital by actual employment.[12]

The *Economic Report of the President, 1979* appears to have it both ways. On page 117 it states that "in recent years . . . the ratio of capital to labor inputs has *not increased at all:* the *labor force* has expanded rapidly while growth in the capital stock has slowed. *This* decline in capital intensity has been one cause of the lower rate of productivity growth typical of this period." (Italics mine.) On page 126, however, "the U.S. capital labor-ratio grew at an average annual rate of nearly 3 percent between 1948 and 1973. Since then the growth of this ratio has declined more than 1 percentage point." This would apparently leave a growth rate of nearly 2 percent; the statement here is apparently based on actual hours worked.

The correct procedure depends, as always, on the purpose. Thus Peter Clark, formerly of the staff of the Council of Economic Advisers, correctly used potential employment to compute a cyclically adjusted capital per worker when he sought to estimate what output per worker would be if employment were at the potential level.[13] But to explore reasons for the observed slowdown in the growth of actual output per worker or hour one must use actual employment, as Jerome Mark has done, and as is done here in analyzing actual output per worker.[14] Fixed capital did not contribute much to the decline in the growth of actual output per worker.

If actual employment had suddenly jumped to its potential level in 1976, capital would have restrained output per worker, and it presumably did so during the sharp employment expansion of 1977–78. But it is not clear that any fundamental change in the capital-labor ratio was in progress. It is likely that, as in the past, if fast employment expansion had continued until employment and output reached their potential levels, it would soon have been followed by rapid expansion of the capital stock as well.

If this is so, and if one also takes into consider-

10. Statement by G. William Miller before the Senate Committee on Finance, 95 Cong. 2 sess., September 6, 1978.

11. Statement of Jerome A. Mark before the Joint Economic Committee, 95 Cong. 2 sess., June 8, 1978.

12. Other differences pertain to time periods, parts of the economy covered, choice between employment and man-hours as the denominator of the capital-labor ratio, and choice between gross and net stock in the numerator.

13. Peter K. Clark, "Capital Formation and the Recent Productivity Slowdown," *Journal of Finance*, vol. 23 (June 1978), pp. 965–75.

14. Use of potential employment could be defended only if the capital stock were spread out among work stations in the same way as if the economy were operating at the potential level. This would imply that capital had been installed for potential new workers who had not found jobs and that this capital stood idle. But this does not describe the situation in 1973–76 or thereafter.

ation that developments discussed in the characterization of slower productivity growth during 1969–73 as temporary, inevitable, or even welcome were also present in 1973–76, a considerable drop in the growth rate of NIPPE might have been accepted without great concern. But there can be no justifi-

cation for viewing a reversal of the actual size, much of it unexplained, with equanimity. Possible reasons for the part of the drop that has not been explained are considered in chapter 9. But first, the measured sources of growth in the economy as a whole will be examined.

➤➤✕◀◀

Sources of Growth and Potential Output in the Economy as a Whole

➤➤✕◀◀

Growth rates of national income, potential national income, national income per person employed, and potential national income per person potentially employed all dropped sharply after 1973 in the economy as a whole. This chapter examines the sources of these declines, as well as changes in growth rates during other recent periods, against the background of experience in longer and earlier periods. The gap between actual and potential national income is also explored.

Derivation of Sources of Growth

Estimates of the sources of growth in the whole economy are derived from those for the four sectors. Table 6-3 provided the contribution that each growth source in the three smaller sectors made to the growth rate of national income in the whole economy. Estimates for nonresidential business were obtained in the same way: the amount that each source contributed to the growth rate in that sector, shown in table 7-1, was multiplied by the weight of nonresidential business in the whole economy, shown in table 6-3. Nonresidential business is 75 to 79 percent of the economy, depending on the period. The total contribution of each growth source, which is shown in table 8-1, is the sum of the numbers for the separate sectors.

Most individual growth sources, in fact, contributed to growth in only one sector. The contribution of such a source to the growth rate of total national income equals the product of (1) its contribution to the growth rate of the sector in which the source appears and (2) the weight of that sector. The contributions of sources that appear only in nonresidential business are 75 to 79 percent as large as their contributions to the growth rate of nonresidential business national income. Labor input and some of its components appear both in nonresidential business and general government, households, and institutions. Capital input appears in three sectors, but its detailed components in only one each.

The main reason that estimates shown in table 8-1 differ from corresponding estimates I gave for periods up to 1969 in *Accounting for Growth* is not revisions but the change from 1958 prices to 1972 prices in the measurement of constant price output. This change raised the weight of general government, households, and institutions by more than two-fifths. Most of the offset was in nonresidential business. The change in base year also made necessary one departure, explained later, from the usual procedure of calculating contributions. It affects the meaning of the unallocated component of labor input, which now includes the effects of employment shifts between sectors.[1]

The estimates for potential national income are derived in the same way as those for actual national income, except that data on a potential basis are used.

The tables that refer to national income per person employed (NIPPE) detail the determinants that have produced changes in NIPPE in the economy as a whole. For example, if the national income provided by the stock of dwellings increases more than total employment, this raises NIPPE even though there is no employment in the dwellings sector. If the education of persons employed in business advances, this contributes to a rise in output in nonresidential business and hence in the whole economy, but the contribution to the growth of NIPPE in the whole economy is necessarily smaller than the contribution to the growth of NIPPE in nonresidential business because the extra output it made possible is divided among more people.

---

1. See note 4 in this chapter.

Table 8-1. Sources of Growth of Total Actual National Income, Selected Periods, 1929–76
Contributions to growth rates in percentage points

Item	Longer periods			Shorter periods						
	1929–76	1929–48	1948–73	1929–41	1941–48	1948–53	1953–64	1964–69	1969–73	1973–76
National income	**2.98**	**2.49**	**3.65**	**2.07**ᵃ	**3.21**ᵃ	**4.64**	**3.12**	**4.45**	**2.91**	**0.58**
Total factor input	**1.82**	**1.52**	**2.13**	**1.32**	**1.90**	**3.15**	**1.44**	**3.08**	**1.78**	**1.23**
Labor	1.36	1.42	1.42	1.39	1.54	2.34	0.80	2.28	1.14	0.77
Employment	1.09	1.01	1.22	0.78	1.42	1.60	0.55	2.36	1.12	0.66
Hours	−0.24	−0.22	−0.24	−0.18	−0.28	−0.02	−0.30	−0.26	−0.33	−0.46
Average hours	−0.51	−0.68	−0.40	−0.71	−0.65	−0.23	−0.39	−0.48	−0.49	−0.58
Efficiency offset	0.19	0.39	0.07	0.49	0.25	0.10	0.00	0.11	0.12	0.12
Intergroup shift offset	0.08	0.07	0.09	0.04	0.12	0.11	0.09	0.11	0.04	0.00
Age-sex composition	−0.08	0.01	−0.14	0.04	−0.04	0.06	−0.08	−0.29	−0.33	−0.19
Education	0.41	0.38	0.41	0.42	0.30	0.36	0.40	0.37	0.50	0.67
Unallocated	0.18	0.24	0.17	0.33	0.14	0.34	0.23	0.10	0.18	0.09
Capital	0.46	0.10	0.71	−0.07	0.36	0.81	0.64	0.80	0.64	0.46
Inventories	0.09	0.06	0.12	0.03	0.12	0.17	0.08	0.17	0.09	0.03
Nonresidential structures and equipment	0.18	0.00	0.32	−0.08	0.13	0.35	0.25	0.42	0.31	0.24
Dwellings	0.17	0.04	0.24	0.00	0.09	0.28	0.25	0.22	0.18	0.22
International assets	0.02	0.00	0.03	−0.02	0.02	0.01	0.06	−0.01	0.06	−0.03
Land	0.00	0.00	0.00	0.00	0.00	0.00	0.00	0.00	0.00	0.00
Output per unit of input	**1.16**	**0.97**	**1.52**	**0.75**	**1.31**	**1.49**	**1.68**	**1.37**	**1.13**	**−0.65**
Advances in knowledge and n.e.c.	0.73	0.46	1.10	0.24	0.83	1.04	1.07	1.02	1.22	−0.58
Improved resource allocation	0.26	0.28	0.29	0.20	0.39	0.40	0.26	0.35	0.11	−0.01
Farm	0.21	0.26	0.20	0.18	0.39	0.31	0.20	0.19	0.06	0.01
Nonfarm self-employment	0.05	0.02	0.09	0.02	0.00	0.09	0.06	0.16	0.05	−0.02
Legal and human environment	−0.04	0.00	−0.04	0.00	0.00	0.00	−0.01	−0.05	−0.13	−0.34
Pollution abatement	−0.02	0.00	−0.02	0.00	0.00	0.00	0.00	−0.02	−0.08	−0.18
Worker safety and health	−0.01	0.00	−0.01	0.00	0.00	0.00	0.00	0.00	−0.04	−0.09
Dishonesty and crime	−0.01	0.00	−0.01	0.00	0.00	0.00	−0.01	−0.03	−0.01	−0.07
Dwellings occupancy ratio	0.01	0.02	−0.01	0.01	0.03	−0.02	−0.01	0.01	0.00	0.02
Economies of scale	0.27	0.21	0.32	0.12	0.36	0.36	0.24	0.43	0.32	0.19
Irregular factors	−0.07	0.00	−0.14	0.18	−0.30	−0.29	0.13	−0.39	−0.39	0.07
Weather in farming	0.00	−0.01	0.00	−0.02	0.02	0.00	−0.01	0.00	0.01	−0.02
Labor disputes	0.00	0.00	0.00	0.00	0.00	0.00	0.00	0.00	0.01	0.00
Intensity of demand	−0.07	0.01	−0.14	0.20	−0.32	−0.29	0.14	−0.39	−0.41	0.09

Sources: Derived from tables 2-2, 2-9, 6-3, and 7-1.
n.e.c. Not elsewhere classified.
a. Based on data excluding work relief employees. When based on data including work relief employees, growth rates are 2.21 in 1929–41 and 2.97 in 1941–48.

Sources of Growth of Output over Long Periods

Estimates for the longer time spans are useful to indicate the main sources of long-term growth and their relative importance. For this purpose potential national income is more appropriate than actual. The growth rate of actual national income differs from that of potential national income in any time span only because the first and last years of a period happen not to be comparable with respect to demand pressures.

Total National Income

In the first three columns of table 8-2 the sources of growth of potential national income are pro-

vided for the whole period from 1929 to 1976 (when the growth rate was 3.2 percent), for 1929–48 (when the rate was 2.5 percent), and for 1948–73 (when the rate was 3.9 percent). In these periods increases in total labor, capital, and land input were responsible for about three-fifths of the growth and increases in output per unit of input for about two-fifths. More exactly, the input percentages were 60.7 in 1929–76, 61.5 in 1929–48, and 56.6 in 1948–73. Estimates for 1973–76, when the growth rate of only 1.6 percent a year was more than accounted for by the increase in inputs, appear in the last column of the table. This period, which will be examined later, is so different—either because it is very special or because it represents the first phase of a new era—that data covering both

Table 8-2. Sources of Growth of Total Potential National Income, Selected Periods, 1929–76
Contributions to growth rates in percentage points

Item	Longer periods			Shorter periods						
	1929–76	1929–48	1948–73	1929–41	1941–48	1948–53	1953–64	1964–69	1969–73	1973–76
National income	**3.18**	**2.52**	**3.87**	**2.34**	**2.84**	**4.74**	**3.21**	**4.53**	**3.79**	**1.60**
Total factor input	**1.93**	**1.55**	**2.19**	**1.67**	**1.34**	**3.00**	**1.63**	**2.80**	**2.18**	**2.20**
Labor	1.46	1.46	1.48	1.74	0.96	2.18	1.00	1.97	1.56	1.76
Employment	1.22	1.05	1.28	1.34	0.57	1.35	0.84	1.94	1.58	1.97
Hours	−0.24	−0.21	−0.23	−0.19	−0.24	−0.03	−0.28	−0.24	−0.28	−0.44
Average hours	−0.51	−0.68	−0.38	−0.75	−0.54	−0.20	−0.40	−0.02	−0.43	−0.63
Efficiency offset	0.19	0.39	0.06	0.48	0.23	0.08	0.02	0.08	0.10	0.15
Intergroup shift offset	0.08	0.08	0.09	0.08	0.07	0.09	0.10	0.10	0.05	0.04
Age-sex composition	−0.10	0.00	−0.15	−0.02	0.05	0.11	−0.13	−0.24	−0.41	−0.39
Education	0.41	0.38	0.41	0.37	0.36	0.37	0.37	0.40	0.48	0.58
Unallocated	0.17	0.24	0.17	0.24	0.22	0.38	0.20	0.11	0.19	0.04
Capital	0.47	0.09	0.71	−0.07	0.38	0.82	0.63	0.83	0.62	0.44
Inventories	0.09	0.06	0.12	0.02	0.13	0.18	0.07	0.18	0.08	0.03
Nonresidential structures and										
equipment	0.19	0.00	0.32	−0.07	0.14	0.35	0.25	0.43	0.31	0.23
Dwellings	0.17	0.04	0.23	0.00	0.09	0.28	0.25	0.22	0.18	0.21
International assets	0.02	−0.01	0.04	−0.02	0.02	0.01	0.06	0.00	0.05	−0.03
Land	0.00	0.00	0.00	0.00	0.00	0.00	0.00	0.00	0.00	0.00
Output per unit of input	**1.25**	**0.97**	**1.68**	**0.67**	**1.50**	**1.74**	**1.58**	**1.73**	**1.61**	**−0.60**
Advances in knowledge and n.e.c.	0.74	0.46	1.11	0.23	0.88	1.04	1.06	1.04	1.24	−0.56
Improved resource allocation	0.28	0.29	0.30	0.33	0.19	0.35	0.31	0.31	0.15	0.11
Farm	0.22	0.27	0.21	0.25	0.28	0.28	0.22	0.18	0.07	0.04
Nonfarm self-employment	0.06	0.02	0.09	0.08	−0.09	0.07	0.09	0.13	0.08	0.07
Legal and human environment	−0.04	0.00	−0.04	0.00	0.00	0.00	−0.01	−0.05	−0.12	−0.32
Pollution abatement	−0.02	0.00	−0.02	0.00	0.00	0.00	0.00	−0.02	−0.08	−0.17
Worker safety and health	−0.01	0.00	−0.01	0.00	0.00	0.00	0.00	0.00	−0.03	−0.09
Dishonesty and crime	−0.01	0.00	−0.01	0.00	0.00	0.00	−0.01	−0.03	−0.01	−0.06
Dwellings occupancy ratio	0.01	0.02	−0.01	0.01	0.03	−0.02	−0.01	0.01	0.00	0.02
Economies of scale	0.27	0.21	0.32	0.12	0.38	0.37	0.24	0.44	0.32	0.18
Irregular factors	−0.01	−0.01	0.00	−0.02	0.02	0.00	−0.01	−0.02	0.02	−0.03
Weather in farming	−0.01	−0.01	0.00	−0.02	0.02	0.00	−0.01	−0.01	0.01	−0.02
Labor disputes	0.00	0.00	0.00	0.00	0.00	0.00	0.00	−0.01	0.01	−0.01

Sources: Derived from tables 2-2, 2-8, 2-9, 6-3, and 7-2.
n.e.c. Not elsewhere classified.

1948–73 and 1973–76 are a mishmash. Examination of past long-term growth will henceforth be confined to 1929–48 and 1948–73.

Capital and advances in knowledge were responsible for the rise by one-half in the growth rate of potential output from 1929–48, a period that spanned the Great Depression and World War II, to 1948–73. The increase in the growth rate was 1.35 percentage points. Capital contributed 0.62 percentage points of this increase; all four components of capital shared in it. "Advances in knowledge and n.e.c." contributed 0.65 percentage points of the increase. This probably was due largely to a more rapid advance in new knowledge relevant to production, but depression-induced restrictions against efficient practices probably contributed to the difference. There probably was also some widening of the gap between actual and best practice in 1929–48, followed by a narrowing at the beginning of the 1948–73 period.[2] The contribution of economies of scale in 1948–73 was 0.11 percentage points bigger than in 1929–48, a consequence of the faster expansion of markets, but it was the changes in the contributions of capital and advances in knowledge that made this faster expansion possible.

2. It is also possible that the estimate for 1929–48 is understated. See *Accounting for Growth*, pp. 81–82.

	Contributions to growth rate of potential national income			
	Percentage points		Percent of growth rate	
	1929–48	1948–73	1929–48	1948–73
All sources	2.52	3.87	100.0	100.0
More work done, with account taken of characteristics of workers except education	1.08	1.07	42.9	27.6
Increased education per worker	0.38	0.41	15.1	10.6
More capital	0.09	0.71	3.6	18.3
Advances in knowledge and n.e.c.	0.46	1.11	18.3	28.7
Improved resource allocation	0.29	0.30	11.5	7.8
Changes in legal and human environment	0.00	−0.04	0.0	−1.0
Dwellings occupancy ratio	0.02	−0.01	0.8	−0.3
Economies of scale	0.21	0.32	8.3	8.3
Irregular factors	−0.01	0.00	−0.4	0.0

The informal tabulation above condenses growth sources into nine groups—they are similar to summary groups used in chapter 7—and shows contributions in 1929–48 and 1948–73.

By this classification, "advances in knowledge and n.e.c.," responsible for 28.7 percent of the growth rate, was the largest single growth source in 1948–73. (Labor input would be if it were not subdivided.) Although this residual series includes the effects of miscellaneous determinants, I consider the estimate of 1.11 percentage points a reasonable approximation of the contribution to growth of measured output made by the incorporation of new knowledge into the productive process in this period. It should be remembered that procedures of output measurement are such that the contribution of advances in knowledge is confined to the business sector, and that it includes nothing for the wider range of choice that new and improved products provide to consumers.

More labor input, excluding the contribution of education, was the second biggest growth source in 1948–73 and easily the biggest if one goes back to 1929. It contributed 1.07 percentage points to the 1948–73 growth rate, some 27.6 percent of the total. Table 8-2 shows the detail for this estimate. The increase in employment would have contributed 1.28 percentage points in the absence of changes in working hours or labor composition. The shortening of working hours offset 0.23 points of this amount.[3] Another 0.15 points were offset

3. This offset is itself the net result of three estimates. If a reduction in working hours, regardless of its cause, reduced labor input proportionately, hours shortening would have subtracted 0.38 percentage points from the growth rate. But as explained in chapters 3 and 6, reductions in working hours are partly offset by higher output per hour (the "efficiency offset"). Also, the shift of full-time workers from farming or nonfarm self-employment, where hours are long, to nonfarm wage and salary employment, where they are shorter, is not considered to reduce labor input. (Inclusion of the "intergroup shift offset" prevents this.)

by a decline in the proportion of the total hours worked in the business sector that are provided by males in the prime working ages. Finally, the "unallocated" component of labor input added 0.17 percentage points to the contribution of labor.[4]

4. The "unallocated" component arises mainly in general government, households, and institutions. The estimates conform to the method of output measurement in this sector in the NIPA; this has changed since the publication of *Accounting for Growth*, so the estimates are conceptually changed. Estimates for 1929–47 also differ conceptually from those for 1947–76 (see chapter 6).

In *Accounting for Growth* the "unallocated" component referred *only* to changes in employment composition *within* general government, households, and institutions. The change in base year from 1958 to 1972 necessitated its expansion in the present study to include the effect of shifts in the division of employment between that sector and nonresidential business. The explanation follows.

The contribution of employment is defined as the amount by which the growth rate would have been reduced if employment had not changed while other output determinants, including the distribution of employment between the two sectors, had changed as they actually did. Apart from the usual small interaction term, this is the product of (1) the growth rate of employment in the economy as a whole and (2) the weight of labor in the economy as a whole, measured as the sum of (a) the product of the labor weight in nonresidential business and the nonresidential business sector's weight in total national income and (b) the weight of the "government, households, and institutions" sector's weight in total national income. This procedure was used in the present study to obtain the contribution of employment.

In *Accounting for Growth* I used a different procedure that gave virtually the same answer. The contribution of employment was measured as the sum of (1) the product of (a) the growth rate of employment in nonresidential business, (b) the labor share in nonresidential business, and (c) the nonresidential business sector's weight; and (2) the product of (a) the growth rate of employment in nonresidential business and (b) that sector's weight.

With the change from 1958 to 1972 prices, the two procedures give different answers. They are substantially different in two early periods. This results from the combination of two aspects of the data. First, with the deflation procedure followed in the NIPA, the value of output contributed by each worker becomes far higher in general government, households, and institutions than in nonresidential business as one moves back in time. Second, in 1929–41 (on an actual basis) and 1948–53 (on both actual

| | Contributions to growth rate of potential NIPPE | | | |
| | Percentage points | | Percent of growth rate | |
	1929–48	*1948–73*	*1929–48*	*1948–73*
All sources	1.20	2.25	100.0	100.0
Labor input per worker, except education	0.03	−0.21	2.5	−9.3
Education per worker	0.38	0.41	31.7	18.2
Capital per worker	−0.12	0.43	−10.0	19.1
Land per worker	−0.06	−0.05	−5.0	−2.2
Advances in knowledge and n.e.c.	0.46	1.10	38.3	48.9
Improved resource allocation	0.29	0.30	24.2	13.3
Changes in legal and human environment	0.00	−0.04	0.0	−1.8
Dwellings occupancy ratio	0.02	−0.01	1.7	−0.4
Economies of scale	0.21	0.32	17.5	14.2
Irregular factors	−0.01	0.00	−0.8	0.0

This includes an implicit allowance for the effect of increased education of workers employed in government, households, and institutions that is not included in the contribution of education.

The increase in capital contributed 0.71 percentage points to the 1948–73 growth rate, 18.3 percent of the total. Of this amount, capital in the nonresidential business sector contributed 0.44 points (nonresidential structures and equipment 0.32 points and inventories 0.12 points). The increase in the services provided by the stock of dwellings contributed 0.23 percentage points and an increased flow of earnings from abroad 0.04 points.

The pervasive upward movement in the distribution by amount of education of labor in the nonresidential business sector was the fourth major growth source. It contributed 0.41 percentage points to the 1948–73 growth rate, 10.6 percent of the total.

The two major growth sources remaining were improved resource allocation (chiefly the shift of workers from farming), which contributed 7.8 percent of the total, and economies of scale resulting from expansion of the markets that business serves,

and potential bases) the share of government, households, and institutions in total employment increased sharply.

The amounts included in the "unallocated" component of labor input as a result of intersectoral employment shifts, which correspond to the difference between the results of the two methods, follow (in percentage points):

Period	Actual	Potential
1929–76	0.04	0.03
1929–48	0.07	0.07
1948–73	0.05	0.05
1929–41	0.14	0.05
1941–48	−0.03	0.06
1948–53	0.27	0.31
1953–64	0.06	0.03
1964–69	0.02	0.03
1969–73	0.03	0.04
1973–76	−0.02	−0.07

8.3 percent. Contributions of other determinants were minor.

Thus in the economy as a whole, as in nonresidential business, the major sources of growth of potential output were advances in knowledge, more work, more capital, more education, resource reallocation, and economies of scale.

The growth rate of actual output was below that of potential output by 0.03 percentage points in 1929–48 and by 0.22 points in 1948–73. By source, the 1929–48 difference is due to slower growth of actual than of potential employment, while the 1948–73 difference is due in part to employment but even more to reduction of the intensity of utilization of employed labor, capital, and land.

National Income per Person Employed

The sources of growth of NIPPE in the economy as a whole are shown in table 8-3 and those of potential national income per person potentially employed in table 8-4. The latter data are condensed in the informal tabulation above.

The results for 1948–73 are fairly similar to those for nonresidential business, which were reviewed in chapter 7. The contributions of components of output per unit of input (except the dwellings occupancy ratio) and of education are smaller on a whole-economy basis because these determinants make no contribution in the other sectors. Capital contributes more and labor input, other than the education component, subtracts less than in nonresidential business alone.

Retardation in Growth of Total Output

During the postwar era periods of fast growth of total national income have alternated with periods of slow growth. On a potential basis, the very high 1948–53 growth rate of 4.7 percent was followed

Table 8-3. Sources of Growth of Actual National Income per Person Employed, Selected Periods, 1929–76
Contributions to growth rates in percentage points

Item	Longer periods			Shorter periods						
	1929–76	1929–48	1948–73	1929–41	1941–48	1948–53	1953–64	1964–69	1969–73	1973–76
National income per person employed	**1.60**	**1.21**	**2.12**	**1.09**ᵃ	**1.41**ᵃ	**2.60**	**2.42**	**1.45**	**1.50**	**−0.22**
Total factor input	**0.45**	**0.25**	**0.60**	**0.34**	**0.12**	**1.12**	**0.75**	**0.09**	**0.37**	**0.44**
Labor	0.27	0.41	0.20	0.61	0.12	0.74	0.25	−0.08	0.02	0.11
Hours	−0.24	−0.22	−0.24	−0.18	−0.28	−0.02	−0.30	−0.26	−0.33	−0.46
Average hours	−0.51	−0.68	−0.40	−0.71	−0.65	−0.23	−0.39	−0.48	−0.49	−0.58
Efficiency offset	0.19	0.39	0.07	0.49	0.25	0.10	0.00	0.11	0.12	0.12
Intergroup shift offset	0.08	0.07	0.09	0.04	0.12	0.11	0.09	0.11	0.04	0.00
Age-sex composition	−0.08	0.01	−0.14	0.04	−0.04	0.06	−0.08	−0.29	−0.33	−0.19
Education	0.41	0.38	0.41	0.42	0.30	0.36	0.40	0.37	0.50	0.67
Unallocated	0.18	0.24	0.17	0.33	0.14	0.34	0.23	0.10	0.18	0.09
Capital	0.23	−0.11	0.45	−0.23	0.07	0.45	0.52	0.27	0.39	0.35
Inventories	0.04	0.00	0.06	−0.02	0.04	0.08	0.05	0.07	0.04	0.02
Nonresidential structures and equipment	0.07	−0.11	0.18	−0.16	−0.02	0.16	0.19	0.15	0.20	0.18
Dwellings	0.11	0.01	0.18	−0.02	0.04	0.21	0.22	0.08	0.11	0.18
International assets	0.01	−0.01	0.03	−0.03	0.01	0.00	0.06	−0.03	0.04	−0.03
Land	−0.05	−0.05	−0.05	−0.04	−0.07	−0.07	−0.02	−0.10	−0.04	−0.02
Output per unit of input	**1.15**	**0.96**	**1.52**	**0.75**	**1.29**	**1.48**	**1.67**	**1.36**	**1.13**	**−0.66**
Advances in knowledge and n.e.c.	0.72	0.45	1.10	0.24	0.81	1.03	1.06	1.01	1.22	−0.59
Improved resource allocation	0.26	0.28	0.29	0.20	0.39	0.40	0.26	0.35	0.11	−0.01
Farm	0.21	0.26	0.20	0.18	0.39	0.31	0.20	0.19	0.06	0.01
Nonfarm self-employment	0.05	0.02	0.09	0.02	0.00	0.09	0.06	0.16	0.05	−0.02
Legal and human environment	−0.04	0.00	−0.04	0.00	0.00	0.00	−0.01	−0.05	−0.13	−0.34
Pollution abatement	−0.02	0.00	−0.02	0.00	0.00	0.00	0.00	−0.02	−0.08	−0.18
Worker safety and health	−0.01	0.00	−0.01	0.00	0.00	0.00	0.00	0.00	−0.04	−0.09
Dishonesty and crime	−0.01	0.00	−0.01	0.00	0.00	0.00	−0.01	−0.03	−0.01	−0.07
Dwellings occupancy ratio	0.01	0.02	−0.01	0.01	0.03	−0.02	−0.01	0.01	0.00	0.02
Economies of scale	0.27	0.21	0.32	0.12	0.36	0.36	0.24	0.43	0.32	0.19
Irregular factors	−0.07	0.00	−0.14	0.18	−0.30	−0.29	0.13	−0.39	−0.39	0.07
Weather in farming	0.00	−0.01	0.00	−0.02	0.02	0.00	−0.01	0.00	0.01	−0.02
Labor disputes	0.00	0.00	0.00	0.00	0.00	0.00	0.00	0.00	0.01	0.00
Intensity of demand	−0.07	0.01	−0.14	0.20	−0.32	−0.29	0.14	−0.39	−0.41	0.09

Sources: Derived from tables 2-2, 2-6, 2-9, 3-1, 4-1, 6-3, 6-4, 7-1, and G-2.
n.e.c. Not elsewhere classified.
a. Based on data excluding work relief employees. When based on data including work relief employees, growth rates are 0.89 in 1929–41 and 1.76 in 1941–48.

by a much lower rate of 3.2 percent in 1953–64, another very high rate of 4.5 percent in 1964–69, and a rate of 3.8 percent, about the postwar average to that time, in 1969–73. Then came the 1973–76 period when growth fell to only 1.6 percent a year.

Differences among the first four of these five periods were due almost entirely to fluctuations in the growth rate of total factor input (table 8-2). Output per unit of input contributed 1.7 percentage points to the growth rate in the two periods of fastest growth and 1.6 points in the other two periods. The fluctuation in the contribution of total factor input was due mainly to labor input. The contribution of capital was only 0.2 percentage

points larger in the periods of fastest growth than in those of slower growth.[5]

The fifth period, 1973–76, was entirely different. A growth rate far below any previous period was experienced despite a contribution from total factor input that was as large as in 1969–73 and much larger than in 1953–64. Output per unit of input

5. Labor input was not only directly responsible for most of the fluctuation in the growth rate but also an important influence upon the rest. The amount of employment expansion influences the demand for capital. Moreover, fluctuations in the rate of input growth were responsible for those in the rate of market expansion and hence in gains from economies of scale, and economies of scale were responsible (on a net basis) for the small part that output per unit of input did play in the growth rate fluctuations.

Table 8-4. Sources of Growth of Potential National Income per Person Potentially Employed, Selected Periods, 1929–76
Contributions to growth rates in percentage points

Item	Longer periods			Shorter periods						
	1929–76	1929–48	1948–73	1929–41	1941–48	1948–53	1953–64	1964–69	1969–73	1973–76
National income per person potentially employed	1.63	1.20	2.25	0.66	2.12	3.01	2.16	2.04	1.81	−0.80
Total factor input	0.38	0.23	0.58	−0.01	0.62	1.28	0.59	0.33	0.21	−0.19
Labor	0.24	0.41	0.20	0.40	0.39	0.83	0.16	0.03	−0.02	−0.21
Hours	−0.24	−0.21	−0.23	−0.19	−0.24	−0.03	−0.28	−0.24	−0.28	−0.43
Average hours	−0.51	−0.68	−0.38	−0.75	−0.54	−0.20	−0.40	−0.42	−0.43	−0.62
Efficiency offset	0.19	0.39	0.06	0.48	0.23	0.08	0.02	0.08	0.10	0.15
Intergroup shift offset	0.08	0.08	0.09	0.08	0.07	0.09	0.10	0.10	0.05	0.04
Age-sex composition	−0.10	0.00	−0.15	−0.02	0.05	0.11	−0.13	−0.24	−0.41	−0.39
Education	0.41	0.38	0.41	0.37	0.36	0.37	0.37	0.40	0.48	0.58
Unallocated	0.17	0.24	0.17	0.24	0.22	0.38	0.20	0.11	0.19	0.03
Capital	0.19	−0.12	0.43	−0.34	0.26	0.51	0.45	0.37	0.29	0.09
Inventories	0.03	0.00	0.07	−0.04	0.09	0.10	0.04	0.09	0.03	−0.03
Nonresidential structures and equipment	0.05	−0.12	0.17	−0.23	0.07	0.18	0.16	0.20	0.14	0.06
Dwellings	0.10	0.01	0.16	−0.04	0.08	0.22	0.20	0.10	0.08	0.10
International assets	0.01	−0.01	0.03	−0.03	0.02	0.01	0.05	−0.02	0.04	−0.04
Land	−0.05	−0.06	−0.05	−0.07	−0.03	−0.06	−0.02	−0.07	−0.06	−0.07
Output per unit of input	1.25	0.97	1.67	0.67	1.50	1.73	1.57	1.71	1.60	−0.61
Advances in knowledge and n.e.c.	0.74	0.46	1.10	0.23	0.88	1.03	1.05	1.03	1.23	−0.57
Improved resource allocation	0.28	0.29	0.30	0.33	0.19	0.35	0.31	0.31	0.15	0.11
Farm	0.22	0.27	0.21	0.25	0.28	0.28	0.22	0.18	0.07	0.04
Nonfarm self-employment	0.06	0.02	0.09	0.08	−0.09	0.07	0.09	0.13	0.08	0.07
Legal and human environment	−0.04	0.00	−0.04	0.00	0.00	0.00	−0.01	−0.05	−0.12	−0.32
Pollution abatement	−0.02	0.00	−0.02	0.00	0.00	0.00	0.00	−0.02	−0.08	−0.17
Worker safety and health	−0.01	0.00	−0.01	0.00	0.00	0.00	0.00	0.00	−0.03	−0.09
Dishonesty and crime	−0.01	0.00	−0.01	0.00	0.00	0.00	−0.01	−0.03	−0.01	−0.06
Dwellings occupancy ratio	0.01	0.02	−0.01	0.01	0.03	−0.02	−0.01	0.01	0.00	0.02
Economies of scale	0.27	0.21	0.32	0.12	0.38	0.37	0.24	0.43	0.32	0.18
Irregular factors	−0.01	−0.01	0.00	−0.02	0.02	0.00	−0.01	−0.02	0.02	−0.03
Weather in farming	−0.01	−0.01	0.00	−0.02	0.02	0.00	−0.01	−0.01	0.01	−0.02
Labor disputes	0.00	0.00	0.00	0.00	0.00	0.00	0.00	−0.01	0.01	−0.01

Sources: Derived from tables 2-2, 2-8, 2-9, 3-2, 4-1, 6-3, 6-4, and G-2.
n.e.c. Not elsewhere classified.

actually dropped in absolute terms and made a negative contribution to growth.

The pattern of fluctuations in the growth rate of actual national income was similar to that in potential national income but the decline from 1964–69 to 1969–73 was larger. This dropped the actual growth rate much below the potential rate in 1969–73 and the difference continued in 1973–76. Because of the effect of fluctuations in intensity of demand on intensity of utilization, changes in the contribution of output per unit of input were somewhat larger on an actual than on a potential basis over the first four periods, but they did not coincide with changes in the growth rate of output. Total factor input, mainly labor input, was responsible for fluctuations in actual as well as potential output growth before 1973.

Table 8-5 shows the amount by which the contribution of each growth source in each of the three most recent short periods differed from its contribution in the long period from 1948 to 1973. Differences are provided for both potential and actual national income. This presentation makes it easy to examine the unusual features of the three recent periods.

In the 1948–73 period used as a base, the growth rate of actual national income was 0.22 percentage points below that of potential national income, but the contributions of only two sources differed by more than 0.01 percentage points. These were employment and fluctuations in intensity of utilization due to demand intensity.

The 1964–69 Period

In the rapid expansion from 1964 to 1969, the growth rate of potential national income was 0.66 percentage points (17 percent) higher than in 1948–73. Labor input was responsible for 0.49

Table 8-5. Sources of Growth of Total Potential and Actual National Income: Differences between Contributions to Growth Rates in Recent Short Periods and in 1948–73

Excess over contributions in 1948–73 in percentage points

Item	1964–69		1969–73		1973–76	
	Potential	Actual	Potential	Actual	Potential	Actual
National income	**0.66**	**0.80**	**−0.08**	**−0.74**	**−2.27**	**−3.07**
Total factor input	**0.61**	**0.95**	**−0.01**	**−0.35**	**0.01**	**−0.90**
Labor	0.49	0.86	0.08	−0.28	0.28	−0.65
Employment	0.66	1.14	0.30	−0.10	0.69	−0.56
Hours	−0.01	−0.02	−0.05	−0.09	−0.21	−0.22
Average hours	−0.04	−0.08	−0.05	−0.09	−0.25	−0.18
Efficiency offset	0.02	0.04	0.04	0.05	0.09	0.05
Intergroup shift offset	0.01	0.02	−0.04	−0.05	−0.05	−0.09
Age-sex composition	−0.09	−0.15	−0.26	−0.19	−0.24	−0.05
Education	−0.01	−0.04	0.07	0.09	0.17	0.26
Unallocated	−0.06	−0.07	0.02	0.01	−0.13	−0.08
Capital	0.12	0.09	−0.09	−0.07	−0.27	−0.25
Inventories	0.06	0.05	−0.04	−0.03	−0.09	−0.09
Nonresidential structures and equipment	0.11	0.10	−0.01	−0.01	−0.09	−0.08
Dwellings	−0.01	−0.02	−0.05	−0.06	−0.02	−0.02
International assets	−0.04	−0.04	0.01	0.03	−0.07	−0.06
Land	0.00	0.00	0.00	0.00	0.00	0.00
Output per unit of input	**0.05**	**0.15**	**−0.07**	**−0.39**	**−2.28**	**−2.17**
Advances in knowledge and n.e.c.	−0.07	−0.08	0.13	0.12	−1.67	−1.68
Improved resource allocation	0.01	0.06	−0.15	−0.18	−0.19	−0.30
Farm	−0.03	−0.01	−0.14	−0.14	−0.17	−0.19
Nonfarm self-employment	0.04	0.07	−0.01	−0.04	−0.02	−0.11
Legal and human environment	−0.01	−0.01	−0.08	−0.09	−0.28	−0.30
Pollution abatement	0.00	0.00	−0.06	−0.06	−0.15	−0.16
Worker safety and health	0.01	0.01	−0.02	−0.03	−0.08	−0.08
Dishonesty and crime	−0.02	−0.02	0.00	0.00	−0.05	−0.06
Dwellings occupancy ratio	0.02	0.02	0.01	0.01	0.03	0.03
Economies of scale	0.12	0.11	0.00	0.00	−0.14	−0.13
Irregular factors	−0.02	−0.15	0.02	−0.25	−0.03	0.21
Weather in farming	−0.01	0.00	0.01	0.01	−0.02	−0.02
Labor disputes	−0.01	0.00	0.01	0.01	−0.01	0.00
Intensity of demand	...	−0.15	...	−0.27	...	0.23

Sources: Derived from tables 8-1 and 8-2.
n.e.c. Not elsewhere classified.

percentage points of this difference. Changes in employment would have created an even larger difference, 0.66 points, if changes in hours and employment composition had been the same in the two periods. The largest offset, 0.09 points, was from age-sex composition.

Capital, also growing rapidly in 1964–69, was responsible for 0.12 points of the difference from 1948–73 in growth rates. The contribution of capital used in nonresidential business to the growth rate of potential national income in the whole economy was larger by 0.17 points in 1964–69, but the contributions of dwellings and especially of international assets were smaller. Economies of scale contributed 0.12 percentage points more in 1964–69 than in 1948–73 because markets were growing more rapidly as a result of the faster increase in inputs. For no other growth source did contribu-

tions in the two periods differ by more than 0.07 points.

The growth rate of national income on an actual basis was higher in 1964–69 than in 1948–73 for about the same reasons that it was higher on a potential basis, except that the difference between periods in the contribution of employment was even greater. (Unemployment was reduced from 1964 to 1969.) This was partially offset by a sharper decline in intensity of utilization from 1964 to 1969 than from 1948 to 1973.

The 1969–73 Period

Both the growth rate of potential national income and its sources were very much the same in 1969–73 as in 1948–73. Differences between the short and long periods were less than 0.1 percentage points for the growth rate itself and for the contributions of total labor input, of capital input and all of its components, and of output per unit of input and all but two of its components. Even for the exceptions the differences were not much greater. Advances in knowledge and n.e.c. are shown to have contributed 0.13 percentage points more in 1969–73, a difference too small to be granted much significance in a residual estimate. The shift of labor from farming contributed 0.14 percentage points less in 1969–73, an important and lasting change but not of dominant size. Changes in the legal and human environment began to cut into the growth rate, but affected the interperiod difference by only 0.08 percentage points.

Although the change in labor input contributed only 0.08 percentage points more in 1969–73 than in 1948–73, differences for its components, already evident in 1964–69, were more pronounced. The increase in employment would have contributed 0.30 percentage points more in 1969–73 than in 1948–73 in the absence of changes in hours and labor composition. But the change in age-sex composition subtracted 0.26 points more in 1969–73. Much smaller changes occurred in other labor input components. As I have stressed repeatedly, these changes were inseparable results of the same phenomena. If low birthrates during the depression and World War II had not been followed by high birthrates in the early postwar years, and if changes had not occurred in labor force participation rates of young people and women, there would have been no sharp employment increase in the 1969–73 period, no sharp decline in the age-sex composition index, no big increase in part-time employment to reduce average hours, and no reduction in the average age of adult workers to accelerate the rise in the education index.

The actual growth rate in 1969–73 fell 0.88 percentage points below the potential rate in that period, and 0.74 points below the actual rate in 1948–69. From 1969 to 1973 the ratio of actual to potential employment fell sharply and so did intensity of utilization of employed inputs. Of the 0.74 point difference between 1948–73 and 1969–73 growth rates of actual national income, labor input was responsible for 0.28 points, intensity of utilization related to demand fluctuations for 0.27 points, and resource reallocation for 0.18 points. Other differences were much smaller.

The 1973–76 Period

Most growth sources contributed to the collapse in the growth rate of potential national income in 1973–76. The main exception is employment. Potential employment grew very fast in this period. It would have contributed 0.69 percentage points more to the growth rate of potential national income in 1973–76 than in 1948–73 in the absence of changes in hours and labor composition. The increase in the education that workers had received also contributed more, by 0.17 percentage points, in 1973–76, and the change in the dwellings occupancy ratio contributed 0.03 points more.

The growth rate of potential national income dropped 2.27 percentage points from 1948–73 to 1973–76 despite increased contributions from these determinants. Without these offsetting increases the drop would have been 3.16 percentage points. This is the amount ascribable to other determinants, and all except land contributed to it.

An exceptionally large drop in working hours was responsible for 0.21 percentage points of the decline in the growth rate, the age-sex composition of hours worked for 0.24 points, and the unallocated component of labor input for 0.13 points. All four components of capital contributed to the decline: inventories 0.09 points, nonresidential structures and equipment 0.09 points, dwellings 0.02 points, and international assets 0.07 points. The shift of labor from farming contributed 0.17 points and the shift from nonfarm self-employment 0.02 points. Increased costs for pollution abatement were responsible for 0.15 points, costs incurred for worker safety and health for 0.08 points, and costs imposed by dishonesty and crime for 0.05 points. Smaller gains from economies of scale were responsible for 0.14 points of the drop (a very crude estimate). Even the irregular factors contributed: the weather in farming, 0.02 points, and the effect of labor disputes on intensity of utilization, 0.01 points. The remaining 1.67 percentage points appear in the estimate for advances in knowledge and miscellaneous determinants. This drop is explored in chapter 9.

The growth rate of actual output from 1973 to 1976 was 1.02 percentage points below that of potential output. Labor input alone was responsible for 0.99 points of this difference as the ratio of actual to potential employment dropped sharply, and resource reallocation accounted for 0.12 points. A modest increase in intensity of utilization of employed resources offset 0.09 points of these amounts.

The growth rate of actual output was 3.07 percentage points lower in 1973–76 than in 1948–73, a much bigger difference than that in potential rates.

On an actual basis labor input contributed 0.65 percentage points less in 1973–76 than in 1948–73 whereas on a potential basis it contributed 0.28 points more.

Dwindling Growth of National Income per Person Employed

Growth rates of actual and potential NIPPE and their sources during the shorter postwar periods are shown in the last five columns of tables 8-3 and 8-4. On a potential basis, the growth rate shows a steady downward progression: 3.0 percent in 1948–53, 2.2 percent in 1953–64, 2.0 percent in 1964–69, 1.8 percent in 1969–73, and −0.8 percent in 1973–76. On an actual basis the decline was smaller over the whole period and was interrupted from 1964–69 to 1969–73.

The First Four Postwar Periods

During the first four of these periods output per unit of input had little responsibility for the downtrend in potential national income per person potentially employed; it contributed 1.7 percentage points to the growth rate in 1948–53 and in 1964–69 and 1.6 points in 1953–64 and 1969–73 (table 8-4). Changes in the contributions of some individual components of output per unit of input were large relative to their size, but they were moderate relative to the growth rate of total output. They also were largely offsetting.

The contribution made to growth by increases in the amount of capital per person potentially employed in the whole economy did contribute to the downward progression, receding in each period. The whole drop was only 0.2 percentage points, however, from 0.5 points in 1948–53 to 0.3 points in 1969–73. The services provided by dwellings per person potentially employed accounted for almost two-thirds of this reduction.

Most of the slowdown up to 1973 in NIPPE, computed on a potential basis, resulted from changes in working hours and labor composition. Changes in the age-sex composition of hours worked were most important to the downward progression. They raised the growth rate by 0.1 percentage points in 1948–53, then subtracted 0.1 points in 1953–64, 0.2 in 1964–69, and 0.4 in 1969–73. Changes in working hours subtracted only 0.03 percentage points in 1948–53, but about one-fourth of a point

in all three of the following periods. The contribution of education, unchanged from the first period to the second, rose in the last two. This moderated the downward progression of the growth rate at that time. The unallocated component of labor input contributed an extraordinary 0.4 percentage points in 1948–53 as the large increase in the government share of total employment at the time of the Korean hostilities gave an artificial boost to output per worker. It did so because the use of 1972 prices attaches a much higher value to the output of labor in government than of labor in business in 1948–53.[6] In the three following periods the contribution of the unallocated component was only 0.1 or 0.2 percentage points.

The 1973–76 Period

At −0.8 percent, the growth rate of NIPPE on a potential basis in 1973–76 was below its 1948–73 rate by nearly 3.1 percentage points. Total factor input contributed 0.8 percentage points to the decline and output per unit of input, 2.3 points. All growth sources contributed to the decline except education, the dwellings occupancy ratio, and (in the most detailed classification) the efficiency offset to the reduction in hours.

The sources of the reduction are detailed in table 8-6. They were much like those responsible for the slightly smaller drop in the similar series for nonresidential business, which was discussed in chapter 7.[7] In addition, the contributions of dwellings, international assets, and the "unallocated" component of labor input, which do not appear in nonresidential business, all fell from 1948–73 to 1973–76.

Difference between Potential and Actual Growth Rates in 1973–76

From 1973 to 1976 the growth rate of actual national income (0.6 percent) was 1.0 percentage point beneath the growth rate of potential national income (1.6 percent). On a per-person-employed basis the relationship is reversed. The growth rate of actual NIPPE (−0.2 percent) was 0.6 percentage points above that of potential NIPPE (−0.8 percent).

6. See note 4 in this chapter.
7. See the section in chapter 7 on potential and actual sector NIPPE.

The following tabulation shows the differences by source:[8]

Source	Contribution to actual growth rate less contribution to potential growth rate (percentage points)	
	Total national income	*NIPPE*
All sources	−1.02	0.58
Labor	−0.99	0.32
Employment	−1.31	...
Hours	−0.02	−0.03
Age-sex composition	0.20	0.20
Education	0.09	0.09
Unallocated	0.05	0.06
Capital	...	0.26
Inventories	...	0.05
Nonresidential structures and equipment	...	0.12
Dwellings	...	0.08
International assets	...	0.01
Land	...	0.05
Improved resource allocation	−0.12	−0.12
Farm	−0.03	−0.03
Nonfarm self-employment	−0.09	−0.09
Intensity of demand	0.09	0.09

Total National Income

Total actual national income increased less than total potential national income from 1973 to 1976 because actual employment rose much less than potential employment. Indeed, employment more than accounted for the difference: its contribution to the growth rate was 1.31 percentage points smaller on an actual than on a potential basis. A larger decline in actual than potential hours augmented the difference by another 0.02 points.

However, the difference between actual and potential employment changes was concentrated among young people, women, and the less educated. This offset 0.29 percentage points of the employment difference.

Because the divergence between actual and potential employment was confined to nonfarm business wage and salary workers, it also affected the distribution of employment among uses. The ratio of business employment to total employment dropped on an actual basis and rose on a potential basis; the ratio of farm employment to total business employment dropped less on an actual basis

than on a potential basis; and the ratio of nonfarm self-employment to total nonfarm business employment rose on an actual basis and fell on a potential basis. By affecting the "unallocated" component of labor input the first of these differences tended to make the actual growth rate higher than the potential rate to the extent of 0.05 percentage points, but the latter two, which affected the resource allocation components, worked the other way, reenforcing by 0.12 percentage points the shortfall of the actual rate from the potential rate.

All these differences in the contributions of labor and resource allocation reflect the smaller increase in actual than in potential employment or the larger decrease in average hours. Of themselves, they would have dropped the growth rate of actual national income 1.11 percentage points below that of potential national income, but 0.09 points were offset by a little more intensive use of employed labor, capital, and land in 1976 than in 1973.

Both 1973 and 1976 were years of relatively low utilization. That this was so in 1973 is not surprising. Low utilization and productivity is typical of business cycle peaks, especially years such as 1973 in which output fails to expand much or even declines during most of the year and employment does not adjust promptly.[9] The tendency was further accentuated in 1973 because, for a business cycle peak, unemployment was high.[10] The year 1976 was well into the expansion phase of the business cycle, a time when utilization of employed resources is typically favorable to high output per unit of input. But the recovery was from such a deep output trough that 1976 intensity of utilization, though up sharply from 1974 and 1975, held only a small margin over 1973.

National Income per Person Employed

From the discussion of total national income and the preceding text table, it is easy to see why actual NIPPE grew more rapidly than potential NIPPE from 1973 to 1976. The difference between growth rates of actual and potential employment, responsible for the contrary differential in total national income, does not directly affect NIPPE.

8. Entries are omitted for sources whose contributions on actual and potential bases differ, if at all, only by minor amounts that result from differences in sector weights or from interaction terms and rounding.

9. See appendix I.

10. Whether unemployment was high and intensity of utilization of employed resources low only because demand was inadequate to induce larger output or also because not enough raw materials were available to allow production of desired end products for which demand was unsatisfied was debated in 1973 and early 1974. My estimates do not resolve this question.

Table 8-6. Sources of Growth of Potential and Actual National Income per Person Employed: Differences between Contributions to Growth Rates in Recent Short Periods and in 1948–73

Excess over contribution in 1948–73 in percentage points

Item	1964–69		1969–73		1973–76	
	Potential	Actual	Potential	Actual	Potential	Actual
National income per person employed	−0.21	−0.67	−0.44	−0.62	−3.05	−2.34
Total factor input	−0.25	−0.51	−0.37	−0.23	−0.77	−0.16
Labor	−0.17	−0.28	−0.22	−0.18	−0.41	−0.09
Hours	−0.01	−0.02	−0.05	−0.09	−0.20	−0.22
Average hours	−0.04	−0.08	−0.05	−0.09	−0.24	−0.18
Efficiency offset	0.02	0.04	0.04	0.05	0.09	0.05
Intergroup shift offset	0.01	0.02	−0.04	−0.05	−0.05	−0.09
Age-sex composition	−0.09	−0.15	−0.26	−0.19	−0.24	−0.05
Education	−0.01	−0.04	0.07	0.09	0.17	0.26
Unallocated	−0.06	−0.07	0.02	0.01	−0.14	−0.08
Capital	−0.06	−0.18	−0.14	−0.06	−0.34	−0.10
Inventories	0.02	0.01	−0.04	−0.02	−0.10	−0.04
Nonresidential structures and equipment	0.03	−0.03	−0.03	0.02	−0.11	0.00
Dwellings	−0.06	−0.10	−0.08	−0.07	−0.06	0.00
International assets	−0.05	−0.06	0.01	0.01	−0.07	−0.06
Land	−0.02	−0.05	−0.01	0.01	−0.02	0.03
Output per unit of input	0.04	−0.16	−0.07	−0.39	−2.28	−2.18
Advances in knowledge and n.e.c.	−0.07	−0.09	0.13	0.12	−1.67	−1.69
Improved resource allocation	0.01	0.06	−0.15	−0.18	−0.19	−0.30
Farm	−0.03	−0.01	−0.14	−0.14	−0.17	−0.19
Nonfarm self-employment	0.04	0.07	−0.01	−0.04	−0.02	−0.11
Legal and human environment	−0.01	−0.01	−0.08	−0.09	−0.28	−0.30
Pollution abatement	0.00	0.00	−0.06	−0.06	−0.15	−0.16
Worker safety and health	0.01	0.01	−0.02	−0.03	−0.08	−0.08
Dishonesty and crime	−0.02	−0.02	0.00	0.00	−0.05	−0.06
Dwellings occupancy ratio	0.02	0.02	0.01	0.01	0.03	0.03
Economies of scale	0.11	0.11	0.00	0.00	−0.14	−0.13
Irregular factors	−0.02	−0.25	0.02	−0.25	−0.03	0.21
Weather in farming	−0.01	0.00	0.01	0.01	−0.02	−0.02
Labor disputes	−0.01	0.00	0.01	0.01	−0.01	0.00
Intensity of demand	...	−0.25	...	−0.27	...	0.23

Sources: Derived from tables 8-3 and 8-4.
n.e.c. Not elsewhere classified.

But the offset that it creates (its net effect on other components of labor input and on resource allocation) and the rise in intensity of utilization do.

This is not the entire story. Capital and land input per person employed are also affected by the difference between actual and potential increases in employment. It will be recalled that potential output in any year is defined as the output that would be obtained if the unemployment rate were at 4 percent, intensity of utilization were at the rate that on the average would be associated with a 4 percent unemployment rate, and "other conditions had been those that actually prevailed in that year." "Other conditions" include capital, as explained in chapter 2, and of course land, so total capital and land input are the same on a potential as on an actual basis. All components of capital and land input per person employed therefore would necessarily have risen less or declined more if employ-

ment had increased at the high potential rate instead of the lower actual rate.

Of the 0.58 percentage points by which the growth rate of actual NIPPE exceeded that of potential NIPPE, capital and land together account for 0.31 percentage points, labor input and resource reallocation for 0.20 points, intensity of utilization related to intensity of demand for 0.09 points, and minor differences due to weighting, and so on, for an offsetting −0.02 points.[11]

11. It may be observed that the combined contributions of labor, capital, land, and resource reallocation are always such as to produce differences between actual and potential growth rates of NIPPE that are opposite in direction from those introduced between actual and potential national income. However, when changes in intensity of utilization are not only in the same direction as those in unemployment, as in 1973–76, but also large, it is possible for the actual growth rate of either total national income or NIPPE to exceed or fall short of the corresponding potential rate. This happened in three of the seven shorter periods.

Difference between Actual and Potential Output

Knowledge of differences between actual and potential output and input is crucial for the formulation of economic policy, particularly but not only for fiscal and monetary policy. It is indispensable for forecasts and projections of future output, prices, and employment. It is valuable in many quite unrelated types of economic analysis that depend on relationships among time series because the business cycle affects relationships among many types of economic variables, and a series measuring the ratio of actual to potential output is a useful tool to isolate the cyclical influence.

This study provides estimates not only of the gap between actual and potential output but also of its detailed composition. The detail in which the estimates are derived is indeed their distinguishing characteristic and the reason for what I consider to be their superiority over others. The fact that they are not highly current detracts somewhat from their usefulness for policy purposes, but this would be remedied if growth accounting were institutionalized and estimates released annually. In *Accounting for Growth* I suggested that the Bureau of Economic Analysis and the Bureau of Labor Statistics, jointly, might well accept this function. The Panel to Review Productivity Statistics (the Rees Committee) has made a similar recommendation.[12]

The estimates I have prepared refer to a 4 percent unemployment rate. This is lower than nearly all economists, including the writer, consider an appropriate target under present conditions because of its implications for inflation. However, I shall first examine the gap between actual and potential output as defined, and then show how the estimates can be modified to give results for any unemployment rate selected as a target.

For the years 1973 to 1976, tables 2-1, 2-7, and 2-8 yield the series for unemployment and for relationships between actual and potential series in the economy as a whole (national income is in 1972 prices) shown at the top of the next column.

Although actual values were below potential values for all of these series (except unemployment) in all of these years, the relationships among

	1973	1974	1975	1976
Percent of civilian labor force 16 and over unemployed	4.8	5.6	8.5	7.7
Actual as percentage of potential:				
National income	96.0	92.0	90.5	93.2
Labor force	99.5	99.0	97.2	97.7
Employment	98.6	97.4	92.9	94.0
Total hours at work	98.1	96.2	92.1	93.7
Average hours at work	99.5	98.8	99.2	99.6
NIPPE	97.4	94.4	97.4	99.1
National income per hour at work	97.9	95.5	98.2	99.5

them were constantly changing. Particularly striking is the finding that in 1976 the difference between actual and potential was only 0.5 percent for output per hour, while it was still 6.3 percent for hours at work.

The 6.8 percent shortfall of actual national income below potential national income in 1976 amounted to $74.4 billion at 1972 prices. This amount is divided among the determinants of the difference in table 8-7, which also provides similar data for all other years covered by this study. Over one-third, or $25.6 billion, of the 1976 gap was due to less intensive utilization of the labor, capital, and land that was present in business establishments than would have been the case under potential conditions.

The other $48.8 billion was due to actual labor input in nonresidential business being below potential labor input. The shortfall was entirely among wage and salary workers in nonfarm business; this is so by assumption, but it is also approximately correct in fact. Consequently the actual percentage distribution of labor among uses was different than it would have been on a potential basis, and part of the $48.8 billion is classified in the resource allocation categories. The full distribution is shown in columns 4 through 10 of table 8-7.

Other things being equal, the combined effects of the shortfall of actual from potential employment and working hours and of higher actual than potential shares of business employment in farming and nonfarm self-employment would have put actual national income $63 billion below potential national income. They were offset to the extent of $14 billion because the additional hours that would have been worked under potential conditions would have been concentrated among age-sex groups and education groups that contribute least, per hour worked, to the value of output and (to the extent

---

12. National Research Council, Panel to Review Productivity Statistics, Committee on National Statistics, Assembly of Behavioral and Social Sciences, *The Measurement and Interpretation of Productivity* (National Academy of Sciences, 1979).

Table 8-7. Composition of the Gap between Total Actual and Potential National Income, 1929–76[a]

Actual less potential in billions of 1972 dollars

Year	Total national income gap (1)	Intensity of demand, effect on output per unit of input (2)	Total labor input, resource allocation, and unallocated (3)	Labor input — Employment (4)	Hours (5)	Age-sex composition (6)	Education (7)	Farm (8)	Nonfarm self-employment (9)	Unallocated (10)	Addendum: Total GNP gap (11)
1929	4.8	1.6	3.2	2.9	0.5	−0.6	−0.2	0.9	0.5	−0.9	5.3
1940[b]	−24.2	−0.6	−30.6	−30.3	−0.9	3.3	1.1	−5.0	−3.4	3.9	−27.4
1941[b]	1.3	9.3	−13.4	−15.9	1.2	1.4	0.7	−2.3	−1.6	2.6	1.5
1947	−4.5	−5.3	0.8	1.2	−0.2	−0.5	0.0	0.4	0.2	−0.2	−5.1
1948	5.0	2.9	2.1	1.8	0.5	−0.7	−0.1	0.4	0.3	−0.3	5.6
1949	−9.4	−0.8	−8.6	−9.1	−0.8	1.0	0.5	−0.9	−1.1	1.6	−10.7
1950	3.6	8.5	−4.9	−6.2	0.1	0.6	0.4	−0.5	−0.7	1.2	4.1
1951	13.1	7.6	5.5	4.8	1.1	−1.3	−0.1	0.8	0.6	−0.5	14.7
1952	5.3	−1.4	6.7	7.0	0.6	−1.7	−0.3	1.0	0.8	−0.9	6.0
1953	3.8	−3.7	7.5	8.2	0.5	−2.0	−0.4	1.4	1.0	−0.9	4.3
1954	−15.9	−7.2	−8.7	−8.1	−1.6	0.7	0.5	−0.4	−0.9	1.1	−17.9
1955	3.9	4.8	−0.9	−1.3	−0.1	−0.3	0.1	0.2	−0.1	−0.4	4.4
1956	−7.3	−5.7	−1.6	0.2	−1.8	−0.7	0.0	0.3	0.0	0.5	−8.2
1957	−13.9	−10.3	−3.6	−0.8	−2.9	−0.5	0.2	0.1	−0.2	0.5	−15.7
1958	−42.7	−19.6	−23.1	−19.5	−6.0	2.2	1.1	−1.2	−2.1	2.4	−48.3
1959	−20.1	−8.6	−11.5	−10.2	−2.8	1.0	0.6	−0.6	−1.0	1.3	−21.3
1960	−28.2	−14.4	−13.8	−11.2	−4.2	1.1	0.7	−0.6	−1.2	1.4	−31.8
1961	−37.2	−14.8	−22.4	−20.9	−4.1	2.4	1.2	−1.2	−2.0	2.0	−41.9
1962	−18.2	−5.9	−12.3	−12.0	−2.0	1.2	0.7	−0.6	−1.1	1.4	−20.5
1963	−12.3	−0.2	−12.1	−13.5	−0.9	1.6	0.7	−0.6	−1.1	1.6	−13.8
1964	−2.0	5.6	−7.6	−9.7	0.2	1.0	0.5	−0.3	−0.8	1.6	−2.2
1965	10.4	11.6	−1.2	−3.9	1.5	0.2	0.3	−0.1	−0.2	1.1	11.6
1966	17.1	11.8	5.3	3.7	2.0	−0.6	−0.1	0.2	0.4	−0.1	19.1
1967	4.8	2.8	2.0	1.9	0.3	−0.2	−0.1	0.1	0.1	0.2	5.4
1968	10.1	4.5	5.6	4.9	1.3	−0.7	−0.2	0.3	0.4	−0.2	11.3
1969	−5.7	−10.0	4.3	6.0	−0.6	−1.1	−0.2	0.3	0.5	−0.3	−6.4
1970	−43.0	−29.8	−13.2	−11.6	−3.1	1.9	0.3	−0.3	−0.8	0.8	−48.4
1971	−51.9	−27.9	−24.0	−25.4	−2.5	4.3	0.5	−0.6	−1.7	1.3	−58.4
1972	−44.7	−24.0	−20.7	−22.5	−2.2	4.0	0.8	−0.6	−1.4	1.1	−50.3
1973	−41.3	−28.3	−13.0	−12.2	−2.8	2.1	0.7	−0.3	−0.7	0.5	−46.4
1974	−85.5	−58.4	−27.1	−23.1	−7.5	3.2	1.4	−0.6	−1.5	0.7	−96.3
1975	−100.6	−41.7	−58.9	−64.5	−5.4	10.0	3.2	−1.4	−4.1	1.6	−111.0
1976	−74.4	−25.6	−48.8	−55.6	−2.7	8.9	2.7	−1.2	−3.5	1.9	−83.1

Sources: Column 1, table 2-4, column 5: column 2, table 2-4, column 2, sign reversed: column 3, table 2-4, column 3, sign reversed: column 4, table L-5, product of columns 20 and 21 times (ratio of column 1 in table 3-2 to column 1 in table 3-1, minus 1), sign reversed. Columns 5, 6, and 7, same as column 4 except that column 9, 4, or 7, respectively, of tables 3-2 and 3-1 is substituted for column 1. Column 8, table L-5, column 21 times (ratio of column 2 in table 5-2 to column 2 in table 5-1, minus 1), sign reversed. Column 9, same as column 8 except that column 3 of tables 5-2 and 5-1 is substituted for column 2. Column 10, table L-5, column 21 times (ratio of column 13 of table 4-6 to 100.00, minus 1), sign reversed. Column 11, column 1 of this table times the ratio of (1) net domestic product of nonresidential business measured from the income side of the NIPA, to (2) nonresidential business national income, both measured in 1972 prices and according to NIPA concepts. The value of (1) is derived from the NIPA tables as business net domestic product less the residual, both from table 1.12, minus the excess of gross housing product over housing capital consumption allowances with the capital consumption adjustment, both from table 1.21. The value of (2) is equal to business national income from table 1.12 minus housing income from table 1.21.

a. Column 1 equals the sum of columns 2 and 3 (except in 1940–41; see note b). Column 3 equals the sum of columns 4 through 10 except for discrepancies resulting from rounding. Such discrepancies, though trivial, are larger than normal because they include the effects of rounding indexes that enter into the calculation of columns 4 through 10. Data for 1929–59 exclude Alaska and Hawaii.

b. Output of employees on work relief ($6.0 billion in 1940 and $5.4 billion in 1941) is not offset against the gap in nonresidential business in column 3 but is added to column 1. See table 2-4.

of under $2 billion) because of other factors for which an allocation was not made.[13]

It should be noted that the nearly $3 billion of the gap caused by the difference between actual and potential hours is itself, in effect, a net figure.

13. See "Other Indexes" section in appendix M for an explanation of the unallocated column.

Hours of actually employed workers contributed much more to the output gap, but this was offset by the fact that persons who were not employed, but would have been employed under potential conditions, would have worked shorter hours than those who were employed. The actual 1976 average weekly hours of employed persons in nonresidential business were 36.62. Under potential conditions these workers would have averaged 36.94 hours.[14] But when the additional workers are introduced into the calculation, average potential hours drop back to 36.71. If the ratio of the effect on output to the effect on hours was the same for the two adjustments, the hours gap for employed workers contributed $10 billion to the shortfall of actual from potential output, of which $7 billion was offset by exclusion from the actual figures of those who were not employed.

The aggregate data, supplemented by the earlier comments on capital, make it easy to understand why NIPPE was only 0.9 percent lower on an actual than on a potential basis in 1976. The shortfall due to low intensity of utilization was held to 2.3 percent ($25.6 billion out of a $1,091.8 billion potential national income) because output was recovering continuously and fairly smartly throughout the year, a characteristic favorable to high productivity. The difference between actual and potential allocations of labor among sectors and types of work contributed 0.4 percent to the shortfall and hours of employed persons 0.8 percent, bringing the total to around 3.5 percent. The offsets were the low average hours that would have been worked by the additional persons who would have been employed under potential conditions (perhaps 0.6 percent); the less favorable composition of the total hours that would have been worked with respect to age-sex composition (0.8 percent) and education (over 0.2 percent); the absence of additional capital in nonresidential business (0.8 percent) and of more housing or income from abroad (0.4 percent) to accompany the additional workers; and unallocated factors (0.2 percent).[15]

There are, of course, many estimates of potential output. They may be divided between direct estimates, like mine, which are obtained by adjusting actual output to take account of differences between actual and potential conditions, and series that are merely based on an assumed growth rate of potential output from some selected starting point. Among the best known direct estimates are those based on a rule of thumb known as Okun's law, named for Arthur M. Okun. It states that

actual output falls below potential output (at a 4 percent unemployment rate) by a percentage that is three times (originally, 3.2 times) the difference between the actual civilian unemployment rate and 4 percent. Thus if the unemployment rate were 7 percent, actual output would be 9 percent below potential output (3 times the difference between 7 and 4). The ratio of 3 was intended to take account of differences between actual and potential unemployment, labor force, average hours, and all determinants of output per hour. My own analysis indicates that the ratio is unstable because the many determinants of the gap move differently. For example, my estimates imply a ratio of 5 in 1973 and 1974 and approximately 2 in 1975 and 1976, as may be calculated from the preceding text table. Employment and output gaps may even be in opposite directions (as in 1969).[16]

It must be recognized that potential national income, even apart from questions of definition, is a hypothetical figure that is difficult to estimate. The series presented is the best I can calculate, but it obviously is subject to error. It probably is a little more likely to be too high than too low in the 1970s because alternative judgments in calculating the series for the effect of intensity of utilization on output per unit of input would have yielded higher actual index values in recent years, and therefore a smaller gap between actual and potential national income. The size of the labor force adjustment has been considerably debated, but I have no feeling about whether it is more likely to be too small or too big. A larger adjustment would raise total potential national income and lower potential NIPPE, while a smaller adjustment would have the opposite effect.

Gaps between Actual Output and Output Corresponding to Alternative Unemployment Goals

My estimate of the gap between actual and potential national income can readily be adjusted to conform to a potential unemployment rate other than 4 percent. The calculation must be made in two steps. I illustrate with 1976 data.

1. The index that measures the effect on output per unit of input in nonresidential business of

---

14. These numbers are readily calculated from tables 2-7, 2-8, C-1, and L-3.

15. Because numbers in this paragraph are approximations and interaction terms are ignored, the difference between factors operating to lower actual NIPPE (3.5 percent) and those operating to raise it above potential NIPPE (3.0 percent) differs from the directly calculated shortfall of 0.9 percent.

16. See *Accounting for Growth*, chap. 7, for additional discussion. Okun's law refers to GNP and my estimates to national income, but this does not significantly influence the stability of the ratio. To facilitate comparisons of my estimates of the gap with others, they are adjusted to a market-price basis (applicable to either GNP or net national product) in table 4-7, column 11.

"changes in the intensity of utilization of employed resources resulting from fluctuations in intensity of demand" is shown in table 5-1, column 9. Its 1976 value was 99.99. Its potential value at 4 percent unemployment was set at 103.31, based on a regression with the unemployment rate. National income originating in nonresidential business, shown in table 2-6, column 5, was $769.6 billion at 1972 prices in 1976. Hence the output of employed resources would have been $769.6 billion × (103.31 ÷ 99.99), or $795.2 billion under potential conditions. Actual national income was therefore $25.6 billion below potential national income for this reason (table 8-7, column 2). The regression that provides 103.31 as the potential value at 4 percent unemployment provides corresponding values for other unemployment rates: 103.73 at 3.5 percent, 102.90 at 4.5 percent, 102.48 at 5.0 percent, 102.07 at 5.5 percent, 101.65 at 6 percent, 101.24 at 6.5 percent, and so on, with a difference of 0.83 points per percentage of unemployment.[17] Potential output of employed resources when potential is specified at a different unemployment rate is then easily calculated. At 5.0 percent, for example, it is $769.6 billion × (102.48 ÷ 99.99), or $788.8 billion, and the contribution of this determinant to the gap is $19.2 billion. Table 8-8, column 2, shows the corresponding gaps for a range of unemployment rates.

2. Labor input, including its effect on allocation, was responsible for $48.8 billion of the 1976 gap between actual and potential national income in 1972 prices. An exact determination of the corresponding amount when potential unemployment is set at something other than 4 percent would require recalculation in detail, but a decent approximation is readily obtained. The 1976 unemployment rate was 7.7 percent (table 2-1, column 5), 3.7 percent above potential. The potential output gap due to labor input was therefore $13.2 billion per point in the unemployment rate. Relationships with unemployment in a given year are close enough to being linear to allow the use of this figure.[18] Thus if target unemployment is put at 5.5 percent, this second component of the gap is $29.0

Table 8-8. 1976 National Income in 1972 Prices at Alternative "Potential" Unemployment Rates
Billions of 1972 dollars

"Potential" unemployment rate (percent)	Actual 1976 national income (1)	Adjustment for intensity of utilization (2)	Adjustment to labor input[a] (3)	Total gap (4)	Potential national income (5)
3.5	1017.4	28.8	55.4	84.2	1101.6
4.0	1017.4	25.6	48.8	74.4	1091.8
4.5	1017.4	22.4	42.2	64.6	1082.0
5.0	1017.4	19.2	35.6	54.8	1072.2
5.5	1017.4	16.0	29.0	45.0	1062.4
6.0	1017.4	12.8	22.4	35.2	1052.6
6.5	1017.4	9.6	15.8	25.4	1042.8

Sources: Column 1, table 2-1; columns 2 and 3, see text; column 4, column 2 plus 3; column 5, column 1 plus column 4.

a. Includes adjustment to resource allocation and unallocated components.

billion, equal to the $48.8 billion at 4 percent minus (5.5 − 4.0) × $13.2 billion. Table 8-8, column 3, shows 1976 gaps for other potential unemployment rates.[19]

Potential national income at any specified unemployment rate is simply the sum of actual national income and the two adjustments. The preceding text table indicates that in 1976 potential national income was lowered by 1.8 percent each time the unemployment rate used in the definition of potential output is raised by one percentage point.

Calculations like those in table 8-8 can be made with little work for most years for which potential output was calculated.[20] The procedure not only provides appropriate estimates of the gap that corresponds to any selected potential or target unemployment rate but also permits calculation of the amount that the growth rate of potential output would be altered by incorporation of a reader's alternative definition of potential output and his assumptions about changes in the relationship between unemployment and prices. For example, my potential output series has a growth rate of 3.27

17. Because of a paucity of observations, it is not possible to check regression results for years of high unemployment with actual data for years ranging around the selected rates, as was done for the 4 percent rate in appendix L. They are therefore less satisfactory.

18. This procedure cannot be safely used in years in which the gap due to labor input is very small, however. These are years in which the actual unemployment rate is close to 4 percent.

19. *The Budget of the United States Government, Fiscal Year 1980,* p. 46, uses an "unemployment rate at high employment" of 5.1 percent. By interpolation from table 8-8, my estimate of the gap in potential national income in 1972 prices at that rate is found to be $52.8 billion. The Council of Economic Advisers puts the 1976 GNP gap at 5.1 percent unemployment at $70.1 billion in 1972 prices. (*Economic Report of the President, January 1979,* p. 75.) Based on table 8-7, columns 1 and 11, this translates to a national income gap of $62.8 billion, so my estimate of the gap is $10 billion smaller than that of the council, on a comparable basis.

20. See note 19 for exceptions.

percent from 1966 to 1976. Suppose one wished, as some do, to define potential as output at the lowest unemployment rate that would not cause the pace of inflation to change from whatever it is at a given date. Suppose he estimated that an unemployment rate of 4 percent would have kept the 1966 inflation rate unchanged and that an unemployment rate of 6 percent would have kept the much higher 1976 inflation rate unchanged. By substituting $1,052.6 billion (from table 8-8, column 5) for $1,091.8 billion as 1976 potential output, he would secure a growth rate (from $791.6 billion in 1966) of 2.89 percent. He could, of course, use unemployment rates other than 4 percent in both terminal years.

If one wishes to identify potential output with an unemployment rate that would yield the *same* rate of inflation in 1966 and 1976, there is no doubt that that unemployment rate would have risen greatly, and that by such a definition the growth rate of potential output was very much less than when potential is identified with 4 percent unemployment.

Comparison with Recent Estimates of the Council of Economic Advisers

For many years the President's Council of Economic Advisers (CEA) has prepared estimates of potential GNP. In the 1979 *Economic Report of the President,* CEA revised its series. For recent years the revision was downward. There had been a previous large downward revision of these years in the 1977 CEA report.

Almost all the 1979 revision and much of the earlier revisions resulted from a reappraisal of the

numbers, but the concept has also been amended.[21] The CEA identifies potential output with a varying unemployment rate that is intended to hold constant the degree of tightness in the labor market. This rate for the civilian labor force 16 years of age and over rose from 4.9 percent in 1973 to 5.1 percent in the years from 1975 through 1978.

Table 8-9, row 1, shows the unemployment rate that the CEA uses for each of the years from 1973 through 1976. Row 2 shows my estimates of the values of potential national income that correspond to these rates. They were obtained by the procedure described in the explanation of table 8-8. They fall $20 billion or more below my standard potential national income series based on an unvarying 4 percent unemployment rate. (See table 8-9, row 6.) Their use, however, would change the 1973–76 growth rate of potential output only from 1.60 percent to 1.59 percent.

The CEA's estimates of the gaps between actual and potential GNP that correspond to its potential unemployment rates were converted to a national income basis to permit a series for potential national income to be calculated.[22] It is shown in table 8-9, row 3. The potential national income implied by the latest CEA estimates exceeds my estimate by $10.0 billion or 9.0 percent in 1976 and about

21. The excess of potential GNP over actual GNP in 1973, measured in 1972 prices, was lowered from $30 billion to −$7 billion and then to −$8 billion. The excess in 1976 was lowered from $156 billion to $99 billion, and then to $70 billion. (*Economic Report of the President, January 1979*, p. 75, and ibid., January 1977, p. 54.)
22. There is some question about the appropriate treatment of the statistical discrepancy in the national accounts, and of revisions in the data, to make the CEA series and mine comparable. The range of uncertainty is a few billion dollars.

Table 8-9. Comparison of Council of Economic Advisers and Denison Series for Potential Output, 1973–76
Value data in 1972 prices

Item	1973	1974	1975	1976	1973–76 growth rate
1. CEA potential unemployment rate	4.9	5.0	5.1	5.1	...
Potential national income at CEA potential unemployment rate:					
2. Denison	1,020.8	1,040.1	1,034.9	1,070.2	1.59
3. CEA (implied)	992.7	1,019.1	1,045.7	1,080.2	2.86
4. Difference (2 − 3)	28.1	21.0	−10.8	−10.0	...
5. Potential national income at 4 percent unemployment, Denison	1,041.1	1,063.4	1,055.9	1,091.8	1.60
6. Row 2 minus row 5	−20.3	−23.3	−21.0	−21.6	...

Sources: Row 1, *Economic Report of the President, January 1979*, p. 75; row 2, computed by the same method as table 8-8; row 3, actual national income in 1972 prices from table 2-1, column 2, plus national income gap computed as product of CEA gap for GNP from ibid., p. 75, and the ratio of column 1 to column 11 of table 8-7; row 5, table 2-1, column 4.

as much in 1975. The difference is not at all regular, however. The CEA series is $28.1 billion, or 2.8 percent, *below* mine in 1973 and 2.0 percent below it in 1974.

Erratic differences between the series are to be expected. The CEA assumes smooth increases in potential output. In the 1973–78 period it uses an increase in GNP of 3.0 percent each year. In contrast, my method of estimation allows irregular and abrupt changes. The movement of my potential national income retains all changes in actual national income except those that are due to fluctuations in the ratio of labor at work to available labor, or to fluctuations in the intensity with which employed inputs are used as a result of fluctuations in demand. From 1973 to 1976 changes in my potential national income are far more irregular than is usual, and they include an actual decline in 1975.

The CEA's 3 percent growth rate for GNP seems to be based on consideration of the 1973–78 period as a whole and the CEA's expectations for the years immediately ahead, but the same rate is also used for 1973–76. It translates into an estimated 2.86 percent for national income. My estimates yield a 1.60 percent national income growth rate for 1973–76, so there is a difference of up to 1.3 percentage points between the rates. If my series were available through 1978, it would show a higher rate for 1973–78 than for 1973–76, so it would differ less from the CEA's series in that period.

The CEA gives only a limited breakdown of its 3.0 percent GNP growth rate, dividing it among "a 2.5 percent annual growth in potential employment, a 0.5 percent per year decline in annual hours per employee, and a 1 percent per year growth in productivity."[23] My estimates for the whole economy, computed from table 2-1, show 1973–76 growth rates of 2.4 percent for potential employment and −0.8 percent for average potential hours; together they explain 0.4 percent of the difference between the 1973–76 growth rates of potential national income. It may be recalled that hours dropped by an unusually large amount in this period, an irregularity that the CEA's procedure cannot capture.

The CEA's estimate that potential GNP per potential hour grew 1.0 percent a year compares with my 1973–76 growth rate of 0.0 percent in

potential national income per potential hour; even after allowance for the difference between GNP and national income, these estimates may be as much as 0.9 percentage points apart. Part of the difference is due to the CEA's basing the rate on a longer time period than 1973–76. One may surmise that two other factors are among those responsible for the CEA's higher rate. First, the CEA may have inferred the rate from an actual rather than a potential series for recent years without taking into account that changes in the distribution of labor by age, sex, and education and changes in capital input per worker or per hour were much more favorable on an actual than on a potential basis from 1973 to either 1976 or 1978.[24] Alternatively, the CEA may not consider that there was such a difference, either because of some conceptual disagreement—for example, the CEA has not specified its concept of potential capital stock with respect to cyclical movements in it—or disagreement about the facts. Second, on the basis of experience during the period it considered, 1.0 percent is a bit generous even for actual output per hour. The Bureau of Labor Statistics series for actual GNP per hour in the whole economy, on which the CEA relies, grew 0.85 percent a year in 1973–76 and 0.88 percent in 1973–78.[25] The CEA was expecting the same change in 1979 as in 1978 and a 1.1 percent increase in 1980.[26] If the CEA's anticipations are realized, then the actual growth rate in this series over the whole seven-year period from 1973 to 1980 will be 0.84 percent.[27]

The thrust of the 1979 CEA report is similar to mine despite differences in detail. Under the heading, "The Productivity Slowdown," the CEA reported:

Productivity growth in 1978 showed a very marked slowdown from accustomed rates, adding substantially to inflationary pressures and raising fundamental concerns about underlying trends. . . . The slow productivity growth over the past 2 years adds to the accumulating evidence that the underlying trend in productivity growth since 1973 has been substantially lower than in earlier periods. Between 1948 and 1965, productivity growth in the private nonfarm sector averaged 2.6 per-

23. *Economic Report of the President, January 1979*, p. 74.

24. According to my series, the 1973–76 growth rate of potential output per hour was 0.55 percentage points below that of actual output per hour for these and other reasons, as already explained.

25. Computed from indexes provided by the Bureau of Labor Statistics, January 30, 1979.

26. *Economic Report of the President, January 1979*, pp. 93, 109.

27. The CEA projects annual increases of 2.0 percent by 1982; ibid., p. 109.

cent per year. In 1965–73 this rate declined to 2.0 percent. Since 1973, private nonfarm productivity growth has averaged less than 1 percent per year. . . .[28]

The CEA rightly stresses the profoundly adverse impact of low productivity growth on living standards, the intensity of conflicts over the division of national income, the adequacy of resources available for government programs, and inflation. Because of its effect on inflation, low productivity also enlarges the shortfall of actual below potential output and employment that prudence demands be maintained.

28. Ibid., p. 67.

-»>×«<-

CHAPTER NINE

The Unexplained Portion of the Decline in Output per Unit of Input

-»>×«<-

The contribution of advances in knowledge and miscellaneous determinants to growth rates in nonresidential business, as measured by the residual series, fell from 1.4 percent a year in the 1948–73 period to −0.8 percent a year in the 1973–76 period. Annual estimates pinpoint the decline in 1974 and 1975. From 1973 to 1975 the residual dropped by a total of 4.2 percent, whereas it would have increased by 2.8 percent if the 1948–73 rate had continued. After a gain in 1976 that was moderately above average, but probably swollen by calendar effects, the performance of the residual again was poor in 1977 and 1978 according to preliminary indications. There is no doubt that the contribution over the whole 1973–78 period was far below that in 1948–73, even though the exact amount after 1976 has not been estimated.

That I do not know why the record suddenly turned so bad after 1973 must be obvious, because the effects of all output determinants that I could measure continuously are excluded from the residual. Perhaps it would be wisest to end with this statement, but I find that to do so leads to insistent questions about what *might* have been responsible and to requests for comments on specific suggestions. This chapter takes up these matters.

One general point needs stressing. According to my estimates there is no unexplained drop in productivity change until 1974. I consider this timing

an important clue in any attempt to unravel the mystery surrounding the retardation. But nearly all the possible reasons advanced for a productivity slowdown would be much more likely to take effect gradually than to cause a sudden reversal. This counts heavily against them. Nevertheless, I have included such suggestions in the following discussion. Most were proposed by observers who, if they had in mind any specific data at all, were trying to explain the slackening in growth that began about 1967 in the Bureau of Labor Statistics series for output per hour.

Of course, "coming events cast their shadows before," and the onset of fundamental changes that were to lead to decline may have been discernible in advance of the actual event. But the unexplained decline itself does not appear until 1974.

Determinants of output for which I have provided specific estimates fully accounted for the slackening of productivity growth until 1974. These determinants do not affect the residual series for the contribution of advances in knowledge and miscellaneous determinants and will not be taken up again. Examples are the change in age-sex composition, the growth in capital, and the shift of labor from farming. From the almost limitless list of possible influences on the residual series, I have selected suggestions that have been or may be seriously suggested as important causes of productivity slowdown. Inevitably there is some overlapping among the suggestions examined.

Suggestions Affecting Advances in Knowledge

The first part of this chapter is concerned with four suggested explanations that pertain to advances in knowledge. The next two sections are concerned with thirteen suggested explanations relating to miscellaneous output determinants.

Curtailment of Expenditures on Research and Development

Secretary of Commerce Juanita Kreps, formerly professor of economics at Duke University, has stated that a "probable source of the slowdown in productivity is the dramatic reduction in expenditures for research and development."[1] John W. Kendrick of George Washington University, an

---

1. "Tax Policy and the Supply Side," address before the American Economic Association and the American Finance Association in Chicago, August 29, 1978. The secretary also pointed to regulatory costs.

expert in productivity analysis, has repeatedly called attention to the decline in R&D. The conclusions of a two-day meeting held by the American Association for the Advancement of Science were summarized in the *Washington Post* as follows: "The United States is losing its competitive edge in technology because American industry is spending less on research and because the Federal government withdrew much of its support for industrial research at the ends of the Apollo space program and the Vietnam War."[2]

Expenditures for organized R&D in the United States have been much larger in the postwar period than ever before, and within the period, expenditures rose rapidly until the mid-1960s. How one describes their subsequent behavior depends on the series he chooses to emphasize.

If expressed as a percentage of gross national product, total R&D expenditures rose from 0.95 percent in 1955 to a peak of 2.97 percent in 1964, then slipped gradually to 2.27 percent in 1976 and 1977. The drop was mainly in expenditures financed by the federal government, largely for defense and space programs whose connection with productivity advance is slight. Expenditures financed by other sources (mostly industry but including universities and nonprofit organizations) continued to climb throughout the 1960s, rising from 0.99 percent of GNP in 1963 and 1964 to 1.15 percent in 1969 and 1970. They then slipped, but only to 1.07 percent, in 1972 and 1973 before recovering to 1.11–1.13 percent every year from 1974 through 1977.[3] I have quoted percentages of GNP because this practice is widespread, but its rationale is not clear. Just because the size of the economy is, say, twice as big, does it take twice as much R&D to obtain the same annual productivity gain? Doubtless it would take twice as much R&D if an economy doubled its size by producing twice as many products, each with a unique technology, and no more of any one product. But why should more R&D be needed if growth occurs by expanding the average output of products rather than their number? An invention that cuts 1 percent from the production cost of 5 million automobiles should do as much for 10 million.

Total R&D expenditures themselves, when expressed in constant (1972) dollars, rose rapidly until 1966, when they reached $28.5 billion, then less rapidly until 1968, when they peaked at $29.8 billion.[4] Expenditures in all years from 1969 through 1976 were in the range of $27.7 billion to $29.6 billion, so that in the whole 1966–76 period they were essentially flat. In 1977, constant-dollar expenditures reached a record $30.2 billion. Within the total, R&D that was financed by industry increased rapidly until 1969, when it reached $11.5 billion, then more slowly to $13.2 billion in 1976 and $13.9 billion in 1977. Its annual growth rate was 6.5 percent in 1960–69 and 2.0 percent in 1969–76.[5] R&D financed by universities (including state and local governments) and nonprofit organizations increased steadily to $1.1 billion in 1976. R&D financed by the federal government jumped rapidly to $17.3 billion in 1964, peaked at $18.2 billion in 1967, fell to $14.4 billion in 1974, and recovered to $14.6 billion in 1976 and $15.2 billion in 1977.[6]

The number of scientists and engineers employed in R&D, computed on a full-time equivalent basis, peaked at 558,000 in 1969, fell 7 percent to 521,000 in 1973, and recovered to 550,000 in 1976 and a record 571,000 in 1977. The pattern in industry was similar: a drop from a peak of 386,000 in 1969 to 353,000 in 1972, then a recovery to 372,000 in 1976 and to 390,000 in 1977. The industry figure includes personnel employed in business who are engaged in federally funded research, including defense and space.[7]

Kendrick constructed a series for the "stock" of knowledge acquired from all components of domestic organized R&D by cumulating past expenditures and applying an obsolescence rate. This series, measured in constant prices, increased at annual rates of 9.6 percent a year from 1948 to

---

2. Thomas O'Toole, *Washington Post*, June 21, 1978. The experts also referred to increased government regulation and an outdated patent policy.

3. National Science Board, National Science Foundation, *Science Indicators, 1976* (Government Printing Office, 1977), p. 207, and unpublished current and revised data. In this terminology the whole business sector is covered by the word "industry."

4. The conversion of R&D expenditures to a constant price basis is subject to considerable possible error. The National Science Foundation, whose data I cite, uses the GNP implicit deflator.

5. Private R&D expenditures for pollution abatement, which appear mainly in the industry total, were an unchanging $0.5 billion a year from 1972, the first year for which estimates are available, through 1976. Current-dollar data are from *Survey of Current Business*, vol. 58 (February 1978), p. 12. They were deflated by the GNP implicit deflator.

6. National Science Board, *Science Indicators, 1976*, p. 207, and unpublished current and revised data. Values in 1972 prices are current dollar values divided by the GNP implicit deflator.

7. Ibid., p. 206, and unpublished current and revised data.

1966 and 5.2 percent from 1966 to 1973, when it ends.[8]

Like the United States, other advanced countries sharply increased R&D spending, both in absolute terms and as a percentage of GNP, until about 1965. During the middle and late 1960s total R&D spending began to increase less than GNP not only in the United States but also in the United Kingdom, France, and Canada, and after 1970 in West Germany. In Japan R&D spending continued to increase as a percentage of GNP but more slowly than before.[9] The absolute amount of foreign R&D spending measured in constant prices increased throughout the period.

To consider the impact of changes in R&D on output per unit of input, it is first necessary to recall that only certain types of advances in knowledge raise output per unit of input as it is actually measured, namely, those that allow the same amount of measured output to be obtained with less input. Advances that do so are those that reduce the unit cost of final products that are already in existence.

Advances leading to the introduction of new products for final sale from the business sector (primarily to households and government) do not have this effect, no matter whether the new products are color television sets, space rockets, atomic-powered aircraft carriers, tastier biscuits, or microwave ovens for household use. After their introduction, total measured product will be the same as if the labor, capital, and land devoted to their production were used instead to produce previously existing products. When products with new features—for example, refrigerators with automatic ice makers and stoves with self-cleaning ovens—are introduced, they qualify as new products in this formulation. Thus R&D that is directed toward new final products for civilian or military use, even if highly successful in meeting its objectives, does not contribute to the growth of measured output per unit of input except insofar as it may have some incidental offshoots that cut the costs of existing final products. Nearly all federally financed R&D is in this category and so is the larger part of industry-financed R&D. Only R&D that is directed either toward new processes, which may be roughly identified with research to reduce a firm's own costs, or toward new *intermediate* products and capital goods has an objective that, if achieved, raises measured output per unit of input.[10]

Organized R&D in the United States is only one of many points of origin for advances in knowledge that raise output per unit of input, but fortunately it is one (the only one) for which a separate estimate of the contribution to growth has been hazarded. In 1961 I compounded a series of plausible assumptions and guessed that one-sixth of the total contribution of advances in knowledge was the contribution of domestic R&D.[11] A more recent and somewhat more solidly based attempt to estimate this contribution was made by Zvi Griliches of Harvard University.[12] Griliches estimated that R&D was contributing no more than 0.3 percentage points to the growth rate of private domestic GNP as of 1966 and probably considerably less; his maximum estimate equals less than one-fourth of my estimate of the contribution being made by advances in knowledge at that time.[13]

The main elements in these and similar calculations are the value of R&D expenditures for projects that, if successful, can be expected to raise output per unit of input; the social rate of return on such projects; and sometimes the rate of obsolescence on knowledge gained from previous R&D.[14] The value of pertinent R&D expenditures is too small to yield Griliches a contribution above 0.3 points even though his estimate of them is deliberately generous and the social rate of return is high.

The large gap between estimates of the contributions of advances in knowledge and of R&D expenditures does not imply that the estimates are inconsistent. As already stressed, organized R&D

8. John W. Kendrick, *The Formation and Stocks of Total Capital* (New York: National Bureau of Economic Research, 1976); and idem, "Total Investment and Productivity Developments," paper prepared for the Joint Session of the American Finance Association and the American Economic Association, New York, December 30, 1977.

9. National Science Board, *Science Indicators, 1976,* pp. 5, 184.

10. I have discussed this important aspect of output measurement more extensively in earlier books. See especially *Sources of Growth*, pp. 155–57 and 231–46.

11. Ibid., pp. 239–46.

12. "Research Expenditures and Growth Accounting," in B. R. Williams, ed., *Science and Technology in Economic Growth* (New York: Halsted Press for the International Economic Association, 1973).

13. He also estimated that if R&D were capitalized instead of expensed, the growth rate of output and the contribution of R&D would both be 0.2 percentage points higher.

14. The largest sample of cases for rates of return has been built up by Edwin Mansfield of the University of Pennsylvania and his associates. See Edwin Mansfield and others, "Social and Private Rates of Return from Industrial Innovations," *Quarterly Journal of Economics,* vol. 91 (May 1977), pp. 221–40. See also Edwin Mansfield, "Research and Development, Productivity Change, and Public Policy," in *Relationships between R&D and Economic Growth/ Productivity* (National Science Foundation, November 9, 1977).

conducted in the United States is only one source of advances in knowledge. Managerial and organizational knowledge of how to produce at low cost stems from sources that are unrelated to expenditures measured in series for R&D. The observation and ingenuity of persons engaged in production and distribution contribute new technological knowledge. So do individual inventors. All types of knowledge originate in all countries, not only the United States.

If R&D contributed no more than 0.3 percentage points to the growth rate in the mid-sixties, retardation of such expenditures could have contributed little, if anything, to the decline of productivity growth even if the percentage of GNP spent on R&D of all types were the relevant series and the period from 1964 peak to 1976 trough were the relevant time span. The drop in the percentage was about one-fourth, so if the 0.3 percentage points contribution of R&D to the growth rate of output were reduced proportionally, it would decline by less than 0.1 percentage points. Expenditures financed from private sources, measured in constant prices, are a more pertinent series for R&D. Since this series did not decline at all, there is no assurance that R&D spending contributed anything to the decline in productivity growth. Griliches, using a somewhat broader series for R&D spending relevant to productivity growth, suggested that the change in R&D spending from the 1966 rate to the 1970 rate might reduce its contribution by 0.1 percentage points, with the effect perhaps delayed until the mid-1970s. The range from 0.0 to −0.1 percentage points covers the probable change in the contribution.

Kendrick estimated higher contributions from organized R&D than did Griliches or I: the percentage point contributions were 0.85 in 1948–66 and 0.71 in 1966–73.[15] The high estimates stem from counting in the "stock" all R&D performed in the business sector, including all that is devoted to new and improved products and all that is financed by the federal government. As justifications, Kendrick mentions spin-offs and the prevalence of learning curves for all new products, regardless of their buyers, but I do not believe the procedure is tenable.[16] Even so, Kendrick obtains

a reduction in the contribution only slightly in excess of 0.1 percentage points during the period he covered.

Roger E. Brinner of Data Resources, Inc., has, so far as I am aware, the only estimates that show a much larger decline.[17] His estimate of the contribution of R&D falls by 0.2 percentage points from the 1960–65 period to the 1965–70 period, and then an additional 0.2 percentage points from the 1965–70 period to the 1970–75 period, when he puts the contribution at only 0.05 percentage points.[18] This unusual set of results apparently stems from the combination of two features of his estimates. First, like Kendrick (whose stock series is Brinner's starting point), Brinner counts government-financed R&D, so he has gross additions to knowledge from R&D declining. Second, the amount of old knowledge that he eliminates from the stock, presumably because it is rendered obsolete by new knowledge, is related to the stock of knowledge rather than to the amount of new knowledge, so it rises even when new knowledge falls. This procedure would permit R&D to contribute negatively to growth.[19]

To conclude, as I have, that R&D probably is not responsible for much of the productivity re-

15. Kendrick, "Total Investment and Productivity Developments."

16. In "Research Expenditures and Growth Accounting," p. 80, Griliches says that "if one expands the boundaries of the relevant concept of R and D, one should probably adjust the estimated rates of return downward accordingly. . . ." (Kendrick does not do so.) If one adopted

this alternative, he would need to use a higher rate of return in the seventies than in the sixties because the proportion of R&D that is largely irrelevant declined. Kendrick actually uses a lower rate in 1966–73 than in 1948–66, and this contributes to the decline in his estimate of the contribution.

17. I disregard in this book attempts to ascertain the results of R&D spending on the economy as a whole by correlation analysis because results are too tenuous. Problems are described in Zvi Griliches, "Issues in Assessing the Contribution of Research and Development to Productivity Growth," Harvard Institute of Economic Research Discussion Paper 641 (August 1978). For a comprehensive discussion of efforts to arrive at results of R&D see all the papers (by Edwin Mansfield, M. Ishaq Nadiri, Nestor E. Terleckyj, George C. Eads, and John W. Kendrick) in *Relationships between R&D and Economic Growth/Productivity*.

18. Roger Brinner, *Technology, Labor, and Economic Potential* (Lexington, Mass.: Data Resources, Inc., 1978), p. 102.

19. Whether obsolescence should be deducted at all in calculating the contribution of R&D to growth is a question that need not be resolved here, but I shall note that such a deduction seems questionable to me (except when obsolescence results from demand shifts rather than new knowledge). This is because the social rates of return used in such calculations are based on sample studies in which the output obtained when the fruits of an R&D project are available is compared with the output obtainable from the same inputs when the fruits of that project are not available but all other existing knowledge, including any made obsolete by the new knowledge, is available. If R&D expenditures are multiplied by such a net rate of return to obtain the increase in output that they permit, where is the overstatement that the obsolescence deduction is meant to eliminate?

tardation is not to deny that expansion of R&D is a promising way of promoting future productivity growth. Available studies, though limited in scope, indicate that the social rate of return on R&D is high.[20] This, when combined with the inability of firms financing successful R&D to capture more than a fraction of that return for themselves, provides justification for policies to either raise that fraction or increase governmental support.

Decline in Opportunity for Major New Advances

In the postwar period, advances in knowledge and, in consequence, the growth rate have been exceptionally large by past standards. Many have regarded this period as beginning a new era, to be characterized by exponential growth at a high rate for an indefinite time. But it is arguable that in the long sweep of history a slackening of the advance in knowledge might reasonably be anticipated quite apart from any reduction in research, and the postwar growth rate may appear as a temporary bulge.

The postwar jump in productivity is attributed by some to the crest of a wave of new advances in knowledge made possible by science-based technology, the so-called "second industrial revolution." In their view this wave has passed. This view can be based on reasoning such as that of Orio Giarini, who stated that "we are more and more coming to the point where science-based technology, at least in certain sectors, has exploited all the major possibilities made available by the scientific advances of the last century," and that we may have to wait decades for the reservoir to be replenished.[21] Other observers, also envisaging a drop in the contribution of new knowledge, rely on Schumpeter's belief that innovations typically come in waves as an idea spreads and is applied in many fields, and they suppose that we have come to the end of such a wave.

F. M. Scherer of Northwestern University, former director of the Bureau of Economics of the Federal Trade Commission, suggests, though cautiously, that both explanations may be correct (and their effects exacerbated by the slowdown in R&D expenditures and contracting career opportunities

for scientists). To indicate a slackening rate of advance in technological knowledge, he points out that the number of patents issued to domestic corporations peaked in 1971 and declined 20 percent by 1976. Scherer notes that if patents lag three years behind inventions, this would date the invention peak as 1968.[22]

I have no trouble accepting the possibility of declining opportunities for technological advances, but the diversity of the economy should ensure that the resulting retardation of growth would be gradual. The residual shows no sign at all of retarded growth up to 1973. It is not plausible that declining opportunity for new advances could be responsible for much of the sudden drop in the residual from 1973 to 1975.

Decline of Yankee Ingenuity and Deterioration of American Technology

"There is today a pervasive perception that the dynamic vitality of the U.S. economy is faltering. This perception appears to be founded on two concerns: first, that America is not as productive as it used to be; and second, that we are somehow not as inventive either." So reads the box summarizing a 1978 *Washington Post* article, "Something's Happened to Yankee Ingenuity."[23]

Have Americans become less ingenious? To answer this question one would have to isolate possible deterioration in American ingenuity from the possibility, which Giarini regards as a fact, that the remaining problems that would need solving to expand output are more stubborn than those encountered in the recent past.[24] He would also have to disentangle changes in the speed with which Yankee ingenuity solves problems of production and distribution from possible lengthening of lags between solution and implementation as a result of new government regulations and other institutional changes. In fact, the main reason for suspecting a decline in Yankee ingenuity seems to be the retardation of productivity growth, a development for which there are many alternative suggestions. Irwin B. Margiloff, industrial executive and engineer, and Delbert Tesar of the University of Florida

---

20. See citations in note 13.
21. Orio Giarini, "Economics, Vulnerability and the Diminishing Returns of Technology," *The Geneva Papers on Risk and Insurance*, no. 6 (October 1977), p. 10. Dr. Giarini is secretary general of the International Association for Risk and Insurance Economics Research and formerly was a division head of the Battelle Institute of Geneva.

22. F. M. Scherer, "Technological Maturity and Waning Economic Growth," *Arts and Sciences* (Northwestern University, Fall 1978), pp. 7–11. The accuracy of patents as an index of inventions, it should be noted, has been debated for many years.
23. Bradley Graham, *Washington Post,* September 3, 1978.
24. Giarini, "Economics, Vulnerability and the Diminishing Returns of Technology," p. 18.

believe long-run deterioration of American technology is responsible for poor productivity performance, but the deterioration they have in mind set in much too early to explain the recent productivity slowdown.[25]

Increased Lag in the Application of Knowledge Due to the Aging of Capital

The "best" practice possible with the knowledge available at any given time may be distinguished from the average practice actually in use. Translating this distinction into a classification suitable for growth analysis, one may distinguish in principle between the contribution made possible by advances in knowledge as such and the contribution (positive or negative) that may be made by a change in the lag of average practice behind the best known.

The residual series under discussion, insofar as

it measures the contribution of advances in knowledge, is an estimate of the effects of incorporating new knowledge into the productive process. It therefore includes the effect of changes in the "lag." It is widely suggested that the lag has increased and that this is a reason for the poor performance of productivity.

The most common basis for this belief is that fixed capital formation has declined. This is thought to be germane because it affects the average age of structures and equipment, the carriers of much new technology. Many observers think this was a very important factor. But in chapter 4, I showed that even if the effect on output per unit of input were that which the assumptions of an extreme vintage model would imply, changes in the average age of capital could have reduced the growth rate of the residual by less than 0.2 percentage points from the 1948–73 period to the 1973–76 period. I also explained why the actual effect was far less.

A change in the average age of capital is not the only possible reason to suspect a change in the lag in the application of knowledge. In particular, government regulations may delay or prevent remunerative projects using new technology, a possibility I discuss in the context of government regulation.

Suggested Effects of Government Regulation and Taxation

A variety of explanations for the retardation of output per unit of input would affect miscellaneous determinants. These are often overlapping, and they could be classified and grouped in alternative ways. In this part of the chapter I consider suggested effects of government regulation and taxation. The various ways in which government may have reduced output per unit of input are examined here under seven headings.[26]

Diversion of Input to Comply with Government Regulation, Except Pollution and Safety

The most direct way that government regulation affects measured output per unit of input is by requiring business to divert labor, capital, and land from production of measured output to tasks required to comply with regulations. Under this heading I shall discuss diversion of input other than that

---

25. Margiloff says that a decline in the public's expectation of technological innovation has led society to seek to meet problems by turning to financial solutions (pouring in money) and to improvements in management technique. Technology, he laments, has been left to set its own goals without guidance from the public, with adverse effects on productivity. He argues that it is possible to identify desired rates of change of productivity, particularly in manufacturing and construction, and that a suitable structure of recognition for achievements in these directions would result in having professionals strive to meet these needs, rather than less socially important ones that often enjoy more public and professional acclaim. He contrasts the great advances in the art of construction during the nineteenth century with their absence in the twentieth. He points to a lessened attraction of engineering for the brightest young people, relative to the sciences. He regrets the absence of awards for technology comparable to the Nobel prizes for science and reports that the American Institute of the City of New York "was founded to spur the development of what we now call civilian technology and did so for about a hundred years." About fifty years ago the institute dropped activities that related to technology and began to sponsor the high school science fairs, no longer participating "in spurring or rewarding in any way the development of technology, which was its original function." Other organizations acted in much the same way. But it seems clear that the developments Margiloff describes are very long run and would not have produced a sudden recent change in productivity. (Irwin B. Margiloff, "When Technology Falters," address to the 142nd Annual Meeting of the American Institute of the City of New York, February 4, 1970, and correspondence with the author.)

Tesar reports that companies had hired expert designers from Central Europe to compensate for American inactivity in machine science during the first half of the twentieth century but that they no longer do so. He states that machine science never enjoyed a significant portion of research funding even in periods of research expansion; the National Science Foundation supported little basic research in mechanical engineering and mechanics. According to Tesar, the weakness of U.S. mechanical technology is especially damaging currently in the field of high-quality consumer products and in light industry. (Delbert Tesar, "Mission Oriented Research for Light Machinery," *Science*, vol. 201 [September 8, 1978], pp. 880–87.)

26. Both the Ford and Carter administrations recognized these effects and tried to minimize them when legislation permitted. For a brief discussion of some of the steps taken or recommended, see *Economic Report of the President, January 1979*, pp. 85–91, 94, 130–31, and 162.

imposed by programs for pollution abatement and worker safety and health. The excluded programs deducted an estimated 0.35 percentage points from the 1973–76 growth rate. This was eliminated before arrival at the residual series; the drop of nearly 2.2 percentage points in the growth rate of the residual from 1948–73 to 1973–76 was in addition to effects of these programs. There are, however, other programs that impose similar resource costs, and for which requirements are new or have become more stringent. In the field of consumer protection are regulation of food and drugs by various agencies and regulation by the Consumer Product Safety Commission created in 1972 to protect the buyers of consumer goods from unnecessary hazards.[27] Other regulations, such as the national speed limit, are designed to conserve energy or force utilities and manufacturers to substitute one fuel for another; these began only after 1973. Costs in these and other relatively new areas have not been estimated, but they surely increased relative to national income from 1973 to 1976 and contributed to the decline in the residual. However, Robert W. Crandall, senior fellow of the Brookings Institution, states that of the agencies entrusted with social regulation, the two having the largest impact on business costs are the Occupational Safety and Health Administration (OSHA) and the Environmental Protection Agency (EPA), both covered by my estimates for pollution abatement and worker safety and health.[28] This tends to be supported by the 1977 incremental costs imposed on forty-eight large companies by six programs. Incremental costs to these companies imposed by requirements of Equal Employment Opportunity Commission (EEOC) regulations, the Department of Energy, the Employee Retirement Income Security Act, and consumer protection activities of the Federal Trade Commission, together, were 19 percent as large as the incremental costs imposed by the EPA and the OSHA.[29]

I should be surprised if the increase in the total resource costs, except paperwork costs, of all other

27. The costs of regulation of motor vehicles, aside from recalls, do not affect the residual. See chapter 5.
28. Robert W. Crandall, "Federal Government Initiatives to Reduce the Price Level," in Arthur M. Okun and George L. Perry, eds., *Curing Chronic Inflation* (Brookings Institution, 1978), p. 183.
29. Arthur Andersen and Company, *Costs of Government Regulation Study for the Business Roundtable* (Business Roundtable and Arthur Andersen and Co., 1979). The concept of incremental costs differs from mine in the case of capital costs; capital outlays are counted instead of the sum of depreciation and the net opportunity cost of invested capital.

regulatory programs together affected the change in output per unit of input as much from 1973 to 1976 as the two for which I made estimates. But it is also likely that these costs have been rising sharply.

Government-Imposed Paperwork

Filing reports, making and preserving records, and compiling data in order to meet government requirements also absorb resources that could otherwise be used to produce measured output. Most of these costs are associated with tax collection or with regulatory activities—for example, railroad rate or pension fund regulation—that do not otherwise require diversion of an appreciable amount of input from the production of measured output.

The Commission on Federal Paperwork estimated that paperwork necessary to meet the requirements of the federal government cost American business $25 billion to $32 billion in 1976.[30] This is 2.4 to 3.1 percent of 1976 nonresidential business national income. The requirements of state and local governments may have raised the percentage by one-fourth to one-half, bringing it into the 3.0–4.6 percent range.[31]

Estimates of the total hours required to meet federal reporting requirements, assembled from agency reports by the Office of Management and Budget (OMB), suggest that business reports to the federal government required perhaps 530 million hours a year as of January 1977.[32] This is only 0.2 percent

30. See U.S. Commission on Federal Paperwork, *A Report of the Commission on Federal Paperwork, no. 6: Final Summary Report* (GPO, 1977), pp. 5, 66. The estimate, the sum of estimates for small and large firms, is based on small samples. Though crude, it is apparently the best available. Inclusion of an additional $354 million estimated to be spent by farms (p. 64) would not change the rounded aggregate.
31. A report by Peat, Marwick, Mitchell and Co., commissioned by the Office of Management and Budget, indicated that one-third of the government paperwork burden on small businessmen comes from state and local governments. A survey of small Wisconsin foundries found that 21 percent of costs allocated by level of government were for state and local governments and 79 percent for the federal government; the amount allocated excludes 34 percent of cost that was for consultants to ensure compliance and not divided by level of government. (*Efforts to Reduce Federal Paperwork,* Hearing before the Subcommittee on Oversight of the Senate Committee on Government Operations, 94 Cong. 1 sess. [GPO, 1976], pp. 27, 53.)
32. This is a rough estimate that I derived from *Paperwork and Red Tape: New Perspectives—New Directions,* A Report to the President and the Congress from the Office of Management and Budget (GPO, 1978). The page references in the description that follows refer to that report. An estimate of 465 million hours as of March 31, 1977, was obtained as the sum of the following components: one-fourth, including farms (p. 15), of 126 million hours (p. 34) to complete forms for departments and agencies subject to

of total hours worked in nonresidential business in 1976 and thus suggests a much smaller paperwork burden than do the dollar estimates; it seems, in fact, incredibly small.[33]

Whether the higher or lower percentages for the level of the paperwork burden are accepted, changes in the burden cannot have increased enough to depress productivity significantly from 1973 to 1976 if the OMB's percentage distribution of the man-hour estimates is anywhere near correct. OMB analyses indicate that major changes in the burden are the result of changes in programs.[34] Tax forms account for perhaps four-fifths of all the hours and there were no major changes in the tax area; all the principal tax forms go back to at least

1963.[35] The number of public use reports subject to OMB review, which excludes tax forms, peaked in 1944, 1952, and 1973 because of economic controls (wage and price controls in all three periods and, in the first two, production and resource allocation regulations as well). Statistical series for the number of such reports were disrupted after 1973 as responsibility for reviewing reports for regulatory commissions and certain other agencies was transferred from the OMB to the General Accounting Office. But it is known that elimination of wage and price controls had reduced reporting considerably by 1976. Although new types of government regulation created new paperwork requirements, the OMB estimates that the total hours outside the tax area nevertheless declined from 1973 to 1976.[36]

Thus the evidence indicates that paperwork can be eliminated as a significant source of productivity decline from 1973 to 1976, although it may have been a factor—but not a major one—if one goes back to 1966. The general impression of the burden of paperwork may be exaggerated because, in Herbert Kaufman's phrase, red tape is universally an "object of loathing."[37]

Regulation and Taxation: Diversion of Executive Attention

The profitability of a business is now greatly affected by the way it responds to rapid changes in government action, not only with respect to regulation but also to provisions in the tax laws that discriminate among different types of income and different business costs. Under these conditions it is not surprising that top management and other business people of great talent devote more and more of their time to the firm's interaction with government and correspondingly less time to its interaction with competitors, customers, and suppliers, and to its internal operation. This can hardly fail to impair efficiency and productivity in the ordinary sense of these words.

A burgeoning of regulation during the past decade has affected practically all the domestic and foreign activities of businesses in every indus-

OMB review; 95 percent (assumed) of 237 million hours (p. 14) for Internal Revenue Service (IRS) forms W-2 (wage and tax statements for employees), 941 (employers' federal tax return for employees), and 1099 (recipients of interest and dividends); one-tenth (assumed) of 149 million hours (p. 14) for IRS form 1040 (individual income tax long form); none of 33 million hours (p. 14) for IRS form 1040A (individual income tax short form); three-fourths (assumed) of 184 million hours (pp. 14, 34) for other forms (including the corporate income tax) that are required by the IRS and other agencies that are exempt from review of forms; and all of 43 million hours (p. 34) for forms for independent regulatory commissions and agencies subject to General Accounting Office review.

Total hours per year required of all respondents fell from 870 million as of January 31, 1977, to 785 million as of March 31, 1978 (p. 34). If hours needed for business reports changed in the same proportion, their number was 530 million as of January 31, 1977.

33. In 1965 the Subcommittee on Census and Government Statistics of the Committee on Post Office and Civil Service of the House of Representatives concluded that "the wide disparity between agency estimates for minimum time required to complete a report and respondents' estimates for the same report for the most part casts serious doubts on the realism of the agency estimates. . . . the subcommittee can only conclude that not only are some agencies completely unrealistic concerning the cost to the public of their paperwork undertakings but, also, that—ostrich-like—they would prefer not to know such costs." (*The Federal Paperwork Jungle: A Report on the Paperwork Requirements Placed upon Business, Industry, and the Public by the Federal Departments and Agencies*, H. Rept. 52, 89 Cong. 1 sess. [GPO, 1965], pp. 45–46.) Several instances of verified understatement are cited in Commission on Federal Paperwork, "Study of Federal Paperwork Impact on Small and Large Businesses" (July 1977), pp. 35, 36, 40.

34. Testimony of Robert H. Marik, Associate Director of the Office of Management and Budget, in *Hearings on HR 16424 to Establish a Commission on Federal Paperwork*, Hearings before the House Committee on Government Operations, 93 Cong. 2 sess. (GPO, 1974), pp. 34–36. Marik gave a breakdown by source of the increase of 50 percent that occurred between December 1967 and June 1974 in the reporting burden on American business caused by required forms other than tax forms. Occupational safety and health programs, expanded social security (especially medicare and medicaid), manpower programs, aircraft and airport regulations, and equal employment opportunity led the list.

35. This fraction is based on the OMB data cited in note 32. Estimates from the Commission on Federal Paperwork, "Study of Federal Paperwork Impact on Small and Large Businesses," imply a smaller fraction, since they show IRS forms to be responsible for 75 percent of the costs to small business (tables 6 and I-3) and apparently much less for large business (p. 46). (Small business costs are about three-fifths of the estimated total.)

36. *Paperwork and Red Tape*, p. 30.

37. Herbert Kaufman, *Red Tape: Its Origins, Uses, and Abuses* (Brookings Institution, 1977), p. 4.

try, so much so that Senator Lloyd Bentsen, Chairman of the Joint Economic Committee's Subcommittee on Economic Growth and Stabilization, calls federal regulation "America's number one growth industry."[38] Failure to learn of and conform to regulations can have serious legal consequences, including criminal penalties.[39] Failure to find the cheapest way to conform can be expensive. Failure to learn of proposals for new laws or regulations and to participate in hearings and use other channels to help shape their final form can bring permanently higher costs or loss of markets. So can failure to foresee changes in laws and regulations and to take timely action in advance to minimize losses or maximize gains from the change.[40]

Not only laws and regulations actually proposed or made effective are pertinent; one must guess at what may be proposed in the future. In the words of Irwin L. Kellner, vice-president and economist of Manufacturers Hanover Trust, not only have laws, rules, regulations, and regulatory agencies leaped upward in number, but they "have become increasingly unpredictable of late. Unlike economic, technological, or other uncertainties indigenous to the private free enterprise system, political uncertainties tend to be sudden, swift, and unprecedented."[41] Now that price and wage controls have been introduced once in peacetime, business must (and does) consider the possibility that such controls will be repeated and must position itself appropriately. The spring and summer 1978 quarterly surveys of businessmen conducted by the U.S. Chamber of Commerce showed a majority anticipated mandatory wage and price controls

within two years. In the same year regulation displaced taxation as the greatest concern of respondents to the chamber's surveys.

Glen McLaughlin, vice-president for finance of Four Phase Systems, Inc., of Cupertino, California, says

corporations have been burdened with regulatory excess to the point of stifling normal improvement in efficiencies. Business leaders can and will continue to assume additional taxes and regulations; however, as each new tax and each new regulation is imposed, another layer of incentive to perform is removed and otherwise creative efforts are diverted to nonproductive, but lucrative, jobs of avoiding taxes and doing battle with bureaucrats. This is a tremendous waste of national resources; however, it is occurring at an accelerating rate.[42]

George C. Eads of the Rand Corporation suggests that the change in emphasis among the activities that are required for a business to prosper must also affect the type of person who will emerge to manage firms. Presumably more emphasis will be placed on knowledge of the law, the legislative process, and public relations and less on production, sales, and internal management.[43]

Concern about government regulation is not confined to top management. Professor Murray L. Weidenbaum of St. Louis University points out that

virtually every major department of the typical industrial corporation . . . has one or more counterparts in a federal agency that controls or strongly influences its internal decision making: OSHA for "production"; the Consumer Product Safety Commission for "marketing"; several agencies concerned with safety and efficiency rather than sales promotion for "advertising"; EEOC for "personnel"; IRS, SEC [Securities and Exchange Commission], and the credit agencies for "finance"; EPA for "research and development"; and so on.[44]

Government Regulation: Delay of New Projects

Government regulatory requirements for applications, permits, and reports give rise to delays between first consideration and completion of projects, and the spread of regulation has undoubtedly lengthened delays substantially in recent

38. *Notes from the Joint Economic Committee,* vol. 4 (May 16, 1978).

39. Francis A. Allen of the University of Michigan School of Law states that "criminal provisions are routinely included in most pieces of regulatory legislation" and that "there are few, if any, regulatory areas of importance in which the possibility of criminal punishment is lacking." *Regulation by Indictment: The Criminal Law as an Instrument of Economic Control,* William K. McInally Memorial Lecture, Graduate School of Business Administration, the University of Michigan (1978), p. 9.

40. The number of proposed and final actions that affected the iron and steel industry and that were published in the *Federal Register* in a two-year period (1974 and 1975) came to 19,464. They consisted of 333 proposed new agency regulations, 5,390 proposed amendments to existing regulations, 581 final agency regulations, and 13,160 final amendments to existing regulations. Many of these also affected many or most other industries. Data from Council on Wage and Price Stability, "Catalog of Federal Regulations Affecting the Iron and Steel Industry," in Commission on Federal Paperwork, "Study of Federal Paperwork Impact on Small and Large Businesses," p. 15.

41. Manufacturers Hanover Trust, *Business Report,* Autumn 1977, p. 2.

42. McLaughlin rates the regulatory burden second, after the tax legislation of 1969 and subsequent years (relating to capital gains taxes and qualified stock options), as a source of productivity slowdown. The quotation is from a letter to the author, dated March 7, 1978.

43. George C. Eads, "Achieving 'Appropriate' Levels of Investment in Technological Change: What Have We Learned?" in *Relationships Between R&D and Economic Growth/Productivity* (National Science Foundation, November 9, 1977).

44. Murray L. Weidenbaum, *Government-Mandated Price Increases* (American Enterprise Institute for Public Policy Research, 1975), p. 100.

years.[45] The difficulty of coordinating several permits from different agencies may result in long delays or even abandonment of projects.[46] The time span between administrative receipt of an application and a decision is often long, and delays are greatly extended by judicial appeals. Delays resulting from government regulation not only slow the introduction of new ideas and new technology but also reduce the flexibility of firms in dealing with recurrent changes in production and marketing conditions.

Increased delays stemming from increased regulation unquestionably contributed to the recent retardation of productivity growth. No estimate is available of the amount by which it did so.

Regulation and Taxation: Misallocation of Resources[47]

Efficiency is greatest when individuals and jobs are properly matched (the round pegs are in the round holes) and when total input is allocated among uses in such a way as to maximize output. Government regulations and various provisions of the tax code affect resource allocation, and hence output, in many ways.

Because of privacy legislation, which denies confidentiality to appraisals of students, government employees, and other groups, prospective employers must find references of less value. Civil rights legislation has added new criteria for hiring, promotion, and release of workers that may affect resource allocation positively in the long run yet in the short run be adverse to the selection of the best person for each job. It also adds to costs of personnel management.[48]

45. Weidenbaum believes there has been not only a spread of regulation but also a lengthening of "regulatory lag" for old types of regulation. (Murray L. Weidenbaum, *The Costs of Government Regulation of Business,* A Study Prepared for the Use of the Subcommittee on Economic Growth and Stabilization of the Joint Economic Committee [GPO, 1978], p. 15.)

46. John K. Evans, president of the Hampton Roads Energy Company, planned to build a $500 million oil refinery in Hampton Roads. He was unable to obtain any decision concerning a permit (the last he needed) from the Corps of Engineers for more than three years after filing an environmental impact statement, and his project was placed in jeopardy because his marine resources and air permits were both about to expire. (Statement submitted to the Energy and Power Subcommittee of the House Committee on Interstate and Foreign Commerce; letter to the Department of Energy on June 14, 1978; and letter to the author dated June 21, 1978.)

47. See also the section headed "Capital Gains Provisions of the Revenue Act of 1969."

48. See Carol J. Loomis, "A.T.&T. in the Throes of Equal Employment," *Fortune,* January 15, 1979, pp. 44–57, for an examination of telephone industry experience under a consent decree.

At the macro level the discriminatory effects of the investment tax credit have already been described (chapter 4); the tax code is packed with other provisions that discriminate among types of expenditures and kinds of activity. New government regulations, like old ones, contain provisions to protect special interests. Other provisions serve only to appeal to uninformed prejudices; an example is congressional prohibition of the exportation of surplus Alaskan oil from the West Coast to Japan, and the offsetting importation of oil on the Atlantic and Gulf Coasts.

Perhaps the aspect of regulation most adverse to efficient resource allocation is increased uncertainty. I do not refer now to the effect this uncertainty is sometimes said to have on the *amount* of investment; rather, I am concerned here with its effect on *composition.* The enormous change in the scope of regulation is sometimes said to have placed nearly all business in the category of regulated industries. When an investment decision must be made, the way that regulations will be applied in the specific instance and the length of time that will be required to secure all necessary regulatory decisions so that a project may proceed are important but unknown determinants of cost. Moreover, the difficulties of deciding the characteristics of a project or of determining the future benefits from it are accentuated by the prospect that regulatory conditions may change once a facility is in use, altering the optimal combination of inputs and conceivably even banning the sale of products. It is a reasonable inference that the allocation of the capital stock among types and uses must depart further from the optimal allocation at any given time than it would if regulations were less pervasive, changing, and uncertain in application. The wedge introduced by regulation between costs and benefits that are anticipated and those that are realized probably is increasingly widened as the planned life of investment lengthens, so regulation probably moves the distribution of investment toward shorter-lived assets, as is frequently asserted. But this is only a detail within the general picture.

The Effects of High Tax Rates on Incentives and Efficiency

Beryl W. Sprinkel, economist and executive vice-president of the Harris Trust and Savings Bank, believes that

the reason for the poor performance of our economy [that is, significantly deteriorating productivity trends in the past dozen years, accompanied by accelerating inflation] has been the growing burden of government.

The tax burden at all levels of government in 1966 was 33 percent of national income. This past fiscal year the tax burden rose to a record 39.2 percent of national income. Although voters perceive taxes paid as the cost of government, the real economic cost is represented by the share of national income devoted to government outlays. This figure rose from 34 percent of national income in fiscal 1966 to 41 percent last year.[49]

One way a large government share might reduce output is by contributing to inflation, which (as explained in a later section) may impair efficiency. It was inflation that Colin Clark, the Australian author of *The Conditions of Economic Progress,* forecast as the disastrous result if government expenditures exceeded 25 percent of national income.[50] Subsequently others have forecast various dire consequences, including impaired growth, at some higher percentage. The assertion that high taxes diminish incentives to work and to save is commonplace.

Herbert Stein, professor of economics at the University of Virginia and former chairman of the President's Council of Economic Advisers, examined this view, which he described as follows:

The argument that increased government spending, as a share of GNP, slows down the rate of growth of real output runs along familiar lines. The higher taxes needed to finance the higher spending would weaken incentives to work and to invest, and would absorb funds that otherwise would have been saved and invested. If the government borrows to finance its expenditures, that will crowd out private investment. A more recent version of this view is that the absorption of productive resources by the government cuts the supply of resources available to produce investment goods and marketable consumption goods, which will reduce private investment especially, since workers will resist reducing their consumption of marketable goods. Another aspect to be considered is that increased government spending absorbs workers into public employment, where productivity is low and growing slowly if at all, and that this restrains the growth of total output.[51]

If the consequences of large budgets asserted in this argument were confined to a reduction of the labor and capital used in nonresidential business, they would not reduce output per unit of input

in the sector.[52] They would do so only if the effect on labor took the form of people working less hard while at work or refusing promotions.

But Stein in any case finds little support in the American experience for any of the processes he described, whether they would affect output per unit of input or not. In particular, "no stagnation of growth was evident during the period of high and rising government expenditures." Nor is any effect on the private saving rate or much, if any, on employment to be observed. Stein finds that the evidence suggests that the effects of government spending and taxes on economic growth during the period from 1956 to 1973 were "at least uncertain and probably small."[53]

The period after 1973 was one of poor growth and productivity performance but not one in which the government share shot up abruptly. Federal, state, and local government expenditures, which rose from 24.8 percent of GNP in 1956 to 31.0 percent in 1973, went to 33.5 percent in 1976 and 32.5 percent in 1978. The increase from 1973 to 1976 was partly due to the business cycle. Government receipts were 26.1 percent of GNP in 1956, 31.0 percent in 1973, 31.6 percent in 1976, and 32.4 percent in 1978.[54]

I agree with Stein that the general size of government budgets has not had a substantial adverse effect on growth and productivity. This does not necessarily mean, of course, that there would be no such effect from a further increase, such as has recently been experienced in several European countries. In the Netherlands, the three Scandinavian countries, and the United Kingdom, general government expenditure reached 44 to 51 percent of gross domestic product in 1975, compared with 34 percent in the United States.[55]

Capital Gains Provisions of the Revenue Act of 1969

William F. Ballhaus, president of Beckman Instruments, Inc., ascribes the recent slowdown in growth and productivity to the provisions of the Revenue Act of 1969 that affected capital gains.

49. *Tax Reductions—Economists Comments on H.R. 8333 and S. 1860,* prepared for the House Committee on Ways and Means, 95 Cong. 2 sess. (GPO, 1978), p. 85.

50. Colin Clark, "Public Finance and Changes in the Value of Money," *Economic Journal,* vol. 45 (December 1945), pp. 370–89.

51. Herbert Stein, "Spending and Getting," in William Fellner, ed., *Contemporary Economic Problems, 1977* (American Enterprise Institute for Public Policy Research, 1977), p. 74. The "more recent version" to which Stein refers is that developed by Robert Bacon and Walter Eltis with respect to Great Britain. Eltis applies it to the United States and Canada as well. See Walter Eltis, "Are Canada and the United States Following Great Britain?" *New International Politics,* vol. 2 (July 1977).

52. Output per hour would be reduced if investment were impaired.

53. Ibid., pp. 74, 77.

54. These are based on NIPA definitions. Percentages for 1948 and 1973 are from Stein, "Spending and Getting," p. 65. Those for 1976 and 1978 were computed from the *Survey of Current Business,* vol. 58 (July 1978) and vol. 59 (March 1979).

55. Organization for Economic Cooperation and Development, "Public Expenditure Trends" (February 2, 1978), p. 13.

Previously, only half of long-term capital gains (then gains on assets held six months or more) were subject to the federal individual income tax, and the rate on this half was limited to 50 percent, so the top effective marginal rate was 25 percent.[56] The Revenue Act of 1969, effective January 1, 1970, deleted the 50 percent rate ceiling; this raised the effective rate for high-income individuals from 25 percent to 35 percent. For a small number whose income was largely from sources given preferential tax treatment, the effective marginal rate could be higher, as much as 49.1 percent, as the result of a new minimum tax provision of the law or even 52.3 percent for a few individuals with large foreign tax credits. In addition the period for which assets had to be held for gains on them to qualify as long-term rather than short-term gains (which are taxed like ordinary income) was to be increased, but this provision became effective only in 1977.[57]

Ballhaus sees the increased taxation of capital gains as the cause of reduced investment.[58] He also sees it as the cause of reduced spending for research and development.[59] Even if he is correct, these two effects probably contributed little to the slowdown in the *residual*. Less investment reduces capital input, not output per unit of input or the residual, although it does affect output per hour.[60] Less R&D would reduce the residual, but R&D has already

been rejected as a probable cause of very much of the productivity slowdown.

But Ballhaus has a third effect: taxation of capital gains biases the distribution of investment and R&D away from the more risky undertakings. This would be another cause of misallocation of resources that would reduce the residual. It seems inescapable that capital gains taxation has such a tendency, and therefore that higher capital gains taxation increases the tendency. This statement does not rely on an assumption that investors are averse to risks. A $1 million investment certain to repay $1.1 million has the same expected return as a $1 million investment that has nine chances of becoming a total loss and one of repaying $11 million, and the two investments are equally advantageous to society. But if the government shares in gains but not in losses, the safer investment promises the higher return to the investor. Ballhaus assigns a particularly strategic role to individual investors in small companies and states that equity investment in small companies declined after 1969 and almost vanished in 1973–75.

The argument that high capital gains taxation impedes growth became central in 1978 to the case for Congressman William A. Steiger's proposal to restore the situation that existed before the Revenue Act of 1969. The tax bill actually passed in 1978 was not much less favorable than his proposal for any taxpayer and was even more favorable for most. Sixty percent of long-term gains, as against the previous 50 percent, was exempted from income tax and this together with changes in the minimum tax and the enactment of a new "alternative minimum tax" reduced the highest effective marginal tax rate on capital gains to 28 percent. If the 1969 change in capital gains taxation was an obstacle to growth, that obstacle has been removed.

However, the 1969 law raised the tax yield from capital gains at 1978 income levels by less than $1 billion (from $7,544 million to $8,483 million), according to Treasury Department estimates. The small size of the extra tax burden suggests that the misallocation resulting from it, though doubtless present, was not large.

Other Suggestions Affecting Miscellaneous Determinants

In this part of the chapter I consider six additional causes that have been suggested for retardation of the growth rate of productivity and that would affect my residual series. Like suggestions considered in the preceding section, their effects, if any,

---

56. A temporary surtax raised the percentage to 26.875 in 1968 and 27.5 in 1969.

57. Both the old and new laws permitted capital losses to be deducted from capital gains. But only a token amount of capital losses could be deducted against other income (and this small benefit was halved by the 1969 act). Losses exceeding gains in one year could be used to offset gains in a future year. The government paid no interest on a backlog of capital losses waiting to be deducted from future gains. Since there was no negative income tax, the government made no payment to a taxpayer whose cumulated total income (including capital gains and losses) was negative. Consequently the government is said to share in gains but not in losses.

58. John Cobbs, "The Tax that is Killing Investment," *Business Week*, January 16, 1978, p. 14.

59. William F. Ballhaus, "Personal Investment is Necessary for R&D Growth," *Industrial Research/Development*, April 1978, pp. 84–87.

60. It really is not clear that capital gains taxation curtails total investment by business in real assets more than other taxes, despite claims during the 1978 tax debate that the repeal of capital gains taxes would raise stock values by enormous amounts and hence cut the cost of equity financing. In a 1978 U.S. Chamber of Commerce survey of businessmen, 48 percent said they would increase investment if capital gains taxes were reduced; 82 percent said they would do so if the investment tax credit were increased, 78 percent if the corporate tax rate were reduced, 78 percent if faster depreciation write-offs were allowed, and 71 percent if the investment tax credit were extended to structures. ("Fear of Recession Grows Stronger," *Nation's Business*, October 1978, p. 45.)

would be on miscellaneous determinants of output, including aspects of labor and resource allocation for which specific estimates were not prepared.

"People Don't Want to Work Any More"

The press recently quoted me as stating—as I have here—that productivity had declined, in part for reasons that were mysterious. The result was long-distance calls informing me, usually with the patronizing air used in speaking to children and the simpleminded, that the trouble is obvious: "People don't want to work any more." Sometimes the comment was more pointed: "Young people don't work like we did at their age." This is without doubt the number one popular explanation of low productivity. It is also shared by some professional economists.

Thus Arthur F. Burns, then chairman of the Board of Governors of the Federal Reserve System and previously president of the National Bureau of Economic Research and chairman of the Council of Economic Advisers, devoted most of his 1977 commencement address at the University of South Carolina to this theme.[61] "Careful study [of labor force composition and capital per worker] still leaves a substantial part of the recent productivity slowing unexplained," he stated. "Other adverse influences apparently have been at work as well. My own judgment is that we have been undergoing a change in our societal values and attitudes that has contributed significantly to poorer job performance in recent years. I advance that as a hypothesis only, not as an established fact. It is a hypothesis, however, for which there is regrettably a considerable body of supportive evidence."[62]

The attitudes and behavior that trouble Burns and so many others are highly visible. And the difficulty of finding reliable workers for jobs that are particularly hot, dirty, noisome, arduous, or regarded as menial can scarcely be denied, though this may be more the result of improved alternatives than of changes in workers' preferences.

Yet I am skeptical that a sudden drop in willingness to work is responsible for the recent retardation of productivity, whether that is dated after 1966 or after 1973. My skepticism is largely attributable to having heard similar generalizations all my life and having read them in the works of observers who wrote long before my birth. It was well before 1967 that I wrote, "Like the supposed decline in the spirit of enterprise, there seems always to be a popular belief that people are less willing to 'put in a hard day's work' than they used to be, but this is scarcely evidence."[63]

These generalizations, moreover, are also common in other countries, including those with excellent records for raising productivity. And they are not new there either. Thus the Tokyo *Mainichi Daily News* editorialized on April 7, 1976:

> Opinions have been expressed at offices and factories that today's young people are not eager to work. The view is not anything new. Every generation seems to say the same thing about its youths. Still, young people must seriously ponder the allegation. . . . We . . . exhort the newly employed young people to tackle their work with due seriousness.
>
> A government survey shows that two-thirds of today's youth want to live a carefree life to their personal taste outside concern about work. If they want to take a job, however, they are required to care more seriously about work. A switch is needed in their life style concept.

Testimony about a similar observation in Germany comes from Walter W. Heller, another former chairman of the Council of Economic Advisers and an expert on the puritan ethic, who dissents from the Burns view about "this supposedly weakening work ethic." Heller noted: "Ludwig Erhard used to tell me that 'the world-famous German diligence has disappeared.' He told me that in the fifties, and he told me that in the sixties, and now I am hearing it in the seventies." Burns's very interesting response to Heller was: "It has been true each time."[64]

It is indeed possible, as those quoted have suggested, that always and everywhere work effort has declined and has curtailed productivity growth. If so, my residual persistently understates the contribution of advances in knowledge. It is also possible, as Solomon Fabricant has suggested, that over long periods work effort has fluctuated and that the impressions reported all refer to the declining phases

---

61. "The Significance of Our Productivity Lag," May 14, 1977.

62. As evidence of "a lessened sense of industriousness on the part of our work force," Burns cited only high and rising absenteeism and an increase in time paid for but not worked. Neither bears directly on effort while at the workplace, although they may be indicative of a change in attitudes.

63. *Sources of Growth*, p. 166. For a history of the survival of the work ethic despite changes in the character of work as factories spread, and of the perceived need constantly to denounce laziness and profligacy, see David T. Rodgers, *The Work Ethic in Industrial America, 1850–1920* (University of Chicago Press, 1978).

64. "Tax Revolt: The Lady or the Tiger," *Public Opinion*, vol. 1 (July-August 1978), p. 60.

of these cycles.[65] But neither pattern, even if they were accurate descriptions, would explain a downturn in recent years in my residual.

Is there any reason at all for a recent (post-1966 or post-1973) sudden sharp decline in work effort from its past trend, whatever that trend may be? One possibility, perhaps slight, was suggested in *Accounting for Growth*. "Programs to hire the 'hard core' unemployed that do not require them to meet as stringent performance standards as those applied to the ordinary work force pose a possible danger: acceptance of lower standards for a special group in an establishment may reduce performance standards for the rest of the work force in that establishment."[66] Hiring to meet objectives of legislation to promote equal employment opportunities has a similar potential. "On the other hand," as I wrote, "such programs may help to remove irrelevant hiring tests or other forms of disguised discrimination."[67]

My series for average hours, which enters into the calculation of total input, measures time spent at the workplace. The Survey Research Center at the University of Michigan reports that time records kept by a small sample of married men showed the ratio of time actually worked to time at the workplace to have been 2 percent lower in 1974–76 than in 1965–66.[68] Whether there was a change in trend, and if so, when it occurred, cannot be ascertained from these data. The concept of time actually worked is obviously a difficult one for many categories of workers.

I have no desire to minimize the importance of work effort. In *Why Growth Rates Differ* I suggested that higher intensity of work in the United States than in at least several of the European countries may well help to account for the higher level of productivity in the United States. I also stated that an "inability to answer the simple question—how hard do people work?—and to compare different places and dates, is probably the most serious gap in my measure of labor input."[69] It is quite possible that a decline in work effort contributed something to the retardation of productivity, although this has not been demonstrated; but it is unlikely to have been a major cause of the suddenly retarded growth of the residual after 1973.[70]

Impairment of Efficiency by Inflation

Inflation is widely thought to impair growth of output per hour or per worker by reducing saving and investment.[71] In my classification this effect would be captured by the contribution of capital and would not reduce output per unit of input or the residual series. A consequence of inflation that would do so is rendering rational calculations by businessmen more expensive and less accurate. When prices are changing rapidly, information about prices charged in different markets and outlets is quickly outdated.[72] So is knowledge about wage rates and interest rates. The problem is intensified if, as stated by the Bank for International

---

65. *Special Study on Economic Change*, Hearings before the Joint Economic Committee, 95 Cong. 2 sess. (GOP, 1978), pt. 2, p. 535.

66. *Accounting for Growth*, p. 79.

67. Ibid.

68. F. Stafford and G. Duncan, "The Use of Time and Technology by Households in the United States" (July 1977), table 4. A much larger decline was reported for married women.

69. *Why Growth Rates Differ*, pp. 112–14.

70. I briefly discussed effort and incentives in the context of economic growth in *Sources of Growth*, pp. 166–69, and *Why Growth Rates Differ*, pp. 112–14. The literature on the general topic of influences affecting work effort is limitless. It has apparently burgeoned in the past decade as "quality of working life" has become a popular catch phrase and as the relationship between work satisfaction and productivity has received renewed attention. Two studies of interest, both of which summarize broad experience, are Raymond A. Katzell and Daniel Yankelovich, with others, *Work, Productivity, and Job Satisfaction* (New York: Psychological Corporation, January 1975); and Swedish Bernard J. White reported that "survey results over the last Employers' Confederation, *Job Reform in Sweden* (Stockholm: Grofisk Reproduktion, 1975). Whatever the relationship, work satisfaction seems not to have changed. forty years have been remarkably consistent in finding that from 80% to 90% of working people report moderate to high satisfaction with their jobs. Only 10% to 20% report actual dissatisfaction." ("Does Bureaucracy Deserve Its Bad Reputation?" *Dividend*, the Magazine of the Graduate School of Business Administration, University of Michigan, Winter 1977, p. 8.)

71. For example, Robert C. Turner of Indiana University, a former member of the Council of Economic Advisers, considers inflation "the most serious economic threat to economic expansion in the United States" because it reduces investment incentives and may reduce the propensity of individuals to save. (Committee on Ways and Means, *Tax Reductions—Economists Comments*, p. 97.) George Terborgh, a leading expert on the investment process, stresses the adverse effect that inflation exerts on business earnings after tax because business, in his opinion, does not usually base prices on replacement costs and because of its effects on tax liabilities. (George Terborgh, *Corporate Earning Power in the Seventies: A Disaster* [Machinery and Allied Products Institute, August 1977].) Arthur Okun says "the gap [created by inflation] between actual, historical costs of old plant and equipment and current or predicted costs of new facilities creates agonies in capital budgeting and weakens investment." (Arthur M. Okun, "The Great Stagflation Swamp," address to the Economics Club of Chicago, October 6, 1977.)

72. Arthur M. Okun, "Inflation: Its Mechanics and Welfare Costs," *Brookings Papers on Economic Activity*, 1975:2, pp. 351–401.

Settlements, "a high average rate of inflation almost certainly entails an increased variance of individual price changes."[73] As Arthur M. Okun, senior fellow of the Brookings Institution and a former chairman of the Council of Economic Advisers, says, inflation "disturbs a valuable set of institutions that economize on information, prediction, and transaction costs through continuing employer-worker and buyer-seller relationships."[74] Many others have pointed out that inflation erratically affects the tax burden, especially that of firms, because the tax system is based on nominal incomes and book profits.[75]

In his Nobel lecture Milton Friedman of the University of Chicago discussed limitations of indexing as a method of minimizing the impact of inflation on efficiency. Inflation that is high on the average tends to be extremely variable in its rate, and

increased variability shortens the optimum length of unindexed commitments [which would itself increase transaction costs] and renders indexing more advantageous. But it takes time for actual practice to adjust. In the meantime, prior arrangements introduce rigidities that reduce the effectiveness of markets. An additional element of uncertainty is, as it were, added to every market arrangement. In addition, indexing is, even at best, an imperfect substitute for stability of the inflation rate. Price indexes are imperfect; they are available only with a lag and generally are applied to contract terms only with a further lag.

These developments clearly lower economic efficiency.[76]

Friedman also effectively stated the general argument that inflation contributes to inefficiency.

A second related effect of increased volatility of inflation is to render market prices a less efficient system for coordinating economic activity. A fundamental function of a price system . . . is to transmit compactly, efficiently, and at low cost the information that economic agents need in order to decide what to produce and how to produce it, or how to employ owned resources. The relevant information is about *relative* prices—of one product relative to another, of the services of one factor of production relative to another, of products relative to factor services, of prices now relative to prices in the future. But the information in practice is transmitted in the form of *absolute* prices—prices in dollars or pounds or kroner. If the price

level is on the average stable or changing at a steady rate, it is relatively easy to extract the signal about relative prices from the observed absolute prices. The more volatile the rate of general inflation, the harder it becomes to extract the signal about relative prices from the absolute prices: the broadcast about relative prices is, as it were, being jammed by the noise coming from the inflation broadcast. . . . At the extreme, the system of absolute prices becomes nearly useless, and economic agents resort either to an alternative currency or to barter, with disastrous effects on productivity. . . .

These effects of increased volatility of inflation would occur even if prices were legally free to adjust— if, in that sense, the inflation were open. In practice, the distorting effects of uncertainty, rigidity of long-term contracts, and the contamination of price signals will almost certainly be reinforced by legal restrictions on price change. In the modern world, governments are themselves producers of services sold on the market: from postal services to a wide range of other items. Other prices are regulated by government and require government approval for change: from air fares to taxicab fares to charges for electricity. In these cases, governments cannot avoid being involved in the price-fixing process. In addition, the social and political forces unleashed by volatile inflation rates will lead governments to try to repress inflation in still other areas: by explicit price and wage control, or by pressuring private businesses or unions "voluntarily" to exercise "restraint," or by speculating in foreign exchange in order to alter the exchange rate.[77]

That inflation impairs productivity seems certain. But I have no idea how much it may have done so from 1973 to 1976.

Lessening of Competitive Pressure and Changes in the Quality of Management

According to my calculations, output per unit of input in the United States surpassed that in Western Europe (in 1960) and Japan (in 1970) by a much wider margin than is explained by determinants whose effects I could calculate separately.[78] In discussing the difference between the United States and Europe, I listed less intense competitive pressures in Europe among probable causes, noting that "less competition means that inefficient firms and inefficient management are under less pressure to minimize costs and less likely to be displaced by those who can do better." I also wrote: "In the field of 'managerial knowledge' it is probably futile to distinguish between what management knows and what management does with the knowledge it has; but somewhere in this area, I suspect, lies an important part of the explanation for the productivity

73. Bank for International Settlements, *47th Annual Report* (Basle, Switzerland: June 13, 1977), p. 48.

74. Arthur M. Okun and George L. Perry, "Editors' Summary," *Brookings Papers on Economic Activity,"* 1975:2, p. 252.

75. For an extended discussion, see Henry J. Aaron, ed., *Inflation and the Income Tax* (Brookings Institution, 1976).

76. Milton Friedman, "Nobel Lecture: Inflation and Unemployment," *Journal of Political Economy,* vol. 85 (June 1977), p. 466.

77. Ibid., pp. 466–67.

78. *Why Growth Rates Differ,* pp. 289–95; and Edward F. Denison and William K. Chung, *How Japan's Economy Grew So Fast: The Sources of Postwar Expansion* (Brookings Institution, 1976), pp. 110–11.

differential."[79] Competitive pressure clearly affects management quality but is not the only influence on it. I have suggested that increased competition and improved management probably contributed to the increase over time in efficiency in France. Eleanor M. Hadley of George Washington University and the U.S. General Accounting Office concluded that increased competition had done so in Japan.[80]

When I examined American economic growth in 1961, I quoted Edward S. Mason and Theodore J. Kreps to the effect that either there had not been a change in monopoly or the size of the competitive area in America or it was impossible to know whether there had been any change.[81] This seems still to be the case.

The only broad quantitative measures available refer to concentration in manufacturing industries. The four-firm concentration ratio for an industry is the percentage of the industry's shipments made by the four firms with the largest value of shipments. A summary measure can be obtained by computing weighted average concentration ratios for all manufacturing industry, letting each individual industry's four-firm ratio be weighted by the value added originating in that industry. F. M. Scherer has provided such ratios for several years:[82]

1947	35.3
1954	36.9
1958	37.0
1963	38.9
1972	39.2

Although there is some increase in concentration, it is small from 1963 to 1972. The increase up to 1963 seems to result mainly from changes in industry composition and weights; with constant weights and constant industry definitions—but unavoidably, much less complete coverage—the percentages are those shown below:

1947	38.0
1954	38.1
1958	...
1963	37.9
1972	38.5

I am aware, of course, that some observers believe the breadth and strength of competition has declined. Sometimes this belief is related to the argument of a previous section, which described how the need to interact with the government has diverted executive attention from competition and other conventional concerns. Other alleged effects of regulation (including financial regulation) are the heightening of barriers against the entry of new firms and the elimination of small firms that are unable to afford compliance costs (although the latter seems to be more a forecast of things to come than a description of events up to 1976). Conglomerate mergers, which peaked in number and value in 1966–68, are sometimes suspected of having lessened competition, but Peter O. Steiner of the University of Michigan, who cites the Bureau of Economics of the Federal Trade Commission and Jesse W. Markham of Harvard in addition to his own analysis, found no major effect of this type.[83] On the other side, it is pointed out that foreign competition has become much more intense. Also, recurrent and persistent underutilization of resources since 1969 has cut into profits and made for a highly competitive situation.

Burton H. Klein of the California Institute of Technology places great emphasis on competition —or to use his term, "rivalry," which he particularly associates with battles for market shares—as the engine driving firms to improve technique and especially to lower costs.[84] He regards the early postwar "golden age" as "primarily the result of a highly competitive economy generating a wide diversity of ideas." As Klein sees it, the situation has changed, evidently since about 1965. "The dynamism of the American economy is highly dependent upon new firms. . . ." Klein believes the entry of new firms has become rare, primarily because of the unavailability of risk capital for new firms. "Openness" of firms, which in Klein's terminology is the opposite of a closed hierarchical system that is resistant to new blood and radical new ideas, has diminished. "A decline in openness," he reports, "has caused large firms to become more structured and, as such, less able to deal with risk. Moreover, the change in internal incentives results

79. *Why Growth Rates Differ*, p. 292.
80. Eleanor M. Hadley, *Anti-Trust in Japan* (Princeton University Press, 1970), pp. 438, 442.
81. *Sources of Growth*, pp. 193–95.
82. Data are from the forthcoming revised edition of F. M. Scherer, *Industrial Market Structure and Economic Performance*, first published by the Rand Corporation in 1971. The first text table excludes newspapers and ordnance, and the second also excludes the numerous industries for which data conforming to constant definitions were not available.

83. Peter O. Steiner, *Mergers, Motives, Effects, Policies* (University of Michigan Press, 1975), pp. 320–22. U.S. Federal Trade Commission data for mergers are summarized in Bureau of the Census, *Statistical Abstract of the United States 1978* (GPO, 1978), p. 580, and preceding issues of the *Abstract*. After an extended period of low activity, conglomerate mergers again increased in the last half of the 1970s.
84. See Burton H. Klein, *Dynamic Economics* (Harvard University Press, 1977). The quotations that follow are from pp. 182–83.

in the selection of managers with quite different personality characteristics. And there is a good deal of evidence that imaginative scientists and engineers are being replaced with business school graduates and lawyers, that is, by people who perform the same function in modern societies as did genetic inbreeding in feudalistic societies."[85] It is evident that Klein blames loss of rivalry for alleged managerial changes that others ascribe to government regulation.

Managerial behavior is, of course, subject to many influences. For example, Alfred Rappaport of Northwestern University believes that executive compensation systems often instill a drive to produce short-term results, influencing management to forgo investment in capital equipment and R&D and to take other actions, such as corporate takeovers, that sacrifice longer-term earnings to secure short-term accounting profits of less value to the firm.[86]

The Rise in Energy Prices

The sharp drop in the growth of the residual series coincided with the sudden increase in OPEC oil prices at the end of 1973 and in early 1974. Explanations that ascribe the productivity drop to the oil price increase are therefore exceptional in that they account for the timing of the drop.[87] In one study described later in this section Rasche and Tatom even estimated the effect to be of a size about equal to the amount by which growth of the residual deteriorated. To be able to accept this estimate would be doubly satisfying because it would not only solve the productivity mystery but also would be somewhat reassuring for the future. For even if a one-time fuel price increase permanently lowers the level of productivity, it should not reduce the subsequent growth rate once the transition is completed. Unfortunately, the Rasche-Tatom estimate appears to be many times too big, for reasons explained below, and I do not think

that much of the productivity slowdown can be ascribed to energy prices.

It is necessary to distinguish three effects of the oil price increase. First, the increase in the price of imported oil was the main component of a deterioration in the terms of trade that reduced the nation's command over goods and services by about 1 percent but did not in the first instance affect national income or productivity.[88] If buyers had been willing and able and had been permitted by the government simply to pay the higher price without changing fuel consumption, national income per unit of input would not have been altered. Hence the "terms of trade" effect can be ignored here. Second, the government did intervene, with controls over fuel consumption and choice of fuels, to try to reduce present and future imports. These were among the many new controls discussed earlier. Third, the high price of energy resulting from the higher price of imported oil probably caused nonresidential business to use less energy per unit of labor, capital, and land.[89] The question that must be explored here is, how much? And what was the effect on output per unit of input? This section describes some studies.

The usual way to approach the subject is to treat energy as if it were a factor input. Energy gets about 5 percent of the total input weight in the business sector, according to Roger Brinner.[90] Data from the Nuclear Energy Policy Study Group, when combined with estimates by Sam H. Schurr and Joel Darmstadter of Resources for the Future, yield 4.6 percent, calculated as follows: The study group put the cost of primary energy in 1975 at $70 billion.[91] Schurr and Darmstadter state that

---

85. I am reminded that Erik Lundberg, the Swedish economist, ascribed this role to engineers, though only those above 40 years of age. In recent years Lundberg, describing Sweden, has written about a tendency for business to select "managers that correspond to a *soft type*—not strong in maximizing profits and enforcing efficiency—but good at dealing with trade unions, caring for stable employment and not least in getting money (soft loans and subsidies) from Government." (Letter from Lundberg to author, February 26, 1979.)

86. Alfred Rappaport, "Executive Incentives vs Corporate Growth," *Harvard Business Review,* vol. 56 (July-August 1978), pp. 81–88.

87. This was observed in the *Economic Report of the President, January 1977,* p. 55.

88. See chapter 2.

89. The high price of energy and government controls presumably forced some existing capital out of use. In the absence of information about this, no reduction was made in the Bureau of Economic Analysis capital stock series, so if this happened, the effect was to reduce growth of the residual rather than of capital input.

90. "Energy inputs represent only approximately 5 percent of total factor costs." Roger Brinner, *Technology, Labor, and Economic Potential* (Data Resources, Inc., 1978), p. 74.

91. It estimated primary energy use at 70 quads (a quad is 10^{15} British thermal units) and the average price of energy at $1.00 per million BTU. (*Nuclear Power Issues and Choices,* Report of the Nuclear Energy Policy Study Group sponsored by the Ford Foundation [Ballinger, 1977], p. 49.) The Bureau of Mines and the Energy Information Administration put the average price of domestically produced mineral fuels at 85.4 cents per million BTU. (U.S. Department of Energy, Energy Information Administration, *Annual Report to Congress,* vol. 3: *Statistics and Trends of Energy Supply, Demand, and Prices* [GPO, 1978], p. 19.) Inclusion of imported fuel and hydro and nuclear power and exclusion of exports would probably bring this figure to $1.00.

"no more than 60 percent of yearly energy use goes to the [nonresidential] business sector."[92] Hence the value of primary energy used by nonresidential business can be put at $42 billion in 1975, which was 4.6 percent of a $916 billion nonresidential business national income.[93] This percentage is based on energy prices after the oil price increase; before the increase it was smaller.

Given the weight of energy, the effect on output per unit of input of any given percentage decline in energy use by nonresidential business depends on the elasticity of substitution between energy, on the one hand, and labor and capital, on the other. If the elasticity of substitution is unity and the weight of energy is 5 percent, a 1 percent reduction in energy consumption with no change in labor and capital would reduce output by 0.05 percent and output per unit of input by the same percentage.

To be sure, this approach has difficulties. The amount by which the price rise may have reduced fuel consumption in nonresidential business is hard to estimate. One reason is that it is not easy to say what would have happened to total energy consumption after 1973 in the absence of a price change, because earlier experience was not uniform.[94] The ratio of total energy consumption to GNP has declined in the long run—say, since 1920—but not steadily; there was little net change from about 1953–54 to 1973. Short-run fluctuations in the ratio have been sizable, reflecting in part effects of the business cycle and war. Worse, a suitable time series for actual energy consumption by nonresidential business has not been compiled for either the historical or recent period.[95] Much of the energy supply is used to heat, air condition, and illuminate dwellings and government buildings; for cooking and household appliances; and to operate consumer and government motor vehicles, planes, and ships. The remainder—that is, nonresidential business use—may not have

moved as the total did. Partly because of these difficulties, only rough impressions of the elasticity of substitution are available.

Moreover, energy is not really a factor input but is itself the product of labor, capital, and land (natural resources). At the point where it reaches the user, most of its value consists of the earnings of the labor and capital required to transform a natural resource into the form needed by energy users and move it to where it is needed. Additional energy can always be provided by adding labor and capital, although it may require the use of poorer natural resources requiring more labor and capital.

This suggests another approach to the question. Suppose 20 percent of energy were imported and higher import prices caused imports to be cut by one-fourth (5 percent of consumption). The loss could be made good without changing consumption by raising domestic energy production from 80 percent to 85 percent of consumption. Suppose the cost in labor and capital per unit of energy were as much as twice as high for the additional energy as for existing domestic production. If 80 units of labor and capital were required to produce 80 percent of consumption, 90 units would be required to produce 85 percent of the same consumption. The labor and capital requirement for domestic energy production per unit of energy would be raised to 105.9 percent (90 ÷ 85) of the original requirement. This would leave business with as much energy as ever. If domestically produced energy were initially 4 percent of nonresidential business output and input, output per unit of labor and capital in nonresidential business would be reduced by 4 percent of 5.9 percent, or 0.24 percent. This figure could be reduced by some substitution of labor and capital for energy. These import substitution numbers are only illustrative, but they suggest the dimensions of the effect.

I turn now to actual estimates that have been made of the effect of the energy price increase on the course of productivity after 1973. George L. Perry, a senior fellow of the Brookings Institution, has made what I regard as the most reasonable calculation.[96] Perry prepared a time series for nonresidential business use of energy, measured in Btu's, that begins in 1949. It covered about three-fifths of the total; the main omissions were com-

92. "The Energy Connection," *Resources,* no. 53 (Fall 1976), p. 5.

93. See also citations given below (to articles by Ridker, Watson, and Shapanka of Resources for the Future and by Hogan and Manne of Stanford University), which give 4 or 5 percent as the energy share.

94. See Jack Alterman, *The Energy/Real Gross Domestic Product Ratio: An Analysis of Changes during the 1966–1970 Period in Relation to Long-Run Trends,* BEA Staff Paper 30 BEA-SP 77-030 (BEA, October 1977). See also Sam H. Schurr, "Energy, Economic Growth, and Human Welfare," *EPRI Journal,* vol. 5 (May 1978), pp. 14–18.

95. Noteworthy is the absence of any such series in U.S. Department of Energy, Energy Information Administration, *Annual Report to Congress,* vol. 3, 1978: *Statistics and Trends of Energy Supply, Demand, and Prices.*

96. George L. Perry, "Potential Output: Recent Issues and Present Trends," in Center for the Study of American Business, *U.S. Production Capacity: Estimating the Utilization Gap,* Working Paper 23 (1977), pp. 6–13 (Brookings Reprint 336).

mercial uses of petroleum for heating and transportation. For the 1949–73 period (as well as for subperiods) he related this series for energy use to gross business product, the ratio of actual to potential gross business product, and the trend in the ratio of energy use to output (which is downward by 1.3 percent to 1.6 percent a year). He then used three alternative equations based on these data to predict the ratio of energy use to business GNP in 1976. They predicted declines from 1973 to 1976 of 7.3, 7.0, and 5.3 percent, respectively. The actual decline was 10.2 percent. The difference of 2.9 to 4.9 percent between actual and predicted reductions is an estimate of the reduction one can ascribe to higher energy prices or other unspecified factors, including government controls. Perry considers this a maximum estimate because the equations assume a constant downtrend through 1973 in energy per unit of business product, whereas the decline was actually accelerating. (If the estimated 1973–76 decline in the absence of the price rise is understated for this reason, the effect of the price rise on energy use is overestimated.) Perry next estimates that the value of the energy saved by the 2.9 percent to 4.9 percent reduction was $2.4 billion to $4.1 billion, based on the 1976 general price level but (appropriately) at the average of the 1973 and 1976 ratio of the price of energy to the general price level.[97]

Because Perry is interested in output per hour worked rather than output per unit of input (and also to avoid explicit estimates of elasticities of substitution), he uses a variant of the income share approach at this point. He reasons as follows:

Even if business is assumed to have accomplished all this saving by substituting labor for energy, not much extra labor could have been used in this process. $4.1 billion is 0.5 percent of employee compensation in the business sector. $2.4 billion is 0.3 percent. Since an unknown amount of the substitution must involve capital as well as labor, the added labor input would be smaller still. . . . Finally, some part of the energy saving must have involved no substitution of other inputs at all: lowering thermostats to 68 degrees in winter and raising them to 75 degrees in summer or turning out every other light in hallways are obvious examples, but there must have been less obvious examples of "waste" that were eliminated only after the OPEC crisis made firms more energy conscious. . . . I know of no way to pin down the answer more accurately; but on the basis of the evidence here, it seems unlikely that higher energy prices have caused more than a 0.2 percent loss of labor

productivity and potential output between 1973 and 1976.[98]

When Perry reduced the initial 0.3–0.5 percent to 0.2 percent in order to obtain the effect of the higher energy price on labor productivity (output per hour), he took into account both the substitution of capital for energy and the conservation of energy without loss of production. To estimate the effect on output per unit of input (my objective here), only the second reduction should be made. A reduction from a midpoint 0.4 percent estimate to 0.3 percent is reasonable for 1976. This would mean that higher energy prices reduced the growth rate of the residual from 1973 to 1976 by 0.1 percentage points. This is a significant amount, but less than one-twentieth of the drop for which an explanation is needed.

The conclusion that output per unit of input would be cut 0.3 percent by a 3.9 percent reduction in energy use in nonresidential business (the midpoint of Perry's estimates) is broadly similar to—indeed, even above—two other estimates. Ronald G. Ridker, William D. Watson, Jr., and Adele Shapanka, all of Resources for the Future, wrote: ". . . we believe that the following rule will prove to be in the ball park. According to this rule, a 10 percent reduction in net industrial and commercial energy use per unit of output, over what would otherwise have occurred had the pre-1973 trend in the ratio prevailed, results in a 0.5 percent decline in GNP during a transition period of ten to fifteen years."[99] William W. Hogan and Alan S. Manne of the Institute for Energy Studies at Stanford University estimated the decline in output would be 0.4 percent from a 10 percent reduction in energy.[100] Moreover, the Council of Economic Advisers points out that the short-term effect is less than the longer-term effect. "Widespread declines in productivity growth rates would only occur as adjustment of production methods to economize on energy took place. Actually, adjustment to the new oil prices has been extremely slow."[101]

Before Perry's study, Robert H. Rasche and John A. Tatom of the Federal Reserve Bank of St.

---

97. His reason for averaging relative prices before and after the increase is the same as mine for averaging share weights at the beginning and end of a period when I compute the percentage change in total factor output.

98. Perry, "Potential Output," pp. 11–12.
99. "Economic, Energy, and Environmental Consequences of Alternative Energy Regimes, An Application of the RFF/SEAS Modeling System," in Charles J. Hitch, ed., *Modeling Energy-Economy Interactions: Five Approaches* (Resources for the Future, 1977).
100. "Energy-Economy Interactions: The Fable of the Elephant and the Rabbit?" in Hitch, *Modeling Energy-Economy Interactions*, p. 248.
101. *Economic Report of the President, January 1979*, p. 71.

Louis estimated that the increase in the price of energy permanently reduced economic capacity, or potential output, by 4 to 5 percent.[102] This would mean a reduction of 5 or 6 percent in potential nonresidential business national income and in my residual series. Their estimate flowed from what are, conceptually, two equations. One assumes that the elasticity of demand for energy used in production is unity, so that each 10 percent increase in the price of energy relative to the price of output reduces energy input by 9.1 percent. The other assumes a Cobb-Douglas-type production function in which energy is treated as an input along with labor and capital. Energy is given a weight of 12 percent, so each drop of 9.1 percent in energy consumption reduces GNP by 1.1 percent. Lacking data on energy consumption, Rasche and Tatom condensed the two equations, estimating that each 10 percent increase in the relative price of energy reduces output by 1.1 percent.

Although the condensation of the equations eliminates the calculation of energy input, it is easy to calculate that the assumption of unit elasticity of demand implies that the 57 percent increase in the relative price of energy from 1973 to 1976 reduced energy use by 36 percent relative to what it would otherwise have been (since $100 \div 1.57 = 64$). The Rasche-Tatom estimate of the productivity loss assumes that this actually happened. Although the size of the actual reduction is uncertain, it is obvious that it did not remotely approach such a magnitude. Rasche and Tatom radically overestimated the size of the quantity response to the price increase. A second reason the Rasche-Tatom result is so high is their use of a 12 percent weight for energy, which they based on a finding that "the share of energy costs in total factor costs . . . was quite stable throughout the 1960s at around twelve percent of total factor costs." The estimate cited refers only to manufacturing.[103] It is far above any of the estimates for nonresidential business or the whole economy that I have located.

If Perry's estimate that the use of energy was reduced by 2.9 to 4.9 percent were substituted for the implied Rasche-Tatom estimate of 36 percent, and if Brinner's 5 percent weight were substituted for their 12 percent, then the second Rasche-Tatom formula would yield 0.14 to 0.25 percent as the reduction in output per unit of input in 1976 that stemmed from the energy price increase.[104]

Another sizable estimate has recently appeared. Edward A. Hudson of Data Resources, Inc., and Dale W. Jorgenson of Harvard University analyzed the impact of higher energy prices by using their "dynamic general equilibrium model of the U.S. economy."[105] A feature of the model is its reliance on a close relationship between the quantity of capital and energy use—that is, energy and capital are considered complements with a low elasticity of substitution between them. But a high degree of substitution is thought to exist between energy and capital, on the one hand, and labor, on the other. The model "was used to simulate two economic growth paths over the 1972–1976 period. In the first simulation, actual values of the exogenous variables, including world oil prices, were employed as the basis for model solution. . . . In the second simulation, 1972 energy prices were employed over the whole 1972–1976 period." Since all other exogenous variables were the same, "the differences in simulated economic activity can be attributed solely to the impact of the oil price increase."[106] These differences include the effects of the impact of the oil price increase on demand as well as on production relationships.

Their model results showed energy consumption 8.8 percent lower in 1976 with the energy price

102. Robert H. Rasche and John A. Tatom, "The Effects of the New Energy Regime on Economic Capacity, Production, and Prices," *Federal Reserve Bank of St. Louis Review*, vol. 59 (May 1977), pp. 2–12; and idem, "Energy Resources and Potential GNP," *Federal Reserve Bank of St. Louis Review*, vol. 59 (June 1977), pp. 10–24. The range cited is from the introduction to the first article. Slightly different results based on different periods and data are provided elsewhere in these articles.

In the same articles Rasche and Tatom present a potential output series. To avoid misunderstanding, I stress that my disagreement with them is not over their conclusion that growth of potential output was sharply curtailed after 1973 but with their attribution of the change to the higher price of oil.

103. The particular use made of the estimate by Rasche and Tatom is in an analysis of manufacturing, but the manufacturing results are applied to the whole economy.

104. An interesting feature of the Rasche-Tatom analytical framework is that the output reduction is the result of a change—not of an *increase*—in the relative price of oil. A decrease in the price of oil would have had the same effect. A change in the relative prices of labor and capital, in either direction, also reduces output in this framework, as the authors clearly realize, since they calculate the cost of such a change. All this is rather baffling because the authors do not have in mind temporary costs of adjustment. On the contrary, they insist that the impact of the oil price increase on the American economy is "profound and permanent." Given that any change in either direction reduces output, one might expect that productivity would drop again if the price of oil were now to fall, but in another puzzling sentence the authors state that the only way potential output could be restored is for the relative price of oil to return to its old level, a statement that in another context would seem entirely reasonable.

105. Edward A. Hudson and Dale W. Jorgenson, "Energy Prices and the U.S. Economy, 1972–1976," *Data Resources U.S. Review*, September 1978, pp. 1.24–1.37.

106. Quotations appear in ibid., p. 1.25.

increase than without, real GNP 3.2 percent lower, and energy consumption per unit of GNP 5.8 percent lower. The energy estimates refer to all uses of energy, not just business use, so the 5.8 percent reduction is not necessarily comparable to Perry's 2.4–4.9 percent; still, it is in the same ball park. The model showed labor input lower by 0.5 million jobs or just over 0.5 percent with the energy price increase than without it, and GNP per unit of labor 2.57 percent lower. Capital input evidently was 3.0 percent lower.[107] The base to which the percentage reduction in capital refers is unclear. If it includes all nonresidential and residential business capital and land (that is, all nonlabor input) the reduction in total factor input is about 1.23 percent because the weights, gross of depreciation, in the economy as a whole, are about 0.72 for the drop of something over 0.5 percent in labor and 0.28 for the 3.0 percent drop in "capital."[108] With total energy use reduced 8.8 percent, energy per unit of factor input is lowered by 7.7 percent. With GNP reduced 3.2 percent, GNP per unit of factor input is lowered by 2.0 percent. If, as seems reasonable, 1973 GNP was unaffected, the rise in energy prices would then have reduced the growth rate of GNP per unit of input in the whole economy by almost 0.7 percentage points from 1973 to 1976.

The implied drop of 2.0 percent in GNP per unit of labor, capital, and land as the result of a mere 7.7 percent decline in total energy consumption per unit of labor, capital, and land is puzzling. Suppose business use of energy fell by the same percentage (7.7) per unit of input as total use. The value of energy used in nonresidential business does not exceed 4 percent of total factor input in the whole economy. The usual procedure would then yield a reduction in output per unit of labor, capital, and land of only 0.3 percent (7.7×0.04). Hudson and Jorgenson obtain a result seven times as large. The disparity is partly due to different estimates of elasticities of substitution, but it does not seem that this could be the whole explanation. Both the difference in elasticities and the cause of the remainder of the difference need more explanation than has been made available.

My citation of several studies may create the false impression that the scale of investigation of the effect of the energy price increase on past output has been substantial. In fact, study of the actual effect of the change in the energy situation on total output and productivity since 1973 is minuscule even in comparison with the resources devoted to trying to guess at its implications for the twenty-first century. More research specifically devoted to measuring the effects already experienced is needed. Pending such research, the estimate that the energy price increase reduced the growth rate of my residual by about 0.1 percent a year from 1973 to 1976 is reasonable.

The Shift to Services and Other Structural Changes

Whenever productivity is discussed at any length, someone will assert that opportunities to raise productivity are less for services than for commodities, that the service share of the economy is rising rapidly, and that the overall rate of productivity advance must therefore decline. I examined this allegation in a long article in 1973 and concluded that within the *nonfarm* nonresidential business sector it simply has no substance.[109] The most obvious, though not the only, reason is that within this sector there was no appreciable shift to the services. This is so whether one considers employment classified by industry or output classified by end product. The *shift* of employment from *farming* to other commodity and service industries did affect productivity. Because the shift reduced misallocation, its effect was favorable and its diminishment therefore unfavorable. But the amount was estimated in the present study and is excluded from my residual series.

In the same article I stressed that a classification based on commodities and services is in any case

---

107. In the Hudson-Jorgenson calculations, the 3.2 percent drop in GNP would in itself cause a proportional 3.2 percent drop in the demand for and use of "capital services," and therefore a 3.2 percent drop in capital stock. The drop in capital services from this cause is valued at $15.5 billion. However, the higher energy price induces changes in the composition of demand and substitutions among labor, capital, and energy that provide a small offset, reducing the drop in capital services to $14.5 billion. Hence the percentage drop in capital services and capital stock was 3.2 percent $\times$ 14.5 ÷ 15.5, or 3.0 percent.

108. The calculation is $(0.72 \times 0.54) + (0.28 \times 3) = 1.23$. The numerator for the 0.72 labor share is the sum of (1) national income in general government, households, and institutions (table 2-5, column 2); and (2) the product of national income in nonresidential business from table 2-5, column 5, and the labor share in that sector from table G-2, column 2. The denominator is the sum of (1) national income (table 2-5, column 1); and (2) "capital consumption allowances with capital consumption adjustment" from NIPA, table 1.9, row 2. If the percentage reduction in capital refers only to fixed residential and nonresidential capital, which seems likely, the reduction in total factor input is less.

109. Edward F. Denison, "The Shift to Services and the Rate of Productivity Change," *Survey of Current Business*, October 1973, pp. 20–35 (Brookings reprint T-003).

inappropriate because industries or products classified in each group are completely lacking in homogeneity with respect to productivity change—or to almost anything else. Both groups contain industries of fast and slow productivity growth.

The Bureau of Labor Statistics has also explored the effect of the shift to the services. Jerome A. Mark, its assistant commissioner for productivity and technology, noted in testimony before the Joint Economic Committee that services can be defined very narrowly to include only business or personal services, or (as I defined them) very broadly to include all noncommodity-producing industries. In either case the effect of the shift was trivial. Under the narrow definition the effect of shifts in hours to the services was −0.01 percentage points in 1947–76, zero in 1947–66, and −0.02 in 1966–76. By the broad definition it was slightly positive: 0.01 percentage points in 1947–76, zero in 1947–66, and 0.04 in 1966–76.[110]

Quite apart from such calculations and the inappropriateness of a commodity-service dichotomy, in the article previously cited I raised "a fundamental objection to the procedure of analyzing the behavior of components in the past in order to judge future productivity trends within nonfarm nonresidential business. This objection is to the implicit assumption that components which gain or lose share of employment or total input, and which have above average or below average productivity gains in one period, will have the same characteristics in the next period."[111]

I went on to say:

Suppose we classify nonfarm nonresidential business or a major portion of it by detailed components, whether by industry or by end product. Available evidence suggests that over any time span that is long and terminated by years that are representative we are likely to find that employment and other input measures increased by an above average amount in components whose productivity increased by an above average amount. This is not really surprising. One reason is that components toward which demand shifts secure the greatest productivity gains from economies of scale. Another is that new components typically both increase their shares and have large productivity gains. A third is that demand appears typically to be so elastic that declining relative prices resulting from above average productivity gains raise volume more than enough to offset the saving in employment and

other inputs that results from above average productivity gains.[112]

And finally:

If this relationship holds, components with above average productivity gains during a period will be found to have bigger shares of employment or total input at the end of a period than at its beginning. Does this mean we should expect ever-rising rates of productivity growth in the sector as a whole? Of course not. Such a tendency would be present only if at every date the components which had high rates of productivity gain and increased their shares of input or employment in previous periods will again have high rates of productivity gain, and increase or at least not reduce their shares, in the period to come. There is no such continuity. Industries rise and fall.

Suppose, instead, that in some period or by some classification the relationship is the opposite: that components with fast-rising productivity in a period systematically lose their shares of inputs. Would this mean an ever-falling rate of productivity increase? No, for the same reason.[113]

Possible Errors in the Data

The change in the course of national income per person employed was so sudden and sharp after 1973 that some observers have wondered whether it really happened. They ask whether some development might have introduced a sudden error into the output measure.

An error in real output could result from an incorrect series for output valued in current prices or from errors in price data used for deflation. Output (national income) in current prices is measured in two ways. In one, GNP is first estimated, as the sum of expenditures for final products (personal consumption expenditures, gross private domestic investment, net exports, and government purchases). To obtain national income, capital consumption, indirect business taxes, and business transfer payments are then subtracted from GNP and subsidies are added. The second way, on which my series is based, is to add the several types of earnings from current production (employee compensation, proprietors' earnings, rental income of persons, corporate earnings, and net interests). The two estimates agree rather well from 1973 to 1976.

110. Jerome A. Mark, "Productivity Trends and Prospects," *Special Study on Economic Change*, Hearings before the Joint Economic Committee, 95 Cong. 2 sess. (GPO, 1978), pt. 2, p. 485.

111. Denison, "The Shift to Services," p. 34. The reasoning applies equally to a comparison of two past periods.

112. Ibid. "Both [W. E. G.] Salter and [John] Kendrick found that industries that reduced *factor* input per unit of output most also reduced *materials* input per unit of output most. This is important in explaining the finding, because factor inputs are only part of the total costs of an industry and a given percentage reduction in factor input costs alone would yield a much smaller percentage reduction in price." (Ibid., note 25, p. 34.)

113. Ibid., p. 34. In the same article I explain why it is a mistake to suppose that within nonresidential business the accuracy of series for commodity-producing industries is greater than that for service-producing industries.

There is, nevertheless, one reason to suspect that national income in current prices may be unusually subject to error in 1973–76. It pertains to the inventory valuation adjustment, which enters into the estimates obtained by both methods.[114] Estimates of the inventory valuation adjustment are needed to obtain the change in nonfarm business inventories (a component of gross private domestic investment, which enters into the first estimate) and nonfarm proprietors' earnings and corporate earnings (components of the second estimate). The inventory valuation adjustment is difficult to measure and it was unusually big from 1973 through 1976 as the result of large price movements. At the same time, difficulties in its estimation were increased by widespread changes in business accounting practices (shifting from first-in-first-out to last-in-first-out accounting). As a result, output in current prices was more susceptible to measurement error, in either direction, than usual. Even so, an error in the current-dollar figures large enough to alter the productivity picture materially would surprise me greatly. With respect to the possibility of systematic downward bias in the current-dollar series after 1973, I am not aware of any development likely to lead to such a bias.

The price data used for deflation are ordinarily subject to greater error than the current-dollar measures. The period under discussion was one of unusually large price change, and this may have made the data unusually prone to error. I do not know that price indexes are subject to greater error when prices are changing sharply than when they are relatively stable, but such a relationship seems plausible. For some components of fixed investment and government purchases from business there may be timing discrepancies between a price index and the current dollar figure it is used to deflate; the former, for example, may refer to new contracts, the latter to deliveries or work done. Error from timing mismatches becomes more difficult to avoid if prices fluctuate widely.

In the period under review there is also a special consideration: price data may have been affected by price controls. Price controls tend to cause understatement of reported prices, which would cause measures of real output to be overstated. Controls of fluctuating severity were in effect from August 15, 1971, through April 1974. Conse-

quently output in this period may be overstated relative to earlier and later years. This would make the 1969–73 growth rate too high and the 1973–76 rate too low. If 1973 prices were understated by one-half percent, for example, the growth rates of output and the residual would be 0.13 percentage points too high in 1969–73 and 0.17 points too low in 1973–76. Unless the price bias were bigger than this, the retardation in the growth rate of the residual would still be confined to the 1973–76 period.[115]

The Federal Reserve Board index of industrial production is sometimes compared with components of real GNP that roughly correspond to its coverage.[116] With respect to changes from 1973 to either 1976 or 1977, and based on the data available at the end of 1978, the series happen to be in close agreement; the industrial production index actually yields growth rates slightly (about 0.1 percent a year) lower than the GNP series.[117]

There is no way to determine the accuracy of the output data conclusively; only impressions can be offered. Mine is that statistical errors in output measurement may have contributed *something* to the observed productivity slowdown that this chapter has explored, but it is improbable that they contributed materially to it.

The growth rate of national income per person employed would be affected by errors in employment data as well as in the output series, except to the extent that inconsistencies are eliminated by measuring current dollar output from the income side of the national accounts.[118] The growth rate of the residual would also be affected by noncompensating errors in the series measuring effects of other determinants. Random errors in these series,

---

114. The inventory valuation adjustment is the difference between (1) the change in the physical volume of inventories valued in prices of the current period and (2) the change in the value of inventories reported by business.

115. A discussion of other potential biases in price series used in deflation that might have caused overstatement of the decline in real output in 1974–75 is found in the appendix to Victor Zarnowitz and Geoffrey H. Moore, "The Recession and Recovery of 1973–1976," *Explorations in Economic Research*, Occasional Papers of the National Bureau of Economic Research, vol. 4 (Fall 1977), pp. 471–557. To affect the 1973–76 movement of the residual, such a bias would have to affect the output series differently than in previous cyclical swings (otherwise it would be picked up in the series for intensity of utilization) and, to have an appreciable effect, would also have to affect price movements in the downswing without being offset in the recovery. None of the suggestions offered seem likely to qualify.

116. The GNP series includes all "goods" components, personal consumption expenditures for electricity and gas, and 40 percent of structures, minus gross farm product and margins on the sale of used cars.

117. The relative position of the intervening years differs substantially, with industrial production showing 1974 higher and 1975 lower relative to 1973 and 1976 than does the GNP series.

118. See p. 15 and *Accounting for Growth*, pp. 164–65.

if not offsetting, consequently could cause the amount of retardation in the residual to be overstated—or understated.[119]

It is sometimes suggested that growth of an illegal economy, or a barter economy, has caused a large amount of production to disappear from the scope of the NIPA. I have not been able to visualize how this might have occurred in such a way as to instill a sudden sharp downward bias in output per unit of input when output is measured by adding the several types of earnings from current production.

Summary and Clues

Seventeen suggested reasons for the slowdown in my residual series were explored in this chapter. I rejected a few suggestions, expressed skepticism about some, had no opinion about others, and characterized the rest as probably correct but individually able to explain only a small part of the slowdown. No single hypothesis seems to provide a probable explanation of the sharp change after 1973.

It is possible, perhaps even probable, that everything went wrong at once among the determinants that affect the residual series. Just as many determinants whose effects were separately estimated contributed to the drop in the growth rate of national income per person employed from 1948–73 to 1973–76, so may the rest of the drop have resulted from many of the circumstances discussed in this chapter, with each subtracting one- or two-tenths of a point from the growth rate. Several developments may have combined to slow the advance in knowledge itself, and others to retard the incorporation of new knowledge into production. Similarly, inflation, regulation, soaring energy prices, high taxes, and changing attitudes may have conspired to exert the large adverse impact on the miscellaneous determinants of output that forced the residual series into an actual decline.

The finding that the unexplained slowdown in productivity growth started only after 1973 not only is an important clue in itself but also permits

one to arrive at another: the slowdown was typical of the main industrial branches of the economy rather than focused in one or two areas for which one might seek special explanations. Table 9-1 compares the growth rates of real GNP per hour at work in 1948–73 with the rates from 1973 to both 1976 and 1978.[120] In ten of the eleven branches, including both nondurable and durable goods manufacturing, the growth rates of GNP per hour in both 1973–76 and 1973–78 were much below the 1948–73 rate.[121] The only exception is communication (mainly the telephone industry).[122] It seems safe to infer that the decline in the residual was also general.

International comparisons provide an opportunity to obtain still another clue. To do so, however, it would be necessary to develop up-to-date estimates of the sources of growth in other advanced countries comparable to mine for the

119. The depth of the 1974–75 recession dropped the index for intensity of utilization due to fluctuations in demand below the previous range of experience (in the period for which it has been calculated). If its drop was underestimated, this would cause the residual to be underestimated in those years. But if that were the cause of the 1974–75 drop, it should have been followed by an exceptionally strong advance in the recovery period, which did not happen. See also pages 186 and 188.

120. Edward F. Renshaw used the same body of data to reach a similar conclusion in "A Note on the Aggregate Learning Curve for the U.S. Economy and the Persistent Gap Between Actual and Potential GNP" (1978).

121. Government and government enterprises; finance, insurance, and real estate; and private households are excluded because the data have no independent meaning and are chiefly outside nonresidential business. Nonprofit institutions were not eliminated, and this accounts for the low 1948–73 growth rate in services.

122. By dividing the postwar period at 1967 instead of 1973 and comparing 1950–67 with 1967–77, the Council on Wage and Price Stability concluded from the same data source that a reduction in the growth rate of productivity did not occur in manufacturing but was confined to construction and most of the service divisions. (Council on Wage and Price Stability, *Executive Office of the President News,* October 4, 1978.) The council's conclusion that retardation was concentrated and confined to nonmanufacturing industries is questionable, however, even if one is concerned with longer periods such as those the council examined because the result was entirely dependent on the exact choice of periods. If the council had divided the period at 1965, 1966, or 1968 instead of 1967, it would have obtained a decline in the growth rate of manufacturing productivity, and the declines would have been larger if the period had begun in 1948 instead of 1950. To illustrate with an extreme case, the growth rate of output per hour in manufacturing dropped by 0.74 percentage points from 1948–65 to 1965–77 according to the series the council used. Jerome Mark has shown that the decline in the rate of growth of output per man-hour from 1947–66 to 1966–76 was general among sixty-two detailed industries for which the Bureau of Labor Statistics published series. Forty-six had lower growth rates of output per hour in 1966–76 than in 1947–66, one had the same rate, and fifteen had higher rates. (Mark, "Productivity Trends and Prospects," table 1, p. 484.) An unpublished compilation provided by Mark in February 1979 also shows that fifty-three of seventy-four industries had lower growth rates from 1973 to 1977 (or 1976 if 1977 was not available) than from 1947 (or the earliest subsequent date for which the series was available) to 1973. The proportion was the same, three-fourths, in manufacturing and nonmanufacturing industries.

Table 9-1. Gross National Product in 1973 in Constant (1972) Prices and Growth Rates of Gross National Product per Hour Worked, 1948–73, 1973–76, and 1973–78, by Industry[a]

Industry[b]	GNP, 1973 (billions of 1972 dollars)	Growth rates (percent)		
		1948–73	1973–76	1973–78
Agriculture, forestry, and fisheries	35.9	4.5	1.1	2.0
Mining	19.2	3.6	−6.6	−4.8
Contract construction[c]	58.3	1.6	0.9	−1.1
Manufacturing: nondurable goods	124.1	3.3	2.0	2.3
Manufacturing: durable goods	189.0	2.6	1.1	1.1
Transportation	50.6	3.0	0.1	0.8
Communication	32.0	5.2	8.4	7.1
Electric, gas, and sanitary services	30.0	5.4	1.4	0.7
Wholesale trade[c]	88.9	3.3	−1.3	−0.6
Retail trade[c]	123.1	2.4	1.1	1.1
Services[d]	137.9	1.0	−0.2	0.1

Source: Calculated from NIPA, tables 6.2, 6.11, and (to eliminate hours in private households) 6.10. Utilizes data from the July 1979 *Survey of Current Business.*
  a. Hours worked by unpaid family workers are excluded when GNP per hour worked is computed.
  b. Excluding finance, insurance, and real estate; private households; and government and government enterprises.
  c. Classification for 1948–73 growth rate differs slightly from classification used for 1973–76 and 1973–78.
  d. Excludes private households; includes nonprofit institutions.

United States.[123] If the residual series for other countries showed no retardation, it would suggest a localized cause for the decline in the United States. But if most other countries experienced a similar setback, this would strengthen the case for causes (such as inflation) that have been widespread.

The top panel of table 9-2 compares growth rates of output per employed civilian in the whole economy in the United States and six other large industrial countries. In the United States the growth rate per employed civilian dropped by about two percentage points from either 1950–73 or 1960–73 to either 1973–76 or 1973–77. The rate also dropped in all six other countries shown. The drop was smaller than in the United States only in Germany. It was about the same in Canada, France, and the United Kingdom. In Japan and Italy it was much larger. It should be recalled, however, that all these countries shared in the world recession after 1973.

The bottom of table 9-2 compares output per hour in manufacturing in 1973–76, 1973–77, and 1973–78, with rates in 1950–73 and 1960–73 for ten countries besides the United States. Among the six large foreign countries, all except Germany experienced an unambiguous drop in the rate. The drop was less than in the United States in France and larger in Canada, Japan, Italy, and the United

Kingdom. Among the four smaller countries the rate dropped appreciably in Sweden. If the recent years are compared with 1960–73, the rate also dropped substantially (though much less than in Sweden) in Denmark and the Netherlands, but not very much in Belgium.

These data show that sharp declines in the growth rates of national income per person em-

123. My study for eight Western European countries (*Why Growth Rates Differ*) ended with 1962, that for Canada by Dorothy Walters (*Canadian Growth Revisited, 1950–67,* Staff Study 28 [Economic Council of Canada, 1970]) ended in 1967, and that for Japan by William Chung and me (*How Japan's Economy Grew So Fast*), in 1971.

Table 9-2. Selected Growth Rates in Industrial Countries
Percent per annum

Country	Growth rates				
	1950–73	1960–73	1973–76	1973–77	1973–78
Real gross domestic product per employed civilian					
United States	2.1	2.1	−0.1	0.3	n.a.
Canada	2.6	2.4	0.4	0.5	n.a.
Japan	7.8	8.8	2.3	2.7	n.a.
France	4.6	4.6	2.7	2.9	n.a.
West Germany	5.0	4.4	3.3	3.3	n.a.
Italy	5.3	5.8	0.8	−0.2	n.a.
United Kingdom	2.5	2.6	0.4	0.4	n.a.
Output per hour in manufacturing					
United States	2.7	3.2	1.2	1.5	1.7
Canada	4.2	4.6	1.3	2.1	2.5
Japan	9.7	10.0	1.4	2.4	3.5
Belgium	n.a.	7.0	6.7	6.6	n.a.
Denmark	5.2	7.0	6.2	5.2	4.7
France	5.3	5.7	4.7	4.8	4.8
West Germany	5.8	5.5	6.0	5.5	5.1
Italy	6.6	7.2	3.0	2.4	2.6
Netherlands	6.2	7.4	5.4	4.9	n.a.
Sweden	5.3	6.7	0.9	0.5	1.5
United Kingdom	3.1	3.9	0.1	−0.2	0.2

Sources: U.S. Department of Labor, Bureau of Labor Statistics, Office of Productivity and Technology, "Comparative Real Gross Domestic Product, Real GDP per Capita, and Real GDP per Employed Civilian, Seven Countries, 1950–77" (June 1978); "Output per Hour, Hourly Compensation, and Unit Labor Costs in Manufacturing, Eleven Countries, 1950–1978" (July 10, 1979).
n.a. Not available.

ployed and of output per hour in manufacturing were widespread. They do not prove that this pattern carries over to the residual, but it may. It would be worthwhile to find out.[124]

124. The adjustment for intensity of utilization is likely to be very difficult in several countries because it has become increasingly difficult or expensive to lay off unneeded workers. A decline in demand is likely to be matched to a lesser extent by a drop in input and to a greater extent by a drop in output per unit of input than was formerly the case or is now the case in the United States.

Another way to learn more about the causes of the slowdown in the residual is to investigate intensively the suggestions I have reviewed in this chapter. Although some are not readily amenable to research, many are, and properly focused investigations on each of them would be valuable.

Finally, the mere accumulation of experience as time elapses will be helpful. Knowledge of the path of the residual series for output per unit of input over the next few years should assist in the identification of causes.

Appendixes

APPENDIX A

-->>><<<---

Measures of Actual Output

-->>><<<---

The derivation of actual national income in current and constant prices in the economy as a whole, the four sectors, and the farm and nonfarm components of nonresidential business is described in the sources given for tables in chapter 2. The NIPA data used for 1929–72 are provided in U.S. Department of Commerce, *The National Income and Product Accounts of the United States, 1929–74 Statistical Tables, A Supplement to Survey of Current Business* (Government Printing Office, 1977); for 1973–76, in the *Survey of Current Business* for July 1977; for 1977, in the *Survey of Current Business* for July 1978; and for 1978, in the *Survey of Current Business* for February 1979. Corrections of constant-price national income in years from 1929 to 1946 that were published in the August 1978 *Sur-*

vey of Current Business were introduced. (For 1941 a preliminary figure was used.) Since 1975–76 data do not incorporate revisions introduced in the July 1978 *Survey of Current Business,* they are not exactly comparable to those for other years, but differences are minor. Data for 1925–28 plotted in figure 2-1 are estimates derived from NIPA, table 1.23.

The series for command over goods and services in constant prices (table 2-1, column 3) was derived in the following steps:

1. Net exports of goods and services in 1972 market prices were obtained from NIPA, table 1.2.

2. To secure an alternative series for net exports in 1972 market prices, net exports in current market prices (NIPA, table 1.1) were divided by the implicit deflator for imports (NIPA, table 7.1).

3. The amount by which the alternative procedure changes net exports at market prices was obtained as series 2 minus series 1.

4. Nonresidential business net national product at 1972 market prices was derived from NIPA tables 1.12 and 1.21.

5. The percentage by which the alternative procedure changes nonresidential business net national product at market prices was obtained by dividing series 3 by series 4.

6. The amount by which the alternative procedure changes net exports at factor cost in constant prices was estimated by multiplying nonresidential business national income in 1972 prices (from table 2-5) by series 5.

7. Command over goods and services at 1972 factor cost is the sum of national income in 1972 prices (from table 2-1) and series 6.

APPENDIX B

Estimates of Actual Employment

Employment estimates in table 2-7, were prepared by the procedures described in *Accounting for Growth,* appendix C, except for minor changes dictated by alterations in the NIPA that the Bureau of Economic Analysis (BEA) introduced in 1976. They replace table C-1 in *Accounting for Growth.*

Tables C-2 and C-3 in *Accounting for Growth,* which present 1929–69 series for persons 14 and over from the Current Population Survey (CPS), are unchanged and are not reproduced here. Similar data for 1970–77 can be derived from January issues of the Bureau of Labor Statistics' (BLS) *Employment and Earnings* by adding data for 14- and 15-year-olds to those for older workers.

Table C-4 in *Accounting for Growth* is replaced by table B-1 in the present book. It shows the derivation of total employment. The movement of employment is based mainly on the same establishment reports as are the earnings included in national income, because this procedure yields an employment index as consistent as possible with the output series. Establishment reports measure jobs rather than

persons, but my series is reduced to the average level of employment reported in the CPS. The result is a series for the number of persons employed that I believe to be as accurate as can be obtained.

Columns 6 and 8 of table B-1 permit comparison of the two types of employment data. These columns are conceptually the same but different statistically. Strings of years in which the CPS series for civilian employment (column 6) exceeds the establishment-based series adjusted to the same average level (column 8) alternate with strings of years in which it is lower. The CPS series is close to the establishment-based series in 1947, higher in 1948–50, lower in 1951–57, higher in 1958–65, lower in 1966–70, higher in 1971–72, about the same in 1973–74, and again higher in 1975–76. There are also unexplained irregular discrepancies between the annual movements of the two series within these periods.[1]

Tables C-5 and C-6 in *Accounting for Growth* showed the derivation of farm employment and the number of nonfarm self-employed and unpaid family workers, while table C-7 showed the derivation of employment in general government, households, institutions, and the rest of the world. No changes in procedure have been introduced. (However, data are revised.) In accordance with a change in the NIPA, the rest-of-the-world industry now includes Americans temporarily employed abroad by business, while foreigners temporarily employed in the United States are subtracted. Table C-8 in *Accounting for Growth* showed BLS data for unpaid absences and an alternative index of total employment that made use of these data. The BLS has continued to report unpaid absences for one week in May each year (also in November 1970), and it remains true that these data do not help to reconcile establishment and CPS series.

1. Known incomparabilities in the CPS employment series do not consistently help to explain differences. After 1969 they included additions to CPS employment of about 301,000 in January 1972 and 60,000 in March 1973. An additional 236,000 were added in January 1978.

Table B-1. Derivation of Total Employment, 1929, 1940–41, and 1947–76

Thousands

Year	Civilian employment, based mainly on establishment reports					CPS civilian employment (6)	Ratio, column 6 to column 5 (7)
	Full-time and part-time employment (1)	Active proprietors of unincorporated enterprises (2)	Unpaid family workers (3)	Civilian employment overseas (4)	Total domestic (5)		
	Excluding Alaska and Hawaii						
1929	37,375	10,320	1,670	0	49,365	n.a.	n.a.
1940a	...	...	...	...	...	...	...
1940b	37,874	10,150	1,786	0	49,810	n.a.	n.a.
1941a	...	...	...	...	...	...	...
1941b	41,946	10,090	1,948	0	53,984	n.a.	n.a.
1947	48,176	10,199	1,941	96	60,220	57,860	0.96081
1948	49,398	10,211	1,860	96	61,373	59,166	0.96404
1949	48,028	10,064	1,862	92	59,862	58,472	0.97678
1950	49,880	9,996	1,740	85	61,531	59,798	0.97184
1951	52,710	9,699	1,697	76	64,030	60,836	0.95012
1952	53,529	9,637	1,685	76	64,775	61,085	0.94303
1953	54,724	9,475	1,612	77	65,734	61,997	0.94315
1954	53,293	9,329	1,592	74	64,140	60,941	0.95012
1955	55,163	9,149	1,732	76	65,968	62,996	0.95495
1956	56,948	8,981	1,809	77	67,661	64,762	0.95715
1957	57,362	8,821	1,765	77	67,871	65,065	0.95866
1958	56,076	8,611	1,607	77	66,217	64,020	0.96682
1959	57,872	8,428	1,633	76	67,857	65,636	0.96727
1960	...	...	...	64	...	66,448	...
	Including Alaska and Hawaii						
1960	58,988	8,311	1,586	64	68,821	66,737	0.96972
1961	59,083	8,189	1,565	65	68,772	66,852	0.97208
1962	60,657	8,027	1,452	65	70,071	67,903	0.96906
1963	61,754	7,746	1,350	66	70,784	68,867	0.97292
1964	63,309	7,681	1,337	64	72,263	70,416	0.97444
1965	65,760	7,561	1,332	65	74,588	72,239	0.96851
1966	69,256	7,312	1,203	68	77,703	74,127	0.95398
1967	70,808	7,235	1,174	72	79,145	75,608	0.95531
1969	72,808	7,149	1,153	71	81,039	77,209	0.95274
1969	74,964	7,228	1,160	71	83,281	79,221	0.95125
1970	75,124	7,119	1,105	69	83,279	79,989	0.96049
1971	75,357	7,150	1,110	63	83,554	80,501	0.96346
1972	77,660	7,228	1,088	61	85,915	83,116	0.96742
1973	81,109	7,304	1,063	63	89,413	85,886	0.96055
1974	82,480	7,495	961	65	90,871	87,408	0.96189
1975	80,964	7,449	942	62	89,293	86,172	0.96505
1976	83,595	7,416	879	63	91,827	88,844	0.96751

Sources: Column 1, NIPA, table 6.7, total minus military, federal government work relief, and state and local government work relief; column 2, unpublished NIPA series provided by Bureau of Economic Analysis; column 3, 1929–69 data from *Accounting for Growth*, table C-4; column 3, 1970–76 data from Bureau of Labor Statistics, *Employment and Earnings* (January 1977), tables 21 and 34 and corresponding tables from January issues, 1971 to 1976; column 4, sum of (1) U.S. citizens employed abroad by the U.S. government, for which the BEA provided data based on the Civil Service Commission series, and (2) U.S. citizens employed abroad by private enterprises, which is a component of the NIPA series for employment in the rest-of-the-world industry and was supplied by the BEA from work sheets; column 5, sum of columns 1, 2, and 3 minus column 4; column 6, 1947–69 data from *Accounting for Growth*, table C-3; column 6, 1970–76 data, same as column 3; column 8, column 5 times 0.96157, the average value of column 7 in 1947–75; column 9, column 4 plus column 8; column 10 is the NIPA military employment series (published until 1975), excluding reserve personnel, and was provided by the BEA; and column 11, column 9 plus column 10.

n.a. Not available.

a. Includes work relief employment. Estimates in column 8 obtained by adding 2,830,000 persons on work relief in 1940 and 2,209,000 in 1941, as reported in NIPA, table 6.7, to the following line

b. Excludes work relief employment.

c. Ratio to following row assumed the same as in column 6.

	Estimated employment		
Domestic civilian (8)	Total civilian (9)	Military (10)	Total (11)
47,468	47,468	261	47,729
50,726	50,726	549	51,275
47,896	47,896	549	48,445
54,118	54,118	1,676	55,794
51,909	51,909	1,676	53,585
57,906	58,002	1,599	59,601
59,014	59,110	1,468	60,578
57,562	57,654	1,604	59,258
59,166	59,251	1,694	60,945
61,569	61,645	3,124	64,769
62,286	62,362	3,638	66,000
63,208	63,285	3,545	66,830
61,675	61,749	3,326	65,075
63,433	63,509	3,025	66,534
65,061	65,138	2,848	67,986
65,263	65,340	2,786	68,126
63,672	63,749	2,632	66,381
65,249	65,325	2,543	67,868
65,889ᵉ	65,953	2,516	68,469
66,176	66,240	2,516	68,756
66,129	66,194	2,598	68,792
67,378	67,443	2,800	70,243
68,064	68,130	2,723	70,853
69,486	69,550	2,720	72,270
71,722	71,787	2,732	74,519
74,717	74,785	3,156	77,941
76,103	76,175	3,421	79,596
77,925	77,996	3,517	81,513
80,081	80,152	3,463	83,615
80,079	80,148	3,096	83,244
80,343	80,406	2,738	83,144
82,613	82,674	2,403	85,077
85,977	86,040	2,295	88,335
87,384	87,449	2,202	89,651
85,861	85,923	2,154	88,077
88,298	88,361	2,123	90,484

➵➵❮❮❮

Total and Average Hours Worked

➵➵❮❮❮

Table 2-1, column 9, and table C-1 provide total hours worked and hours worked per person employed, classified by sector and class of worker.

Estimates for nonresidential business and for households and nonprofit institutions were prepared in the way described in *Accounting for Growth*, appendix E; they are based on employment estimates prepared as part of the NIPA and on estimates of average hours prepared by the Bureau of Labor Statistics. Revisions in my series stem from revisions in these data.[1] The unpublished BLS ratios of "hours at work" to "hours paid for" that are described in *Accounting for Growth*, page 183, are now available for 1952 through 1974; I extrapolated their trend backward to 1947 and forward to 1976.

Data from NIPA, table 6.10 have been substituted for the series formerly used for civilian and military employees of general government, and for the rest-of-the-world industry. This change is required for consistency with the new NIPA series for national income created by government and rest-of-the-world labor, and hence for analysis of labor input in these subsectors. The new NIPA series for total hours worked by civilian government employees runs one-fifth lower than the series I previously used, which had been benchmarked on the Current

1. For wage and salary workers in nonfarm business, weekly hours worked per person employed are lowered about 0.3 hours in an average year, of which about 0.1 hours is due to lower estimates of weekly hours per job and nearly 0.2 hours to a higher average ratio of employed persons to jobs. (See ratios provided in table B-1, source of column 8, and in *Accounting for Growth*, table C-4, source of column 6.)

Population Survey. The Bureau of Economic Analysis uses 39.54 hours a week for military personnel on active duty (I had previously used forty) and forty hours for rest-of-the-world labor. Hours worked by military reservists, which average around five a week, have been added to total military hours. (Reservists are not added to my series for the number of persons employed.)

Table C-1. Weekly Hours at Work per Person Employed and Total Weekly Hours, 1929, 1940–41, and 1947–76[a]

| | Weekly hours at work per person employed[b] | | | | | | Total weekly hours at work in nonresidential business (millions) | | |
| | | | Nonresidential business | | | | | Nonresidential business | |
Year	Whole economy (1)	General government, households, and institutions (2)	Total (3)	Farms (4)	Nonfarm self-employed and unpaid family workers (5)	Wage and salary workers in nonfarm business (6)	Farms (7)	Nonfarm self-employed and unpaid family workers (8)	Wage and salary workers in nonfarm business (9)
				Excluding Alaska and Hawaii					
1929	48.5	43.9	49.17	54.6	53.9	46.2	539.41	269.78	1,220.76
1940[c]	42.4	35.1	44.21	53.1	47.8	40.5	472.06	251.99	1,082.03
1940[d]	43.4	38.9	44.21	53.1	47.8	40.5	472.06	251.99	1,082.03
1941[c]	42.7	35.5	44.55	52.5	48.9	41.4	468.00	260.41	1,258.73
1941[d]	43.5	38.3	44.55	52.5	48.9	41.4	468.00	260.41	1,258.73
1947	41.7	35.9	42.72	50.1	47.8	40.2	397.15	290.50	1,451.34
1948	41.4	35.3	42.50	50.1	47.9	40.0	392.36	295.45	1,470.26
1949	40.9	35.2	41.96	49.1	47.9	39.4	376.01	293.41	1,389.51
1950	40.9	35.2	41.99	48.4	47.9	39.7	363.12	295.56	1,449.74
1951	40.8	35.6	41.97	49.0	47.9	39.8	346.96	296.10	1,548.65
1952	40.6	35.8	41.78	48.6	47.8	39.6	334.37	298.04	1,573.57
1953	40.4	35.7	41.53	49.1	47.8	39.3	325.88	296.55	1,602.42
1954	40.0	35.3	41.12	48.3	47.8	38.9	319.72	290.78	1,527.01
1955	40.0	34.9	41.22	47.6	48.0	39.2	309.10	292.71	1,587.61
1956	39.7	34.5	40.96	46.5	48.8	39.0	290.15	301.26	1,628.11
1957	39.2	34.3	40.34	45.4	47.7	38.5	269.06	299.52	1,612.81
1958	38.8	34.0	40.01	45.0	47.1	38.2	254.59	293.46	1,532.42
1959	39.0	33.8	40.27	45.2	46.8	38.6	250.66	288.94	1,604.78
1960	38.8	33.8	40.02	45.2	46.8	38.4	238.09	290.97	1,609.58
				Including Alaska and Hawaii					
1960	38.8	33.8	40.02	45.2	46.8	38.4	239.18	292.05	1,615.79
1961	38.5	33.5	39.78	44.7	46.2	38.2	229.71	288.94	1,597.49
1962	38.5	33.4	39.88	45.4	46.4	38.3	223.33	285.01	1,644.11
1963	38.4	33.3	39.83	45.6	45.9	38.4	211.72	276.24	1,674.21
1964	38.3	33.1	39.77	44.8	46.0	38.4	195.54	278.18	1,721.49
1965	38.3	33.0	39.85	45.5	46.0	38.6	188.87	277.51	1,799.13
1966	37.8	32.6	39.45	45.4	46.1	38.2	170.98	273.09	1,876.63
1967	37.4	32.9	38.82	45.0	45.5	37.6	162.95	267.01	1,885.92
1968	37.2	32.7	38.63	45.3	45.8	37.4	161.27	265.05	1,928.78
1969	37.0	32.7	38.39	45.2	45.2	37.2	154.58	270.47	1,985.77
1970	36.5	32.3	37.81	44.5	44.4	36.7	147.29	263.89	1,950.99
1971	36.3	32.0	37.65	44.7	44.2	36.5	144.14	267.40	1,933.93
1972	36.3	31.9	37.67	44.3	43.7	36.6	142.38	266.35	2,005.07
1973	36.2	31.9	37.49	44.0	43.5	36.5	140.05	270.43	2,104.60
1974	35.8	31.6	36.99	43.7	42.7	36.0	138.98	271.88	2,111.15
1975	35.4	31.4	36.64	44.2	42.0	35.6	139.57	267.56	2,017.49
1976	35.4	31.4	36.62	43.9	41.9	35.7	137.40	267.78	2,098.74

Source: See text of appendix C.

a. See table 2-1 for additional data on total hours at work.

b. Hours worked by military reservists not on full-time active duty are included in the numerator in the computation of hours per person in the whole economy but excluded in the computation of columns 2 to 6.

c. Including persons on work relief.

d. Excluding persons on work relief.

—»>X«<—

Nonresidential Business: Composition of Hours Worked, by Age and Sex

—»>X«<—

The index for the effect of age-sex composition of hours worked on labor input was constructed in almost the same way as that used in *Accounting for Growth* and described in appendix F of that book. There were minor changes in the weights, however, and in 1961 and subsequent years minor changes in the distributions of hours worked.

The Hourly Earnings Weights

Hourly earnings of employed civilians other than government wage and salary workers, classified by age and sex, were estimated for 1967 in *Accounting for Growth*, pages 187–89. They were reestimated in the present study by an identical procedure but with the underlying data corrected. The explanation is as follows:

The main statistics used are the mean earnings and mean incomes of full-time year-round workers, as calculated by the Bureau of the Census from data collected in the Current Population Survey (CPS). Up to 1967 means were calculated from grouped data by the use of midpoints for class intervals. Starting in 1968 mean incomes were calculated from individual responses. Comparisons indicated the procedures were not comparable. The Census

Bureau subsequently retabulated the 1967 data, using individual responses.[1] This sharply reduced the relative hourly earnings of females 14–19 and appreciably changed those of some other groups. Incorporation of the revised data is necessary not only to improve the 1967 estimates but also to make possible valid comparisons with other years.

With income and some earnings information now available annually from 1967 through 1974, it was decided to base weights on an average of years rather than on only one. Hourly earnings for each age-sex cell in 1967 were extrapolated to 1968–74 by the estimated mean annual earnings of full-time year-round workers, excluding government workers, in that cell.

These earnings data could be computed directly from *Current Population Reports* for each sex, but without an age breakdown. However, mean annual *incomes* of full-time year-round workers of each sex (including government workers) were available by age. For each sex the ratio of average income in each age group to average income in all ages combined was calculated for full-time year-round workers. This ratio was multiplied by the mean earnings of year-round workers, excluding government workers, of that sex to secure a preliminary series for mean annual earnings of full-time year-round workers, excluding government workers, in each sex-age group. This series was used to extrapolate the final 1967 estimate of mean earnings of full-time year-round workers. The resulting series was used in turn to extrapolate average hourly earnings.

Presumably because of sampling errors, the CPS mean incomes of sex-age groups fluctuate erratically. This is especially true of means for the groups with the smallest numbers of year-round full-time workers, which are the youngest and oldest age groups of each sex. The erratic year-to-year fluctuations in the earnings differentials derived from them obviously have no real-world counterpart. For this reason it is desirable to base the weights on an average of years. Moreover, despite their erratic nature these data must be used to judge whether any

1. The original income data were published in *Current Population Reports: Consumer Income,* series P-60, no. 60, "Median Income in 1967 of Male Year-Round Full-Time Workers 25 Years Old and Over, by Years of School Completed, for the United States" (Government Printing Office, June 30, 1969). The revised income data for males 25 and over were published by age in ibid., no. 92, "Annual Mean Income, Lifetime Income, and Educational Attainment of Men in the United States, for Selected Years, 1956 to 1972" (GPO, March 1974), p. 20; for other age-sex groups the Bureau of the Census provided unpublished data. I revised 1966 mean *earnings* in each sex-age group by the same percentage the Bureau of the Census revised in 1967 mean income in the same age-sex group.

change has occurred in relative earnings. To aid in this appraisal, average percentage differentials were calculated for various time periods. I concluded that average earnings of five demographic groups have not changed relative to one another. These are males 35–64 and 65 and over, and females 25–34, 35–64, and 65 and over. These groups include the most important differential, that between males and females 35–64. I also concluded that earnings in the remaining five groups have declined relative to the first five.[2]

Two sets of weights were selected, one for use in 1929–70, the other for use in subsequent years. They are shown in table 3-5. For the five groups whose weights are not changed the 1967–74 average was used in both periods. For the other five groups the 1967–70 average was used in 1929–70 and the 1971–74 average in 1970–76. The new 1929–70 weights differ from the previous weights for 1929–69 because of the improved method of calculating means that the Bureau of the Census adopted and of the use of four- or eight-year averages in place of a single year.

The Distributions of Hours Worked

Percentage distributions of hours worked in non-residential business among ten age-sex groups are shown in table 3-6. Aside from small adjustments affecting years beginning with 1961, the distributions for 1929–69 are the same as those shown in *Accounting for Growth* (table F-5) and described there, and the estimates for 1970–76 were derived from CPS annual averages by the same procedure as that used to obtain the 1966–69 estimates in *Accounting for Growth* (page 195). The adjustments described in the following paragraphs eliminated discontinuities in CPS data.

Starting in January 1972 the Bureau of Labor Statistics (BLS) substituted population controls by age, race, and sex that were extrapolated from the 1970 census for controls extrapolated from the 1960 census. *Employment and Earnings,* February 1972, gives January 1972 employment data by age and sex on both bases. This permits the effect on the hours distributions, as shown in table 3-6, to

2. The change for males 14–19 is small and uncertain and might have been disregarded except for the general pattern of decline in relative earnings of the younger age groups.

be calculated. In percentage points the effects of the change were as follows:

Age	Males	Females
14–19	0.02	0.00
20–24	0.09	0.06
25–34	−0.18	−0.03
35–64	0.00	0.02
65 and over	0.00	0.02
Total	−0.07	0.07

The CPS data for 1972 needed no adjustment because the new control data were used throughout the year. Adjustments of percentage distributions required for the years 1970 and 1971 were the same as the changes for January 1972. Adjustments were then reduced by one-tenth each year back to 1961; 1960 is unchanged. This is similar to my adjustment when 1950 Census Bureau controls were introduced. (See *Accounting for Growth,* pages 194–95.)

For a second change in control totals, introduced in March 1973, the BLS did not publish age-sex data before and after the change, but it is possible to approximate the effect of the change for four age-sex groups. The effect on age-sex proportions was found to be trivial and no adjustment for this change was made.

A third change in CPS data, the introduction in January 1974 of the "inflation-deflation" method of extrapolating population controls from the 1970 census, necessitated an adjustment to the 1970–73 data. Based on the ratio of employment by the new method to employment by the old method in January 1974, and my 1973 distribution of business hours, the new BLS procedure changed the percentage distributions of nonresidential business hours by age and sex by the following amounts in January 1974:

Age	Males	Females
14–19	0.00	0.02
20–24	−0.18	−0.05
25–34	−0.08	0.00
35–64	0.23	0.02
65 and over	0.03	0.01
Total	0.00	0.00

I adjusted the annual averages by the following percentages of these amounts: 1970, 6 percent; 1971, 33 percent; 1972, 60 percent; 1973, 88 percent. These are the percentages of the time from the census month to January 1974 that had elapsed by midyear. No adjustment was needed in 1974 or thereafter.

⇛⇚

Nonresidential Business: Employment and Hours, by Sex and Work Status

⇛⇚

Tables 3-7, 3-8, and 3-9 correspond to tables G-1, G-2, and G-3 in *Accounting for Growth*. As explained there, the estimates are constructed in two steps. A set of estimates based on the Current Population Survey is first developed. These CPS-based estimates are then adjusted to control totals for employment, based in the present study on table 2-7, columns 4, 6, and 7, and for total hours worked, based on table C-1, columns 7–9. Changes from *Accounting for Growth* in tables 3-7 to 3-9 stem mainly from revisions in the control totals.

The CPS-based estimates for 1947–60 are the same as those used in *Accounting for Growth*. Preliminary CPS-based estimates for 1970–71 and final ones for 1972–76 were developed by the same procedure that is described for 1966–69 estimates in *Accounting for Growth* (pages 201–03). The CPS-based estimates for 1961–69 used in *Accounting for Growth* and the preliminary estimates for 1970–71 were adjusted so as to introduce gradually—rather than abruptly in January 1972, as in the original CPS data—the adjustment of CPS weights to conform to the 1970 census of population. (See the last section of appendix D.)

Efficiency indexes for changes in hours of work, shown in table 3-1, columns 5 and 6, were constructed for each sex by the same procedures that are described in *Accounting for Growth* (pages 35–43 and appendix H). The weights for females used in combining these indexes are shown in table F-5, column 6.

To facilitate computation of the efficiency offset to changes in hours of full-time nonfarm wage and salary workers, hours in each year were initially expressed as efficiency equivalents to an hour of work in 1960, based on the curve described in chapter 3. These efficiency equivalents are shown in table E-1, which differs from table H-1 in *Accounting for Growth* only because 1960 hours (table 3-7) have been revised and because the range of hours shown has been extended to cover levels in recent years.

Table E-1. 1960 Efficiency Equivalents to Average Weekly Hours of Nonfarm Wage and Salary Workers Used in Construction of "Intragroup" Efficiency Indexes

Males		Females	
Average weekly hours	*Efficiency equivalents*	*Average weekly hours*	*Efficiency equivalents*
Postwar values		*Postwar values*	
...	...	36.9	37.30
...	...	37.0	37.38
...	...	37.1	37.47
40.8	41.15	37.2	37.55
40.9	41.23	37.3	37.63
41.0	41.32	37.4	37.71
41.1	41.40	37.5	37.79
41.2	41.48	37.6	37.88
41.3	41.56	37.7	37.96
41.4	41.63	37.8	38.03
41.5	41.71	37.9	38.11
41.6	41.78	38.0	38.18
41.7	41.85	38.1	38.25
41.8	41.93	38.2	38.33
41.9	42.00	38.3	38.40
42.0	42.08	38.4	38.48
42.1	42.15	38.5	38.55
42.2	42.23	38.6	38.63
42.3[a]	42.30	38.7[a]	38.70
42.4	42.37	38.8	38.77
42.5	42.43	38.9	38.83
42.6	42.50	39.0	38.90
42.7	42.56	39.1	38.96
42.8	42.63	39.2	39.03
42.9	42.69	39.3	39.09
43.0	42.76	39.4	39.16
43.1	42.83	39.5	39.23
...	...	39.6	39.29
...	...	39.7	39.36
...	...	39.8	39.42
...	...	39.9	39.48
Prewar values		*Prewar values*	
43.6	43.14	40.4	39.78
44.1	43.43	40.7	39.96
48.8	45.29	45.1	41.17

Source: See section in chapter 3 on intragroup changes in hours of full-time workers.

a. 1960 level.

➤➤❬❬❬

Nonresidential Business: Labor Input Index for Education

➤➤❬❬❬

The education index (table 3-1, column 7) is the same from 1929 to 1969 as in *Accounting for Growth* except that the series is now expressed with 1972 instead of 1958 as 100 and except for a slight change in 1969 resulting from the use of new weights for the education categories after March 1969.[1]

Derivation of 1969 Earnings Weights

The first half of this appendix is concerned with the 1969 standardized earnings and weights that are shown in table 3-12. Their derivation was generally similar to that of the 1959 earnings and weights (described in *Accounting for Growth*, appendix I, part 1), but some changes were necessary.

Comparison of 1960 and 1970 Census Tabulations

The main data source for 1959 was *Census of Population, 1960, Occupation by Earnings and Education*, Subject Report PC(2)-7B (Government Printing Office, 1963), which provides the mean earnings of men aged 25 to 64 in the experienced civilian labor force of 1960 who had earnings in 1959. The corresponding census volume for 1970, *Earnings by Occupation and Education*, PC(2)-8B (GPO, 1973), provides similar but not identical information for the experienced civilian labor force of 1970 that had earnings in 1969. Both reports are based on the 5 percent sample of the whole population.

The 1970 tabulations are more satisfactory in four ways, of which the fourth is much the most important.

1. Means of annual earnings were calculated from actual data (slightly rounded) reported on the individual schedules. This is more accurate than the 1960 procedure, which used grouped data.

It is possible that the change impaired comparability of the two censuses with respect to earnings differentials in the highest education groups, particularly between those with 4 years of college and those with 5 or more years.

2. Persons with 4 years of college are separated from those with 5 or more years of college in all tabulations, whereas in 1960 they were combined in tabulations by race.

3. The 1970 tabulations provided data for Negro men.[2] (Both the 1960 and 1970 tabulations provided data for all men and for white men. Data for nonwhite men were obtainable by subtraction.) In analyzing the 1970 data I used earnings of Negroes in place of those for nonwhites (as in analyzing the 1960 data) because Negroes are a more homogeneous group. The small group of nonwhites other than Negroes were simply omitted from the 1969 analysis.

4. Both censuses provided data for men 25–64 who were in the experienced civilian labor force at the census date and who had earnings in the preceding year. The 1970 census provided, in addition, data confined to men in this category who worked fifty to fifty-two weeks in 1969. This is a marked improvement. It permitted men who worked only part of the year to be omitted from the start in the analysis of 1969 earnings, whereas it was necessary to base the initial analysis of 1959 earnings on data for the whole group and then to make a summary adjustment to eliminate the effect of part-year workers on earnings differentials.

In two respects the 1970 tabulations were less satisfactory than the 1960 tabulations.

1. Men 35 to 44 years of age were combined with those 45 to 54 years of age.

---

1. Weights used to combine separate series for males and females were revised in all years, but the revisions were too small to affect the education index.

2. Data for men of Spanish origin were also provided but could not be used since they overlap data for whites and Negroes.

Table F-1. Mean 1969 Annual Money Earnings of Males in the Experienced Business Labor Force in April 1970 Who Worked 50–52 Weeks in 1969, by Age, Farm or Nonfarm Attachment, Race, Region, and Years of School Completed[a]

Dollars

Age group	Work attachment	Race	Region	*Years of school completed*					
				Elementary	*High school*		*College*		
				0–8[b]	1–3	4	1–3	4	5 or more
25–34	Nonfarm	White	North	7,552	8,468	9,095	9,935	12,208	13,345
25–34	Nonfarm	White	South	6,223	7,244	8,114	9,022	11,599	12,780
25–34	Nonfarm	Negro	North	6,342	6,695	7,460	8,073	9,586	12,226
25–34	Nonfarm	Negro	South	4,474	5,028	5,757	6,444	7,601	9,855
25–34	Farm	White	North	5,346	6,373	7,158	7,316	9,349	*
25–34	Farm	White	South	3,917	5,235	6,194	7,653	8,503	*
25–34	Farm	Negro	North	2,561	*	*	*	*	*
25–34	Farm	Negro	South	2,491	3,019	3,278	*	*	*
35–44	Nonfarm	White	North	8,280	9,350	10,473	12,451	16,256	19,284
35–44	Nonfarm	White	South	6,926	8,520	9,643	11,431	15,271	19,206
35–44	Nonfarm	Negro	North	6,859	7,346	8,019	8,726	11,125	16,487
35–44	Nonfarm	Negro	South	4,751	5,599	6,253	6,969	8,820	13,476
35–44	Farm	White	North	6,334	7,581	8,375	9,356	9,603	*
35–44	Farm	White	South	4,371	6,169	7,165	9,225	10,397	*
35–44	Farm	Negro	North	3,418	*	*	*	*	*
35–44	Farm	Negro	South	2,669	3,315	4,274	*	*	*
45–54	Nonfarm	White	North	8,534	9,725	10,983	13,720	19,036	25,325
45–54	Nonfarm	White	South	7,006	8,792	10,113	12,596	17,040	23,277
45–54	Nonfarm	Negro	North	6,868	7,148	7,593	8,745	11,125	16,487
45–54	Nonfarm	Negro	South	4,691	5,448	5,921	6,983	8,820	13,476
45–54	Farm	White	North	6,328	7,117	7,948	8,505	10,455	*
45–54	Farm	White	South	4,510	6,001	7,311	9,264	10,397	*
45–54	Farm	Negro	North	3,816	*	*	*	*	*
45–54	Farm	Negro	South	2,548	3,020	3,894	*	*	*
55–64	Nonfarm	White	North	8,008	9,294	10,383	12,750	17,711	22,846
55–64	Nonfarm	White	South	6,614	8,292	9,869	12,333	16,603	22,141
55–64	Nonfarm	Negro	North	6,560	7,219	7,336	8,415	9,363	14,455
55–64	Nonfarm	Negro	South	4,479	5,141	6,132	6,219	8,067	13,899
55–64	Farm	White	North	5,608	6,434	6,796	8,518	9,577	*
55–64	Farm	White	South	4,102	5,652	6,236	7,272	9,425	*
55–64	Farm	Negro	North	3,518	*	*	*	*	*
55–64	Farm	Negro	South	2,343	*	*	*	*	*

Source: Derived from data in U.S. Bureau of the Census, *Census of Population, 1970, Earnings by Occupation and Education,* Subject Report, PC(2)-8B (GPO, 1973), tables 3 and 4. Partly estimated.

a. Persons with no money earnings in 1969 are excluded.

b. Includes persons with no education.

* Less than 400 persons, or the Census Bureau shows means for only one of the two farm occupations, and this one employs less than 75 percent of the farm total.

2. Men with 0–7 years of education were combined with those having 8 years of education.

Derivation of 1969 Earnings Differentials before Division of the Group with 0–8 Years of Education

In deriving 1969 weights the first step was to compute mean 1969 money earnings of year-round male workers in the experienced business labor force in each education category classified by age, farm or nonfarm work attachment, color, and region. These data, shown in table F-1, are similar to those for 1959 shown in table I-2 of *Accounting for Growth,* with the major exception that the 1969 data refer to men who worked fifty to fifty-two weeks in 1969. In addition, data for Negroes replace those for nonwhites and the categories of 0–7 years and 8

years of education are combined, while college graduates are divided into two groups.[3]

3. As in 1960, the farm occupations are "farmers and farm managers" and "farm laborers and foremen." The occupations eliminated as primarily nonbusiness differ slightly from the 1960 list. They are clergymen; social and recreation workers; teachers, college and university; elementary school teachers; secondary school teachers; air traffic controllers; radio operators; inspectors, except construction; public administration; officials and administrators, public administration, n.e.c.; school administrators, college; school administrators, elementary and secondary; firemen, fire protection; policemen and detectives; and private household workers. Because of the small numbers of Negroes in some of these occupations, full occupational detail was not available for them. To eliminate nonbusiness occupations from the data for Negroes it was sometimes necessary to deduct slightly different occupational groupings, or to substitute data for nonwhites for data referring to Negroes.

The Census Bureau report omits mean earnings in cells containing less than 400 people (20 in the sample). Missing means were estimated if needed to eliminate a small group from a large one; specifically, to eliminate individual nonbusiness occupations and to deduct the two farm occupations to secure nonfarm business aggregates. The necessity for such estimation does not appreciably impair the means for nonfarm business workers. Means for farm workers are shown only when the Census Bureau reports mean earnings for both farm occupations (requiring at least 400 persons in each), or if only one occupation is reported, it contains at least three times as many persons as the other. In the latter case the missing mean was estimated. Most cells in the Negro farm rows are omitted because their numbers were too few to meet this test. Also omitted here are means for both white and Negro men in the farm category who had 5 or more years of college. Not only were the numbers in these cells small but, in addition, a significant fraction consisted of government employees who should be omitted.

As in 1960, the nonfarm occupational detail in the regional tables of the 1970 Census Bureau report is too limited to use. It was again necessary to estimate the means for nonagricultural business occupations in each region as the product of (1) mean earnings in all nonagricultural occupations in the region in the corresponding age-race-education category and (2) the national ratio of mean earnings in primarily business nonagricultural occupations to mean earnings in all nonagricultural occupations in that category.

The preceding description applies to 25–34, 35–54, and 55–64 age groups. The 35–54 age group is subdivided in table F-1. In each work attachment-race-region-education category it was assumed that the ratios of the mean earnings of men 35–44 and 45–54 to the mean earnings of men 35–54 were the same in 1969 as in 1959.[4] The mean 1959 earnings of the detailed age groups are from *Accounting for Growth*, table I-2. The 1959 means for the combined (35–54) age groups were computed from the worksheets for *Accounting for Growth*.

4. The main underlying assumption is that the relative earnings of the two age groups did not change within detailed cells. Because the 1959 data, unlike those for 1969, include part-year and part-time workers it is also necessary to assume that within detailed cells, the percentage of workers in these categories was the same in the two age groups. The effect on the final standardized earnings differentials of errors in these assumptions should be trivial because overstatement for an education category in one age group is approximately offset by understatement in the other.

Unlike the situation in 1959, the data for 1969 in table F-1 require no adjustment to eliminate the effects of intermittent employment because the tabulations used are confined to men who worked fifty to fifty-two weeks. At first sight an adjustment for part-time work seems necessary because it is known that the percentage of employed persons who work full time in a given week increases (with certain irregularities) as education level increases the fact is, however, that nearly all part-time male workers either are outside the 25–64 age bracket or are not full-year workers. In either case they are excluded from the 1969 earnings data I use. Among all males in the 22–64 age bracket who worked fifty to fifty-two weeks in 1969, some 98.2 percent were full-time workers.[5] Since a considerable number of men 22–24 are students employed part time, the full-time percentage for men 25–64 was even higher.

Preliminary Division of the Group with 0–8 Years of Education into Two Parts

To obtain mean earnings separately for men with 0–7 years of education and with 8 years of education in each of the thirty-two categories listed in table F-1, it was assumed that the ratios of the mean earnings of men with 0–7 years of education and with 8 years of education to the mean for men with 0–8 years of education were the same in 1969 as in 1959. The implied assumption that the ratio is the same for year-round workers (to whom the 1969 data pertain) is the same as for all workers (to whom the 1959 data pertain) is not satisfactory because part-year employment is likely to be more common in the 0–7 than in the 8-year education category. Consequently the average earnings of men with 8 years of education are overstated and those with 7 years are understated. This error is corrected subsequently but not in the detail shown in table F-1.

Weighted Average of Earnings Differentials

The next step was to compute a weighted average of earnings "indexes" based on table F-1 and the separate estimates, just described, for men with 0–7 and 8 years of education. For each of the thirty-two lines in the table, average earnings at each level of education were expressed as a percentage of av-

5. U.S. Bureau of the Census, *Current Population Reports*, series P-60, no. 95, "Supplementary Report on the Low-Income Population 1966 to 1972" (Government Printing Office, 1974).

erage earnings in the same line at the 8-years-of-education level. These thirty-two "indexes" were then weighted by total earnings of men in the thirty-two categories. Observations were available for categories with 99.8 percent of the total weight for all education levels except 5 or more years of college, for which the percentage was 96.3.

Corrected Division of the Group with 0–8 Years of Education into Two Parts

The weighted index just described showed the correct relationship between standardized earnings of full-time year-round workers with 0–8 years of education and groups with more education, but the figures for those with 0–7 years and 8 years of elementary education, separately, were biased, as explained earlier. To correct them I turned to income data for 1969 collected in the Current Population Survey (CPS).[6] This source gives the mean money income of men with 0–7, 8, and 0–8 years of education, both for all men with money income and for men with money income who were year-round full-time workers. Data are available for each of the ten-year age brackets I use but without detail by work attachment, race, and religion.

For each age group, I expressed mean income of all men with money income at the 0–7 and 0–8 years of education levels as a percentage of the mean income of men with 8 years of education. A weighted average of the percentages was computed, based on the earnings weights for the age groups. A similar weighted average was also computed for mean incomes of year-round full-time workers. The ratios of the income indexes for year-round full-time workers to those for all men with income were multiplied by the preliminary earnings indexes described earlier to obtain corrected indexes of earnings for year-round full-time workers having 0–7 and 0–8 years of education, expressed with earnings at 8 years of education equal to 100. The indexes for the remaining education groups had then to be restated with the new, adjusted earnings at the 8-year level taken as 100. Therefore, the indexes obtained previously for all high school and college education groups were multiplied by the ratio of the new index for the group with 0–8 years of education (earnings at 8 years = 100) to the preliminary index. The relative earnings among all education groups except the 0–7- and 8-year groups were unchanged by this procedure.

Division of the Group with 0–7 Years of Education into Three Parts

Separate indexes of standardized earnings in full-time equivalent business employment were needed for men with 0, 1–4, and 5–7 years of education. Earnings data are not available in this amount of educational detail but estimates had been made for 1959.[7] Changes from 1959 to 1969 in differentials among education groups in the mean income (as distinguished from earnings) of males with income were used to estimate changes in earnings differentials.

Income distributions for males with income were available for 1959 from *Census of Population, 1960, Educational Attainment,* Subject Report PC (2)-7B (GPO, 1963), table 6; and for 1969 from *Census of Population, 1970, Educational Attainment,* Subject Report PC(2)-5B (GPO, 1973), table 7.[8] In addition, data on number of persons, mean income, and median income were available for 1969. Data for number of persons and median income were also available for 1959, but mean income was missing and had to be estimated—sometimes from size distributions and sometimes by applying the 1969 ratio of mean income to median income to 1959 median income. The Census Bureau tables for both years provided income data from which the desired cross-classification by school years completed, age, race, and regional groupings could be obtained, but information needed for a breakdown by farm or nonfarm attachment was lacking.

Despite the devotion of much effort to developing earnings indexes for men with 0, 1–4, and 5–7 years of education, these estimates are subject to appreciable error. The results indicate that standardized earnings of the group with 5–7 years of education bore almost the same relationship to earnings of men with 8 years of education in 1969 as in 1959, but that the relative earnings of men with 1–4 years of education, and especially men with no education, rose sharply over the decade.

Complete Standardized Earnings Index

Table 3-12, column 2, shows the complete set of standardized earnings differentials for 1969. The broad range from 5–7 years of elementary school to 4 years of college covered 92 percent of full-time equivalent business employment of males, and 97

---

6. Ibid., no. 75, "Consumer Income" (GPO, December 14, 1970), table 47.

7. *Accounting for Growth,* table I-4 and pp. 225–26.
8. In the 1960 volume, see pp. 88–90 and 107–09; in the 1970 volume, see pp. 150–52 and 175–78.

percent of females in that year. Within that range, differentials had narrowed modestly since 1959. Standardized earnings in the highest education group within this range exceeded those in the lowest by 110.8 percent in 1959 and by 104.6 percent in 1969, a drop of one-eighteenth. The differential between men with no education and those with 1–4 years of education is estimated to have been cut by more than one-half. This is not an estimate meriting much confidence; although the differential in the average *income* of *all men with income* was greatly reduced, it is possible that this was not accompanied by a large reduction in the full-time earnings differential, as is supposed here. The earnings differential between men with 4 years of college and those with 5 or more years of college fell from 31.2 percent to 24.3 percent, or by more than one-fifth. Despite the possibility of errors in 1959 means for the top group stemming from the use of grouped data in their calculation, there is little doubt that this differential narrowed—but it is not clear why.

Adjustment for Academic Aptitude and Socioeconomic Status of Parents

The final step in obtaining 1969 weights was to adjust the standardized earnings to eliminate the part of the percentage differentials between men in adjacent education groups that would have been present even if the men did not differ in amount of education. This part is due to differences between education groups with respect to the academic aptitude of the men and the socioeconomic status of their parents. The percentages by which earnings of men at each education level would have exceeded earnings of men at the next lower level if their education were the same were estimated for 1959.[9] The same percentages were used for 1969, so the entire reduction in earnings differentials from 1959 to 1969 is ascribed to the education component. An exception was made for the differential between men with 4 years of college and those with 5 or more years of college. The latter group is open-ended and includes individuals with a one-year masters degree, or no degree, as well as those with many years of specialized training in medicine or other professions. These categories differ greatly not only in amount of education and the men's investment in it but also in academic aptitude, socioeconomic status, and earnings. Given the large reduction from 1959 in the size of the standardized earnings differential between the two top education groups, the fact that a large part of the differential in 1959 was

9. See *Accounting for Growth*, pp. 228–41.

ascribed to academic aptitude and socioeconomic status, and the uncertainty as to how the mix within the top group had changed by 1969, it seemed best to depart from the procedure used for the rest of the distribution. In this case I reduced the differential due to education and the differential due to aptitude and status by the same percentage (21) from 1959 to 1969.[10]

Evidence from the Current Population Survey

Statements that the earnings advantage of college graduates over high school graduates has greatly diminished in recent years have been widely publicized.[11] If they were correct, the education weights derived for 1969 might need further adjustment before being used in the 1970s.

The best data to evaluate this question are those reported in the Current Population Survey on the mean incomes of full-time year-round male workers, classified by age. These data are available annually from 1967 through 1975. They have several merits. They are mean (rather than median) incomes, refer to year-round full-time workers, cover the whole educational range, are available by age, are available annually, and are based on a representative sample. They are greatly inferior, however, to decennial census data for the derivation of earnings weights. They refer to income rather than earnings. Nonbusiness occupations cannot be eliminated. Cross-classification by work attachment, race, or region is not possible. Most serious, the data are highly erratic, presumably because the sample is small.

For each of the ten-year age brackets used elsewhere, I calculated the mean income of men at each education level as a percentage of the mean income

10. To actually calculate the 1969 weights, I repeated the calculations in *Accounting for Growth*, table I-13, columns 1 and 5 to 9, and substituted 1969 standardized earnings percentages (from table 3-12) for 1959 percentages in column 1, leaving column 6 unchanged except for the substitution of 10.36 for 13.12 in the "College, 5 or more" line.

11. They are based mainly on the work of Richard B. Freeman. See Richard B. Freeman, "Overinvestment in College Training?" *Journal of Human Resources,* vol. 10 (Summer 1975), pp. 287–311; Richard B. Freeman and J. Herbert Holloman, "The Declining Value of College Going," *Change,* vol. 7 (September 1975), pp. 24–31; Stephen B. Dresch, "Human Capital and Economic Growth: Retrospect and Prospect," *U.S. Economic Growth from 1976 to 1986: Prospects, Problems, and Patterns,* Studies Prepared for the Joint Economic Committee, 95 Cong. 1 sess. (GPO, 1977), vol. 11, *Human Capital,* pp. 112–53; and "Who Needs College?" *Newsweek,* April 26, 1976, pp. 60–64, 69. Contrary evidence is presented by David R. Witmer in "Is the Value of College Going Really Declining?" *Change,* vol. 8 (December 1976), pp. 46–47, 60–61; and "Better Data, Better Results; Illustrations in Rate of Return Computations" (December 21, 1976).

of men with 8 years of education each year. Because data in even this detail are erratic, the data for any single year or any single age group cannot be used as a satisfactory estimate. Table F-2 shows data that have been averaged in two ways. First, simple averages of the percentages for the four age groups were computed for each year. Second, the annual percentages so obtained were averaged for the periods 1967–70 and 1971–75. For the former period, averages from which the 1968 and 1969 data are omitted are also shown. Comparison of columns 1 and 2 shows it makes but little difference whether all years or only the first and last years of the 1967–70 period are used except for the category with 4 years of college, and it is because of that category that column 2 is shown.

Examination of the original figures for the separate age groups convinced me that the 1968 and 1969 data for men with 4 years of college must be discarded.

The 55–64 age class causes the most trouble. Mean dollar earnings of men 55–64 years of age in the three college education classes are reported as follows:

	Years of college		
	1–3	*4*	*5 or more*
1967	10,122	12,631	16,417
1968	10,436	18,315	17,445
1969	12,566	16,676	17,636
1970	12,904	16,080	19,509
1971	14,427	16,613	21,065
1972	15,796	19,399	23,380
1973	16,420	21,390	23,523
1974	17,470	21,814	25,706
1975	18,848	24,937	25,685

The 1968 mean of $18,315 for men with 4 years of college in the 55–64 age group is far too high. It exceeds the mean for men with 5 or more years of college—the only case in the entire set of detailed data, covering seven education categories in four age groups for nine years, where income fails to rise with education. It is also far above the means for the same group in any other year until 1972, whereas in other categories income was rising steadily. Unless there was an error in processing the data, a Rockefeller—or several of them—must have entered the sample. This age group more than accounts for a seventeen-point annual rise, from 195.1 percent in 1967 to 212.5 percent in 1968, in the average ratio of earnings in this category to those of men with 8 years of education. The mean income of men in this age group who had 4 years of college is reported still to have been above 1970

Table F-2. Mean Income of Year-Round Full-Time Workers, by Years of School Completed[a]

Mean income of men with 8 years of education = 100 percent

Years of school completed	1967–70 average (1)	1967 and 1970 average (2)	1971–75 average (3)
Elementary			
0–7 years	81.2	80.8	84.0
8 years	100.0	100.0	100.0
High school			
1–3 years	113.1	113.5	112.1
4 years	131.7	131.9	131.4
College			
1–3 years	156.8	157.0	156.1
4 years	201.0	193.5	192.2
5 or more years	228.4	230.6	218.7

Sources: Data for 1967–72, U.S. Bureau of the Census, *Current Population Reports*, series P-60, no. 92, "Annual Mean Income, Lifetime Income and Educational Attainment of Men in the United States for Selected Years, 1956 to 1972" (GPO, 1974), p. 20; for 1973, ibid., no. 97, "Money Income in 1973 of Families and Persons in the United States" (GPO, 1975), pp. 122–24; for 1974, ibid., no. 101, "Money Income in 1974 of Families and Persons in the United States" (GPO, 1976), pp. 116–18; and for 1975, ibid., no. 105, "Money Income in 1975 of Families and Persons in the United States" (GPO, 1977), pp. 195–97.

a. Percentages shown are averages of percentages for each of four ten-year age groups of men 25–64 years of age.

and 1971 in 1969, a pattern that is not credible. The 1969 figure also continued to look too high relative to 1969 averages for other education groups.[12]

The unacceptably big differential between reported incomes of high school and college graduates in 1968 and 1969 and the correspondingly small differential between college graduates and those with 5 or more years of college are reflected in the following tabulation:

	Mean income		
	1967 and		
	1967–70	*1970*	*1971–75*
College, 4 years, as percent of high school, 4 years	152.6	146.8	146.3
College, 5 or more years, as percent of college, 4 years	113.9	119.2	113.7

When 1968 and 1969 are omitted, annual data from 1967 to 1975 for incomes of men with 4 years of college show no trend relative to incomes of those with 4 years of high school.[13]

Once the 1968–69 averages for men with 4 years

12. Unlike the 1968 situation, in 1969 the averages for men with 4 years of college also look aberrantly high in the 35–44 and 45–54 age groups. However, it is the 55–64 group that causes most of the difficulty.

13. This evidence in itself does not necessarily contradict the belief that the differential received by new college graduates over new high school graduates has diminished. Indeed, the data underlying table F-2 show a clear, if erratic,

of college are discarded, the income data for 1967 to 1975 do not suggest any change in weights in the broad range from elementary school graduates through college graduates. The data in table F-2 are consistent with a continuation of the narrowing of differentials that was observed from 1959 to 1969 between this group and the small group with 0 or 1–4 years of elementary school and the group with 5 or more years of college, but the evidence is too indirect to warrant changing the 1969 weights at this time. A contrary decision would scarcely alter the labor input index for education.

Distributions by Amount of Education

Percentage distributions of full-time equivalent business employment in table 3-10 for dates up to March 1970 are from *Accounting for Growth*, table I-15. The main sources for later dates are the Bureau of Labor Statistics (BLS) Special Labor Force Reports (which are reprints from the *Monthly Labor Review* with detailed statistics added).[14]

I obtained distributions of persons 18 and over in March 1971 and March 1972 by the same procedures I used to obtain those for March 1962 through March 1970, which are described in *Accounting for Growth*, pages 244–46. To preserve continuity without revising earlier distributions,

the preliminary occupational distributions of various categories of workers in the nonbusiness sector and of those in the business sector continued to be based on *Census of Population, 1960*. (See *Accounting for Growth*, point 4, pages 245–46.) Where NIPA data were needed to extrapolate the numbers of workers in the various categories, the series as they existed before the January 1976 NIPA revisions were used.

The distributions of persons 16 and over from March 1972 to March 1976 were obtained by generally similar methods, but differences between the two distributions shown for March 1972 are not due solely to the addition of 16- and 17-year-olds to the coverage because the procedural changes below were introduced at the same time.

The procedure for eliminating nonbusiness employment described in *Accounting for Growth*, subsection A on pages 245–46, was changed as follows (the identifying letters and numbers refer to those used in that source):

A2a. An adjustment to eliminate 16–17-year-olds from the number of government wage and salary workers reported in CPS reports was no longer needed.

A2b, c, d. The numbers employed in "private education" and in "welfare, religious, and nonprofit organizations" in 1970 were obtained, by sex, from *Census of Population, 1970, Detailed Characteristics, U.S. Summary*, PC(1)-D1 (GPO, 1971). They were extrapolated to later years by the new NIPA series for full-time equivalent employment in "educational services, n.e.c." (not elsewhere classified) and "nonprofit membership organizations, n.e.c." As previously, the composition of employment by sex in these industries was altered on the basis of changes in the division by sex of total nonagricultural civilian employment.

A3. Occupational distributions as of 1970 for each of the four categories of civilian workers other than private household workers were obtained, by sex, from the *Census of Population, 1970* volume cited. (The four categories are "government wage and salary workers," "private education," "welfare, religious, and nonprofit organizations," and "all other.") These distributions were applied to the totals obtained in step 2 to secure preliminary 1972–76 distributions by occupation (similar to those described for earlier periods in *Accounting for Growth*). The occupational detail was increased by treating separately male "physicians, dentists, and related practitioners" and "transport equipment operatives" of both sexes.

---

reduction in that differential if the 25–34 age group alone is considered. On the other hand, CPS data for the 18–24 age group, which includes most men entering the full-time labor force for the first time, show an equally clear, if equally erratic, increase in the differential. On this point the data are inconclusive.

It may be noted in passing that it is dangerous to infer anything about changes in income or earnings differentials by amount of education in this period without giving consideration to age. Because the earnings of young people dropped relative to those of mature workers, and young workers have more education, a decline in differentials by amount of education for combined age groups would show up even in the absence of a change in differentials within separate age groups.

14. Specifically, William V. Deutermann, "Educational Attainment of Workers, March 1971," no. 140 (Reprint 2771); Deutermann, "Educational Attainment of Workers, March 1972," no. 148 (Reprint 2842); Deutermann, "Educational Attainment of Workers, March 1973," no. 161 (Reprint 2941); Beverly J. McEaddy, "Educational Attainment of Workers, March 1974," no. 175 (Unnumbered reprint from *Monthly Labor Review*, February 1975); Bob Whitmore, "Educational Attainment of Workers, March 1975," no. 186 (Unnumbered reprint from ibid., February 1976); and Kopp Michelotti, "Educational Attainment of Workers, March 1976," no. 193. In addition, unpublished tables that underlie those published in these reprints in the form of percentage distributions were obtained from the BLS. For March 1972, tables were secured from the BLS that permitted all tabulations that are used to be derived for persons 18 years of age and older as well as for persons 16 and over.

Table F-3. Civilians 16 and 18 Years of Age and Over: Unemployment Rates and Education Quality Indexes, Based on Years of Education, by Sex, Survey Dates, 1968–76
Weight of persons with 8 years of education = 100

Sex, age, weights, and date	Percent unemployed (1)	Education quality indexes based on years of education			Percent by which column 3 exceeds column 2 (5)	Ratio of column 4 to column 3 (6)
		Civilian labor force (2)	Civilian employment (3)	FTE business employment (4)		
Males						
18 and over, 1959 weights						
March 1968	2.96	129.02	129.38	126.92	0.28	0.9810
March 1969	2.59	129.78	130.09	127.52	0.24	0.9802
March 1970	3.74	130.55	130.93	128.13	0.29	0.9786
18 and over, 1969 weights						
March 1969	2.59	127.51	127.80	125.45	0.23	0.9816
March 1970	3.74	128.18	128.53	125.99	0.27	0.9802
March 1971	5.47	129.19	129.69	127.23	0.39	0.9810
March 1972	5.29	129.97	130.44	127.89	0.36	0.9805
16 and over, 1969 weights						
March 1972	5.95	129.29	129.91	127.84	0.48	0.9841
March 1973	4.74	130.28	130.78	128.79	0.38	0.9848
March 1974	4.85	131.30	132.84	129.98	0.41	0.9859
March 1975	8.96	132.40	133.62	131.58	0.92	0.9847
March 1976	7.82	133.44	134.44	132.28	0.75	0.9839
Females						
18 and over, 1959 weights						
March 1968	4.23	128.07	128.43	123.65	0.28	0.9628
March 1969	3.98	128.43	128.78	124.04	0.27	0.9632
March 1970	4.90	129.20	129.59	124.74	0.30	0.9626
18 and over, 1969 weights						
March 1969	3.98	126.26	126.56	122.18	0.24	0.9654
March 1970	4.90	126.94	127.29	122.80	0.28	0.9647
March 1971	6.41	127.81	128.24	123.71	0.34	0.9647
March 1972	6.03	128.28	128.66	124.17	0.30	0.9651
16 and over, 1969 weights						
March 1972	6.50	127.61	128.07	124.17	0.36	0.9695
March 1973	5.84	128.50	128.95	124.85	0.35	0.9682
March 1974	6.00	129.61	130.14	126.05	0.41	0.9686
March 1975	9.50	130.19	131.06	127.09	0.67	0.9697
March 1976	8.48	131.10	131.86	127.79	0.58	0.9691

Sources: Data for persons 18 and over, 1959 weights, are from *Accounting for Growth*, table I-17, and comparable data for nine earlier dates are available there. See text for explanations of other rows.
FTE Full-time equivalent.

The following change was made in the weighting of employment categories, which is described in subsection B, pages 246–48, of *Accounting for Growth*.

B2. In the calculation of full-time equivalent employment, persons who usually work full time but worked part time for economic reasons were formerly treated as part-time workers. They are now counted as full-time workers for consistency with tables G-1, G-2, and G-3.

In March 1976 the BLS introduced two changes in the detail of the tabulations:

1. In all tabulations, persons with no years of school completed were combined with those for persons with 1–4 years of elementary school. I subdivided this combined class at various points in the procedure by the use of March 1975 proportions for 1976.

2. In the tabulations on which the adjustment to full-time equivalence is based, persons with 4 years of college were separated from those with 5 or more years of college for the first time since March 1967. The subdivision of these data consequently no longer had to be estimated.[15]

15. The results were compared with those that would have been obtained under the previous extrapolation procedure. For males there was almost no difference, but for females the new data added 0.06 points to the percentage with 4 years of college and deleted 0.06 points from the percentage with 5 or more years of college. To avoid a discontinuity, the size of the correction was interpolated and the percentage distributions for 1971 to 1975 that have already been described were adjusted.

Table F-4. Derivation of Education Quality Indexes for the Business Sector, Based on Years of Education, by Sex, Annually, 1968–76

Sex, age, weights, and year	Index for civilian labor force[a] (1)	Percent of civilian labor force unemployed (2)	Index for civilian employment[a] (3)	Estimated ratio of index for FTE business employment to index for civilian employment (4)	Index for FTE business employment[a] (5)
Males					
18 and over, 1959 weights					
1968	129.24	2.48	129.54	0.9808	127.05
1969	130.00	2.39	130.28	0.9797	127.64
18 and over, 1969 weights					
1969	127.70	2.39	127.97	0.9812	125.56
1970	128.48	3.91	128.86	0.9805	126.34
1971	129.41	4.85	129.86	0.9808	127.36
1972	130.26	4.44	130.68	0.9807	128.16
16 and over, 1969 weights					
1972	129.58	4.95	130.10	0.9843	128.05
1973	130.58	4.13	130.96	0.9851	129.01
1974	131.62	4.83	132.12	0.9855	130.21
1975	132.70	7.88	133.72	0.9845	131.64
1976[b]	133.76	7.04	134.64	0.9839	132.47
Females					
18 and over, 1959 weights					
1968	128.16	4.33	128.52	0.9630	123.76
1969	128.66	4.22	129.00	0.9630	124.23
18 and over, 1969 weights					
1969	126.46	4.22	126.78	0.9652	122.36
1970	127.20	5.37	127.57	0.9647	123.07
1971	127.94	6.40	128.36	0.9648	123.84
1972	128.55	6.07	128.96	0.9647	124.40
16 and over, 1969 weights					
1972	127.88	6.63	128.42	0.9691	124.45
1973	128.83	5.97	129.30	0.9684	125.21
1974	129.77	6.71	130.32	0.9689	126.27
1975	130.46	9.29	131.29	0.9695	127.29
1976[b]	131.37	8.64	132.15	0.9691	128.07

Sources: Rows for persons 18 and over, 1959 weights, are from *Accounting for Growth*, table I-18. Sources for other rows are as follows: Column 1, straight-line interpolation of data from table F-3, column 2, or similar data; increases from March 1976 to March 1977 assumed equal to increases from March 1975 to March 1976. Column 2, BLS, *Employment and Earnings*, various issues. Column 3: column 1 is raised by a percentage equal to 0.0810 plus (column 2 × 0.0542) for males 18 and over, 1969 weights; −0.2251 plus (column 2 × 0.1258) for males 16 and over, 1969 weights; 0.0968 plus (column 2 × 0.0362) for females 18 and over, 1969 weights; and −0.1457 plus (column 2 × 0.0853) for females 16 and over, 1969 weights. Column 4: straight-line interpolation of data from table F-3, column 6, or similar data; 1976 assumed equal to March 1976. Column 5 is the product of columns 3 and 4.

FTE Full-time equivalent.

a. Weight of persons with 8 years of education = 100.

b. Preliminary.

Calculation of Indexes

Indexes of the effect of changes in education on labor input were calculated in the same way as in *Accounting for Growth* (pages 250–59). As stated in chapter 3, however, it was necessary to link three indexes covering survey dates because in March 1969 the weights were changed and in March 1972, 16- and 17-year-olds were added to the distributions. Because the method of interpolating between survey dates to secure annual averages requires taking account of the effect of unemployment on the indexes, it was also necessary to calculate separate regressions between (1) unemploy-

ment and (2) the difference between indexes for civilian employment and the civilian labor force for each period. Tables F-3 and F-4, which are extensions of tables I-17 and I-18 in *Accounting for Growth*, provide the estimates needed to calculate the indexes based on years of education. Data needed to allow for changes in days of education per year were given in table I-20 of *Accounting for Growth* for periods up to 1970. The table can be extended by adding for the 1970–75 period the following rates in columns 1 to 4, respectively: 0.62, 0.58, 0.17, and 0.17. Columns 1 to 5 of table F-5 replace table I-21 in *Accounting for Growth*. All these tables are described in that source. Column 6 of table F-5 shows the female percentages of labor earnings in nonresidential business that were computed in the process of developing the index for age-sex composition. Male percentages are

100.00 minus this column. Averages of percentages in adjacent years were used as weights to combine annual percentage changes in the indexes for the separate sexes.

Table F-5. Indexes of the Effect of Amount of Education on Labor Input in the Business Sector, 1929, 1940–41, and 1947–76
1972 = 100

Year	Before allowance for change in days per year of school		Final indexes			Female share of earnings (6)
	Males (1)	Females (2)	Males (3)	Females (4)	Both sexes (5)	
1929	82.50	87.85	75.85	80.98	76.64	10.03
1940	86.30	91.68	81.94	87.42	82.79	11.43
1941	86.44	91.80	82.23	87.67	83.08	12.01
1947	87.90	92.69	84.66	89.41	85.42	13.81
1948	88.25	93.02	85.18	89.88	85.94	14.04
1949	88.86	93.50	85.95	90.49	86.69	14.46
1950	89.19	93.77	86.44	90.90	87.17	14.58
1951	89.37	93.95	86.76	91.18	87.48	15.05
1952	89.76	94.16	87.28	91.50	87.98	15.51
1953	90.16	94.29	87.80	91.75	88.45	15.41
1954	90.81	94.66	88.57	92.22	89.18	15.27
1955	91.10	94.65	88.98	92.32	89.55	15.61
1956	91.46	94.74	89.50	92.54	90.01	16.05
1957	91.96	94.85	90.15	92.80	90.60	16.33
1958	92.87	95.24	91.20	93.31	91.57	16.41
1959	93.29	95.43	91.77	93.63	92.10	16.42
1960	93.81	95.92	92.42	94.26	92.74	16.57
1961	94.41	96.57	93.17	95.05	93.50	16.73
1962	94.74	96.78	93.62	95.41	93.94	16.85
1963	95.08	96.70	94.09	95.49	94.34	16.88
1964	95.42	96.78	94.57	95.73	94.78	17.19
1965	95.84	97.20	95.14	96.31	95.36	17.61
1966	96.30	97.46	95.69	96.69	95.87	18.15
1967	96.96	97.63	96.44	97.00	96.54	18.49
1968	97.52	97.99	97.10	97.48	97.17	18.75
1969	97.98	98.36	97.65	97.98	97.72	19.48
1970	98.59	98.92	98.37	98.69	98.43	19.67[a]
1971	99.38	99.55	99.27	99.43	99.30	19.65
1972	100.00	100.00	100.00	100.00	100.00	20.11
1973	100.75	100.61	100.85	100.73	100.83	20.46
1974	101.68	101.46	101.88	101.68	101.84	21.01
1975	102.80	102.28	103.08	102.61	102.98	21.09
1976	103.45	102.91	103.81	103.35	104.09	21.79

Sources: Columns 1 and 2, table F-4, column 5, and *Accounting for Growth*, table 1-18, column 5. Columns 3–6, see text.
a. Based on new weights, as in subsequent years. Based on old weights, as in preceding years, the percentage is 19.62.

Nonresidential Business: Weights for Inputs

In Appendix J in *Accounting for Growth* I describe and appraise distributions of nonresidential business national income by type of income and the weights derived from them that were used to combine inputs in nonresidential business. Similar procedures are used in the present study, so the detailed description and appraisal is not repeated. Changes in the 1929–69 distributions and weights stem from revisions of the data used, including minor conceptual changes in national income.

Income Shares

Table G-1, from which the final weights in table G-2 are derived, shows annual percentage distributions of earnings in the sector, classified by type of input. Their derivation starts from the four-way division of national income originating in the sector that is shown in table G-3. Table G-3 is easier to derive than formerly because NIPA data are now based on the desired series for depreciation, so they no longer need adjustment on that account. Each income flow in table G-3 is allocated among types of input by the same procedure as before.

Asset values, which enter into the allocations, are shown in table G-4.[1] In general they are based

1. The Department of Agriculture was revising its data for land as these estimates were made. The new series is used here starting in 1974. The farmland estimate in 1973 would be $217.2 billion instead of $209.0 billion as shown in table G-4, or 3.9 percent higher, if the new data had been used in that year.

Table G-1. Nonresidential Business: Percentage Distribution of Earnings in the Sector, by Type of Input, 1929, 1940–41, and 1947–76

Year	Total (1)	Labor (2)	Nonresidential structures and equipment (3)	Inventories (4)	Land (5)
	Earnings (percent)				
	Excluding Alaska and Hawaii				
1929	100.00	79.28	10.80	4.51	5.41
1940	100.00	80.41	10.61	4.73	4.25
1941	100.00	76.11	12.64	6.17	5.08
1947	100.00	79.87	9.68	5.66	4.79
1948	100.00	78.13	11.08	5.95	4.84
1949	100.00	79.96	10.84	5.04	4.16
1950	100.00	77.82	12.26	5.51	4.41
1951	100.00	77.72	11.98	5.75	4.55
1952	100.00	80.36	10.67	4.99	3.98
1953	100.00	81.79	10.22	4.50	3.49
1954	100.00	82.20	10.21	4.27	3.32
1955	100.00	79.48	11.98	4.81	3.73
1956	100.00	81.69	10.79	4.20	3.32
1957	100.00	82.67	10.32	3.90	3.11
1958	100.00	83.88	9.58	3.52	3.02
1959	100.00	81.54	11.17	3.99	3.30
1960	100.00	82.65	10.37	3.72	3.26
	Including Alaska and Hawaii				
1960	100.00	82.71	10.33	3.71	3.25
1961	100.00	82.84	10.16	3.65	3.35
1962	100.00	81.32	11.02	3.97	3.69
1963	100.00	80.56	11.40	4.15	3.89
1964	100.00	79.93	11.81	4.28	3.98
1965	100.00	78.38	12.59	4.59	4.44
1966	100.00	78.22	12.60	4.63	4.55
1967	100.00	79.93	11.70	4.25	4.12
1968	100.00	80.07	11.73	4.14	4.06
1969	100.00	81.88	10.63	3.68	3.81
1970	100.00	84.43	9.17	3.07	3.33
1971	100.00	83.86	9.59	3.10	3.45
1972	100.00	82.80	10.12	3.28	3.80
1973	100.00	82.99	9.46	3.28	4.27
1974	100.00	85.99	7.73	2.76	3.52
1975	100.00	84.54	8.79	3.02	3.65
1976	100.00	83.52	9.67	3.18	3.63

Source: See text for derivation.

on the same sources and procedures as before. Bureau of Economic Analysis (BEA) capital stock data in the desired form are more readily available than formerly. The figures for structures and equipment and inventories are the current-price counterparts of the constant price series shown (without detail) in table 4-1, columns 1 and 4. Year-end inventories are now seasonally adjusted. No new data for the value of nonfarm nonresidential land have been obtained since 1966. The ratio of the value of such land to the value of structures is held constant to 1976. (Table J-5 in *Accounting for Growth* shows the ratios and their derivation.)

Table G-2. Nonresidential Business: Weights Used for Inputs in the Sector

Period ending[a]	Total (1)	Labor (2)	Nonresidential structures and equipment (3)	Inventories (4)	Land (5)
1940	100.00	79.13	11.09	4.80	4.98
1941	100.00	78.78	11.36	5.30	4.56
1947	100.00	78.56	10.82	5.78	4.84
1948	100.00	78.32	10.70	6.00	4.98
1949	100.00	78.22	11.41	5.70	4.67
1950	100.00	78.38	11.82	5.40	4.40
1951	100.00	78.97	11.46	5.33	4.24
1952	100.00	79.60	11.02	5.23	4.15
1953	100.00	80.03	11.02	5.01	3.94
1954	100.00	80.60	11.01	4.73	3.66
1955	100.00	81.22	10.87	4.45	3.46
1956	100.00	81.48	10.86	4.30	3.36
1957	100.00	81.61	10.89	4.18	3.32
1958	100.00	82.02	10.70	3.98	3.30
1959	100.00	82.46	10.53	3.80	3.21
1960	100.00	82.34	10.62	3.80	3.24
1961	100.00	82.02	10.70	3.84	3.44
1962	100.00	81.69	10.82	3.89	3.60
1963	100.00	81.08	11.13	4.03	3.76
1964	100.00	80.26	11.60	4.22	3.92
1965	100.00	79.74	11.86	4.32	4.08
1966	100.00	79.56	11.87	4.34	4.23
1967	100.00	79.71	11.78	4.30	4.21
1968	100.00	80.28	11.55	4.14	4.03
1969	100.00	81.08	11.12	3.89	3.91
1970	100.00	81.79	10.71	3.64	3.86
1971	100.00	82.37	10.43	3.44	3.76
1972	100.00	82.77	10.19	3.30	3.74
1973	100.00	82.96	9.73	3.27	4.04
1974	100.00	83.10	9.36	3.29	4.25
1975	100.00	83.17	9.43	3.30	4.10
1976	100.00	83.19	9.71	3.26	3.84

Source: See text for derivation.

a. Entries for 1940 refer to the 1929–40 period and those for 1947 to the 1941–47 period. All others refer to the two-year period ending in the year shown.

Values for corporate and farm structures and equipment shown in table G-4 are generally lower than in *Accounting for Growth,* apparently because estimated service lives are 15 percent shorter.[2] Nonfarm inventory values are a bit higher than before from 1941 forward, farm inventories run lower by a trifling amount, and farmland is scarcely changed.

2. The reduction in the farm component was accentuated by statistical revision of the BEA series. For 1960, for example, my former figure of $38.2 billion was the BEA estimate with depreciation based on 100 percent of Bulletin F service lives. The BEA figure based on 85 percent of Bulletin F service lives was then $33.2 billion. My new figure of $29.2 billion is the new BEA estimate based on 85 percent of Bulletin F service lives.

When the income types shown in table G-3 are divided between labor and nonlabor income, all of column 2 (compensation of employees) is assigned to labor while all of column 3 (income originating in nonfarm corporations, except compensation of employees) is nonlabor income. Columns 4 and 5 must be allocated; my procedure is unchanged from *Accounting for Growth.* The earnings of farm proprietors and property income earned from farm property (table G-3, column 4) are allocated between labor and property earnings in proportion to the amounts (1) that farm proprietors and unpaid family workers would earn from labor if their average compensation were the same as that of paid employees in the business sector and (2) that farm property would earn if the ratio of its earnings to the value of tangible assets were the same as in nonfarm corporations. Earnings of nonfarm proprietors and noncorporate nonfarm property (table G-3, column 5) are allocated by a similar procedure.

Table G-5 shows the ratio of actual earnings to initially imputed earnings—the sum of items 1 and 2 above—in both cases. In farms the actual earnings have always fallen far below this sum, but in the 1970s they came closer on the average than formerly. Since 1968 the ratio has been very erratic because of price fluctuations. In the nonfarm noncorporate sector actual earnings averaged much closer to the sum of items 1 and 2 above, but the ratio fell after 1968.

Property earnings of corporations, nonfarm noncorporate enterprises and farms are allocated among nonresidential structures and equipment, inventories, and land in proportion to asset values from table G-4.

Weights Used for Inputs

Table G-2 shows the weights used to combine inputs in the nonresidential business sector. (The weights alongside 1955, for example, were used to weight 1954–55 percentage changes in the four inputs to secure the 1954–55 percentage change in total input.) The derivation of the corresponding table in the preceding study is described on pages 261–63 of *Accounting for Growth.*

Table G-2 is based on table G-1. It differs in that an attempt is made to smooth out fluctuations in the labor share that result from fluctuations in profits in the course of the business cycle, as well as from the effects of wartime controls on prices and

Table G-3. Nonresidential Business: National Income Originating in the Sector, and Distribution among Types of Income, 1929, 1940–41, and 1947–76

Billions of dollars

| Year | Total (1) | Compensation of employees (2) | Income, except compensation of employees | | |
			Originating in nonfarm corporations (3)	Earnings of farm proprietors and property used on farms (4)	Earnings of non-farm proprietors and noncorporate nonfarm property (5)
Excluding Alaska and Hawaii					
1929	71.5	43.9	10.3	7.3	9.9
1940	65.8	41.9	9.3	5.3	9.3
1941	86.7	52.8	14.6	7.5	11.8
1947	167.4	107.2	21.1	16.9	22.2
1948	189.8	118.3	27.4	19.1	25.0
1949	180.2	115.9	25.1	14.0	25.2
1950	200.6	127.4	31.3	15.1	26.8
1951	228.7	146.7	35.3	17.6	29.1
1952	236.6	157.4	32.7	16.7	29.8
1953	247.5	169.9	32.7	14.5	30.5
1954	244.2	166.2	31.8	13.9	32.3
1955	269.5	181.7	41.3	12.9	33.6
1956	284.3	197.2	39.1	12.9	35.1
1957	294.8	206.9	38.3	12.7	36.9
1958	291.2	204.8	34.2	14.9	37.3
1959	319.8	223.3	44.5	12.4	39.6
1960	327.4	233.1	42.7	13.3	38.3
Including Alaska and Hawaii					
1960	328.6	234.1	42.7	13.3	38.5
1961	334.6	238.8	42.8	14.1	39.0
1962	360.4	255.3	50.4	14.4	40.2
1963	379.5	268.6	55.3	14.4	41.3
1964	407.6	287.4	61.8	13.4	45.1
1965	445.9	309.7	72.3	16.2	47.7
1966	489.5	341.5	79.8	17.5	50.6
1967	509.1	362.8	76.6	16.0	53.7
1968	554.5	398.2	83.8	16.3	56.3
1969	595.5	438.3	81.2	18.5	57.5
1970	610.3	462.7	71.4	18.6	57.6
1971	650.9	490.3	79.5	19.4	61.7
1972	724.6	540.5	93.1	24.9	66.1
1973	817.3	609.6	96.1	42.1	69.5
1974	862.2	669.6	84.8	34.8	73.0
1975	916.5	701.6	103.7	33.0	78.2
1976	1,033.8	788.5	129.9	28.8	86.6

Source: See text for derivation. Figures are rounded.

wages. The objective is to approximate the shares that would have prevailed in normal circumstances with the rate of utilization of resources at about the 1948–69 average.

The methodology is essentially unchanged from the previous study, to which the reader should refer, but the following comments are needed:

In Step Two (following the writeup in *Accounting for Growth*, page 261) the actual labor shares in the recession years 1949, 1954, 1958, and 1961 were replaced with the average of the percentages for the preceding and following years, as before, but the 1969 percentage was retained. It was difficult to decide what adjustments to introduce after 1969. Business was slack in much if not all of the period. I retained the 1972 and 1973 percentages; replaced the actual ones for 1970 and 1971 with others interpolated between the 1969 and 1972

Table G-4. Nonresidential Business: Estimated Value of Tangible Assets Owned by the Sector, Excluding Dwellings and Sites, 1929, 1940–41, and 1947–76[a]

	Nonfarm corporate				Nonfarm noncorporate				Farm			
Year	Total (1)	Nonresidential structures and equipment (2)	Inventories (3)	Land (4)	Total (5)	Nonresidential structures and equipment (6)	Inventories (7)	Land (8)	Total (9)	Nonresidential structures and equipment (10)	Inventories (11)	Land (12)
1929	110.4	65.9	24.1	20.4	26.2	14.4	5.8	5.9	52.0	7.3	11.0	33.7
1940	88.5	52.8	22.0	13.7	20.6	12.1	4.1	4.4	36.9	5.8	9.3	21.8
1941	98.0	57.6	25.9	14.5	23.1	13.3	5.0	4.8	40.0	6.4	11.1	22.5
1947	164.8	96.9	46.4	21.4	38.1	21.3	10.1	6.7	81.7	11.2	23.8	46.7
1948	193.3	114.7	52.6	26.0	44.4	25.2	11.5	7.7	87.4	14.1	24.6	48.8
1949	206.7	125.7	52.6	28.4	47.1	27.3	11.7	8.0	89.7	16.5	21.4	51.8
1950	221.7	136.4	55.6	29.8	50.4	29.5	12.4	8.5	90.9	18.9	21.8	50.1
1951	250.5	151.2	66.0	33.2	56.2	32.7	14.1	9.4	105.1	21.5	25.4	58.2
1952	271.3	164.1	71.6	35.6	59.2	35.0	14.3	9.9	112.5	23.3	24.8	64.3
1953	282.9	174.1	73.0	35.8	60.7	36.4	14.4	10.0	112.3	24.3	22.4	65.6
1954	292.6	183.2	73.1	36.3	62.6	37.8	14.5	10.2	110.9	24.9	21.0	65.0
1955	308.6	193.4	75.8	39.4	66.5	40.5	14.8	11.2	112.7	25.7	19.1	67.9
1956	344.3	217.2	83.4	43.6	72.8	44.8	15.6	12.4	116.9	26.9	18.0	72.0
1957	372.4	238.0	88.4	46.0	78.1	48.9	16.2	12.9	125.6	27.8	19.6	78.1
1958	385.2	250.7	88.1	46.4	81.3	51.6	16.7	13.0	134.4	28.5	22.9	83.0
1959	397.0	258.5	89.5	49.1	85.0	53.7	16.8	14.4	143.2	28.8	24.2	90.2
1960	411.3	266.0	93.4	51.9	89.0	56.2	16.7	16.1	148.9	29.2	24.2	95.5
1961	423.2	272.4	96.3	54.6	92.7	58.7	16.1	17.9	152.6	30.0	24.9	97.7
1962	437.2	279.5	100.3	57.5	97.0	61.2	15.8	20.0	159.7	30.7	25.8	103.2
1963	455.6	288.7	106.0	60.9	102.2	64.3	15.6	22.3	167.4	31.9	26.8	108.7
1964	479.0	301.4	112.9	64.8	108.3	68.3	15.3	24.7	175.5	33.3	26.3	115.9
1965	514.6	322.4	121.6	70.6	117.4	73.6	15.8	27.9	186.4	35.0	27.7	123.7
1966	567.0	353.5	134.9	78.5	128.9	80.4	16.7	31.8	200.1	37.6	29.3	133.2
1967	624.6	389.3	149.5	85.7	139.9	87.7	17.1	35.1	211.0	40.6	29.0	141.3
1968	685.1	429.1	161.8	94.3	153.4	96.6	17.2	39.6	224.2	44.0	29.8	150.4
1969	760.1	478.2	176.3	105.6	171.4	108.3	17.5	45.6	238.7	48.0	31.9	158.9
1970	839.5	531.4	189.5	118.6	189.1	120.1	18.1	51.0	249.1	52.3	32.6	164.2
1971	911.1	580.5	199.3	131.3	204.2	129.5	19.5	55.2	262.2	56.2	34.2	171.8
1972	988.5	630.7	212.9	144.9	220.4	139.2	21.6	59.6	286.0	59.9	40.7	185.4
1973	1,114.6	706.8	242.6	165.2	247.2	155.7	24.1	67.4	330.4	66.0	55.4	209.0
1974	1,318.9	825.0	300.0	193.9	284.0	179.0	26.6	78.4	429.3	75.8	64.1	289.4
1975	1,497.3	941.7	337.2	218.4	313.1	199.5	26.7	86.9	452.9	85.4	62.9	304.6
1976	1,605.5	1,018.5	355.4	231.6	330.2	212.1	27.1	91.0	499.5	91.8	61.9	345.8

Source: See text for derivation.

a. Classified by ownership except that property used on farms is classified in "farm" regardless of ownership. Data are averages of values at the beginning and end of the year.

actual percentages; and replaced the 1974 to 1976 actual ones with the 1973 actual percentage. The labor weight each year is a five-year moving average of the shares so adjusted (Step Three) apart from adjustments having to do with the level of the series (Step Four) and with Alaska and Hawaii (Step Five).

In Step Four (still following the writeup in *Accounting for Growth*) a uniform adjustment was introduced to restore the average 1948–69 level of

the adjusted percentages to the average 1948–69 level of the original percentages. The average 1948–76 level of the labor share is allowed to remain lower after the adjustments than in the original data of table G-1 because the average actual level in 1970–76, like that in the 1930s, is regarded as abnormal because of underutilization.

Figures in table G-2 are averages of the adjusted percentages for the year shown and the preceding year.

Table G-5. Proprietors' and Property Earnings: Ratio of Actual Earnings to Unadjusted Imputed Earnings, Farm and Unincorporated Nonfarm Subsectors of Nonresidential Business

Year	Farm	Nonfarm noncorporate
1929	0.519	1.035
1940	0.413	0.958
1941	0.464	0.981
1947	0.564	1.014
1948	0.656	1.003
1949	0.508	1.028
1950	0.503	0.981
1951	0.550	0.972
1952	0.531	0.980
1953	0.469	0.969
1954	0.461	1.043
1955	0.376	0.964
1956	0.394	0.976
1957	0.403	0.981
1958	0.498	0.998
1959	0.358	0.964
1960a	0.398	0.912
1961	0.422	0.898
1962	0.397	0.870
1963	0.381	0.858
1964	0.330	0.871
1965	0.367	0.859
1966	0.392	0.867
1967	0.371	0.913
1968	0.357	0.901
1969	0.421	0.865
1970	0.475	0.866
1971	0.466	0.852
1972	0.525	0.827
1973	0.818	0.798
1974	0.667	0.801
1975	0.575	0.775
1976	0.425	0.770

Sources: See text.

a. Alaska and Hawaii are included beginning 1960. Without them, the 1960 farm ratio is the same and the nonfarm noncorporate ratio is 0.910.

Nonresidential Business: Gains from Reallocation of Resources

Columns 2 and 3 of table 5-1 (which measure the gains from reallocating labor away from agriculture and nonfarm self-employment) and all columns of table H-1 were estimated by the procedures described in *Accounting for Growth*, appendix N. The corresponding series in that book appear in tables 6-1 (columns 2 and 3), N-1, and N-4.[1]

1. Table H-1 differs slightly from the corresponding tables in *Accounting for Growth* in that overlapping estimates are shown for 1966 and (in a footnote) 1970, whereas the levels of the earlier estimates were adjusted to those of the later series in *Accounting for Growth*.

Table H-1. Series Used in Estimation of Gains from Reallocation of Resources and Related Series, 1929, 1940–41, and 1947–76

Year	Constant 1972 prices (1)	Current prices (2)	Full-time and part-time (3)	Full-time equiv-alent, weighted by sex (4)	Labor input (5)	Nonfarm self-employed and unpaid family workers: share of full-time equivalent employment, weighted by sex, in nonfarm nonresidential business[a] (6)
1929	9.32	12.10	23.93	24.72	22.42	15.21
1940	10.09	9.63	21.75	23.44	21.22	16.16
1941	9.24	10.12	19.78	20.97	18.93	14.57
1947	6.68	11.75	15.83	16.19	14.53	14.48
1948	6.78	11.67	15.43	15.77	14.15	14.52
1949	6.60	9.35	15.61	16.11	14.46	15.10
1950	6.21	8.93	14.94	15.36	13.77	14.81
1951	5.34	8.98	13.56	13.90	12.44	13.98
1952	5.38	8.27	13.03	13.45	12.03	13.83
1953	5.43	6.97	12.39	12.82	11.45	13.46
1954	5.66	6.78	12.73	13.20	11.80	13.82
1955	5.42	5.74	12.23	12.50	11.17	13.41
1956	5.25	5.46	11.52	11.51	10.27	13.26
1957	5.05	5.23	10.96	11.02	9.38	13.21
1958	5.53	6.11	10.87	10.90	9.71	13.62
1959	4.94	4.80	10.40	10.44	9.31	13.06
1960	5.18	5.00	9.95	9.93	8.84	12.97
1961	5.23	5.17	9.66	9.80	8.73	13.04
1962	4.91	4.92	9.12	9.16	8.15	12.58
1963	4.85	4.69	8.54	8.50	7.56	12.11
1964	4.47	4.13	7.90	7.85	6.98	11.98
1965	4.33	4.42	7.30	7.31	6.49	11.38
1966[b]	4.86	4.32	6.41	6.45	5.72	10.68
1966[c]	4.86	4.32	6.41	6.50	5.77	10.57
1967	3.95	3.86	6.07	6.17	5.47	10.33
1968	3.75	3.61	5.84	5.95	5.28	10.03
1969	3.79	3.78	5.54	5.56	4.92	10.05
1970	4.06	3.76	5.29	5.41	4.79[d]	9.99
1971	4.23	3.65	5.17	5.27	4.66	10.12
1972	4.07	4.07	5.02	5.15	4.58	9.90
1973	3.78	5.80	4.74	4.90	4.34	9.64
1974	3.76	4.75	4.67	4.88	4.32	9.73
1975	4.07	4.31	4.77	5.02	4.45	10.06
1976	3.68	3.49	4.58	4.81	4.25	9.76

Sources: Column 1, table 2-6; column 2, table 2-5; column 3, table 2-7; other columns, see text.
a. Percentages also used for labor input.
b. Comparable to earlier years.
c. Comparable to later years.
d. Comparable to later years. The number comparable to earlier years is 4.80.

⇥⟫⟪⇤

Effects of Varying Intensity of Demand on Output per Unit of Input

⇥⟫⟪⇤

Total factor input measures the labor, capital, and land that are present in business establishments and available for use. It is not affected by short-term fluctuations in the intensity with which these "employed" inputs are used. The effects on output of such fluctuations in intensity of use consequently appear in the series for output per unit of input (table 5-1, column 1).

The main reason that intensity of use fluctuates is that intensity of demand varies from time to time. The index shown in table 5-1, column 9, measures the effect on output per unit of input of fluctuations in intensity of use stemming from variations in demand pressure. This appendix describes the index.

Reasons for Fluctuations

Business responds to changes in the strength of demand for its products by changing its production and inputs, but output per unit of input is also affected because changes in output and input are not proportional. This is partly because fluctuations in demand, and hence in output, are not foreseen accurately enough nor far enough in advance to adjust inputs to what they would be if production

requirements were known for distant future periods. Decisions affecting the inputs present on any given day must be made at times ranging from the start of that day, in the case of some types of casual labor, to many years earlier, in the case of some capital goods. Fluctuations in output per unit of input also result from the presence of overhead costs. It is almost impossible to vary some inputs at all in the short run; others can be varied, but less than output; and still others could be varied as much as output, but the process of doing so would itself entail costs so substantial as to make the process uneconomic. Even if a firm knew many years in advance what its production would be in September 1976, the firm could not plan that September's inputs to accord with the month's production if it were out of line with production in other periods. Most fluctuations in individual firms and establishments are random and offsetting, or seasonal, and scarcely affect annual aggregate series, but general changes in the strength of aggregate demand have a great effect.

A brief examination of the reasons why individual inputs, as measured, do not vary as production does is useful in order to indicate both the nature of the problem and the complexity of the relationship whose effects must be measured.

Labor

My measure of labor input takes full account of short-term changes in total hours worked as well as in the composition by sex, age, and education of those who work them. However, a great deal of labor is of an overhead character, since workers remain on the job in slack periods. There is a substantial element of "indivisibilities" in labor. Although it may be possible quickly to add or lay off a proportion of the production workers in large departments of manufacturing establishments or to vary their working hours as the need for their services changes, it usually is not possible, so long as operations continue at all, to vary the number of hours of executive or supervisory personnel (including self-employed persons) or of large numbers of other workers, ranging from the corporation president's secretary to locomotive engineers on scheduled trains and clerks in any but the largest stores. Moreover, firms do not adjust changes in labor finely to changes in production, even to the extent that the presence of indivisibilities allow. To find, hire, and train workers is expensive. If it is expected in periods of slack that more workers will be needed again in the future, it may be deemed cheaper to retain present employees than to seek new ones when they are needed again. To dismiss employees is also expensive because of merit rating provisions in unemployment compensation tax laws, and sometimes of provisions for dismissal pay. It is, moreover, unpleasant. In periods of unexpected expansion of demand it may be impossible to add personnel quickly. Even if this is possible, it may be deemed desirable to wait to see whether the expansion is more than ephemeral; in the meantime the pace of work tends to quicken and to exceed that likely to be sustainable over an extended period.

Fixed Capital

The input of fixed capital is measured by the capital stock. The stock at any time reflects the expectations existing at some series of past dates concerning present and future needs. The stock of capital is not reduced when production falls or the rate of its increase slackens, and even the increase in the stock of fixed capital can be checked only with a considerable lag because of the time involved in ordering, manufacturing, and installing equipment, and in building structures.

The contribution of fixed capital to current net output is its contribution to current gross output less depreciation on existing assets. Depreciation is related—entirely as measured in this study, and largely in fact—to the passage of time and not to the intensity of use. Consequently variations in the contribution of fixed capital to net output that are associated with changes in the intensity of its use are the same as those in its contribution to gross output in absolute amount, but even larger in percentage terms.

Inventories

Inventory input is also measured by the stock. The stock can and does vary with the level of activity because firms adjust their holdings to their requirements, but there is no presumption that adjustments are proportional. Moreover, the first response of stocks to an unexpected change in business activity is usually perverse. Trade stocks and manufacturers' inventories of finished goods pile up when sales decline, and are drawn down when sales increase. Only with a lag, if at all, are firms able to bring inventories to desired levels.

Land

Land input, too, is measured by the stock. The series actually adopted does not vary at all.

It is obvious that changes in the intensity of utilization of inputs can importantly affect the annual series for output per unit of input. It is also obvious that the relationships are complex. It can be stated in very general terms that productivity is likely to be high when demand is strong and has recently strengthened, especially if the strengthening was unanticipated or not expected to continue, and to be low when the opposite conditions prevail, but timing and magnitudes are unpredictable. It is also clear that there is no way to measure directly the intensity of use of the several inputs. Under these circumstances the only solution available is to find another series that moves like the intensity of utilization, and from which its effect on output per unit of input can be inferred.

When undertaking the estimates for *Accounting for Growth,* I concluded that profit, or more exactly the ratio of nonlabor earnings in corporations to corporate national income, has the desired characteristic.

When overhead labor costs are spread over a smaller number of units of output because demand falls or is unexpectedly low, or because labor is hoarded, the ratio of nonlabor earnings to national income in corporations is reduced simultaneously with productivity. Because depreciation is measured as a function of time rather than of volume, depreciation cost per unit of output varies inversely with utilization of fixed capital; short-term reductions in the rate of utilization of fixed capital adversely affect both the ratio of nonlabor earnings to national income and output per unit of input. Costs ascribable to inventories and land, and the costs of fixed capital input that correspond to its net earnings weight, also are relatively fixed in the short run. These costs are included in nonlabor earnings along with "pure" profit, but because these assets are relatively fixed in the short run, variations in their utilization cause fluctuations in the ratio of nonlabor earnings (inclusive of these costs) to national income that are much like those that would be observed in a purer measure of profit.

Having concluded on a priori grounds that short-term changes in the utilization of employed resources would affect the nonlabor share and output per unit of input in much the same way, the next step was to test whether the data supported the expectation. They were found to do so, and more accurately than any alternative series. Consequently the nonlabor share provided a measure of changes in the intensity of utilization of inputs that could be used to derive, by correlation analysis, the desired series for the effect of intensity of use on output per unit of input. The results were modified to eliminate the consequences of any possible irregularities in the relationship between wage and price movements.

A similar approach is used in the present study, but some changes in detailed procedures were dictated by the data available, and special characteristics of the period since 1969 raised some new procedural questions.

Statistical Series Used

Table I-1 shows the statistical series used in the analysis. The first column shows nonlabor earnings as a percentage of national income originating in nonfinancial corporations. Nonlabor earnings include "corporate profits before tax with inventory and capital consumption adjustments" and "net interest." Labor earnings consist of compensation of employees.[1]

Data are now available for prices and employee compensation that are more consistent with data for the nonlabor share than those I used in *Accounting for Growth*. The price series shown in table I-1, column 2, is the implicit deflator for national income originating in nonfinancial corporations. Column 3 shows compensation per hour worked in nonfinancial corporations. To obtain this series in 1958–76, the Bureau of Labor Statistics (BLS) series for compensation in nonfinancial corporations per hour paid for was divided by the ratio for all nonfarm business wage and salary workers of hours worked to hours paid for (see page 155). The 1958 index value was extrapolated back to 1948 by John Gorman's series for compensation per hour worked in nonfinancial corporations.[2] Column 4 shows the ratio of the hourly

compensation index to the price index. It is in this form that the wage-price data will be used in further analysis.

Column 6 shows the refined series for productivity that is obtained when the influence on output of all inputs and of all the components of output per unit of input previously considered have been eliminated. Column 5 is the same except that the influence of labor disputes—which affect intensity of utilization and income shares in the same way as intensity of demand—is not eliminated.

The 1948–73 Period

This section describes the derivation of the series for the effect of intensity of use on output per unit of input in 1948–73. This period appears to me to be homogenous in the sense that there was no ascertainable change in the underlying trends of the three variables that will be used—the nonlabor share, the ratio of hourly compensation to price, and adjusted output per unit of input—or in relationships among the three.

Computation of Trend Lines

The first step was to compute least squares trend lines for columns 1, 4, and 5 of table I-1. This required the selection of time periods over which to compute trends. In *Accounting for Growth* the 1947–69 period was used. This was satisfactory because the years toward the beginning of the period were similar to those toward the end with respect to the inclusion of years of strong and weak demand, and hence of high and low nonlabor shares and adjusted productivity. A concentration of weak years at the beginning of the period would bias the trend upward over time, while a concentration at the end of the period would bias it downward; concentrations of strong years would have the opposite effect.[3] In the present study I again computed trend values from 1947–69 data.[4] The chief alternative, 1947–73, was rejected because the years at the end of the period were, on the average, years of weak demand. Their inclusion tilts the trends of the nonlabor share and adjusted productivity downward, unjustifiably in my opinion. However, to permit the sensitivity of results to the choice between these periods to be observed,

1. Column 1 differs from the corresponding series used in *Accounting for Growth* in the following respects:

a. Depreciation was formerly based on Bulletin F service lives, whereas it is now based on service lives 15 percent shorter. Price indexes used to calculate depreciation in current prices have also been changed.

b. Data used in *Accounting for Growth* referred to the entire corporate sector, whereas those now used refer to nonfinancial corporations. This change was made, even though output-per-unit-of-input data include finance, because financial organizations not organized for profit are classified as corporations in the NIPA; their addition in successive revisions of the NIPA has impaired the significance of share data for financial corporations.

c. There have also been revisions of a strictly statistical nature.

2. "Nonfinancial Corporations: New Measures of Output and Input," *Survey of Current Business*, vol. 52 (March 1972), pp. 21–28.

3. The levels at which trend lines are set do not affect my results; only slopes matter.

4. The 1947 value for column 5 of table I-1 was corrected from 66.45 to 66.34 after the trend was calculated. The corrected value was used in obtaining the 1947 utilization index itself.

Table I-1. Series Used in Analyzing the Effect of Changes in Intensity of Utilization on Output per Unit of Input in Nonresidential Business, 1929, 1940–41, and 1947–76

| | Nonfinancial corporations | | | | Nonresidential business | |
| | | | | | Adjusted output per unit of input with the effect of work stoppages: | |
Year	Nonlabor share of national income (percent) (1)	Implicit deflator for national income (1972 = 100) (2)	Compensation per hour worked (1972 = 100) (3)	Ratio of hourly compensation index to implicit deflator (4)	Not removed (1972 = 100) (5)	Removed (1972 = 100) (6)
1929	21.79a	n.a.	n.a.	n.a.	57.55	57.53
1940	22.19	n.a.	n.a.	n.a.	58.39	58.37
1941	26.16	n.a.	n.a.	n.a.	62.63	62.64
1947	20.74	n.a.	n.a.	n.a.	66.34	66.35
1948	23.25	62.75	29.80	0.4749	67.63	67.65
1949	21.96	63.96	31.31	0.4895	67.50	67.55
1950	24.36	64.14	32.64	0.5089	71.39	71.43
1951	23.84	67.08	35.27	0.5258	71.69	71.69
1952	21.03	68.59	37.35	0.5445	71.61	71.70
1953	19.51	68.83	39.61	0.5755	72.54	72.55
1954	19.22	70.57	41.14	0.5830	72.39	72.39
1955	22.32	71.23	42.64	0.5986	75.84	75.85
1956	19.98	73.79	45.29	0.6138	76.27	76.29
1957	18.91	76.02	48.11	0.6329	76.77	76.77
1958	17.34	78.13	50.00	0.6400	76.33	76.34
1959	19.96	78.85	51.85	0.6576	79.76	79.89
1960	18.42	79.09	54.19	0.6852	79.81	79.81
1961	18.28	79.25	56.06	0.7074	80.72	80.70
1962	19.82	79.26	58.29	0.7354	84.16	84.16
1963	20.67	78.98	60.22	0.7625	86.25	86.24
1964	21.51	79.57	62.80	0.7892	89.32	89.32
1965	22.66	80.15	64.78	0.8082	92.35	92.35
1966	22.30	81.97	68.69	0.8380	93.92	93.92
1967	20.66	84.00	72.72	0.8657	93.20	93.23
1968	20.36	86.21	77.84	0.9029	95.49	95.52
1969	18.22	89.57	83.29	0.9299	95.67	95.70
1970	15.39	93.34	89.06	0.9541	94.07	94.15
1971	16.09	97.12	94.66	0.9747	96.00	96.04
1972	17.02	100.00	100.00	1.0000	100.00	100.00
1973	16.42	104.67	108.38	1.0354	101.50	101.50
1974	13.92b	117.27	119.18	1.0163	97.16	97.20
1975	15.92b	129.96	131.77	1.0139	95.86	95.87
1976	17.12b	136.88	143.30	1.0469	100.29	100.31

Sources: Column 1, NIPA, table 1.15, one minus row 24 divided by row 23; column 2, NIPA, table 1.15, row 23 divided by row 40; column 3, see text; column 4, column 3 divided by column 2; column 5, table 5-1, column 1 divided by the product of columns 2 through 7; column 6, column 5 divided by table 5-1, column 8.

n.a. Not available.

a. See p. 189 for adjusted value.

b. See table I-7 for adjusted values.

the calculations were repeated with 1947–73 trends substituted for 1947–69.

Extension of the period to include 1974–76 would be wholly unacceptable. This was a time of very serious recession. Its inclusion at the end of the period would tilt trends downward very sharply and unjustifiably. This is in addition to the fact that two of the trends appear to have changed after 1973 so that no single trend line could fit the entire 1947–76 period.

The first six columns of table I-2 show the annual deviations of each of the series from its trend value, with alternative estimates for each of the three based on trends computed from periods ending in 1969 and in 1973. The trends for the nonlabor share are arithmetic so that the trend value changes (falls) by the same absolute amount each year, while the trends for the ratio of employee compensation to price and for adjusted productivity are logarithmic so that the trend value changes (rises) by the same percentage amount each year. Use of logarithmic trends for the last two variables is clearly indicated both on a priori grounds and by the data. Use of an arithmetic trend seems preferable for the nonlabor share but the choice is neither clear nor important to the result.

Table I-2. Deviations of Selected Variables from Trend Values, and Alternative Estimates of the Effect of Intensity of Utilization on Output per Unit of Input, 1948–73

Year	Nonlabor share, trends based on: 1947–69 (N_1) (1)	1947–73 (N_2) (2)	Ratio of employee compensation to price, trends based on: 1948–69 (W_1) (3)	1948–73 (W_2) (4)	Adjusted output per unit of input, trends based on: 1947–69 (P_1) (5)	1947–73 (P_2) (6)	Estimated ratio of actual output per unit of input to output per unit of input if intensity of utilization were at average level, based on:[a] (N_1) (7)	(N_2) (8)	$(N_1$ and $W_1)$ (9)	$(N_2$ and $W_2)$ (10)
	Deviation in percentage points		Deviation in percentage of trend value		Deviation in percentage of trend value					
1948	1.634	1.056	−0.607	−0.690	1.281	0.880	1.0163	1.0098	1.0133	1.0071
1949	0.439	−0.052	−0.690	−0.770	−0.640	−0.973	1.0036	0.9985	1.0007	0.9959
1950	2.934	2.530	0.079	0.020	3.291	3.007	1.0302	1.0249	1.0296	1.0244
1951	2.509	2.193	0.229	0.172	1.953	1.735	1.0256	1.0214	1.0258	1.0251
1952	−0.206	−0.435	0.610	0.554	0.100	−0.054	0.9968	0.9947	0.9993	0.9967
1953	−1.631	−1.773	3.081	3.044	−0.333	−0.424	0.9821	0.9813	0.9945	0.9922
1954	−1.826	−1.881	1.215	1.180	−2.238	−2.268	0.9800	0.9803	0.9853	0.9847
1955	1.369	1.401	0.741	0.724	0.672	0.702	1.0134	1.0133	1.0160	1.0155
1956	−0.876	−0.757	0.114	0.114	−0.487	−0.396	0.9899	0.9915	0.9906	0.9920
1957	−1.851	−1.645	0.063	0.079	−1.546	−1.396	0.9798	0.9826	0.9806	0.9833
1958	−3.326	−3.033	−1.916	−1.901	−3.782	−3.577	0.9648	0.9689	0.9585	0.9633
1959	−0.611	−0.231	−2.317	−2.228	−1.176	−0.905	0.9926	0.9967	0.9838	0.9889
1960	−2.056	−1.589	−1.339	−1.297	−2.803	−2.477	0.9777	0.9832	0.9732	0.9791
1961	−2.101	−1.547	−1.270	−1.215	−3.374	−2.991	0.9772	0.9836	0.9730	0.9798
1962	−0.466	0.175	−0.501	−0.447	−0.977	−0.524	0.9941	1.0008	0.9923	0.9993
1963	0.479	1.207	0.000	0.066	−0.252	0.266	1.0040	1.0113	1.0039	1.0113
1964	1.414	2.229	0.318	0.407	1.534	2.124	1.0139	1.0218	1.0148	1.0227
1965	2.659	3.561	−0.419	−0.321	3.185	3.848	1.0273	1.0356	1.0247	1.0336
1966	2.394	3.383	0.084	0.191	3.147	3.872	1.0244	1.0338	1.0240	1.0337
1967	0.849	1.925	0.220	0.336	0.608	1.377	1.0079	1.0187	1.0085	1.0194
1968	0.644	1.808	1.324	1.449	1.319	2.156	1.0058	1.0175	1.0108	1.0222
1969	−1.401	−0.150	1.142	1.285	−0.224	0.662	0.9844	0.9975	0.9893	1.0020
1970	−4.136	−2.798	0.590	0.750	−3.569	−2.653	0.9566	0.9712	0.9600	0.9744
1971	−3.341	−1.916	−0.388	−0.225	−3.271	−2.293	0.9646	0.9799	0.9641	0.9796
1972	−2.316	−0.804	−0.941	−0.764	−0.962	0.100	0.9750	0.9910	0.9721	0.9886
1973	−2.821	−1.222	−0.576	−0.394	−1.194	−0.073	0.9699	0.9868	0.9685	0.9858

Source: See text.

a. Ratios include effects of work stoppages. "Average level" refers to period to which regressions were fitted. See table I-3 for ratios that are comparable for columns 7 to 10.

I now designate the deviation from its trend of the nonlabor share (measured in percentage points) by N, the deviation from its trend of the ratio of compensation per hour worked to prices (measured in percent) by W, and the deviation from its trend of adjusted output per unit of input (measured in percent) by P. I use the subscript "1" when trends are based on 1947–69 or 1948–69 (used for the wage-price ratio because 1947 is not available) and "2" when they are based on 1947–73 or 1948–73. The formulas for trend values that were used in computing N, W, and P are as follows when log refers to natural logarithms, and t to time (in years):

For N_1: trend value is
$$21.80644 - 0.09503t \quad t_1 = 1947$$
For N_2: trend value is
$$22.55778 - 0.18206t \quad t_1 = 1947$$

For W_1: the log of the trend value is
$$-0.76983 + 0.03117t \quad t_1 = 1948$$
For W_2: the log of the trend value is
$$-0.76880 + 0.03106t \quad t_1 = 1948$$
For P_1: the log of the trend value is
$$4.16686 + 0.01723t \quad t_1 = 1947$$
For P_2: the log of the trend value is
$$4.17205 + 0.01662t \quad t_1 = 1947$$

Estimation of Effect of Fluctuations in Utilization on Output per Unit of Input

On the basis of these data I next estimate the ratio of actual productivity each year to what productivity would have been if intensity of utilization were at its average level during the period on which the estimate is based. I designate this ratio U.

The simplest procedure, and one that is rather satisfactory when judged against the difficulty of the problem, is to correlate P, the deviation of adjusted output per unit of input from its trend, with N, the deviation of the nonlabor share from its trend. The difference between the actual value of P and the "calculated" value of P (the value that is calculated from the regression) is an estimate of the amount by which P differs each year from what it would have been if utilization had been at its average intensity level. The regressions are based on the same time spans as those from which trends were computed, except that the year 1947 was omitted, partly because it is out of line and partly because 1947 wage-price data are not available for subsequent steps.

If the correlation is based on 1948–69 data (and 1947–69 trends), the following relationship and value for r^2 (r^2 corrected for degrees of freedom) is obtained:

$$(1) \quad \log U = -0.00100 + 0.01049 \, N_1$$
$$\bar{r}^2 = 0.872$$

The values of U obtained from this formula are shown in column 7 of table I-2. The figure of 1.0163 for 1948, for example, means that output per unit of input was 1.63 percent higher than it would have been if intensity of utilization had been at the 1948–69 average.

If, instead, the correlation is based on 1948–73 data (and 1947–73 trends), the following relationship is obtained:

$$(2) \quad \log U = -0.00094 + 0.01009 \, N_2$$
$$\bar{r}^2 = 0.872$$

The values of U so obtained are shown in column 8 of table I-2.

The estimates can be improved, on the average, by introducing the wage-price ratio as a second independent variable in the equations. The rationale follows.

It is first necessary to stress again, as I did in *Accounting for Growth*, that none of the correlation between the nonlabor share and adjusted productivity, which I ascribe to the influence of intensity of utilization on both, is due to short-term wage-price movements being related to both. In *Accounting for Growth* I showed that annual changes in adjusted output per unit of input were highly correlated with annual changes in the nonlabor share but not correlated at all with annual changes in the wage-price ratio. These results were obtained again in the present study. When annual percentage changes in adjusted productivity (table I-1, column 5) are correlated with annual changes in the nonlabor share (table I-1, column 1) values

obtained for $\bar{r}^2$ are 0.808 for 1948–49 to 1968–69 changes, and 0.824 for 1948–49 to 1972–73 changes. But when annual percentage changes in adjusted productivity are correlated with annual percentage changes in the ratio of hourly compensation to prices (table I-1, column 4), values of $\bar{r}^2$ for the same periods are zero. As an additional test, the deviation of the wage-price ratio from its trend was compared with the deviation of the nonlabor share from its trend. Values of $\bar{r}^2$ are again zero for both periods.

The reason for devoting attention to the wage-price ratio is the possibility that erratic fluctuations in it, including any due to wage and price controls, might introduce random fluctuations in the nonlabor share that do not result from changes in intensity of utilization. This would introduce an error in the estimated value of U, which measures the effect of intensity of utilization on productivity, if it is estimated from the nonlabor share alone.

One can both test for the presence of such a tendency and reduce any error it causes by introducing as a second independent variable W, the deviation from its trend of the ratio of compensation per hour worked to price. Based on 1948–69 data the relationship is

$$(3) \quad \log U = -0.00101 + 0.01018 \, N_1$$
$$+ 0.0039392 \, W_1 \qquad \bar{r}^2 = 0.922$$

Evidently the suspected tendency is present because introduction of the wage-price ratio raises $\bar{r}^2$ from 0.872 to 0.922. The unexplained percentage of the deviations of adjusted productivity from its trend is thus reduced by two-fifths, from 12.8 percent to 7.8 percent. The positive sign for the wage-price ratio, W_1, in the equation is expected. When W_1 is erratically high the nonlabor share, N_1, will be erratically low. Intensity of utilization, U, will then be underestimated if it is calculated from the nonlabor share alone. Values of U computed from this formula are shown in column 9 of table I-2. These are the results that I shall actually use.

A similar equation was computed from 1948–73 data:

$$(4) \quad \log U = -0.00093 + 0.0098605 \, N_2$$
$$+ 0.0034633 \, W_2 \qquad \bar{r}^2 = 0.904$$

Computed values of U are shown under "N_2 and W_2" in column 10 of table I-2.

Examination of Results

The columns at the right side of table I-2 cannot be compared readily because the average levels

Table I-3. Alternative Estimates of the Effect of Fluctuations in Intensity of Utilization on Output per Unit of Input and of the Semiresidual, 1948–73

Year	Estimated ratio of actual productivity to productivity if intensity of utilization were at its average 1948–73 value based on:[a]				Indexes of the semiresidual (1972 = 100) when intensity of utilization is based on:[b]			
	N_1 (1)	N_2 (2)	N_1 and W_1 (3)	N_2 and W_2 (4)	N_1 (5)	N_2 (6)	N_1 and W_1 (7)	N_2 and W_2 (8)
1948	1.0219	1.0099	1.0189	1.0071	64.89	66.37	64.88	66.38
1949	1.0091	0.9986	1.0062	0.9959	65.57	66.99	65.56	67.00
1950	1.0359	1.0250	1.0353	1.0244	67.57	69.03	67.41	68.90
1951	1.0312	1.0215	1.0315	1.0251	68.15	69.55	67.94	69.38
1952	1.0023	0.9948	1.0048	0.9967	70.05	71.35	69.67	71.03
1953	0.9875	0.9814	1.0000	0.9922	72.02	73.26	70.91	72.28
1954	0.9854	0.9804	0.9907	0.9847	72.02	73.18	71.42	72.67
1955	1.0190	1.0134	1.0216	1.0155	72.96	74.17	72.56	73.82
1956	0.9953	0.9916	0.9961	0.9920	75.12	76.23	74.85	76.00
1957	0.9852	0.9827	0.9860	0.9833	76.40	77.43	76.11	77.19
1958	0.9701	0.9690	0.9638	0.9633	77.15	78.07	77.42	78.34
1959	0.9981	0.9968	0.9892	0.9889	78.35	79.30	78.82	79.73
1960	0.9831	0.9833	0.9786	0.9791	79.59	80.44	79.72	80.58
1961	0.9826	0.9837	0.9784	0.9798	80.53	81.32	80.64	81.44
1962	0.9996	1.0009	0.9978	0.9993	82.55	83.34	82.46	83.27
1963	1.0095	1.0114	1.0094	1.0113	83.76	84.52	83.52	84.31
1964	1.0195	1.0219	1.0204	1.0227	85.89	86.63	85.57	86.34
1965	1.0329	1.0357	1.0304	1.0336	87.65	88.37	87.61	88.32
1966	1.0300	1.0339	1.0297	1.0337	89.39	90.03	89.16	89.82
1967	1.0134	1.0188	1.0141	1.0194	90.16	90.67	89.84	90.38
1968	1.0133	1.0176	1.0164	1.0222	92.56	93.00	91.82	92.34
1969	0.9898	0.9976	0.9948	1.0020	94.76	95.04	94.01	94.38
1970	0.9619	0.9713	0.9653	0.9774	95.89	95.99	95.26	95.44
1971	0.9699	0.9800	0.9694	0.9796	97.04	97.08	96.80	96.88
1972	0.9804	0.9911	0.9775	0.9886	100.00	110.00	100.00	100.00
1973	0.9752	0.9869	0.9738	0.9858	102.04	101.93	101.88	101.79

Source: Tables I-1 and I-2; see text for explanation.
a. Ratios include effects of work stoppages.
b. Semiresidual excludes effects of work stoppages.

to which the ratios refer are not the same. Table I-3, columns 1 to 4, shows the same data with each column restated as a ratio to its own 1948–73 average.

The index that is obtained by dividing output per unit of input by the indexes for all determinants examined so far, including changes in intensity of utilization resulting from both labor disputes and fluctuations in demand intensity, may be called the semiresidual. It measures the combined effects of changes in all remaining determinants—the size of markets, knowledge of how to produce at low cost, and many others. Columns 5 to 8 of table I-3 show indexes of the semiresidual corresponding to each of the four series for intensity of utilization.

Growth rates over various postwar periods are shown in table I-4 for all the series in table I-3. I have already indicated my decision to use results based on trends and relationships in 1948–69 (or 1947–69). In all periods, growth rates of the index for intensity of utilization would be about 0.1 percentage points higher and those for the semiresidual

about 0.1 percentage points lower if the 1948–73 (or 1947–73) period were used. This is so whether the formulas based on both N and W or those based only on N are used. This is also true in periods not shown. Consequently the answer to the important question of whether there was any change in the underlying trend of output per unit of input is not affected by the choice. Differences between periods would be unchanged by use of the longer time span.[5]

Comparison of columns 1 and 3, 2 and 4, 5 and 7, or 6 and 8 in table I-4 shows that growth rates

5. Another possibility would be to use deviations from the 1947–69 trends, as I have done, but base the regression line on 1948–73 instead of 1948–69. When both N and W are used, this regression line is:

$$\log U = 0.00030 + 0.0091918\,N_1 + 0.0033435\,W_1;\ \bar{r}^2 = 0.882$$

This formula would reduce the amplitude of variation in the utilization ratios. The highest ratio to the 1948–73 average (in 1950) would be reduced from 1.0353 to 1.0318 and the lowest ratio (in 1958) increased from 0.9638 to 0.9676. Ratios in the middle range would scarcely be affected.

Table I-4. Alternative Estimates of the Effect of Fluctuations in Intensity of Utilization on Output per Unit of Input and of the Semiresidual: Growth Rates in Selected Periods, 1948–73

Percent per annum

Period	Effect of intensity of utilization based on:				The semiresidual when intensity of utilization is based on:			
	N_1 (1)	N_2 (2)	N_1 and W_1 (3)	N_2 and W_2 (4)	N_1 (5)	N_2 (6)	N_1 and W_1 (7)	N_2 and W_2 (8)
1948–73	−0.19	−0.09	−0.18	−0.09	1.83	1.73	1.82	1.72
1948–69	−0.15	−0.06	−0.11	−0.02	1.82	1.72	1.78	1.69
1948–53	−0.68	−0.57	−0.37	−0.30	2.11	2.00	1.79	1.72
1953–64	0.29	0.37	0.18	0.28	1.61	1.54	1.72	1.63
1964–69	−0.59	−0.48	−0.51	−0.41	1.99	1.87	1.90	1.80
1969–73	−0.37	−0.27	−0.53	−0.41	1.87	1.77	2.03	1.91

Source: Computed from table I-3.

over the whole 1948–73 period are almost the same whether or not the wage-price ratio is added as a second independent variable but that some subperiods are affected—as, of course, are year-to-year changes. Inclusion of this variable seems clearly desirable although this does not imply improvement in every single year.[6] Henceforth I shall be concerned only with the series that is based on N_1 and W_1.

Examination of the Years 1948 to 1969

The estimates from 1948 through 1969 are compared with those obtained in *Accounting for Growth* in table I-5. The small part of the fluctuations in intensity of utilization that is due to labor disputes was removed, so the ratios in columns 3 and 4 refer to the part due to fluctuations in demand.

Years are ranked from highest to lowest utilization according to the new estimates. In both estimates 1950 was highest and 1958 lowest. Column 8 indicates that the average ranking of the years changed only 1.6 places; thus the general picture is much the same as before. Revisions in the actual ratios were more appreciable. The average change was 0.6 percent and two years, 1953 and 1954, changed by more than 1 percent. In considering these changes it should, of course, be recalled that this is a very volatile series.

In *Accounting for Growth* I attached a brief characterization to each year, which I have here

repeated unchanged in column 2, and I examined all the years to ascertain whether their positions seemed reasonable on the basis of all collateral evidence. I concluded that in general they did but noted a few qualifications. The new ordering seems to fit other evidence, as described in *Accounting for Growth*, at least as well and perhaps a bit better than the old.

The year 1948 stands out because utilization was much higher than in other years in which the business cycle peaked; utilization is typically low in such years. In *Accounting for Growth* I argued that higher utilization in 1948 was reasonable, partly because the average level of utilization was high following World War II due to the long curtailment of capital formation, but mainly because in contrast to other peak years output expanded strongly until almost the end of the year. I suggested, however, that utilization would not, perhaps, be expected to be "quite so high as my estimate implies." In the new estimates the 1948 ratio is still high but has been lowered from 1.019 to 1.014.

The ranking of 1949 far above other trough years was justified in *Accounting for Growth* in part by an unusually rapid decline in total hours worked and in part by the high 1948 utilization rate from which the 1949 decline began. The change in the ratio from 1948 to 1949 is the same in the new estimates as in the old. The 1949 ratio itself is still much above other recession years but has been lowered from 1.007 to 1.002.

All four "war boom" years are now distinctly above any other years. The year 1951, ranked sixth in *Accounting for Growth*, has moved up to join the other three.

In *Accounting for Growth* I noted that my results implied that 1969 was a slack year. This re-

6. The semiresidual obtained from the use of both N_1 and W_1 is appreciably smoother than that obtained when only N_1 is used. Of the twenty-five annual changes in the two series, twelve differ by as much as 0.25 percentage points, including six where the difference is as much as 0.40 points. In nine of the twelve, and five of the six, the change obtained from the multiple regression is the closer of the two to the average change over the whole period.

Table I-5. New and Old Estimates of the Effect of Fluctuations in Intensity of Utilization Due to Demand Pressure on Output per Unit of Input, Individual Years, 1948–69[a]

Year (1)	Characterization (2)	Ratio of demand intensity index to its 1948–69 mean			Rank		
		New (3)	Old (4)	Change (5)	New (6)	Old (7)	Change (8)
1950	War boom	1.030	1.036	−0.006	1	1	0
1951	War boom	1.026	1.017	0.009	2	6	+4
1965	War boom	1.025	1.031	−0.006	3	3	0
1966	War boom	1.024	1.033	−0.009	4	2	−2
1955	Expansion	1.016	1.008	0.008	5	8	+3
1964	Expansion	1.015	1.020	−0.005	6	4	−2
1948	Cyclical peak	1.014	1.019	−0.005	7	5	−2
1968	Expansion	1.011	1.004	0.007	8	10	+2
1967	Expansion	1.009	1.011	−0.002	9	7	−2
1963	Expansion	1.004	0.998	0.006	10	11	+1
1949	Trough	1.002	1.007	−0.005	11	9	−2
1952	Expansion	1.001	0.996	0.005	12	12	0
1953	2nd half recession	0.995	0.983	0.012	13	16	+3
1962	Expansion	0.992	0.996	−0.004	14	13	−1
1956	Expansion	0.991	0.994	−0.003	15	14	−1
1969	2nd half recession	0.990	0.982	0.008	16	17	+1
1954	Trough	0.985	0.973	0.012	17	21	+4
1959	Expansion	0.985	0.992	−0.007	18	15	−3
1957	2nd half recession	0.981	0.979	0.002	19	18	−1
1960	2nd half recession	0.973	0.978	−0.005	20	20	0
1961	Trough	0.973	0.978	−0.005	21	19	−2
1958	Trough	0.959	0.965	−0.006	22	22	0

Sources: Columns 3 and 6, computed from table I-3, column 3; columns 2, 4, and 7, computed from *Accounting for Growth*, table O-4, column 3, and table O-5.

a. See page 188 for ratios in later years.

mains the case with the new results, but less so; the ratio is raised from 0.982 to 0.990.

Considered by itself, the ranking of the years in the new estimates is plausible. The first four are years when conflicts in Korea and Vietnam created extreme demand pressure. The next six were all years of strong expansion including one, 1948, which was also a cyclical peak and is so labeled in table I-5. The year ranking eleventh, 1949, was a cyclical trough, but a trough within the immediate postwar period during which the average level of utilization was high. The twelfth to fifteenth years in the ranking, with ratios from 1.001 to 0.991, contain three years of expansion (two of them weak expansion, and one in which output was at a low level) and one year (1953) in which output peaked and turned down. The last seven years include three in which output peaked and turned down and three that are business cycle troughs. The seventh, 1959, was a year of expansion but at a low level of output as business moved up from the worst year of the period, 1958.

Examination of the Years 1970 to 1973

The years 1970 to 1973 were not covered in *Accounting for Growth*. On the scale of table I-5,

column 3, the ratios for these and adjacent years on the scale were:

1960	0.973
1961	0.973
1972	0.972
1973	0.969
1971	0.964
1970	0.960
1958	0.959

All four years stand above 1958 but below all other years. The year 1972 was almost equal to 1960 and 1961, while 1970 was only a little above 1958.

In considering 1970, it is necessary to examine 1969 first. The National Bureau of Economic Research (NBER) dates the 1969 business cycle peak in December, but there was little expansion of business output in early 1969 and a decline after the second quarter.[7] Employment, lagging as usual, continued to expand, so 1969 had been a year of rather lower utilization. In 1970 business national income continued to drop irregularly to a low in the fourth quarter, when it was 3.2 percent lower than it had been six quarters before. Almost all of

7. Quarterly NIPA figures for business national income (including dwellings) in 1972 prices, seasonally adjusted at annual rates in billions of dollars, for the four quarters of 1969 were 712.9, 716.9, 716.4, and 710.9.

1970 was on the downswing of the cycle. Since the 1970 drop came from a below-average level in 1969, it is not surprising to find intensity of utilization in 1970 at the lowest level since 1958.

The next two years came in a period of cyclical expansion. On an annual basis nonresidential business national income in constant prices rose a mere 2.5 percent in 1971 but a robust 7.1 percent in 1972. Even with the latter increase, output remained low compared with past periods; the growth rate of nonresidential business national income was only 2.5 percent a year from 1968, the last year in which utilization was at or above average, to 1972. Although the utilization index rose in 1971 and twice as much in 1972, it too remained low.

In 1973 sector national income, though up 4.9 percent from 1972, increased hardly at all during the year.[8] Employment continued to expand strongly. The BLS series for output per hour in private business dropped in each of the last three quarters of 1973. The utilization rate dipped moderately from 1972 to 1973.

The whole 1969–73 cycle is reminiscent of the period starting in 1957. The NBER dated a peak in August 1957, a trough in April 1958, a peak in April 1960, and a trough in February 1961, after which the long expansion to 1969 set in. As in 1969–73, the utilization ratio did not reach its 1948–69 average in any year of the 1957–60 cycle, nor did it do so until 1963 during the ensuing cycle.

One final observation should be made about 1973. In that year there was general agreement that output gains were slowing down while considerable slack remained in the supply of labor and capital. But there was controversy, continuing well into 1974, about whether demand was insufficient to support a stronger expansion or whether bottlenecks caused by shortages of selected raw materials were the problem. My estimates do not distinguish between these two possible causes of a low rate of utilization of employed resources.

Irregularities in Movement of the Indexes

Table I-6 compares annual percentage changes in adjusted output per unit of input (with effects of work stoppages removed) with those in the semiresidual, the same series adjusted to eliminate the estimated effects of fluctuations in demand intensity. The 1948–73 growth rate of the series after ad-

8. Quarterly NIPA figures for business national income (including dwellings) in 1972 prices, seasonally adjusted at annual rates in billions of dollars, for the four quarters of 1973 were 815.4, 813.4, 814.7, and 817.9.

Table I-6. Percentage Change from Previous Year in Adjusted Output per Unit of Input and in the Semiresidual, 1949–73

Year	Adjusted output per unit of input (1)	The semi-residual (2)
1949	−0.1	1.1
1950	5.7	2.8
1951	0.4	0.8
1952	0.0	2.5
1953	1.2	1.8
1954	−0.2	0.7
1955	4.8	1.6
1956	0.6	3.1
1957	0.6	1.7
1958	−0.6	1.7
1959	4.7	1.8
1960	−0.1	1.2
1961	1.1	1.2
1962	4.3	2.2
1963	2.5	1.3
1964	3.6	2.5
1965	3.4	2.4
1966	1.7	1.8
1967	−0.7	0.8
1968	2.5	2.2
1969	0.2	2.4
1970	−1.6	1.3
1971	2.0	1.6
1972	4.1	3.3
1973	1.5	1.9

Sources: Table I-1, column 6, and table I-3, column 7.

justment was 1.8 percent. It is obvious by inspection that elimination of the estimated effects of variations in intensity of demand eliminates most of the fluctuation in the annual changes. It not only eliminates all six declines but also brings twenty-four out of twenty-five annual changes closer to the 1.8 percent average (all except 1956). The change in the semiresidual differs from the average change by more than one percentage point only in 1956 and 1972. The mean deviation is 0.6 percentage points. Even after effects of intensity of utilization and all the other determinants measured so far have been eliminated, other sources of irregularity remain, so perfect smoothness in the semiresidual should not be sought or expected. In particular, annual changes in the calendar are a source of irregular movements in all existing productivity series, including the semiresidual.

Jumps occurring in table I-6, column 2, in 1952, 1956, 1964, and 1968 probably are correctly ascribed to leap year, but the 1972 jump probably is not. In 1972 there were fifty-two weeks, a Saturday, and a Sunday, a combination that is probably less conducive to high measured output than the extra Friday in 1971.

The 1974–76 Period

The reliability of the demand intensity index drops markedly after 1973, but no error in it is likely to be of such a size and direction that its elimination would alter the very adverse course obtained for the semiresidual. A general description of the period and estimating procedures will precede a detailed discussion of two decisions affecting the estimates.

General Description

Unemployment was high and demand weak throughout the 1974–76 period. The longest and deepest postwar recession carried business activity down from a weak peak in November 1973 to a trough in March 1975, according to NBER dating. The ensuing recovery failed to bring output even close to potential by 1976 or even 1977. The civilian unemployment rate was 5.6 percent in 1974, 8.5 percent in 1975, 7.7 percent in 1976, and 7.0 percent in 1977. Real national income in nonresidential business fell 3.4 percent in 1974 and a further 3.6 percent in 1975. In 1976 it rose 7.7 percent, but this brought it only 0.3 percent above 1973. Its growth rate was only 2.0 percent a year from 1968 to 1976. The BLS series for output per hour in private business, which had begun to fall in the second quarter of 1973, continued to do so through the first quarter of 1975, after which it turned up.

The nonlabor share (table I-1, column 1) was very low in all three years from 1974 to 1976. Even so, for use in estimating intensity of utilization it had to be adjusted downward (as described below) to eliminate the effect of the sudden jump in oil prices at the end of 1973. This was necessary because the price jump lifted the nonlabor share but was not related to utilization.

The previous trend of the nonlabor share was extended to 1976, implying that low utilization was entirely responsible for the large gaps between actual and trend values that the data reveal. This seemed probable, but it is almost equally plausible that the downdrift in trend values accelerated in this period. (See discussion below.) If it did, I increasingly underestimate intensity of utilization of employed resources after 1973 and therefore show too favorable a course for the semiresidual.

But even without allowance for such possible acceleration, the semiresidual portrays a dismal picture of the course of adjusted output per unit of input after the effects of fluctuations in demand are eliminated. If the utilization adjustment in 1973 and 1976 is based on the nonlabor share alone (see

formula 1) the semiresidual stood 1.5 percent lower in 1976 than in 1973.

I cannot improve on this estimate of the change from 1973 to 1976 by introducing W, the deviation from its trend of the wage-price ratio. As stressed earlier, this second independent variable was introduced in 1948–73 only to offset the effect of possible *erratic* movements in wages on year-to-year movements of the nonlabor share. The longer-term rise in the wage-price ratio results from rising productivity and any important change in the growth rate of productivity is matched by a change in the trend of the ratio. It would be absurd to extend the previous trend in the wage-price ratio to 1974–76, when the course of adjusted productivity clearly changed drastically. But it is impossible to estimate a new trend satisfactorily for so short a period.

For 1974 and 1975 two courses were open. One was to base changes in the utilization ratio on the nonlabor share alone, as was done for 1976. The other was to assume that the trend value of the wage-price ratio changed each year after 1973 by a percentage equal to the growth rate of the actual ratio from 1973 to 1976.[9] This permitted W to be calculated, and the utilization ratio could then be calculated from formula 3, as in 1948–73. This procedure made use of the available wage and price data, which seemed especially desirable because of intermittent controls on wages and prices, and it was adopted. There is no certainty that this was the better choice and both sets of estimates will be presented.

The Oil Price Adjustment to the Nonlabor Share

Higher oil prices stemming from developments abroad raised the nonlabor share at a given rate of utilization, and the share was adjusted to remove this effect.

Table I-7 shows national income, nonlabor earnings, and the nonlabor share of national income for nonfinancial corporate business as a whole, oil and gas industries, and all other industries from 1968 to 1976.[10] From 1968 through 1973 the nonlabor

9. As shown in table I-1, the actual ratio was 1.0354 in 1973 and 1.0469 in 1976, a growth rate of 0.369 percent. Application of this rate to the trend value of 1.0414 in 1973 yields trend values of 1.0453 in 1974, 1.0491 in 1975, and 1.0530 in 1976. The actual values in table I-1 fall short of these "trend" values by 0.58 percent in 1973 and 1976, 2.77 percent in 1974, and 3.36 percent in 1975.

10. Consolidation of the three industries named in note *a* of the table minimizes the problem that NIPA industry data classify employee compensation by establishment and property earnings by firm.

Table I-7. Nonfinancial Corporations: Adjustment to Eliminate Effect of Oil Price Increase in 1974–76

Item	1968	1969	1970	1971	1972	1973	1974	1975	1976
National income (billions of dollars)									
1. All industries	403.8	437.0	445.7	476.0	534.8	602.8	642.3	685.8	784.6
2. Oil and gas[a]	9.7	9.6	10.3	10.2	11.3	12.9	21.3	21.1	25.2
3. Other industries	394.1	427.4	435.4	465.8	523.5	589.9	621.0	664.7	759.4
Nonlabor earnings (billions of dollars)									
4. All industries	82.2	79.6	68.6	76.6	91.0	99.0	89.4	109.2	134.3
5. Oil and gas[a,b]	4.7	4.1	4.5	4.3	4.9	6.0	13.0	11.2	13.9
6. Other industries	77.5	75.5	64.1	72.3	86.1	93.0	76.4	97.0	120.4
Nonlabor share (percent of national income)									
7. All industries	20.36	18.22	15.39	16.09	17.02	16.42	13.92	15.92	17.12
8. Oil and gas[a]	48.45	42.71	43.69	42.16	43.36	46.51	61.03	53.08	55.16
9. Other industries	19.67	17.66	14.72	15.52	16.45	15.77	12.30	14.59	15.85
10. All industries minus other industries	0.69	0.56	0.67	0.57	0.57	0.65	1.62	1.33	1.27
Adjusted nonlabor share (percent of national income)									
11. All industries	20.36	18.22	15.39	16.09	17.02	16.42	13.27	15.27	16.47

Sources: Rows 1, 2, 4, and 5 computed from NIPA, tables 1.15, 6.3, and 6.5; row 3, row 1 minus row 2; row 6, row 4 minus row 5; rows 7–9 computed from rows 1–6; row 10, row 7 minus row 9; row 11, 1968–73 from row 7, 1974–76 equals row 7 minus 1973 value of row 10.

a. Includes crude petroleum and natural gas in the mining industry division, products of petroleum and coal in manufacturing, and pipeline transportation in transportation.

b. Absence of data made it necessary to exclude the capital consumption adjustment and include unincorporated enterprises.

share in nonfinancial corporations as a whole exceeded the share in "other industries" by an amount that varied only from 0.56 to 0.69 percentage points. With the sudden increase in oil prices, this difference jumped from 0.65 percentage points in 1973 to 1.62 points in 1974 (table I-7, row 10). Thereafter the difference diminished but remained much higher than before the oil price increase. The oil price increase raised the differential for two reasons. First, even in 1973 the nonlabor share was about three times as high in oil and gas as in other industries.[11] The increase in oil prices raised the weight of oil and gas. Second, the price increase raised the nonlabor share within the oil and gas industries.

An adjusted series for the nonlabor share in 1974–76 was obtained by deducting from the nonlabor share in "all industries" 0.65 percentage points, the amount by which the nonlabor share in "all industries" exceeded that in "other industries" in 1973. An alternative, adding 0.65 percentage points to the share in "other industries," yields much the same result. It may be noted that Department of Commerce capital utilization rates were off about as much after 1973 in petroleum as in all manufacturing.

Nonlabor Share: Trend Values after 1973

The nonlabor share was last as high as its trend value (based on the 1947–69 period) in 1968. It fell short by 2.3 percentage points in 1972, 2.5

11. It should be remembered that depletion is not deducted as a cost in computing nonlabor earnings.

points in 1976, and more in 1970–71, 1973–75, and 1977, if the series adjusted for oil prices is used after 1973. Through 1977 the shortfall was 2.1 or 2.2 points even in the best quarters—the first three of 1976 and the third of 1977. Is this reasonable?

Because business was slack throughout the 1970s there is little reason to doubt that actual nonlabor share in these years was lower than it would have been if utilization had been as intense as it had been on the average in 1947–69. The size of the gap may be overstated. However, there is insufficient evidence to warrant reducing the gap by accelerating the decline in trend values. My uncertainty about whether the nonlabor share has dropped after allowance for the business cycle and utilization is similar to the answer found by Martin Feldstein and Lawrence Summers when they studied an analogous case, the ratio of nonlabor earnings to asset values in nonfinancial corporations.[12] The possibility that the cyclically adjusted nonlabor share has risen can, I believe, be eliminated.[13] Consequently the only reasonable alternative to my series for *N* would progressively raise the index for intensity of

12. See "Is the Rate of Profit Falling?" *Brookings Papers on Economic Activity*, 1:1977, pp. 211–28.

13. It is true that an article written early in the period by Charles L. Schultze implies that the nonlabor share adjusted for the cycle was unusually high as of early 1975. Schultze stated that "at today's price-cost relationships, full employment levels of output and associated levels of productivity would generate very large profits." But the calculation was based on the assumption that productivity had continued to rise at the previous rate after 1973. (See "Falling Profits, Rising Profit Margins, and the Full-Employment Profit Rate," *Brookings Papers on Economic Activity*, 2:1975, p. 449.)

utilization and lower the index for the semiresidual, accentuating further the recent drop observed in the rate of productivity growth after elimination of the effects of changes in intensity of utilization.

Results and Comparison of Alternative Series

When expressed as a ratio to the 1948–69 average, as in table I-5, the 1974–76 values of the index of the effect upon output per unit of input of changes in the intensity of utilization of employed resources resulting from fluctuations in intensity of demand compare with other years of low utilization as shown in the list below. As before, I have entered characterizations of the years. Expansions were, of course, all from a very low level. Utilization was found to be lower in 1974 and 1975 than in any previous postwar year.

1960	0.973	2nd half recession
1961	0.973	Trough
1972	0.972	Expansion
1976	0.972	Expansion
1973	0.969	Late-year recession
1971	0.964	Expansion
1970	0.960	Trough
1958	0.959	Trough
1975	0.949	Trough
1974	0.931	Recession

The demand intensity index is also shown (but with 1973 = 100) in row 1 of table I-8, where it is compared with the series, shown in row 2, that would be derived if it were based only on the nonlabor share (N_1). This would be a reasonable alternative because of the difficulty of estimating W_1 in this period. The alternative series yields higher estimates of the intensity of utilization in 1974 and 1975.

The index of the semiresidual is shown in row 3. It shows an actual decline in 1974, a much sharper

decline in 1975, and an increase in 1976 that at 2.2 percent is above average but probably was artificially inflated by the calendar, which was the most favorable possible in 1976. The drop of 1.5 percent over three years compares with an increase of 5.6 percent that would have been observed if the 1948–73 growth rate had continued.

Had the alternative formula been used for intensity of utilization, the semiresidual would have dropped more sharply in 1974 and risen more sharply in 1976, as is shown by row 4 of table I-8.

Years before 1948

Intensity of utilization in 1929, 1940, 1941, and 1947 was estimated in substantially the same way as in *Accounting for Growth*. The deviation from trend of the nonlabor share in 1947 was based on the 1947–69 trend. The 1947 trend value was also used for the earlier years; that is, the slight downward movement in trend values was estimated to have begun only after 1947. A suitable wage-price series is absent before 1948, so intensity of utilization was estimated from the nonlabor share (see formula 1), and the resulting series was used to extrapolate backward the 1948 index value obtained previously.

A problem was encountered with 1929. Share data used in the present study differ from those used in *Accounting for Growth* because of statistical revisions and because they refer to nonfinancial corporations instead of all corporations. Data for all corporations are conceptually preferable but statistically inferior because they are not confined to corporations organized for profit. The new revised NIPA data yield nonlabor shares for all corporations in 1929–48 that are only moderately different from those used in *Accounting for Growth*, as columns 1 and 2 of table I-9 show.

There usually was also little difference between the shares in all corporations and financial corporations, but columns 2 and 3 in table I-9 show that in 1929 the difference is 1.45 percentage points (as against almost none in 1930 and 1940). Instead of using the 1929 share for nonfinancial corporations, I extrapolated the 1940 share to 1929 by the share for all corporations, which had the effect of raising the 1929 share from 21.79 to 23.27 (column 4). This was based on two considerations. First, the limited data available gave no indication that financial corporations in the not-for-profit category caused the divergent movement. I judge that it re-

Table I-8. Alternative Estimates of Indexes of the Effects of Two Determinants on Output per Unit of Input in Nonresidential Business, 1973–76

1973 = 100

Item	1973	1974	1975	1976
Effect of changes in intensity of utilization of employed resources resulting from fluctuations in intensity of demand:				
1. Based on N_1 and W_1[a]	100.00	96.10	97.96	100.34
2. Based on N_1	100.00	96.85	99.00	100.34
Index of the semiresidual, if demand intensity index is:				
3. Based on N_1 and W_1[a]	100.00	99.62	96.40	98.48
4. Based on N_1	100.00	98.85	95.39	98.48

Source: See text.

a. These are the series shown in table 5-1, with the base year shifted to 1973.

Table I-9. Nonlabor Shares of Corporate National Income, Alternative Series, 1929–48

Percent

Year	All corporations — From Accounting for Growth (1)	All corporations — New NIPA data (2)	Nonfinancial corporations, new NIPA data (3)	Series used (4)
1929	23.32	23.24	21.79	23.27
1930	19.36	19.24	19.22	...
1931	10.52	10.28	10.90	...
1940	21.95	22.16	22.19	22.19
1941	25.86	26.04	26.16	26.16
1947	21.03	20.53	20.74	20.74
1948	23.78	23.18	23.25	23.25

Sources: Column 1, *Accounting for Growth*, tables O-2 and O-6; columns 2 and 3, NIPA, table 1.15; column 4, see text.

flected either profitability of true financial corporations or the earnings of nonfinancial subsidiaries of financial corporations.[14] Second, all available data, including particularly shares in other years of the 1920s, were reviewed in *Accounting for Growth* (pages 308–11) to confirm that the deviation of the nonlabor share from its trend and the resulting estimate of intensity of utilization in 1929 were reasonable. If the 1929 nonlabor share were now to be substantially reduced, it would be necessary either to reduce the estimated trend value of the share in 1929 correspondingly, so that the 1929 value of N_1 would not change, or else to accept estimates that seem less reasonable for the intensity of utilization in 1929.

The indexes of the effect of fluctuations in intensity of utilization due to demand pressure and of the semiresidual in this period appear in table 5-1.

14. Until 1934, tax laws permitted consolidated returns, which put the property earnings of some operating subsidiaries of holding companies, but not their employee compensation, into the finance industry.

APPENDIX J

Economies of Scale

The index of gains from economies of scale (table 5-1, column 11), which is described in a general way in chapter 5, is from table J-1.

Column 1 of table J-1 was derived by dividing the index of output per unit of input (table 5-1, column 1) by the product of the three series for measured irregular factors (table 5-1, columns 7, 8, and 9).

To obtain postwar values for column 2 of table J-1, the output series used to represent the size of markets that business is organized to serve, column 1 was adjusted in the following ways:

First, index values for trough recession years— 1949, 1954, 1958, 1961, 1970, and 1975—were replaced by values interpolated between the previous and following years. Second, for each year-to-year percentage change in column 1 so adjusted, the average of that percentage and the similar percentage for the previous year was substituted. These percentages were then linked to obtain a continuous index. The procedure introduced a degree of smoothing without altering the general pattern of alternation of periods of fast and slow growth, and without using for any date index values for a future date. The 1975 and 1976 index values so obtained were adjusted upward because the index initially calculated barely increased in 1975 and declined in 1976, a pattern considered implausible. Increases of 1.5 percent a year were substituted. The resulting series is shown in table J-1, column 2. Years before 1948 were estimated as described in *Accounting for Growth* (pages 315–17).

To obtain the contribution of economies of scale to each year's change in output, the percentage change in column 2 each year was divided by nine. These annual estimates were then linked to obtain the index of gains from economies of scale, shown in table J-1, column 3.

Table J-1. Nonresidential Business: Estimation of Index of Gains from Economies of Scale
1972 = 100

Year	National income with effects of three irregular factors removed (1)	Income series used to estimate gains from economies of scale (2)	Index of gains from economies of scale (3)
1929	27.06	27.50	86.41
1940	28.29	31.19	87.63
1941	32.46	32.47	88.03
1947	41.84	41.92	90.61
1948	42.37	43.05	90.89
1949	41.63	44.13	91.14
1950	44.35	45.15	91.38
1951	47.53	47.29	91.86
1952	50.15	50.29	92.51
1953	52.36	52.78	93.02
1954	51.36	54.37	93.33
1955	54.06	55.25	93.49
1956	57.17	57.29	93.88
1957	58.33	59.52	94.28
1958	57.67	60.79	94.50
1959	60.99	62.16	94.74
1960	62.24	63.51	94.97
1961	63.01	65.12	95.23
1962	66.05	67.08	95.56
1963	68.21	69.19	95.90
1964	71.56	72.02	96.33
1965	76.10	76.07	96.94
1966	80.60	80.74	97.59
1967	82.87	84.27	98.07
1968	87.03	87.57	98.50
1969	91.38	91.95	99.05
1970	92.22	94.90	99.41
1971	93.95	96.23	99.56
1972	100.00	100.00	100.00
1973	106.35	106.40	100.71
1974	106.96	110.08	101.09
1975	100.95	111.73	101.27
1976	106.35	113.41	101.44

Source: See text of appendix J for derivation.

Growth Determinants in Smaller Sectors

This appendix describes the derivation of series in tables 6-1 and 6-4 that are not described elsewhere.

General Government, Households, and Institutions

Two columns of table 6-1 require additional explanation.

Column 4, Implied Efficiency Offset

The Bureau of Economic Analysis (BEA) measures output changes in households and institutions by the index of full-time equivalent employment rather than by number of hours worked. Column 4 measures the amount by which this procedure prevents changes in average hours in the sector as a whole, measured in column 3, from affecting measured output. It was computed for 1947–76 as described below.

Indexes (1972 = 100) of full-time equivalent (FTE) employment and of total hours worked in households and institutions were computed. The ratio of the former index to the latter, minus 1, was multiplied by national income originating in households and institutions (in 1972 prices) to obtain the amount by which that series would have been below the present estimate if its movement had been based on hours worked instead of FTE employment. This amount (which is negative before 1972) was subtracted from national income in the whole sector to approximate sector national income as it would have been measured if output in households and in-

stitutions had been based on hours worked rather than FTE employment. Column 4 is the ratio of the actual index of sector national income to the index of this alternative sector national income series (with 1972 = 100 in all indexes). When multiplied by column 3 it offsets the part of the drop in average hours that did not reduce measured output.

Before 1947 BEA measured the sector's output differently, so a different approach is needed. A change in hours within any industry-activity component anywhere in the sector did not affect measured output per person employed unless it reflected a change in the ratio of FTE employment to full-time and part-time employment. To obtain the effect of such changes, the 1947 value in 1972 prices of each component was extrapolated back to 1929 by full-time and part-time employment and the results were summed; the calculation was then repeated with FTE employment as the extrapolating index for each component and the results again summed. The ratio of the index of the former aggregate to the index of the latter provides an index of the effect of changes in average hours, other than those of military reserves, on sector output. This is the equivalent of the product of columns 3 and 4 in table 6-1. Division by the index of average hours in column 3 yields column 4, the implied efficiency offset.

Column 6, Other Labor Characteristics

All changes in labor input (or national income) in the sector that do not result from changes in employment or average hours are the consequence of changes in the distribution of total employment and hours worked. An index (table 6-1, column 6) of the effect of such changes in composition is obtained, therefore, by dividing column 7 by the product of columns 1 and 2. After 1947 this index measures the effects of both changes in the weights of different industries or activities and changes in the composition of labor within industrial or activity components of the government part of the sector.[1] Before 1947 it measures only the former.

Services of Dwellings

Only column 3 of table 6-4, the effect of changes in the occupancy ratio, needs to be described here.

The procedure was the same as that used in *Accounting for Growth* (page 28). Revised data consistent with the new NIPA estimates were used, with one exception. The BEA no longer estimates

---

1. Americans employed abroad and foreigners employed here are, in effect, treated as separate industries, the latter being a negative component.

the rental value in current prices of vacant nonfarm dwellings (excluding reserved units). The former estimates, taken from the work sheets for *Accounting for Growth,* were retained for the years 1929 to 1970.[2] To extend the series to 1976 the space rent per unit of vacant units in 1970 was extrapolated by the space rent per unit of occupied nonfarm units (excluding mobile homes but including reserved units). Necessary data for space rent and numbers of units were obtained from BEA work sheets.

2. The 1929–70 estimates of the rental value of occupied (including reserved) nonfarm units (excluding mobile homes) used in *Accounting for Growth* differ only trivially from those used in the 1976 NIPA revisions. It was presumed that any change in the data for vacant dwellings that may be implied by the revisions is also insignificant.

Potential National Income

Potential national income is defined in the same way as in *Accounting for Growth,* except that national income is valued in 1972 prices instead of 1958 prices. It is the value that national income (in 1972 prices) would have taken if (1) the percentage of the civilian labor force 16 years of age and over that is unemployed had been 4 percent; (2) the intensity of utilization of employed resources (aside from effects of labor disputes) had been that which *on the average* would be associated with a 4 percent unemployment rate; and (3) other conditions had been those that actually prevailed in that year.

Potential national income is derived by making the two adjustments to actual national income that are shown in columns 2 and 3 of table 2-4. The procedures are the same as those used in *Accounting for Growth* except for minor changes required by revisions of the data or indicated by the extension of the series to another seven years. That book should be consulted for additional explanation.

Adjustment of Output per Unit of Input for Intensity of Utilization

The first adjustment, shown in table 2-4, column 2, eliminates the effects on output per unit of input of fluctuations in intensity of utilization due to fluctuations in demand. The objective is to obtain the output that resources measured as actually in use would have produced under standardized demand conditions.

For the nonresidential business sector an output series with the proper *movement* could be obtained

by dividing actual national income in this sector by the index shown in table 5-1, column 9. The index measures the effect on output per unit of input of changes in the intensity of utilization of employed resources resulting from fluctuations in the intensity of demand.

To set the *level* of potential output, the value of this index that corresponds to potential conditions must be estimated. It was put at 103.31 when (as in table 5-1) 1972 is 100. This index value corresponds to a 4 percent unemployment rate when a regression line relating the index to the unemployment rate is computed for the 1948–69 period.[1] (At 3.5 percent unemployment the value is 103.73 and at 4.5 percent it is 102.90.)

One way to check this result was to examine years of relatively low unemployment. In one of the years from 1948 through 1976 the unemployment rate was 4.0 percent, in eight it was below 4.0 percent, and in twenty it was above 4.0 percent. To obtain a balanced sample scattered evenly around the 4.0 percent potential level, the twelve years of highest unemployment were discarded. This left seventeen years, in eight of which unemployment was below 4.0 percent and in eight above, with the range from 2.7 to 5.4 percent. In nine of these years the demand intensity index was above 103.31 and in eight it was below 103.31 so the figure selected divides this sample of years as evenly as possible, as it should. In these seventeen years the unemployment rate averaged 4.05 percent and the demand intensity index averaged 103.11. A small adjustment of these results (based on the regression elasticity) suggests that if unemployment had averaged 4.0 percent the demand intensity index would have averaged 103.16. This is reasonably close to the value of 103.31 obtained from the regression.[2]

To obtain column 2 of table 2-4, nonresidential business national income in 1972 prices, from table 2-6, column 5, was multiplied by the ratio of 103.31 to column 9 of table 5-1 (the index of the effect of

---

1. Use of the 1948–73 period would yield 103.02 and 1948–76, 102.90. Regression lines based on these periods were too much influenced by the years of high unemployment after 1969 to be satisfactory for the selection of a low-unemployment index value. On the other hand, an attempt to derive by correlation a rate based only on years of relatively low unemployment (5.2 percent or less) failed because the correlation between unemployment and the demand intensity index, poor even when all years are used, vanished completely when the sample of years was restricted in this way.

2. Use of the sixteen years of lowest unemployment, instead of seventeen, yields 103.19, which is slightly closer. But use of fifteen years would drop the result to 102.93, so the result of this method is somewhat sensitive to the cutoff selected.

fluctuations in intensity of utilization due to fluctuations in intensity of demand). Nonresidential business national income was then subtracted from this product. The adjustment is not necessarily positive when unemployment is above 4 percent and negative when it is below 4 percent, because intensity of utilization is related to changes in demand pressure as much as to the level of unemployment.

Adjustment of Labor Input (Including Allocation of Labor)

Column 3 of table 2-4 shows the second adjustment required to move from actual to potential national income. To obtain it, the amount by which total factor input in nonresidential business would have been different under potential conditions was estimated.[3] It was then necessary to calculate the effect of such a difference in factor input on non-residential business national income. Only the labor component of total input must be adjusted because capital and land inputs are the same on actual and potential bases. Effects of demand-related changes in their utilization are already included in table 2-4, column 2.

The simplifying assumption is made that if the unemployment rate had been 4 percent rather than its actual size, the entire change in employment would have appeared among nonfarm business wage and salary workers. A modification is made in 1940 and 1941 because there would have been no work relief program if unemployment had been at 4 percent. Work relief workers are therefore eliminated from general government, and the value of their output is deducted from actual national income (in table 2-4, column 1). Thereafter, these workers are treated as unemployed (except in calculating the unemployment rate used to estimate the difference between actual and potential labor force).

The following description follows the order of appendix Q of *Accounting for Growth*. It can be shortened here because the methodology is very little changed; see *Accounting for Growth* for fuller explanation. The description refers to postwar years; estimates for prewar years are retained from *Accounting for Growth,* except to incorporate changes in the utilization adjustment and to change the valuation of national income from 1958 to 1972 prices.

Adjustments of Hours Worked by Employed Workers

The total potential hours of nonfarm business wage and salary workers who are actually employed differ from their total actual hours because the percentage employed part time would be different under potential conditions and so would the average hours of both full-time and part-time workers.

PART-TIME EMPLOYMENT. Employed nonfarm business wage and salary workers of each sex are divided between full-time and part-time workers on an actual basis in table 3-7. This division is affected by demand pressure. It is adjusted to a potential basis by transferring the difference between the number actually working part time for economic reasons and the number who would have done so under potential conditions. As in *Accounting for Growth,* the actual numbers working part time for economic reasons were obtained from the Current Population Survey from 1955 on, and in 1947–54 were estimated from regressions between (1) the ratios of the number working part time for economic reasons to the number working full time and (2) the unemployment rate. However, the regressions were recomputed with 1955–73 instead of 1955–69 data and with the unemployment rate corrected for adjustments to the 1970 decennial census. The 1955–73 regressions were also used to estimate the ratios of the numbers working part time for economic reasons to the numbers working full time that are consistent with 4 percent unemployment. At 0.0321 for males and 0.0669 for females, the ratios are scarcely changed from those used in *Accounting for Growth.*[4] Table L-1 shows the numbers transferred from part-time to full-time status to obtain the breakdown under potential conditions.[5]

AVERAGE HOURS OF FULL-TIME AND PART-TIME WORKERS. The method of estimating the average potential hours of employed full-time and part-time workers of each sex was similar to that used in *Accounting for Growth.* There were some differences in detail.

Equations 1 to 4 that appear at the top of page 321 of *Accounting for Growth* were recomputed, using the period 1947–73 instead of 1947–69, and

---

3. The procedure automatically includes the effect of a different allocation of labor.

4. At 3.5 percent unemployment the values are 0.0279 for males and 0.0609 for females. At 4.5 percent unemployment they are 0.0362 for males and 0.0728 for females.

5. Appreciable changes from *Accounting for Growth* (table Q-1) are confined to years before 1955 (chiefly 1949, 1950, and 1954). They stem from revisions in the estimated numbers actually working part time for economic reasons that resulted from the new regressions.

Table L-1. Nonfarm Business: Numbers of Part-Time Wage and Salary Workers Transferred to Full-Time Status to Derive Potential National Income, 1929, 1940–41, and 1947–76

Thousands

Year	Males	Females	Total
Excluding Alaska and Hawaii			
1929	−156	−51	−207
1940	388	231	619
1941	−71	100	29
1947	−41	−20	−61
1948	−61	−30	−91
1949	337	178	515
1950	233	124	357
1951	−187	−100	−287
1952	−256	−144	−400
1953	−287	−161	−448
1954	268	149	417
1955	85	40	125
1956	197	85	282
1957	318	128	446
1958	853	393	1,246
1959	377	234	611
1960	509	275	784
Including Alaska and Hawaii			
1960	511	276	787
1961	639	363	1,002
1962	333	199	532
1963	263	177	440
1964	157	109	266
1965	−4	78	24
1966	−128	−116	−244
1967	−26	−30	−56
1968	−172	−84	−256
1969	−142	−112	−254
1970	73	61	134
1971	161	201	362
1972	96	158	254
1973	2	82	84
1974	179	214	393
1975	610	565	1,175
1976	430	440	870

Source: See text for derivation.

with the new values of the demand intensity index and the unemployment percentages used. In these equations P is potential average weekly hours, A is actual average weekly hours, U is the percentage of the civilian labor force 16 and over unemployed, and I is the percentage by which the demand intensity index exceeds its potential value.

The new equations are:

(1) Males employed full time:
$$P = A + 0.0753 − 0.06543U + 0.14564I$$
$$\bar{r}^2 = 0.70$$

(2) Females employed full time:
$$P = A − 0.0196 − 0.05321U + 0.05846I$$
$$\bar{r}^2 = 0.21$$

(3) Males employed part time:
$$P = A − 0.271 − 0.22996U − 0.11977I$$
$$\bar{r}^2 = 0.08$$

(4) Females employed part time:
$$P = A + 0.018 − 0.0077302U + 0.02158I$$
$$\bar{r}^2 = 0.00$$

As before, correlation is fair for full-time males, who are by far the most important group, and very poor for full-time females. It is nonexistent for part-time workers, but the adjustment for these groups is fortunately of no practical importance.

Potential values of average weekly hours for all groups were calculated in postwar years from the regressions. For full-time workers they are shown in columns 2 and 5 of table L-2.[6]

To derive the regressions, trend values, shown in columns 1 and 4 of table L-2, were needed.[7] They were not (and should not) be used for any other purpose. To obtain them for full-time males and full-time females, the procedure described in *Accounting for Growth* (page 321) was retained through 1969 (but applied to the new "actual" data); the 1967–69 trend values were held unchanged through 1973.[8] (Trend values for 1974–76 were not needed.)

Columns 1 to 3 of table L-3 show, by sex, the difference between the actual and potential total weekly hours of employed workers. They reflect the differences between actual and potential conditions both in the division of employment between full-time and part-time workers and in the average hours of each group. For later use these amounts were allocated among age groups, using the procedure described in *Accounting for Growth* on page 323.

Transfers between Unemployed and Employed Groups

Estimates of the number of unemployed persons who would have been employed under potential conditions and the hours they would have worked,

6. Estimates shown in table L-2 for 1929 were obtained by using the postwar regressions; for 1940, by setting potential hours equal to actual hours; and for 1941, by straight-line interpolation. They were not incorporated into the potential national income estimates for those years; the movement of the prior series was retained.

7. They were used in lieu of potential values, which could be obtained only after the equations were known.

8. For part-time males, a least squares trend based on 1947–73 was used for all years from 1947 to 1973. For part-time females the mean of the 1947–54 actual values was used as the trend value throughout that period, and the mean of the 1955–73 actual values as the trend value throughout that period.

Table L-2. Nonfarm Business: Average Weekly Hours of Full-Time Wage and Salary Workers, by Sex and on a Trend, Potential, and Actual Basis, 1929, 1940–41, and 1947–76

	Males			Females		
Year	Trend (1)	Potential (2)	Actual[a] (3)	Trend (4)	Potential (5)	Actual[a] (6)
1929	...	48.72	48.85	...	45.23	45.21
1940	...	43.71[b]	43.71	...	40.46[b]	40.46
1941	...	43.63[c]	44.12	...	40.38[c]	40.83
1947	43.00	43.16	42.97	39.83	39.90	39.77
1948	43.00	42.83	43.01	39.83	39.80	39.82
1949	43.00	42.69	42.83	39.83	39.66	39.72
1950	43.00	42.67	43.18	39.83	39.84	40.03
1951	42.82	42.84	43.16	39.83	39.78	39.83
1952	42.65	42.71	42.64	39.73	39.70	39.59
1953	42.47	42.34	42.18	39.63	39.40	39.25
1954	42.47	42.55	42.43	39.53	39.62	39.56
1955	42.47	42.24	42.50	39.43	39.60	39.66
1956	42.47	42.54	42.41	39.33	39.64	39.54
1957	42.47	42.27	42.00	39.23	39.20	39.04
1958	42.47	42.37	41.92	39.13	39.46	39.30
1959	42.47	42.53	42.42	39.04	39.41	39.35
1960	42.47	42.63	42.33	38.94	38.90	38.77
1961	42.47	42.65	42.42	38.84	38.85	38.78
1962	42.47	42.64	42.63	38.74	38.71	38.70
1963	42.47	42.61	42.77	38.64	38.58	38.64
1964	42.47	42.79	43.08	38.54	38.14	38.24
1965	42.47	42.69	43.08	38.44	38.51	38.63
1966	42.10	42.32	42.64	38.02	38.17	38.24
1967	42.01	41.99	42.11	37.60	37.70	37.69
1968	42.01	41.81	41.96	37.60	37.54	37.54
1969	42.01	42.13	41.95	37.60	37.70	37.57
1970	42.01	42.02	41.50	37.60	37.54	37.31
1971	42.01	41.79	41.39	37.60	37.30	37.15
1972	42.01	41.98	41.67	37.60	37.50	37.37
1973	42.01	41.97	41.55	37.60	37.41	37.22
1974	...	41.95	40.99	...	37.35	36.96
1975	...	41.24	40.76	...	37.00	36.88
1976	...	41.00	40.81	...	36.99	36.95

Sources: Columns 1 and 4, see text; columns 2 and 5, estimated from columns 3 and 6 by use of formulas 1 and 2 in the text; columns 3 and 6, calculated from data underlying table 3-7.

a. Numbers for years earlier than 1966 differ from those in table 3-7 because they have been linked for continuity.

b. Estimated to be equal to actual hours.

c. Interpolated.

classified by age and sex, were obtained by the procedures described in *Accounting for Growth,* pages 323–27. The total numbers transferred from unemployed to employed are shown, by sex, in table L-4, columns 4 and 5, and their total potential hours in table L-3, columns 4 to 6.

Adjustment of the Labor Force

The size of the labor force is, on balance, negatively associated with the unemployment rate. Differences between the actual labor force and the labor force that would have been present with 4 percent unemployment were obtained, by age and sex, in the same way as in *Accounting for Growth.*

(The estimates for 1929–69 are unchanged.) Totals are shown by sex in table L-4, columns 1 to 3. The estimates are based on elasticities developed by George Perry in 1971. Perry estimated on the basis of 1948–70 experience that each reduction of one percentage point in the unemployment rate increases the labor force by the following percentages of the noninstitutional population in each age-sex group:

Age group	Males	Females
16–19	1.2961	0.9871
20–24	0.9373	0.4991
25–64	0.0106	0.4780
65 and over	0.4393	0.0821

Table L-3. Nonfarm Business: Potential Less Actual Total Weekly Hours of Wage and Salary Workers, by Components, 1929, 1940–41, and 1947–76[a]

Millions of hours

Year	Employed workers			Shift from unemployment to employment			Labor force response to demand for labor			All components		
	Male (1)	Female (2)	Total (3)	Male (4)	Female (5)	Total (6)	Male (7)	Female (8)	Total (9)	Male (10)	Female (11)	Total (12)
1929	−7.3	−1.2	−8.5	−17.4	−4.4	−21.8	−4.8	−6.0	−10.8	−29.5	−11.6	−41.1
1940	11.8	4.5	16.3	181.0	53.1	234.1	26.6	36.4	63.0	219.4	94.0	313.4
1941	−12.6	−1.1	−13.7	96.7	30.4	127.1	8.5	11.7	20.2	92.6	41.0	133.6
1947	3.2	0.6	3.7	−4.7	−1.7	−6.4	−1.2	−2.2	−3.3	−2.7	−3.3	−6.0
1948	−5.6	−1.0	−6.5	−6.5	−2.7	−9.2	−1.7	−3.2	−4.9	−13.8	−6.9	−20.6
1949	4.5	2.9	7.3	32.0	12.6	44.6	8.8	16.9	25.7	45.3	32.4	77.6
1950	−5.8	0.5	−5.4	20.4	8.7	29.0	5.6	11.0	16.6	20.2	20.2	40.2
1951	−10.7	−2.5	−13.2	−13.7	−7.3	−21.0	−4.3	−8.5	−12.8	−28.7	−18.3	−47.0
1952	−4.0	−1.6	−5.5	−18.9	−9.7	−28.5	−6.1	−11.9	−18.0	−29.0	−23.2	−52.0
1953	−2.3	−1.4	−3.7	−21.6	−10.4	−32.0	−7.0	−13.7	−20.7	−30.9	−25.5	−56.4
1954	9.6	3.4	12.9	23.3	10.5	33.9	5.8	11.6	17.4	38.7	25.5	64.2
1955	−3.9	0.1	−3.7	3.8	1.8	5.6	0.8	1.7	2.5	0.7	3.6	4.4
1956	8.5	2.9	11.5	−0.3	−0.2	−0.5	−0.3	−0.5	−0.8	7.9	2.2	10.2
1957	14.7	4.5	19.1	2.1	1.0	3.1	0.4	0.8	1.2	17.2	6.3	23.4
1958	28.7	11.1	38.8	48.6	21.8	70.4	12.3	24.4	36.7	89.6	57.3	146.9
1959	12.3	5.5	17.8	24.0	11.5	35.5	6.3	12.3	18.6	42.6	29.3	71.9
1960	19.6	7.4	26.9	25.7	12.3	37.9	7.0	12.9	19.9	52.3	32.6	84.7
1961	20.1	8.3	28.5	46.9	22.8	69.7	12.6	23.3	35.9	79.6	54.4	134.1
1962	8.5	4.3	12.8	25.8	13.1	38.9	7.1	13.0	20.1	41.4	30.4	71.8
1963	2.3	3.0	5.4	28.1	14.7	42.8	7.7	13.8	21.6	38.1	31.5	69.8
1964	−3.1	0.9	−2.2	19.5	10.8	30.2	5.5	9.6	15.1	21.9	21.3	43.1
1965	−9.9	−1.1	−11.0	7.5	4.4	11.8	2.1	3.6	5.8	−0.3	6.9	6.6
1966	−10.9	−3.5	−14.4	−6.2	−4.0	−10.1	−2.2	−3.6	−5.8	−19.3	−11.1	−30.3
1967	−3.0	−0.6	−3.6	−3.0	−2.0	−5.0	−1.2	−1.9	−3.0	−7.2	−4.5	−11.6
1968	−7.6	−1.8	−9.3	−7.9	−5.1	−13.0	−2.6	−4.3	−6.9	−18.1	−11.2	−29.2
1969	2.9	−0.1	2.7	−9.5	−6.3	−15.8	−3.1	−4.9	−8.0	−9.7	−11.3	−21.1
1970	15.8	4.9	20.7	17.5	10.4	27.9	6.3	10.0	16.3	39.6	25.3	64.9
1971	13.6	6.3	19.9	37.0	21.6	58.6	13.5	21.0	34.5	64.1	48.9	113.0
1972	10.3	5.1	15.4	31.3	18.9	50.2	12.5	18.0	30.5	54.1	42.0	96.1
1973	13.2	5.0	17.1	16.5	10.5	26.9	6.3	9.5	15.8	36.0	25.0	60.8
1974	32.0	11.1	43.1	31.5	20.0	51.5	12.0	18.0	30.0	75.5	49.1	124.6
1975	23.1	12.8	36.0	91.7	55.5	147.2	32.5	50.9	83.5	147.3	119.2	266.7
1976	13.0	9.1	22.1	76.3	48.2	124.5	27.8	42.8	70.6	117.1	100.1	217.2

Source: See text for derivation. Figures are rounded.
a. Includes Alaska and Hawaii beginning in 1960.

He found that the use of lagged relationships, such as making the estimate depend on unemployment in the previous year as well as in the current year, did not improve the estimates.[9]

I did not substitute elasticities that Perry developed in 1977 from data for a different period, 1954–76, which differed in two ways from the elasticities in 1948–70.[10] First, Perry introduced two coefficients for each age-sex group, one to be applied to the previous year's unemployment rate gap and the other to the current year's gap. This greatly changes the movement of the adjustment during and just after years of peak unemployment. Second, the average size of the adjustment is increased. From 1970 to 1976 the new coefficients yield an average shortfall of actual labor force below potential labor force at 4 percent unemployment of 2.3 million as against 1.3 million with the old coeffi-

9. George L. Perry, "Labor Force Structure, Potential Output, and Productivity," *Brookings Papers on Economic Activity, 3:1971,* pp. 533–78; and *Accounting for Growth,* pp. 327–28.
10. George L. Perry, "Potential Output and Produc-

tivity," *Brookings Papers on Economic Activity, 1:1977,* pp. 11–60.

Table L-4. Potential Less Actual Labor Force and Employment, 1929, 1940–41, and 1947–76[a]
Thousands

| | Potential labor force less actual labor force | | | Potential employment less actual employment | | | | | | |
| | | | | Transfers from unemployment | | Adjustment from labor force | | Total adjustment | | |
Year	Total (1)	Male (2)	Female (3)	Male (4)	Female (5)	Male (6)	Female (7)	Male (8)	Female (9)	Total (10)
1929	−271	−123	−148	−374	−105	−118	−142	−492	−247	−739
1940[b]	1,751	752	999	4,390	1,411	722	959	5,112	2,370	7,482
1941[b]	563	241	322	2,365	816	231	309	2,596	1,125	3,721
1947	−93	−33	−60	−114	−47	−32	−57	−146	−104	−250
1948	−139	−49	−90	−161	−73	−47	−86	−208	−159	−367
1949	736	257	479	795	340	247	459	1,042	799	1,841
1950	476	165	311	506	235	158	299	664	534	1,198
1951	−370	−127	−243	−341	−201	−122	−233	−463	−434	−897
1952	−520	−178	−342	−470	−264	−171	−329	−641	−593	−1,234
1953	−599	−206	−393	−540	−285	−197	−378	−737	−663	−1,400
1954	507	174	333	582	289	167	320	749	609	1,358
1955	73	25	48	95	50	24	46	119	96	215
1956	−23	−8	−15	−8	−4	−7	−14	−15	−18	−33
1957	36	12	24	53	29	12	23	65	52	117
1958	1,089	376	713	1,207	607	361	684	1,568	1,291	2,859
1959	553	193	360	600	323	186	345	786	668	1,454
1960	594	210	384	638	348	201	369	839	717	1,556
1961	1,088	387	702	1,167	651	371	674	1,556	1,325	2,881
1962	611	219	392	646	378	210	376	856	754	1,610
1963	666	242	424	709	430	233	407	942	837	1,779
1964	468	173	296	493	317	166	284	659	601	1,260
1965	179	67	112	189	129	64	108	253	237	490
1966	−180	−68	−112	−159	−117	−65	−107	−224	−224	−448
1967	−96	−37	−59	−79	−60	−35	−57	−114	−117	−231
1968	−223	−85	−138	−205	−156	−82	−132	−287	−288	−575
1969	−255	−98	−157	−247	−193	−94	−150	−341	−343	−684
1970	527	204	323	454	322	196	310	650	632	1,282
1971	1,121	437	684	963	672	420	657	1,383	1,329	2,712
1972	959	375	584	814	584	360	560	1,174	1,144	2,318
1973	509	199	310	427	325	191	297	618	622	1,240
1974	962	376	586	817	620	361	562	1,178	1,182	2,360
1975	2,753	1,077	1,676	2,408	1,730	1,034	1,609	3,442	3,339	6,781
1976	2,318	907	1,411	2,012	1,507	871	1,354	2,883	2,861	5,744

Source: See text for derivation.
a. Includes Alaska and Hawaii beginning in 1960.
b. Employment data refer to differences from actual figures that exclude persons on work relief.

cients. The 1976 figures are 4.5 million and 2.3 million.[11] Other investigators regard these differences as big.[12] The coefficients that I used imply that

as of 1976 a one percentage point decrease in the unemployment rate increases the labor force by over 0.6 percent. This percentage is the same as that implied by the procedures used by the Council of Economic Advisers in preparing its 1979 economic report. Use of the new Perry coefficients would have placed the adjustment at the top of the range of plausible estimates; changed, without appearing to improve, the labor force series I derived in *Accounting for Growth;* and required overcom-

11. Numbers cited refer to the difference between the actual labor force and the labor force at 4 percent unemployment. Perry's own estimate of the "gap" between actual and potential labor force is smaller because he uses a higher unemployment figure to represent potential in this period.

12. See comments on Perry's article by Michael L. Wachter, Otto Eckstein, and Peter K. Clark in *Brookings Papers on Economic Activity, 1:1977*, pp. 48–58. The Council of Economic Advisers elasticity of 0.6 that I cite in the following sentence was provided subsequently by Clark. At

the time, he reported, the council was using an elasticity of 0.4.

ing my strong reluctance to let relationships used in estimation be affected by the unusual and difficult 1974–76 period.[13]

To maintain the conditions stipulated for potential output, the adjustment to employment is 96 percent of the labor force adjustment. Table L-4, columns 6 and 7, shows the adjustment to employment in each sex for all age groups combined. As in *Accounting for Growth,* persons in each age-sex group who were added to or subtracted from employment were assigned the same average potential hours as those transferred between employment and unemployment. Table L-3, columns 7, 8, and 9, shows the total hours added or subtracted to allow for labor force response.

Differences between actual and potential hours arising from all causes were next summed, by sex and age; the totals are shown, by sex only, in table L-3, columns 10 to 12. The differences in each age-sex group were then added to actual hours to obtain the total potential hours in each age-sex group of nonfarm wage and salary workers employed in the business sector.

Adjustment of Labor Input and National Income

Table L-5 shows the derivation of the excess of potential over actual national income that is due to labor input. The methodology is the same as that followed for the corresponding table, Q-6, in *Accounting for Growth.* Only two minor comments need be added.

1. In calculating columns 4 and 5 of table L-5, the 1929–70 earnings weights for age-sex groups shown in table 3-5, column 1, were used for 1929–70, and the 1970–76 weights shown in column 2 for 1971–76.

13. The Perry procedure requires predetermining trend values for the labor force at a time that the trend was very difficult to ascertain.

2. The ratios of potential education indexes to actual indexes in table L-5, columns 12 and 13, were based on data from table F-4 and *Accounting for Growth,* table I-18, for (a) persons 18 years of age and over, and 1959 earnings weights, in 1929–68; on (b) persons 18 years of age and over, and 1969 earnings weights, in 1970–71; on (c) persons 16 years of age and over, and 1969 earnings weights, in 1973–76; on (d) an average of ratios of types a and b in 1969; and on (e) an average of ratios of types b and c in 1972.

The excess of potential over actual national income, in 1972 prices, that is due to the difference in labor input is arrived at in table L-5, column 22, and transferred to table 2-4, column 3.

Comment on Years of Peak Unemployment

As noted in *Accounting for Growth* (pages 330–32 and note 25, page 94), potential employment may tend to be overstated in the year of greatest unemployment during a business cycle. In four of six such postwar years (1954, 1958, 1961, and 1975, but not 1949 or 1971) potential employment increased more in the year of highest unemployment than in the following year; the average increase was 1.8 percent as against 1.0 percent in the following year. This suggests the possibility that on the average potential employment might be overstated by 0.4 percent, half the difference, in years of peak unemployment. If there is such a bias, and if it stems from an overallowance for labor force response to unemployment in such years, the effect on output would be divided between overstatement of total potential national income and understatement of potential national income per person potentially employed. No peak unemployment year is the terminal year of a standard period, so the suspected bias does not affect the sources of growth estimates for the periods presented.

Table L-5. Derivation of the Excess of Potential over Actual National Income That Is Due to Labor Input, 1929, 1940–41, and 1947–76[a]
Values in billions of dollars

	Nonfarm business wage and salary workers									All non-	
	Compensation			Ratio of potential to actual				Potential compensation, not adjusted for education		Labor earnings	
				Age-weighted hours		Intragroup hours efficiency index					
Year	Total (1)	Male (2)	Female (3)	Male (4)	Female (5)	Male (6)	Female (7)	Male (8)	Female (9)	Male (10)	Female (11)
1929	42.6	37.7	4.9	0.973	0.950	1.001	1.000	36.7	4.7	51.0	5.7
1940	40.9	35.1	5.8	1.228	1.371	1.000	1.000	43.1	7.9	46.8	6.0
1941	51.6	44.4	7.2	1.083	1.139	1.005	1.004	48.3	8.2	58.1	7.9
1947	104.5	87.5	17.0	0.998	0.991	0.998	0.999	87.2	16.8	115.2	18.5
1948	115.3	96.3	19.0	0.988	0.982	1.002	1.000	95.3	18.7	127.5	20.8
1949	113.1	93.8	19.3	1.040	1.085	1.001	1.001	97.6	21.0	123.3	20.8
1950	124.6	103.1	21.5	1.016	1.051	1.004	1.002	105.1	22.6	133.3	22.8
1951	143.8	118.6	25.2	0.977	0.957	1.002	1.000	116.1	24.1	151.0	26.7
1952	154.5	126.4	28.1	0.977	0.949	0.999	0.999	123.4	26.6	160.6	29.5
1953	167.1	136.9	30.2	0.977	0.945	0.999	0.999	133.5	28.5	171.2	31.2
1954	165.3	135.3	30.0	1.032	1.058	0.999	0.999	139.5	31.7	170.1	30.6
1955	179.1	146.9	32.2	1.000	1.008	1.002	1.001	147.3	32.5	180.8	33.4
1956	194.6	159.2	35.4	1.007	1.005	0.999	0.999	160.2	35.5	195.0	37.3
1957	204.2	166.4	37.8	1.015	1.014	0.998	0.998	168.5	38.2	203.9	39.8
1958	201.9	164.0	37.9	1.076	1.126	0.997	0.999	175.9	42.6	204.2	40.1
1959	220.4	179.3	41.1	1.034	1.062	0.999	0.999	185.2	43.6	218.0	42.8
1960	231.0	187.8	43.2	1.042	1.068	0.998	0.999	195.2	46.1	226.8	45.0
1961	235.5	191.1	44.4	1.064	1.114	0.998	0.999	203.0	49.4	230.8	46.4
1962	252.1	204.7	47.4	1.032	1.062	1.000	1.000	211.2	50.3	243.7	49.4
1963	265.1	215.5	49.6	1.028	1.063	1.002	1.001	221.9	52.8	254.1	51.6
1964	283.9	230.1	53.8	1.015	1.041	1.002	1.000	234.1	56.0	269.8	56.0
1965	306.2	247.2	59.0	0.999	1.012	1.003	1.000	247.6	59.8	288.0	61.5
1966	337.9	271.4	66.5	0.986	0.981	1.002	1.001	268.3	65.3	313.4	69.5
1967	359.1	287.2	71.9	0.995	0.993	1.001	1.000	286.0	71.4	331.7	75.2
1968	394.4	314.3	80.1	0.988	0.982	1.001	1.000	310.8	78.7	360.8	83.2
1969	434.3	343.0	91.3	0.994	0.983	0.999	1.000	340.7	89.7	392.6	95.0
1970	458.4	361.1	97.3	1.027	1.039	0.997	0.999	369.7	101.0	414.2	101.1
1971	486.0	382.4	103.6	1.042	1.076	0.998	1.000	397.6	111.4	438.6	107.2
1972	536.0	420.3	115.7	1.034	1.062	0.998	1.000	434.0	122.8	479.3	120.7
1973	604.3	471.9	132.4	1.022	1.035	0.998	0.999	481.4	136.9	539.5	138.8
1974	663.4	513.2	150.2	1.048	1.067	0.994	0.998	534.9	160.0	585.6	155.8
1975	695.1	534.8	160.3	1.096	1.166	0.998	1.000	584.7	186.9	611.5	163.4
1976	781.2	597.1	184.1	1.073	1.132	0.999	1.000	640.1	208.5	675.3	188.1

Sources: Columns 1–7 and 12–13, see text and *Accounting for Growth*, pp. 328–30 for derivation; column 8, the product of columns 2, 4, and 6; column 9, the product of columns 3, 5, and 7; column 14, column 10 × column 12, minus column 10; column 15, column 11 × column 13 minus column 11; column 16, column 8 minus column 2 plus column 14; column 17, column 9 minus column 3 plus column 15; column 18, the sum of columns 16 and

Education index, ratio of potential to actual Male (12)	Female (13)	Adjustment of potential earnings for education Male (14)	Female (15)	Male (16)	Female (17)	Total (18)	Column 18 as a percentage of column 10 plus column 11 (19)	Labor weight, nonresidential business (20)	Nonresidential business national income in 1972 prices, adjusted to potential utilization (21)	Excess of potential over actual national income due to labor input, 1972 prices (22)	Year
1.002	1.000	0.1	0.0	−0.9	−0.2	−1.1	−1.996	0.794	202.3	−3.2	1929
0.993	0.995	−0.3	0.0	7.7	2.1	9.8	18.505	0.788	209.8	30.6	1940
0.995	0.996	−0.3	0.0	3.6	1.0	4.6	7.035	0.788	241.9	13.4	1941
1.000	1.000	0.0	0.0	−0.3	−0.2	−0.5	−0.346	0.784	310.7	−0.8	1947
1.000	1.001	0.0	0.0	−1.0	−0.3	−1.3	−0.851	0.783	316.2	−2.1	1948
0.998	0.998	−0.3	0.0	3.5	1.6	5.1	3.554	0.782	309.8	8.6	1949
0.998	0.999	−0.2	0.0	1.8	1.1	2.9	1.888	0.786	331.5	4.9	1950
1.000	1.001	0.1	0.0	−2.4	−1.1	−3.5	−1.965	0.793	353.9	−5.5	1951
1.001	1.002	0.1	0.0	−2.8	−1.4	−4.2	−2.234	0.799	373.0	−6.7	1952
1.001	1.002	0.2	0.0	−3.2	−1.6	−4.9	−2.406	0.802	390.6	−7.5	1953
0.998	0.998	−0.3	0.0	3.9	1.7	5.6	2.798	0.810	383.4	8.7	1954
1.000	1.000	−0.1	0.0	0.3	0.3	0.6	0.258	0.814	404.8	0.9	1955
1.000	1.000	0.0	0.0	0.9	0.2	1.1	0.456	0.815	426.4	1.6	1956
1.000	1.000	−0.1	0.0	2.0	0.5	2.5	1.023	0.817	434.4	3.6	1957
0.997	0.997	−0.7	−0.1	11.3	4.6	15.9	6.506	0.823	430.4	23.1	1958
0.998	0.999	−0.4	−0.1	5.6	2.4	8.0	3.073	0.826	453.5	11.5	1959
0.998	0.999	−0.4	−0.1	7.0	2.8	9.8	3.608	0.822	466.2	13.8	1960
0.997	0.997	−0.7	−0.1	11.2	4.9	16.1	5.791	0.819	472.0	22.4	1961
0.998	0.999	−0.4	−0.1	6.1	2.9	9.0	3.058	0.815	494.4	12.3	1962
0.998	0.998	−0.5	−0.1	5.9	3.1	9.0	2.939	0.806	511.2	12.1	1963
0.999	0.999	−0.4	−0.1	3.6	2.2	5.8	1.781	0.799	535.4	7.6	1964
0.999	1.000	−0.2	0.0	0.2	0.7	0.9	0.266	0.796	570.2	1.2	1965
1.000	1.001	0.0	0.0	−3.1	−1.2	−4.2	1.107	0.795	602.4	−5.3	1966
1.000	1.000	0.1	0.0	−1.2	−0.5	−1.7	−0.413	0.799	620.2	−2.0	1967
1.000	1.000	0.1	0.0	−3.3	−1.4	−4.7	−1.060	0.807	651.0	−5.6	1968
1.000	1.000	0.2	0.0	−2.2	−1.6	−3.8	−0.768	0.815	683.2	−4.3	1969
1.000	1.000	−0.2	0.0	8.4	3.6	12.0	2.337	0.821	689.8	13.2	1970
0.999	0.999	−0.4	−0.1	14.8	7.7	22.5	4.116	0.827	704.3	24.0	1971
0.999	0.999	−0.7	−0.1	13.0	7.0	20.0	3.340	0.829	748.6	20.7	1972
0.999	0.999	−0.5	−0.1	9.0	4.4	13.3	1.967	0.830	795.7	13.0	1973
0.998	0.998	−1.0	−0.2	20.7	9.5	30.2	4.071	0.832	800.0	27.1	1974
0.995	0.996	−3.3	−0.6	46.6	26.0	72.6	9.363	0.832	756.3	58.9	1975
0.996	0.997	−3.0	−0.6	40.0	23.7	63.7	7.382	0.832	795.2	48.8	1976

17; column 19, column 18 divided by (column 10 plus column 11) × 100; column 20, annual data that were averaged to obtain the "labor" column in table G-2; column 21, table 2-6, column 5, plus table 2-4, column 2; column 22, the product of columns 19, 20, and 21. Figures are rounded.
a. Includes Alaska and Hawaii beginning in 1960.

APPENDIX M

Nonresidential Business: Indexes of Potential Input and Output

This appendix describes the derivation of the indexes of components of input and output per unit of input on a potential basis that are shown in table 3-2, table 4-6 (columns 10 and 13 only), and table 5-2. Many of these series were first computed with their potential value in 1972 equal to 100 and will be described in that form. For publication in the tables, these series were shifted to the form in which the actual value in 1972 is equal to 100; the method of adjustment is described when it is not obvious.

The detailed information needed to compute the indexes had been obtained in the process of computing corresponding indexes on an actual basis and deriving potential national income, but to obtain many of the indexes on a potential basis the information had to be put together in a different way. Only the indexes that differ from the corresponding indexes on an actual basis are described here.

Labor Input Indexes

Most of the series to be described are components of labor input, which are shown in table 3-2; numbers in the following list refer to columns in that table:

1. *Employment.* Potential employment is from

table 2-8, column 4. Actual employment in 1972, needed to convert the base to an "actual 1972 = 100" basis, is from table 2-7, column 3.

2. *Average weekly hours.* This series is the quotient of columns 3 and 1.

3. *Total weekly hours.* Total potential weekly hours are the sum of total actual weekly hours from table C-1 (sum of columns 7, 8, and 9) and the excess of potential over actual hours from table L-3, column 12.

4. *Age-sex composition of total hours.* As explained in appendix L, the difference between potential and actual total weekly hours (table L-3, columns 10–12) had been estimated by age and sex. This distribution was added to the corresponding distribution of total actual hours to obtain the distribution of potential hours. The distribution of total actual hours was obtained by allocating total actual hours (table C-1, sum of columns 7, 8, and 9) by the age-sex distribution in table 3-6 (or for omitted years, table F-5 in *Accounting for Growth*). From the resulting distributions of potential hours the potential age-sex composition index was calculated in the same way as the corresponding actual index. To place the series on an "actual 1972 = 100" basis, it was calculated that in 1972 the average weight obtained from the potential distribution was 99.36 percent of the average from the actual distribution.

5. *The index for the efficiency of an hour's work as affected by intragroup changes in hours.* For each sex, the percentage by which the potential index exceeds the actual index for full-time nonfarm business wage and salary workers (computed in deriving table L-5, columns 6 and 7) was multiplied by the ratio for that sex of total hours worked by these workers to total hours worked by all workers in nonresidential business. This provided percentage differences between potential and actual indexes for all workers of each sex in the sector. They were weighted by total earnings to obtain the percentage difference for both sexes combined. The index on an actual basis (table 3-1) was adjusted by this percentage each year to obtain the index on a potential basis.

6. *Efficiency of an hour's work as affected by changes in hours due to specified intergroup shifts.* From estimates of employment by sex and full-time or part-time status developed to obtain potential national income, a table on a potential basis was constructed that corresponded to the actual data in table 3-7 ("wage and salary workers in nonfarm business: employment and hours by sex and full-time or part-time status"). Tables 3-8 and 3-9,

which provide similar data for nonfarm self-employed workers and farm workers, are the same on a potential basis as on an actual basis. From these data an index was constructed in the same way as the corresponding index on an actual basis. Comparison of 1972 actual and potential data showed the potential figure to be 100.12 percent of the "actual" figure.

7. *Amount of education.* An index for males based on potential employment was calculated as the product of the index on an actual basis from column 3 of table F-5 and the ratio of the potential to the actual index from column 12 of table L-5. As usual, unrounded data were used. Similarly the index for females is the product of column 4 of table F-5 and column 13 of table L-5. Indexes for the two sexes were weighted in the same way as in the derivation of the education index on an actual basis.

8. *Labor input.* This is the product of columns 3 through 7.

9. *Effect of hours changes.* This is the product of columns 2, 5, and 6.

Other Indexes

Table 4-6, column 10—Potential total factor input. The indexes for input of structures and equipment, inventories, and land are the same on a potential basis as on an actual basis, as are the weights used to combine these inputs and labor input. Total input on a potential basis was calculated in the same way as total input on an actual basis, except that potential labor input was substituted for actual labor input.

Table 4-6, column 13—Potential: discrepancy factor. Since the index for "advances in knowledge and n.e.c." (not elsewhere classified) obtained from the actual estimates is also used as the potential index, there is no residual in the potential series. Consequently the products of the indexes of total factor input and output per unit of input need not equal the index of total output and they do not do so exactly. The index of the discrepancy is calculated by dividing the index of national income by the product of the indexes of total input and output per unit of input.

It is apparent that a discrepancy must arise, except by chance, because construction of indexes of the determinants of potential output required that specific assumptions be introduced with respect to several conditions for which no assumptions were needed to derive potential output itself. Changing these assumptions would change the estimates of total potential input and potential output per unit of input, but not potential output. Among these assumptions are (1) those concerning the size of efficiency offsets to changes in the hours of farm workers and nonfarm self-employed workers, which enter into the measurement of labor input; (2) those concerning the percentages by which output is curtailed by reductions in farm employment and nonfarm self-employment, which enter into the measurement of gains from the reallocation of resources; and (3) those regarding the elasticity of output with respect to the size of markets and to the movement of the series for the size of markets to which production is adapted, both of which jointly govern the index of gains from economies of scale.

The product of the indexes of input and output per unit of input exceeds the national income index in twenty-one of thirty postwar years (including the base year, 1972), so the index for the discrepancy is usually below 100. The product exceeds the national income index by as much as 0.3 percent in only four postwar years and falls short by as much as 0.2 percent in only two. The index of the discrepancy appears to be related to unemployment. It falls farthest below 100 in 1949, 1950, 1958, and 1961 and exceeds it most in 1952 and 1953. During the postwar years the discrepancy is not big enough to raise problems of interpretation. It does not change enough between terminal years of any standard period to introduce serious difficulties in the construction of sources-of-growth tables. Agreement is achieved by forcing the details.

Disagreement is greater in the prewar years, with the discrepancy 0.4 percent in 1929, −1.8 percent in 1940, and −1.1 percent in 1941. The change in the discrepancy factor amounts to only −0.02 percent a year in the 1929–48 period and −0.01 in 1929–76, but it comes to a more troublesome −0.13 percent a year in 1929–41 and 0.17 percent in 1941–48.

Table 5-2, columns 2 and 3—Gains from reallocation of resources from farming and from nonfarm self-employment. The series on a potential basis for gains from the reallocation of labor from farming and from nonfarm self-employment were calculated in the same way as the corresponding actual series. Farm national income, employment, and hours are the same on a potential basis as on an actual basis, as are employment and hours of nonfarm self-employed and unpaid family workers. Data on a potential basis for nonfarm national income, and employment and hours of nonfarm business wage and salary workers, were obtained by subtraction from sector totals. Comparing 1972 actual and potential data, in the same way that adjacent years are compared to derive the indexes, provided the 1972 potential figures with 1972 actual values equal to 100.

Table 5-2, column 9—Changes in intensity of utilization of employed resources resulting from fluctuations in intensity of demand. The potential value of this index is 103.31 in all years. Its derivation is described in appendix L.

Index